TRAVELS WITH THE SAHIB
The Diary of a Not-Quite-Mad-Enough Foreign Service Wife

by
Winifred Denny

Winifred Denny

*for Mary & Hal
with thanks
Carolyn M. Nicholson*

Note for Librarians: a cataloguing record for this book that includes Dewey Decimal
Classification and US Library of Congress numbers is available from the Library and
Archives of Canada. The complete cataloguing record can be obtained from their online
database at:
www.collectionscanada.ca/amicus/index-e.html
ISBN 1-4120-4025-6
Printed in Victoria, BC, Canada

TRAFFORD

Offices in Canada, USA, Ireland, UK and Spain
This book was published *on-demand* in cooperation with Trafford Publishing. On-demand
publishing is a unique process and service of making a book available for retail sale to the
public taking advantage of on-demand manufacturing and Internet marketing. On-demand
publishing includes promotions, retail sales, manufacturing, order fulfilment, accounting and
collecting royalties on behalf of the author.
Book sales for North America and international:
Trafford Publishing, 6E–2333 Government St.,
Victoria, BC v8t 4p4 CANADA
phone 250 383 6864 (toll-free 1 888 232 4444)
fax 250 383 6804; email to orders@trafford.com
Book sales in Europe:
Trafford Publishing (uk) Ltd., Enterprise House, Wistaston Road Business Centre,
Wistaston Road, Crewe, Cheshire cw2 7rp UNITED KINGDOM
phone 01270 251 396 (local rate 0845 230 9601)
facsimile 01270 254 983; orders.uk@trafford.com
Order online at:
www.trafford.com/robots/04-1832.html

10 9 8 7 6 5 4 3 2

To my five greatest accomplishments
and to the author of their being,
I dedicate this memoir of a happy life
for which all of the above are, in
large measure, responsible.

PROLOGUE

"Isn't that just like Dr Denny to go off to India to help all those starving people, and those poor, poor lepers."

I just about choked on my macaroon. The thought of my husband, that quintessential bon vivant, as a combination of Albert Schweitzer and Mother Theresa was too great a stretch of the imagination, even for me. Nonetheless all the ladies gathered for a farewell tea murmured polite assent. I did make some attempt to say that wasn't *actually* the sort of thing he would be doing, but nobody paid much attention. If they but knew the driving force behind this life-changing overseas caper on which we were about to embark. Ulysses had heard the siren's call.

He may well have been listening for some time as a matter of fact, but she sang out loud and clear on a trip to Europe a few months earlier. We had taken our 17-year-old daughter to Switzerland for a year at a school near Montreux, where presumably she would become bilingual, get buffed up a little and be ready for university in 12 months' time. After a tearful (on my part) farewell, we headed for Rome to visit an old friend and former colleague of Doug's, who had abandoned private practice and joined the Overseas Division of Health and Welfare Canada.

We found John and Mildred Graham in a beautiful apartment on one of the seven hills of Rome. The first shock came when our host arrived home at 5.30pm. To a man like Doug, whose day began at 7.00am and, if lucky, ended at 9.00pm, this seemed Nirvana, and I sensed the wheels beginning to spin. Over dinner we were treated to a recital of *la dolce vita*: the educational perks, the travel, the family reunifications and so on. The clincher came, however, as we prepared to leave the next day to continue our travels along the Italian coast. In the midst of farewells, our hostess rushed out to return with a bottle of Johnny Walker Black Label "for your Happy Hour."

I protested: "It is too much... We couldn't possibly...." These effusions were stopped as a hand reached out from behind me, clasped the bottle and announced: "Oh yes we could. They get it duty-free."

That was it. The die was cast. The last banana boat was coming in to dock, and I knew, then and there, who would be on it.

CHAPTER 1

Friday, January 3, 1975 Open a cautious and flu-watery eye. Nothing seems real. I feel I am in a play, and last night's departure for the Airport Inn should have been the last scene before the curtain comes down, and we all go home.

As I become more fully awake, reality returns. Hermione is whimpering quietly by the edge of the bed, her golden spaniel eyes looking at me for some sort of explanation. Why don't I open the door and let her out into the Eden of her own backyard? Is she haunted by memories of last night? She, the dog of impeccable manners, so upset by her imprisonment in the sky kennel that she wet on the hotel's Axminster. Mind you, it was midnight, and nobody was around, but she was humiliated nonetheless.

The same could be said for me, making a dash for the loo, and dramatically emptying the room at our 'seeing-off' party yesterday evening. I should have been prepared, as I had been throwing up with a combination of nerves and flu for the past five days. What a nightmare of organization it has been! Can I ever forgive Doug? I can still see him when the word came from Ottawa that he was 'in', and was to leave for India within the week.

"I'll take my tropical suits and my golf clubs," says he, making it sound onerous and magnanimous at the same time, "and be back for you at Christmas."

What was left unsaid was that the only things I had to concern myself with were sorting out the children, the cars and the house. Oh God, I thought to myself: 20 years of slap-dash housekeeping to be pulled together in two months; 20 years of toys, hair-ribbons, dog-eared comic books ("vintage, Mum, vintage"); 20 years of happy life to be packed, stored, left, walked away from. Was I meant to do this? Was I ready for the Foreign Service? Was it ready for me? I am beset by intimidating visions of a whole super-culture – a film set of morning suits and Givenchy gowns, with everybody looking

1

like Basil Rathbone and Greer Garson – brilliant, witty men, unbelievably beautiful women, with the odd, slightly sinister Soviet Cultural Attaché thrown in for good measure. Into this glamorous scene will I come stumbling like Mrs Cratchit in her "twice-turned gown but brave in ribbons"? It is all too awful! And India, dear Lord, India! What about leprosy, malaria, dengue fever? I realize I know nothing about India, apart from those pictures in the family album of Uncle Jack, a cadaverous figure in shorts, his foot on a tiger. I *like* tigers – do they still do that sort of thing, I wonder?

I decide I think too much, and have seen too many movies. I will try not to fret over the abandonment of my 18- and 17-year-olds in the temptation-ridden freedom of university. I won't think of the twins, finishing off their school year in strange, tidy households. I won't think of the winter woods that lie, waiting, behind our house, nor the snow-covered garden I have just left. I will do as Doug suggests, and think only of high, Halliburton-style adventure, and hear only "the paddles chunkin' from Rangoon to Mandalay".

The plane leaves at 3.00pm, but there is to be yet another send-off at the airport – our four deserted children (oh, unnatural mother) and an assortment of friends, whom I seem to be cherishing more and more with each passing moment.

The hour of departure arrives with the finality of an execution. Tears unshed, but begging for release. Who wants a soppy Mum? We conscientiously stick to talk of our reunion in six months' time. Hilary, still our 'baby' at nine years old, hovers over Hermione. There are a few forlorn last-minute waves, and then we cross the Rubicon.

On the plane, I am feeling worse by the minute, but Hilary has made friends with a young Chinese boy, who invites her to a game of chess. Doug, by now an old hand at all this, relaxes with a drink. We have an unexpectedly festive dinner of Beef Wellington, and Hilary saves half of hers for Hermione, stuffing it, gravy and all, into what she refers to as the 'barf bag', and then into her Snoopy knapsack. We later decide this would be a marvellous way to smuggle diamonds. When we have to disembark for an in-transit stop in Tokyo, the Japanese security men unzip every bag, ponder over a pair of nail scissors, but give one revolted squeeze to the air sickness bag and hurry it through, unopened.

A lot of passengers leave at Tokyo, and I have the luxury of four seats to myself. I stretch out and fall asleep, but wake up as we fly into a magical night-time Hong Kong. The city below is jewel-like – a place of amethyst towers and a sapphire winter sky. As we approach, the surreal curtain disappears and a hopelessly tacky backdrop is revealed. Row upon row of tenements, with long bamboo poles protruding from the windows, and each pole festooned with shirts and trousers and other domestic paraphernalia. The night is dark, and I feel far, far from home.

We break our journey here, and Hilary is beside herself as she waits by the baggage carousel for Hermione to emerge. Finally, there she is – a frantic little dog, a moving oddity among all the matched and monogrammed luggage. Hilary rushes over to release Herm, and is in the act of smothering her with hugs and kisses, when there is a bureaucratic descent. Herm is hustled back into her confinement. Hilary crouches beside her, and holds her paw through the bars until the van arrives and bears the poor little beast off to her overnight quarantine. Our night's shelter is a cut above what awaits Herm, being an opulent hotel in Kowloon. I sink into a bath and very soon after fall into bed. Hilary turns on the TV. It is *Hogan's Heroes* dubbed into Chinese, and it's more than a bit startling to hear Colonel Klink, every inch the German officer, berating Schultz in squeaky Cantonese.

Sunday, January 5 January 4 disappears into limbo somewhere over the International Dateline, and I decide not to chase my brain around trying to figure it out. Have a walk around Kowloon, which looks better and more human somehow in the morning light. There are some elegant hotels, chic shops, and I love the mulberry trees along Nathan Road and the heady smell of roasting chestnuts.

At lunch, the smallness of this new world I have entered is made apparent when a patient of Doug's from Burnaby presents himself at our table. He and his wife are taking an Asian tour as their Christmas present to each other.

After rescuing Herm from her Asian pound, we head once more for the airport and board a Japan Air Lines flight for New

Delhi. Bangkok is little more than an exotic blur, glimpsed from the window, and we are on our last lap. We are circumnavigating the globe, and time is doing its funny thing and catching up with us – or we are catching up with it? Our future is the next stop.

CHAPTER 2

Still Sunday, January 5 It is 6.00pm when we arrive in Delhi. Mildred and John Graham, now based in India, are there to greet us, but not before I take in the sights, sounds and smells of the Delhi airport.

Birds fly in and out, roosting in the ceiling beams and dumping generously on the populace below. Many of said populace seem to have taken up residence. Wrapped in tattered shawls and layers of dhotis, turbaned and shoeless, they curl up on the floor or prop themselves up against the begrimed pillars. The polished corridors of Vancouver International Airport are a lifetime away.

The drive along Palam Road to Vasant Vihar could have been painted by some subcontinental Hogarth. Peering out the car window, I see a spare landscape, dotted here and there with ratty, dust-covered shrubs and trees. The verge is lit by dung fires, around which swaddled figures huddle, some cooking, some sleeping, and all making the January night their own. Even in the enclosed car, the smell which I will forever associate with India seeps through. It is an amalgam of all human odours, plus burning cow dung and a blend of indistinguishable spices.

We go first to the Grahams, who have a nice house in the same neighbourhood as our new home. After a light supper, we are taken to the house that is to be ours for the next two years. I can't see much, but it appears white and squarish from the outside, surrounded by a high wall and a bougainvillea hedge. I spot some scarlet lilies, and a few stiff, regimented marigolds around the door.

Tony, the man Doug has employed as our cook-bearer, is waiting to greet us. He is big and lumbering, very dark and shoeless, and seemingly equipped with a permanent scowl. My heart sinks, until he smiles a transforming smile. We shake hands, and Doug thanks him for waiting up for us on his day off. When Doug takes us upstairs, physical and emotional fatigue has wiped me out. I cannot take in the surroundings. I see only the bed, covers turned back, snowy sheets, a bottle of water on the bedside table. It is enough. It is, for that moment, all that matters in this world – the lure of that waiting bed is the lure of paradise.

Monday, January 6 Wake to brilliant sunshine and the sound of Doug's electric razor from the bathroom. Apprehension, if not actual panic, has me by the hand. What happens now? All the familiar cues are missing, replaced by a lot of strangers milling around downstairs, waiting for me to goof. I'll have to get Doug to fill me in. He emerges from the bathroom to find me making the bed.

"You don't have to do that, the servants make the beds."

"Doug," I begin, "what happens about breakfast? Am I..."

"No, no," he interrupts, "Tony does all that. Come on, let's go down."

Even Doug seems to belong to another planet. Suddenly it seems pompous and pretentious for us to go down together, like a *nouveau* couple in a B-movie. I tell Doug to go on, and I will be down in a minute.

Hesitating to leave the shelter of the bedroom, and feeling more like the second Mrs De Winter with every anxious moment, I finally set out to walk majestically down the staircase. At that precise instant, a barefoot Indian, duster in hand, begins to ascend. We stare at one another. I press myself against the wall, and smile a weak good morning. He, in an equal panic, presses himself against the banister, grinding the duster into his forehead in a kind of salute. We edge past one another in a sort of slow, balletic movement, then we dart – he for the upper landing, me for the dining room.

Doug is already comfortably into his bacon and eggs, when I tell him of my encounter. That was Muni, the cleaner or 'sweeper', he informs me, adding that he, Muni, was probably petrified that his shadow might fall across my path, and I would then consider myself to be 'polluted', in which case it would be goodbye Muni, and goodbye job.

I am overwhelmed at the thought of all this power to create terror, and would happily have sought out Muni to assure him he has nothing to fear from a totally unpolluted me. Doug hastens to let me know that this sort of chummy approach is

We edge past one another in a sort of slow, balletic movement

7

definitely not on and, with a passing peck, leaves for work.

Hilary eventually appears, with Hermione glued to her left heel. Together we decide to 'suss' out the house. It is new and modern, and nice enough in a stark sort of way. I would never have dreamt of dwelling in marble halls (which is what we have) had I known how cold they would feel in the winter.

There is a living room with quite nice furniture, beautiful rugs, some awful pink plastic lighting fixtures that look like tortured tulips, and drapes that I swear Doug picked out with his mother in mind. They are perfectly tasteful, but I have never, repeat never, liked scrolled damask.

I go up to have another look at the master bedroom. In all my years of marriage, I have never had a bedroom that could be even remotely classed as feminine. Our first one boasted a paint-it-yourself plywood suite that had been stained 'deep cedar' but which actually looked like dried ox-blood. Doug's mother had also frugally offered a couple of old bedspreads as curtains and the total effect was definitely 'attic modern'.

So here we are. Doug – having been given free rein in the selection of fabrics and furnishings – had set out to create my dream bedroom. It was, he announced, the least he could do, having dragged me from home and family.

It is tasteful, it is handsome, it is straight out of *Esquire* as the sleeping quarters for an exclusive English gentleman's club in Pall Mall. The favoured brocade frames the windows and the tub chairs are dark forest green, as are the matching bedspreads. I can see that I will have to practice all morning to produce a convincing, "Yes, it is lovely." Ah me!

Hilary consoles me by saying her bedroom also has "old lady" curtains, and suggests we have a tour of the garden. The property is protected by a high stone fence and an iron gate. It being a new house, the garden has yet to mature, but there are indications that one day the wall will be aflame with the bougainvillea I spotted last night.

Inside again, we look over the living room, den, three bedrooms and four bathrooms. There is also a huge storage area or 'godown' in the lower level, and I am assured we will have extra beds for family over-flow when the children arrive.

In the den, I find the list of staff. In addition to Tony, our cook-bearer, and my chum Muni the sweeper, there is a 'dhobi' or laundryman who comes twice a week, a 'mali' or gardener who comes daily, and a 'chowkidar' or night watchman, who comes every eventide to snooze at our gates. I am aghast at the thought of all these bodies, busying themselves with house and garden activities. I hesitate to move from one room to another, and stay rigidly away from an inspection of the kitchen. Yesterday, Doug passed on the information that Tony takes off for two or three hours every afternoon, so I start to plot a stealthy peek this PM.

Around noon, Doug arrives to take us out for lunch and a drive around Delhi. We fall upon him as on a saviour.

I had been warned that India would make Hong Kong look like the ritziest part of well-to-do Vancouver, so my first real glimpse of New Delhi is both a revelation and a relief. It is quite simply and utterly beautiful. The British knew what they were about when they determined, some time around 1912, that this, the eighth City of Delhi, would be the jewel in the Imperial crown as far as capitals were concerned. Sir Edward Luytens, a noted British architect, was hired and magically produced a city that blended Renaissance Europe with the poetry of Mogul architecture. It is lovely, with wide, gracious avenues and flowering boulevards rimmed by magnificent trees. As we approach the great Rajpath, I fight down the feeling that we are in a De Mille epic. It is of such grandeur, from the Purana Quila to the Presidential Palace, a vast extravagance of rose-coloured sandstone.

We drive down the Shanti Path, which houses the Diplomatic Enclave, and I see the Canadian High Commission for the first time. Farther down the road is the Pakistani Embassy, topped by a spectacular lilac-coloured dome. Behind this, as if by special arrangement of a designer, is a glorious blue jacaranda in full bloom. There are roundabouts with flowers and fountains at their centre, encircled by incredible traffic – not many cars, but bicycles, donkeys, oxen carts, cows and the odd camel.

Doug takes us over to the ACSA (American Community Support Association) Lounge for lunch – a favourite watering hole for exiles from below and above the 49th parallel. It's part of the compound that houses most of the US Embassy staff, and has a swimming pool, baseball diamond, New England-style church, Commissary and school. We have hamburgers (probably water buffalo) and milk shakes – all very clean and Yankee Doodle dandy.

Home again, and how quickly one adapts – dinner does not cross my mind until it appears on the table. That night we walk Herm along the street, and breathe in the heady aroma of frangipani and all the night-blooming flowers. The Memsahib has arrived.

CHAPTER 3

Tuesday, January 7 Time for the realities. We have a nine-year-old child for whom we must find a school. I hate to lose her. She has been a little protective padding against the lonely day-time hours, but the poor infant has to be educated.

Our first choice is the British school, looking ahead to 'O' levels and 'A' levels and no-nonsense learning. So, when Doug comes home for lunch, we gather up our fledgling and take her along for an interview with Mrs Boss, the headmistress.

The school looks quite pleasant from the outside. It is shaded by old trees, and the building itself seems rather inviting, with a slight air of *autrefois.* Inside, it is a different story. We are ushered into an ice-cold office, with a malfunctioning heater for which Mrs Boss apologizes. She herself could have come straight out of Central Casting, with her dark ribbed stockings, sturdy oxfords, tweed skirt and twin-sweater set.

The nearby classroom is no improvement over the office. There is a broken air-conditioner dangling from the wall and the chairs are mended with gummed tape. Hilary's face is desolate, and shows clearly that she is harking back to the spiff-plus order of West Vancouver's Cypress Park Elementary. I like Mrs Boss, even if she does seem completely oblivious to the school's all-too-apparent décor deficiencies.

We mention another daughter of 15, who will be coming to India in June. It turns out there will be plenty of room for Barbara but, alas, Hilary falls into their largest age group, the eight to ten year olds. In a couple of years, she explains, these children will be 'going home' to boarding school, but now.... Mrs B spreads her hands in a gesture of helplessness. At this juncture, I am afraid Hilary may do several cartwheels and dance a jig. Mrs. Boss suggests (with a slight curl of the lip) that we try the American School, just a block or two away.

"It is," she says, "claimed by the Principal to be the finest 'plant' in Asia." She patently implies that she, personally, has never equated the groves of academe with factories, but then

11

that is the Americans for you!

We dutifully head for the American School, on the outer edge of the American Compound. It is, indeed, at the other end of the spectrum, décor-wise, as they say in the ad biz. It is built of beautiful cut-stone and is surrounded by courtyards and playing fields, with roomy offices and reception areas. Hilary bucks up perceptibly, and is duly registered to start tomorrow.

Wednesday, January 8 Our first engagement in the Corps Diplomatique. Actually it has nothing to do with the CD, but instead has a direct tie-in with home. A trade officer (seconded from the private sector) and his wife are entertaining a friend of a friend from West Vancouver. A promise to get together has resulted in this invitation to lunch on Tees January Marg.

They live next-door to Birla House, where Gandhi was assassinated on that fateful day, January 30, 1948, hence the street name. It is a lovely road, full of tangled gardens and arching trees. Our hosts occupy a gorgeous old house, with a wide, white verandah, ceiling fans and oodles of turbaned staff running around. There are distinct echoes of a Rumer Godden novel or a film on the twilight of the Raj. Lunch is elegant, and I am impressed by how unobtrusive the servants are and how unflappable. As we are leaving, a snake slithers across the verandah and is instantly snared by a bearer who returns in seconds, bows calmly and opens the car door for us.

The incident brings to mind a story I heard years ago. Back in pre-partition days, a resident commissioner in Lucknow and his wife were entertaining at dinner. The table conversation had included a polite debate about gender reaction in moments of crisis, based on the premise that men will remain cool and act rationally, and women will have hysterics over something as trivial as a mouse.

Things were going swimmingly, when the Memsahib, with no change of expression, moved her head slightly in the direction of her bearer. He bent an ear, and she whispered something to him. She then smiled at her guests and suggested that her husband lead them to the drawing room for coffee.

When they had all left, the bearer returned with another

servant, who carried a forked stick and a Nepalese kukri knife. During the dinner, a cobra had twined itself around the lady's ankle. As she had not moved a muscle, it was now crawling across her shoe, and soon emerged from under the tablecloth. The execution was swift and silent. The lady rejoined her guests and drank her coffee. No one noticed that her cup shook slightly.

I like to think that some long ago nanny recited this tale to an infant Rosemary, or Lavinia, or Sybil, to show them how cold baths and a steady diet of Marmite and semolina pudding could produce English women worthy of the Empire.

It is a full day; we return home, only to change for a reception hosted by the National Film Board entry in the International Film Festival. The place is sprinkled with cultural attachés from various embassies and commissions. I have been told by 'those who know' that *all* Soviet CAs are actually KGB, or spies, or something equally and deliciously sinister. So naturally I am all a-twitter when I find myself talking to the very thing. He is perfectly charming, terribly knowledgeable, and does not ask me one thing about Canada's defence of the Bering Straits. He does, however, discuss films, and asks me if I had seen *Closely Watched Trains*, the Czech entry. Fortunately I have, and so we talk about it and the Russian entry, *The Cranes Are Flying*. To be absolutely honest, he talked and I sort of waffled along. Still, I have now made my début on the international stage (in a manner of speaking) and it was not nearly as terrifying as I had imagined.

Friday, January 10 Another 'first' today. Mildred has invited me to play golf with her and her close chum, the wife of the administrator at the High Commission. My past sorties into this most maddening of all games have not been starry, and I have no reason to believe it will be any different in Delhi. However, played their way, it is not a bad game, even for an ultimate duffer like me. I whack a ball straight into the bush, snake-ridden and dung-laden. No matter – my caddy Sampat Lal retrieves it, spits on it, mounds a neat little pile of grass in the middle of the fairway, and I am off again. He patiently performs similar such services all morning, and earns not only his modest fee, but my eternal gratitude.

I can't say I am particularly enamoured of Mildred's friend. She makes sure I know her husband is a counsellor which, if she only knew, means precious little to me. She also hates India, loathes Indians, and doesn't seem all that keen on me, if it comes to that.

The course, though, is pure heaven, and like every soft-focus picture of India you could ever imagine. We are on the tee, with the first twitter of the birds, and lying before us is a morning pastel of russet temples and lacy trees. Vivid parrots roost in Islamic arches and peacocks shrill on the greens. Golf is relegated to nothing more than a reason for entering this enchanted setting, and my eyes are *never* on the ball.

Saturday, January 11 Hilary's bicycle has been put together, and we ride up and check out our local market. Fresh from the shining shops and plastic purity of our shopping mall back home, the Vasant Vihar plaza is definitely a shock. A cow, solemnly chewing his way through a cigarette packet, guards the entrance. Well, if not exactly an entrance, it is the only spot that is not littered with dung, evidence of betel juice expectorations, fallen bicycles and crouching humans doing heaven knows what.

I spot a barber at his trade. His 'shop' consists of a couple of poles and a flapping blanket. Nearby, a workman is sluicing himself down in a makeshift shower, and a dentist holds his surgery, also *al fresco*, in a choice corner location. Hilary is beside herself with the glamour of it all and darts off to explore further. She is back shortly, tugging at me to come and see "the neatest thing in the whole place."

Does she mean 'neat' as in 'tidy' or 'spruce', or does she mean 'neat' as in the 'coolest'? I strongly suspect the latter, and I am right. She leads me to the butcher shop. It is, as with the barber's establishment, a sort of camping-out affair. The butcher sits cross-legged on the ground, and I rather wish he hadn't. He is barefoot and holds a large knife between his great and second toe. With a kind of awesome rhythm, he brings a rack of chops down onto the knife, and pitches the number required to the waiting customers. Said customers are gathered around him in an admiring circle. Sometimes he misses the waiting hand, but nobody seems disconcerted. They

With a kind of awesome rhythm, he brings a rack of chops down

just pick up their purchases from the reeking earth, tuck them, unwrapped, into their cholas (bags), and Ahmed's your uncle. Whoever told me to let one's bearer do the shopping knew whereof she spoke.

We go to a polo game in the afternoon. A first for me, and I find it quite exciting, although I don't have a clue as to what is going on.

Sunday, January 12 Oh bliss, oh rapture – we are alone! I make breakfast in the still-alien kitchen, and then we are off on a day's adventures. We lunch at the Oberoi Hotel – very posh – then visit the Delhi Zoological Gardens. Hilary and I are enchanted – the tigers are burning bright, even in the darkness of their cages. The white one is magnificent. Hilary snaps a hippo yawning – an awesome sight. I have never liked seeing caged creatures, but I must say for the Delhi Zoo that, inasmuch as possible, they have tried to keep the animals in something close to their natural habitat. Hilary's hippo, for example, is sloshing around in a nice, muddy pool.

In the evening, we are invited to the Grahams for dinner. They have suggested that we swap 'days off'. Salamat, their cook-bearer, is a Muslim, so is off on Fridays, and they will dine with us. Tony, being a Christian, has a free Sunday, and dinner will be at the Grahams. It seems like a good arrangement and means that, in theory, we should never have to don another oven mitt, unless we are so inclined.

Monday, January 13 One week gone by. I gloomily contemplate making a chart like prisoners pent, multiplying 365 by 2, and marking off the days. With Doug off to work and Hilary to school, Hermione and I sit, hand-in-paw, and ponder on the day ahead. I am determined to shake off this "Ruth amid the alien corn" nonsense, and retire to the den where I begin to write letters. Around 11.00am Tony comes in with coffee and informs me that there are flowers in the downstairs bathroom, waiting for Memsahib to arrange. How Edwardian can we get!

I dutifully fulfil this task, and once again go back to my correspondence. Doug, thank goodness, comes home for lunch. Tony retires for his afternoon break, and I take a book upstairs and wonder how long before Hilary will be home.

One of the first pieces of advice Mildred gave me was that I show the servants who is boss. Mildred is no more 'to the manner born' than I, but she does seem to have Salamat whipped into shape. Tony, on the other hand, seems a harder nut to crack. For one thing, Salamat is a timid little man, whereas the large, dark and scowling Tony is more formidable. However, I set out a week ago to do as I was bid. My first morning, Tony had arranged fresh flowers on the coffee table, which I thought was really sweet of him, so I decided not to show him who was boss that day. Tomorrow for sure. The next day, he brought me tea, unasked, and I thought: I can't show him who is boss today after such kindness. So here I am, one week later, and I suspect we both know who is boss, and it isn't me.

As a matter of fact, the boss-showing bit is not the only thing that is not 'me'. Mildred has appointed herself my mentor in guiding me through the labyrinthine ways of the Foreign Service life. It is probably as well, as I realize my arrival was ill timed. The High Commissioner's wife, who is supposed to give newcomers the gen on who's who and what's what, is ill. The pool and cabana – the usual meeting ground – is closed, and Doug has already been 'received' – I am simply his dependent adjunct. Last night, after dinner, Mildred sat me down and set out the ground rules as a caution against my getting ideas above my station.

"We all have our place," she announced, with a clear implication that, as the wife of the senior Medical Officer, hers was superior to mine.

This did not worry me in the slightest, as I have always felt that my 'place' was where I chose to make it. Not so, it seems, in the Foreign Service. There is a distinct pecking order, much as in the military. At the top of the heap is the head of mission, then the second in command, usually the head of chancery. These are followed by counsellors – first, second and third secretaries – with the counsellors usually being the heads of departments. Even the departments are in a descending order of importance: External Affairs, Trade and Commerce, Immigration and, somewhat an afterthought, Health and Welfare. By now, of course, I should be tugging at my forelock and rubbing my hands like Uriah Heep. Instead, and to my shame, I think I displayed a slight twitching of the lip.

Mildred hurried on, unaware of anything amusing. Socially, she explained, we will be invited to the Residence, when fitting – on special occasions, such as Christmas, or for dinners or luncheons involving Delhi's medical elite. We will not, however, be included in the soirées of other Embassy Residences. She did offer a consolation prize, however, by explaining that we *are* officers, and as such will be invited by other officers to functions, and may return the invitations at the same level. The support staff – the guards, communicators, etc – she neglected to mention at all.

Our relations with the local and regional medical community, however, are a different matter, she assured me. Here the H&W doctors come into their own, with the power to hire and fire local Designated Medical Practitioners. Hence, we will be received, wined and dined, and treated with the utmost deference, as the Canadian business is much sought after and is both prestigious and lucrative. At this point, she lowered her voice and added a lot of cautions about avoiding bribes, keeping a watchful eye out for chicanery and so on.

As I am still a bit hazy about Doug's actual duties, I was unaware of these traps. As far as I can gather, his main task is to work hand-in-glove with Immigration, and give a medical thumbs up or down to potential immigrants. He also happens to come with a solid background in the practice of medicine (which a lot of H&W doctors do not) and will, therefore, run a clinic for Canadian staff members, and for any distressed Canadians directed to him by the Consular Service.

It is all a far cry from the easy camaraderie of medical colleagues at Burnaby General Hospital, and the come-one-come-all nature of our social life at home. I thanked Mildred for sharing this with me, but inwardly decided on a wait-and-see policy. At the moment, what India, as a culture and a country, might have to offer far outweighs any worries about who is or who is not coming to dinner.

Wednesday, January 15 I am introduced to the American Commissary. Like the good neighbours they are, the Americans extend the privilege of using their Commissary, as well as the facilities of the ACSA lounge, school and library. I am extremely grateful that Americans abroad remain rigidly American in their habits, particularly when it comes to food. The Commissary is stocked with lots of otherwise impossible-to-get items, plus imported meats and poultry. My heart lifts at the thought of extending Tony's culinary repertoire. The ground rules with regard to liquor are also explained. Canadians are entitled to 30 bottles of alcohol a month, including wine. Each customer must sign for whatever he buys in the course of any given month, and under no circumstances is one allowed to sell or trade this duty-free supply. I can anticipate no problem. Unless you find yourself entertaining every night of the week, 30 bottles a month is a dipso's dream.

Hilary seems a little homesick and mopey, and to cheer her up Doug suggests a trip to the Red Fort in Old Delhi for a *Son et Lumière* show that is being presented tonight.

It is my first trip into Old Delhi, but in the winter twilight, its more obvious horrors are subdued. We enter through the Fort's main gate, which is guarded by a phalanx of vendors, all offering prizes beyond the dreams of Maharajahs for but a few rupees. I am pulled away from these temptations by Doug, and into the wonders within. I rather expected to see a fort, *per se,* but instead it is a series of courts and courtyards, with a covered passageway leading to the palace of Shah Jehan, he of the Taj Mahal, the greatest of all the great Mogul builders and the creator of this, the seventh City of Delhi.

We find our way to a huge central courtyard where the show is being held. It is splendidly done and very informative – taking us through the changing faiths and rulers of all the preceding cities of Delhi. In this respect, Delhi is interesting, if not actually unique, inasmuch as the cities developed side by side, rather than being built one on top of the ruins of the other. It is really so fascinating that I almost forget how cold I am.

When we were leaving the house, I decided it might be a good idea to take a jacket. Hilary and Doug, still with the heat of the day in mind, were openly scornful, but throughout the performance they become extremely matey, trying to wrap themselves up in my sleeves. Hilary actually starts to shiver, and I finally give her my jacket.

It is dark by the time we leave the Fort, and by now I am thoroughly chilled. Snuggling into the warmth of the car, I look out at the street dwellers, their crouching figures casting grotesque shadows in the firelight. How cold they must be in their rags. I am going home to a warm, clean bed in a warm, clean house, and the terrible distance between our lives and theirs is immeasurable and shameful. What is worst of all, I think, is that once I am under the blankets in the same warm, clean bed, I shall probably not give them another thought.

Thursday, January 16 Dr Sharma, a local doctor, and his wife are the first to extend an invitation, and we arrive, as bidden, promptly at 6.00pm at Dr Sharma's office. After sitting in the waiting room for half an hour, he emerges, all smiles and apologies, and whips us off to the hospital, where he must make a call. Another hour of fidgeting in yet another waiting room. The Indian magazines are no more fascinating than copies of the Salvation Army's *Warcry* in Burnaby General Hospital.

After a stop at a pharmacy, it is just before 9.00pm when we finally arrive *chez* Sharma. Mrs S is a lovely lady, and does not turn a single shiny black hair at the fact that we are presenting ourselves three hours after the appointed time.

By now, I am absolutely starving and tuck in to a large (very large) hors d'oeuvre being offered by a turbaned servitor. As so frequently happens after a bit of an abstinence, whatever it was that I have just wolfed down appeases my appetite, and I politely decline a second. Mrs S is distressed and is sure I hate Indian food and that she should have offered something else. To calm her, I accept another. When dinner is finally served, I am absolutely and inelegantly stuffed, but our hostess uses the same sort of culinary moral persuasion she used over the hors d'oeuvres, and I am pressed not only into lavish praise of each course but into additional heapings on my plate.

Anyway, it is an invaluable object lesson, and I know now that 8.00pm can mean anything up until about midnight.

Saturday, January 18 At last our shipment has been released. I have been awaiting it so eagerly that I was sure I would be ecstatic, but I am not. Our things, so right at home, look alien and strangely at odds with their environment – rather like me. Doug has done everything he possibly can to bring Hilary and me into the reality of this new life. I know it will come – but for the moment, it is as though I am on the sidelines, observing someone who looks like me.

Tony is on hand to help me with unpacking, but when I ask him to put something in some particular spot, he gives me that maddening Indian waggle of the head and says, "We should ask the Sahib." What I want to tell him is that the Sahib does not enter into the equation of where household items should go – *I* am telling him, and that is enough.

But I don't. Instead I look disconsolately out the window at the morning parade of heads: turbans, oxen horns above some rumbling carts, a tottering mountain of baskets atop a bicycle, a camel's snooty profile – and ache for the sight of the sea. Herm licks my hand, and I wonder if her faithful little heart is in the green woods of home. I pat her in sympathy and tell her that while a little wallowing won't do us any harm, nor will it do us any good. This pile of boxes is all we have of home, and we had best start looking for it.

Sunday, January 19 Doug has decided that after almost two weeks in India, Hilary and I are sufficiently blooded to see Old Delhi in all its daylight splendour. Contrary to the twilight mirage we had during the *Son et Lumière*, the Red Fort is now revealed in detail. Although some of the romanticism has vanished with the evening mists, I can still see why it is sometimes considered the wonder of all the cities of Delhi. It is absolutely magnificent, and I try to envision it as it must have been, with fountains playing and peacocks wandering across velvet lawns.

The Fort is surrounded by red sandstone walls that have weathered to a rosy softness. We bypass Aurangzeb's defensive barricade (much criticized by his father, Shah Jehan, who scolded his offspring by telling him that he had "made a bride of the palace, and put a veil across her face") and enter through the gate into the main conclave. Seeing India for the first time, as I have, in winter, my overall impression is of a dun-coloured landscape, withered and sere, with only the colours of the resistant flowers to add contrast. Here, inside the Palace City, the scene is ablaze.

We wander through to the Diwani-i-Khas (Hall of Private Audience). One of the many rather officious guides pursues us, trotting along beside us and dodging ahead, spinning tales of the splendour of the carpets, the richness of the drapes and the glory of the fabled Peacock Throne (snatched back to Persia, alas). He launches on the magnificence of the solid silver ceiling but finally loses heart, when he realizes that we are not going to cough up a single rupee.

Now free to ramble on our own, we locate the exquisite Pearl Mosque, and obediently remove our shoes before entering. A boy at the doorway offers some ankle-high floppy slippers, known locally as 'moon boots'. Doug is convinced that they are infested with every germ known to man, but we put them on anyway. The Pearl Mosque was used exclusively by the royal family, rather like the private chapels in England's stately homes.

Outside again, I am amazed to see the lawns being mowed by the primitive means of a cutter pulled by oxen. I am even more amazed to find the place is alive with mystics and entertainers. We stop to observe a levitation at the urging of a swaddled figure, who informs us it is a "holy and sacred" experience offered by "one whose heart is pure". Even the pure in heart, I guess, have to eat, so we pay our handful of rupees and watch. First, a rather grubby red quilt affair covers the saintly body on the ground. There is a lot of chanting and Hindu what-ho-ing, then the quilt rises in the air. As it is supported by several sticks and the quilt is never removed, I am not prepared to accept this 'miracle' at face value, but we applaud politely and bestow our thanks. Hilary is restrained from sneaking a look under the quilt.

We move on to watch snake charmers, dancing monkeys and all the other enchantments being offered. It is a bit like an Asian Coney Island, but the tawdriness of today cannot totally mask the beauty of those delicate minarets, marble domes, elegant avenues and the fountains and pools of Shah Jehan's personal Eden: "If there is a paradise on earth – it is here, it is here, it is here."

After our tour of the Red Fort, Doug leads us across the road to view Chandni Chowk, to be followed by the Street of the Silversmiths. Chandni Chowk is the major market street of Old Delhi, and I am definitely NOT ready for it. It is a horror and an assault on every sense and sensibility. The street is choked with people. Leprous fingers clutch, the halt and the blind and the maimed follow us, begging for money by wailing "Baksheesh" and hawkers with frightful wares keep shoving blue plastic Krishnas under our noses. My pity blends with revulsion and, as yet, I have no emotional immunity.

But if I am not ready, how much less so is Hilary. The poor child finds herself trapped in a jungle of bare, brown legs, and suddenly is confronted, face to face, with a tragic wretch who scoots through the teeming crowds on what appears to be a kind of skateboard. I feel Hilary's grip on my hand tighten and she buries her head in my skirt. What she has seen is a victim of elephantitis – the poor man's face is a blob, a thing of which nightmares are made. My sympathies are everywhere – with him, with Hilary, with me. The crowds and the smells and the clawing fingers have become too much.

"Let's go," I hiss at Doug.

"But you haven't seen the silversmiths yet," he protests.

I'll wait for Birks," I mutter, remembering the hushed luxury of the emporium back home, as we fight our way out to the sanity of the car and the road home.

CHAPTER 4

Monday, January 20 With the arrival of my typewriter, I link up with home in a rash of letters to one and all. Although it is now my third week, I still feel myself to be an uncertain actor, going through the motions, on an alien stage. None of this, of course, do I reveal to my correspondents. I rhapsodize on about the marble halls and the faithful servitors, plus a full description of the wonders we have already seen in this exotic land.

There is another cocktail party on the agenda tonight, and I am beginning to see the diplomatic circle tightening. I wonder if anyone else had the same curious vision of Embassy life as I did.

The very mention of the word 'Ambassador' and I conjured up an endless succession of distinguished-looking characters, dolled up in white tie and tails, or striped trousers and top hats. Furthermore, they are always descending magnificent staircases lined with Cluny tapestries, and inevitably accompanied by divinely beautiful women roped in pearls. Hah!

The reality has proved something of a letdown but, at the same time, an enormous relief. Most of the people I have met so far are really all quite ordinary, with the same warts as the rest of us. Our own High Commissioner and his wife are terribly nice and the souls of probity and honour, but one could not call them physically dazzling. There is even the odd one among the Commission staff who is actually just that – odd.

Prime among the oddities is one lady to whom I am a new and untried ear to be filled with a recital of the events of her life. At one reception last week, I was chatting idly with a small group when there was a sudden mass exodus. I found myself like the boy on the burning deck, whence all but I had fled. My sleeve was being held in a firm, if not actually death's grip, and before I knew it I was being subjected to a full account of the birth of her third child.

My sleeve was being held in a firm, if not actually death's grip

It was not a simple, straightforward tale either, but strayed off at incomprehensible tangents, and I was not even given a chance to show interest with polite interjections such as "what a pity," or "fancy that". It finally dawned on me that the lady was as tight as a tick, and that escape was impossible.

It was at this point that I heard a voice in my ear.

"Run," it whispered, "I'll take over." Could anybody be that noble? Yes, they could. I beetled off.

Sunday, January 21 Sundays are our days of discovery and exploration, and today we begin with the much-vaunted Republic Day Parade. It turns out to be somewhat disappointing – a bust, actually. This year, for the first time, it was decided to eliminate the elephants, camels and all the floats (except for one really tatty affair). There are, instead, a few khaki battalions and some mechanical signs of India's armed might. The Prime Minister Mrs Gandhi drives by in an open car to obligatory cheers but, all in all, the whole affair is more than a bit flat.

We have lunch in the gardens of the Imperial Hotel – very Old Raj – and then head for the Museum of Modern Art, which turns out to be closed on Sundays. The day is beginning to dwindle into disappointment when a visit to the Qutb Minar is suggested.

This wondrous place lies on the outer fringes of Delhi and is, for me, the best thing I have seen so far. I am totally captivated, not just by the awesome Minar (tower), which is classed as the seventh wonder of Hindustan, but by the glorious whole of the entire complex. It reflects a past that makes our present seem off-the-rack and plastic. Where, exactly, it comes in the chronology of Delhi cities, I am not sure, but the tower is traceable to the Afghan period, and soars – all 234 feet of it – above the diverse and fascinating architecture below.

Closer inspection of the tower reveals intricate carving, including passages from the Koran. There are steps inside, and Hilary and I decide to climb the seemingly topless tower. A rash and foolish decision, I think, as I puff my way up.

However, when I can draw a breath, the view is incomparable. I wonder at the long-ago muezzins calling the faithful to prayer, who climbed this Everest of stairs daily.

On the ground once more, I can't get enough. There is an exquisite mosque next to Qutb Minar and we are told it was the first to be built in Delhi at the beginning of the Muslim invasion. There are also wonderful avenues of pillars, both Islamic and pre-Islamic. To me, they look faintly Greek, and I wonder if the conquering Alexander passed this way.

The winter sun casts shadows across our path, which adds no end to the already mystical atmosphere. Just then, I glance up at the great arch near the entrance. A woman in a crimson and gold sari is centred there, standing in a shaft of light. It is worthy of Oscar-winning cinematography, and I fully expect to see the credits roll any time now.

Hilary's goal, through the entire excursion, has been to get us over to the Iron Pillar. It stands in the courtyard of the mosque, and has stood there since the fifth century, when a now obscure Hindu king, Chandar Varman, had it erected. It is 24 feet high and has never rusted. Carved into its shaft are six lines of some ancient language and, needless to say, I am itching to know what they mean. I set myself to wondering where I can dig up a speaker of tongues or a classical scholar who might be able to translate them for me.

The legend of the pillar claims that if you can stand with your back to the column and stretch your arms to encircle it, you will find fame and fortune. Doug manages it and I almost do, but Hilary must resign herself to pursuing her own fortune.

Return home to change for our Sunday dinner at the Grahams. A pleasant surprise! They are entertaining guests from Canada – an Indian doctor and his wife. Also included is a former school friend of the doctor. He is a Mr B D Rao (known as Dinker), a Burmese gentleman resident in Calcutta. He is the managing director of a large company and, as such, has a car and driver at his disposal. He is also a complete charmer, and offers to take the guests on a shopping expedition tomorrow. Calloo-callay, say I, and let's hear it for Dinker.

Monday, January 27 I am up betimes and walk over to the Grahams to join the shopping party. Dinker really is delightful – kind of an Indian David Niven – and his driver takes us to the

Irwin Road shops. These are marvellous and represent the crafts of a number of different regions – Nagaland, Punjab, Haryan et al. I could have lingered longer, but it is lunch time and we are whisked off to the Ashoka Hotel where a sumptuous buffet has been prepared. I love every golden moment, every tender chapati and every spicy morsel.

Unfortunately, Dinker must leave to keep a business appointment, but he bestows both car and driver upon us. We are driven to the Tibetan Market on the Janpath, which is chock-a-block with exotica. I can scarcely contain myself but, alas, Dinker's school chum is monumentally bored, his wife complains of her feet and Mildred is harassed and edgy, so the expedition limps to a retreat.

Tuesday, January 28   After the disappointment of the Republic Day Parade, I am not expecting too much from the Beating of the Retreat. It has all been arranged by Doug's secretary, Raj, who will be joining us. Hilary has been gathered up from school, and we all head for the President's Palace (formerly the Viceroy's home).

It is being held in the vast inner square, and men from the Bengal Lancers line the parade ground. They look magnificent, and Gary Cooper would be proud of them – very impressive discipline. They do not move a muscle throughout the entire ceremony, as regiments solemnly perform manoeuvres. Brass and pipe bands are playing, and the troops perform quick and slow marches with perfect synchronization.

The end is the signal for a brilliant fireworks display. It lights up the twilight sky, and I find tears in my eyes as the regimental buglers on the parapet play *Abide with Me*. The rockets are fired, and the captains and the kings depart. The day dies, as did the Empire, but not without a remembrance of noon.

CHAPTER 5

Saturday, February 1 At the beginning of our second month in India, I try to assess my feelings and changing attitudes.

Today I started my first French lesson. Rather gratified to find Mme Sharma considers me beyond the intermediate stage. Who knows, I may yet win my on-going struggle to become conversationally fluent in French. Besides, with golf, letter-writing, Indian history and French study, perhaps I will be busy enough not to miss the lack of friends. Acquaintances there are a-plenty, and all very pleasant, but it is a shipboard sort of life – a kind of casual camaraderie and joining of common forces against an alien culture.

I wonder about Hilary. She stayed pretty close to home for the first week or so, but she is naturally gregarious and has made quite a number of new friends, mostly American.

She is, I think, the only Canadian child from the Commission in her grade. When she first started at the American Elementary School, she was lumped in with the Canadian miners' children, about whom, I gather, the school elite were being a bit snobbish. I have no idea what all these Canadian miners are doing in Delhi, but imagine it must be some Canadian aid project. In any event, they are the core of the Canadian presence in Grade 4. It seems that most of the Commission offspring are either in their early or middle teens or are pre-schoolers.

Hilary's current best friend is Sue, the child of Peace Corps parents who have a rather laissez-faire attitude toward parenting. As a matter of fact, the American Embassy seems to be brimming over with freewheeling parents. Either that, or I really am the old fogey I strongly suspect I am. Our visits of an evening to the US recreational facilities reveal all sorts of Hilary's classmates wandering around, *sans* parents. One small girl, clinging to the arm of an equally small boy, waves at Hilary.

"Marie is going around with Jake," Hilary confides.

"Going around? At nine years of age??"

Furthermore, for many of these parents and their children, the larger world of India does not seem to exist. When we took one little girl (who had been in India for two years) past the President's Palace, it was all new to her, although it is a spit away from the American Compound. I have to wonder if some of these people feel that they have Main Street, USA, within the confines of the Compound and that is enough for them.

I was always led to believe that in the great days of the Empire the British created their cricket ovals, churches and tearooms in the far corners of the world, and settled into an English style of life. This may be true, but they certainly had nothing on the Americans of the 20th century. However, come to that, I don't have any idea of how adventurous the Canadian expatriates are.

As for us, we are slowly becoming part of the diplomatic social scene, and there always seems to be something on. Tonight it is dinner and bridge at a home in the West End of Delhi. The hostess is she of the other night, from whose recital of birth pangs I was thankfully rescued. Everything is very elegant, although I am beginning to think the Memsahib has a problem, as her eyes start to glaze over quite early in the evening.

In addition to the interesting social scene, I have discovered a new and convenient feature of Delhi life. Services of all kinds come knocking at your door. I used to think it was great to have milk and newspapers delivered at home. Here, countless salesmen present their wares, and various service wallahs present themselves. The barber arrives with his little bag for haircuts; and the tailor, with portable sewing machine, comes to outfit the Sahib with "garments of a truly great elegance." Our resident Savile Row is a Mr Singh, an obliging Sikh, who uses the high point of his turban as a pin cushion. Whenever there is a matter of something being not quite right, he tut-tuts, smiles benignly and assures Doug that he "will tick and will tack, and then will be nice." Not too surprisingly he has become known familiarly in the household as 'Tick Tack'.

He appeared the other night to give Doug a fitting for a pair of dapper white slacks that he'd ordered. There had obviously been some miscalculation as they were distressingly tight around the crotch. This being pointed out, Mr S extracted a large and lethal-looking pin from his turban.

"Do not worry, Sahib, I will tick and will tack...," he began, but was instantly forestalled by Doug who, viewing the pin and the area of correction, categorically refused to be either ticked or tacked.

Sunday, February 2   One of the undeniable pleasures of Sunday to me is the freedom from dodging minions. We can appear *en negligée* and slop around without worrying about what the servants think. Today we opt for lunch at the Akbar Hotel, still selecting with care from the menu, with regard to the delicacy of our western stomachs.

I am rather keen to see Humayun's Tomb, so we make that our first stop. The splendid Mogul architecture seems in such harmony with its surroundings, but then, the surroundings are so much part of whole – the fountains and waterways, the lush gardens and shaded pathways, all background for the splendid domes and arches. Like so many other buildings of the period, Humayun's tomb is red sandstone, but with interstices of black and yellow marble.

One little personal aside pops up. It seems that poor old Emperor Humayun met a singularly un-imperial death, slipping on his library steps and breaking the royal neck. His widow Haji Begum created this wonder of grave and garden, and spent most of her latter years here.

In the Lodi Gardens, we are seduced by the charms of a small and ragged magician who offers us, "Good magic, sahib, for one rupee. Very good magic, two rupees." He appears to be about Hilary's age, and she kneels down beside him in the dust to watch the "very good magic". It is the old shell game, but new to Hilary, and she is entranced.

From the gardens we wander across to the tomb of Isa Khan. I am assuming the Isa was not all that grand, as his tomb, while lovely in itself, is more than a bit run-down. Furthermore his resting place is damned in the guidebook with faint praise. "A fine example of Lodi architecture." I know boom-all about Lodi architecture, but the mood of the place is magical. The winter light is fading a little, though the sun is still warm. There is an old wall, quite beautiful, backed by palm trees and scarlet lilies.

We perch ourselves on a sarcophagus and prepare to hear his story

32

Nobody is around, and so we are startled to see an old man, emerging from the entrance to the tomb. He is very tall and almost transparently thin, and his scholar's face is the colour of old parchment.

"This is my home," he announces, bowing with clasped hands in the traditional *nameste* greeting, "and I am honoured to welcome you."

It is chilly and I am loath to leave the warmth of the sun, but he has greeted us with the politeness of kings and somehow we feel that to decline would be a gross breach of etiquette.

A pile of rags is heaped in the corner; to the left of the crypt is his bed. There are also a few candles, a number of books and some writing materials in evidence. He insists that we have tea and sets himself to the task, while we perch ourselves on a sarcophagus and prepare to hear his story.

Six years ago, he suffered from a long and debilitating illness and, as a result, lost his chair at the university. Normally 'family extension' would have absorbed him into its loosely knit welfare system and he would have become a respected and cared-for elder. However, he had deserted the faith of his fathers some years earlier and become a Christian. At this point, his strict Brahmin family disowned him or, as he described it in the style of a Victorian novel, cast him "into outer darkness." Since then, he has eked out an existence by writing letters for illiterates and polishing up essays for university students.

It is a sad story, and the tomb of the Khan is a dubious residence. He may be a converted Christian, but our host still has the precious Hindu gift of acceptance. This is his karma, and he is at peace with himself. He sees us off with the same warmth and charm with which he welcomed us, and when we, in turn, say goodbye, it as to a friend.

CHAPTER 6

Thursday, February 6 The days are falling into a pattern, as I slowly, slowly begin to put down uncertain roots. Apart from what I buy at the American Commissary, Tony does the bulk of the shopping. All the 'Old India Hands' keep telling me he is probably ripping us off, sneaking staples from the kitchen. I keep dodging the issue.

One of the biggest stumbling blocks in India is the enormity of the gulf between the haves and have-nots. Here are the three of us, with four bathrooms, and the servants have a hole in the ground. The 'OIHs' also keep telling me that our servants consider themselves the Rajahs of the working class, and are the envy of all the street dwellers. I know this is true, but what is also true is that I do not begrudge Tony helping himself to sugar and tea and American-style flour – so why should I make a thing about it?

However, when I happen to stumble on a constant and inexplicably large purchase of eggs (five dozen in one week), I reluctantly concede it is time to draw the line. So today, when Tony comes into the den for money to do the shopping, I suggest he bring me a list beforehand and the bills on his return. I know from his scowl he was sure he had a mark, and he was, of course, perfectly correct. However, despite the fact that I have yet to follow Mildred's dictum on the boss-showing bit, there are times when I feel the stirrings of rebellion. The matter of the eggs is one such time, and last night a big load of iron entered my soul.

A few weeks ago, Tony had taken my bicycle in to be fixed. It seemed all right to me, but he knew someone who would do the necessary "very cheap". He might well have been "very cheap", but he also seemed to be taking eons to do it. Last night, Doug asked Tony to take something over to the Grahams and, purely by accident, I saw Tony taking off on *my* bicycle.

Apparently it had been repaired (or whatever) for ages, and Tony had been swanking around the markets on shining red and chrome, instead of on his own creaking black job. When confronted with this act of perfidy, he just waggled his head, turned his hands palms up and muttered something about it being returned only "minutes ago". Suddenly, it seemed unbelievably petty to pursue the matter further, and I guess we ended in a draw. He knows I know, and I know he knows that I know, and perhaps that is enough.

So my tentative revolt fizzles out, and I content myself by filling my day with French lessons, letter writing, exploring the markets, deplorable efforts at golf, giving and going to parties, devouring books on Indian history, and the not inconsiderable task of keeping track of Hilary as her list of friends grows.

Friday, February 7 It is Open House at the American 'plant' and I go off to see how our fledgling is faring. I need have no fear. She is very much to the forefront in the question-and-answer period, but her teacher, Miss Brooks (yes, really, Miss Brooks) reins her in when necessary, and turns her attention to the silent majority. One of my main worries is allayed. Hilary is adjusting happily to life in India, and doing well at school.

I am glad we do not live on the Compound, because Hilary is soaking up so much more of the Indian scene where we are. She can now identify the cries of each street wallah, has picked up a fair amount of Hindi, and has an on-going battle with the street-corner bicycle wallah. He asks an outrageous amount to fix a flat tire. She counters with an equally outrageous pittance. They argue back and forth and finally settle on a price. Hilary is triumphant, until she discovers a couple of days later that there is a slow leak in the other tire, caused by a suspicious, cleverly placed tack. It is all part of the game, and Hilary returns not unhappily to begin the cut and thrust all over again.

Saturday, February 8 I am shaken to my marrow by the events of the day, and still can't believe I walked away. Doug keeps telling me it was the right thing to do, and his logic is incontrovertible. But it doesn't matter – I still feel awful.

It all begins when we go to Connaught Circus to find Hilary a hard hat for riding. It is late afternoon, and most of the shoppers have left. As we turn the corner toward the store, I step on something soft. At first it appears to be a bundle of rags, but when I look a little closer, I see it is a baby.

I cannot find words to express my horror. I have debased the vocabulary of revulsion by being 'appalled' at the state of a teenager's bedroom; or 'shocked' by a four-letter word from some angel-faced moppet. How does one describe what it feels like to walk on a human infant?

The baby is very small and very still, and flies have already gathered on the waxen eyelids and are probing the tiny nostrils. My first impulse is to pick it up, but Doug stops me. If the baby is dead, what are we going to do with it? If the mother has just drugged the baby into quiet while she toils nearby, we could get ourselves into a lot of trouble.

As Doug points out, the latter is probably the most likely scenario. It is one of the iniquities of an impoverished land that babies are, indeed, drugged by their working mothers. Most of the labourers in Delhi are Rajasthani women. They work on the building sites, carrying bricks and water on their heads, erecting walls in the same timeless fashion that the walls of Jericho were built. No time out is given by their employers to feed or change babies, and babysitters are unheard of. As a result, babies accompany their mothers, and are sedated with a specific type of narcotic weed. The sad thing is that these children grow up functional but, at best, mildly retarded, and the whole cycle begins again. I look down at my own pink-cheeked offspring and send up a silent prayer of thanks.

Monday, February 10 Today I discover Enid. It seems Enid has been an institution in Delhi for longer than any current expat can remember. Her shop is like something out of *The Raj Quartet*. The walls are ancient mahogany, and a huge plate glass mirror awaits to catch every imperfection. There is a vast armoire that looks as though it should contain a collection of Queen Mary's hats. Curtains on a dressing room part and Enid emerges, straight out of *Staying On*.

She is thin to the point of emaciation and her diminished hair is tinted a sort of peach shade. She carries with her a general air of reduced circumstances and a look of total disapproval.

I stop myself from apologizing for bothering her and present my recently purchased fabrics. She grudgingly takes

A huge plate glass mirror awaits to catch every imperfection

my measurements, looks at them as though she were saying, "What could anyone do with these?" I want to defend myself by pointing out that they are my measurements and I am loyal to them. But I can see that Enid is not one for verbal bandying and remain silent.

She totes up the bill and asks for a 150 rupee deposit. With Mildred's cautions in mind, I give her 100 and leave, having just ordered two dresses at 65, two blouses at 45 and two skirts at 55, for a grand total of 330 rupees. Unbelievable. I translate this sum roughly into Canadian currency – it's somewhere around $40.

CHAPTER 7

Saturday, February 13   Our social life is now in full flower, and today is our National Day – every Mission has to have one, and does it really matter that Canada Day is actually July 1? We are all duly grateful, as July 1 could be 110°F in the shade or awash with the monsoons. Doug tells me that all the officers and their 'mems' have been asked to mingle, smile and chat.

Despite the fact that I have now been here for ten weeks, this is my first time at the Residence (His Excellency had already formally received Doug back in November, and Mrs HE has had dengue fever, poor thing.) It (the Residence) is quite impressive – a lovely house with a beautiful garden, big enough to hold the large international crowd that has assembled. There are turbans and fezzes, saris and elegant Chinese cheongsams, as well as the more mundane dress of the westerners.

I do as bid, and mingle and as a result meet some interesting people: Mrs Sharma (our first Indian hostess), several representatives of the World Health Organization, a pleasant lady from the British High Commission whose husband is arranging a golf tournament to which we have been invited, and a white-cassocked priest who is being clutched by my old friend, the sleeve grabber. Having nothing better to hold on to, she has grasped him by the crucifix and is drawing him inexorably and inescapably toward her. Remembering my own rescue, and thinking about 'doing unto others', I decide to try diversionary tactics. All ingratiating smiles, I tell her that someone in the farthest corner of the garden has been asking after her. "No, I didn't get her name. What did she look like? Well, it's a little hard to say... She is wearing sort of a flowered voile..." And from here on, it's every flowered voile for itself, I think, as she dashes off.

The rescued priest is busy adjusting his cassock and mopping his brow. I feel I should ask him for absolution for the amazing fiction I have just perpetrated, but he is giving me

She has grasped him by the crucifix

such a spaniel-like look of gratitude that I feel he is mentally filling out my application for beatification.

Gradually the sun wanes, the band plays *O Canada* and, as usual, I wipe away a furtive tear. The afternoon is over and the honour of the nation has been upheld.

Sunday, February 16   It is the day of the Monkey Golf Tournament at Faridabad Golf Course. We pack a picnic and join two other couples from the Commission. I am not in a deep funk about my shortcomings as a golfer, as it is not a serious affair. Each member of the team is equipped with just one club – either a driver, an iron, a pitching wedge or a putter – and plays a stroke in turn. I am assigned the putter, so nothing much is expected of me.

'HE' the High Commissioner is on the same team as I, and I am reminded all over again what a really nice man he is. All in all, a fun day.

Monday, February 17   Hilary, too, finds herself confronted with the niceties of social life. Today is George Washington's birthday, and the American School is closed. Hilary and her friend Sue are having a lovely time building a dog house of sorts for a pariah dog in the alley behind the house. Doug has issued strict orders about 'pi' dogs, and Hilary promises to keep her distance. This I know to be well-nigh impossible, and just hope for the best.

They are deeply engrossed in this project, when I have to call Hilary in to change for a luncheon to which she has been invited by a school friend. Sue has not been asked, and Hilary is more than reluctant to go. One of those 'in-life-there-are-many-things' chats ensues and – smouldering and muttering – she prepares to leave.

Saturday, February 2   In compensation for the disruption of the dog-house building, Sue has been invited to stay with us for the weekend, and a trip to the Tibetan Market in the Janpath is on the agenda. This has become one of my favourite outings. I love the Imperial Hotel's gardens for tea, and the ingenuity of the totally unscrupulous hawkers in the market. There is one seer who always asks for my "lucky name", this being the key to one's fortune. I try to confuse him by giving him different and exotic names each time, but the fortune remains the same.

Happily, Hilary and Sue have both been invited to a costume party at 6.00pm, so I hurry them off home, get them into their respective costumes and drop them off at the party. We pick them up at the appointed hour, and the parental hosts (another American couple) invite us in. It turns out they have a son at Dartington Hall School in Devon, and I am swept nostalgically away to that not-to-be-forgotten December weekend I spent at Dartington years ago, and my billeting in the 'haunted' Cloisters.

Sunday, February 22   Children keen to go to an open-air 'Paint-In' on Bakhomani Road. Get them up there in a taxi, and tell them to stay until we pick them up. When we return, as agreed, there are no children. My heart sinks, and the mind leaps to conclusions so dreadful they cannot be contemplated. Visions of the Peace Corps parents, tragic and accusing (or even worse, forgiving), beset me. Laid back they may be, but the mislaying of a daughter is not a thing to be shrugged off with a light laugh. We scour the grounds and environs, then return home to address our alternatives. The old 'if-only-they-would-come-home-so-I-can-kill them' returns to me in spades when I see two small girls sitting on the side patio. It turns out that Sue wearied early of self-expression and the wretched little things took a taxi home. There is a garbled tale of the taxi man's all-too-successful efforts to cheat them, of spent allowances and other misfortunes too numerous to recount. We go inside to the shuttered coolness, lemonade is poured, tears are dried and mild lectures are delivered. They are dragged off to an educational exhibit of Indian crafts, but are consoled by the promise of supper at the Commissary café for the obligatory hamburger and fries, to be followed by a movie at the Embassy Theatre.

Thursday, February 27   A full day, full of 'firsts'. By the dawn's early light, I make my first attempt at driving in Delhi. I am incredibly nervous, as if I had never driven before – and the thought of all those camels, oxen carts and bicycles is more than a bit daunting. I drive around Vasant Vihar a couple of times, and then comes the acid test: I drive Doug to the High Commission and return without having dispatched any of Delhi's pedestrian population into premature graves.

In the afternoon, my first brush with royalty as we are invited to a polo match, featuring none other than HRH The Prince of Wales. The announcer, a rotund and sycophantic local with a plummy Oxford accent, is worth the price of admission. He gets quite carried away with every stroke of the princely mallet.

"Oh, I say, an absolutely splendid shot by His Royal Highness," is delivered in ringing tones, followed, alas, by a mumbled, "Oh, bad luck, it just misses."

The last of the 'firsts' in this eventful day occurs at a cocktail party to which we have been invited. It's being given by the CIDA (Canadian International Development Agency) man and his enchanting Vietnamese wife. He is known locally as the 'Sherpa Colonel' because of his work in Nepal.

I still have not found a 'friend of the bosom' and while our hostess is enormously friendly, her English is limited and, as I only pick up about one word in every hundred, I fear she will not become the intimate I am looking for. Despite that, I think a door has opened tonight, just a crack, but it is enough for me to feel there may come a light in the darkness of my social isolation.

I am drifting around the room, a desultory chat here and there, the usual inanities – "How are you enjoying India?", "How long have you been here?", "Children with you?"

"Hello," someone says, and I find myself being addressed by a flowery print, covering a comfortable form topped by what used to be called in the old *Schoolgirl's Weekly* "a jolly face".

"Hello," I say back.

"These parties are pure shit, aren't they?"

Mine has, by and large, been a sheltered life. "Oh, fudge" directed at a parent was considered the pinnacle of rebelliousness, so I was not really prepared for this attractive English Rose to be quite so direct. However, prepared or not, I warm to her.

I mutter something in response about cocktail parties being a useful social device. She expresses another firmly held opinion. We find ourselves a niche behind an Indian screen and we also find an almost instant friendship. I discover she is indeed a woman of strong views, many of them based on hazy but determined convictions.

She is also passionately attached to the word 'fantastic', which peppers her conversation and describes everything from the book she is reading to her entrée into the world of bridge. We touch on both subjects. She is reading a novel about Charles II and Lucy Walters, with whom he (Charles) had a "go" that resulted in the Duke of Monmouth. He (ie Charles II) had a "go" with heaps of others. We then slip from the wayward Charles to Victoria, and did I think she "had it off" with John Brown?

After all the prissy cocktail party conversations, I find my new companion marvellously refreshing. We finally get around to introducing ourselves. She is Monica Barker, and her husband Hamish is the manager of the Chartered Bank in Old Delhi, and do I play bridge? I tell her yes, but so far I haven't found anyone to play with. Her eyes light up with a crusader's zeal, and she lets me know that I have found someone now, and I must come to the British High Commission with her. I have been over this course before, with "you must come sometime..." and nothing happens.

Somehow, I feel it will be different this time.

Friday, February 28 Sure enough, today there is a phone call from Monica – bridge next week at the British High Commission. Bolar Singh, the Chartered Bank driver will pick me up. Am I really about to be launched?

All this gives me pause to wonder about our position at the High Commission. Through a number of circumstances, I have not really formed any comfy friendships: Doug having been here two months before I arrived; Mrs HE, whose duty it is to 'see to' new wives, being ill; the pool being closed.

Doug tells me that the High Commission pool is the general gathering spot for the ladies and children, and once it opens up I will be one of the girls. Well, it opened up a week ago, and I am not one of the girls.

As already mentioned I am glad we do not live on the Compound, as there is, of necessity, a sort of cultural isolation about living in a strictly Canadian environment, with Gurka guards at the gate and the locally-engaged staff restricted as to the use of the facilities.

In addition to the offices of the High Commission, the Compound includes the pool and cabana, a tennis court, and spacious lawns and gardens. There are about four officers' homes in the Compound, and the rest of the living quarters are for the support staff – guards, communicators and technicians. Perhaps herein lies the rub. The officers' residences are larger, better furnished and all in all grander than those of the support staff and I suspect, as in the army, there are invisible social barriers. The doctors are an anomaly – they are not support staff, nor are they diplomats. By the very nature of their profession, there is a degree of respect, but they do not come under the prestigious umbrella of the powerful External Affairs.

So here I am, making my first appearance on the Pool-Cabana stage. I am armed with a hat, sunglasses and a book. The pool shimmers in the sunlight. There are various sun-loungers, tables and umbrellas on the surrounding patio. A group of women are at a table, drinking coffee and long cool drinks. They do not look up as I slip into the cabana. When I emerge, they look in my direction; I smile and say, "Good morning." They smile and say "Good morning" and return to their drinks and their gossip. I find a chaise under a tree, address myself, with every show of the deepest interest, to my book and that is that. I swim and read until it is time to pick up Doug to go home for lunch.

"Well," he says, "how was the pool?"

"Lovely," I reply. What else can I say?

However, if I have yet to make friends among our compatriots, the Indian doctors are putting out the welcome mat in high style. Tonight we are invited to a dinner at the home of Dr and Mrs Khosla. The appointed hour is 8.00pm but, remembering our experience with the Sharmas, we take our time about getting there. We are still the first to arrive.

The rest of the party drifts in slowly. They are a mixed bag of interesting types – an American Naval Attaché and his wife plus her visiting parents, some silent Japanese diplomats, a local lady doctor and her husband, and a rather jolly British

45

Air Force Attaché and his wife.

I find myself sitting next to the last-mentioned gentleman at dinner, and he asks me what I am doing to amuse myself, now that I have a houseful of servants and time on my hands.

"Well, I'm studying French for one thing," I tell him.

"My dear, whatever for?"

"Oh, I don't know. I suppose as a Canadian, I sort of feel it is *un devoir patriotique*."

"Nonsense," he bellows, "they've all got to come to us sooner or later, y'know. To illustrate my point, let me tell you about my lunch the other day at the Ashoka with my opposite numbers at the French and German Embassy. We were discussing this very subject, the Frenchie, Jerry and I, and I picked up a piece of cutlery and set them straight. 'Now my dear chaps, in French, you call this a *cueillir* and in German you refer to it as a *löffel*, but I call it a spoon because that's bloody well what it is.'"

It sounds so English, and his face is absolutely serious, but I detect a redeeming twinkle in his eye.

All in all, I enjoy the evening enormously, and make a date with Mrs K to go shopping with her in Old Delhi.

CHAPTER 8

Sunday, March 2 Hilary's first gymkhana, and I have to admit she acquits herself well, copping three cups: third in musical chairs (a fierce competition vying with, I regret to say, some degree of aggression against equally aggressive Dutch and German competitors), first in the under-10 race and third as the best 'debutante' – at least I think that is what they said. Anyway, she is chuffed as all get out and clutches her cups all the way home.

Monday, March 3 Doug brings back mail from the Commission, including a postcard from my old and very dear friend Sheila Kincaid. I gave the speech at her farewell party when she wound up her career as Director of the Burnaby Art Gallery, and shortly after saw her off on her round-the-world jaunt last November.

The card is from Bombay, and announces that she will be arriving on March 7. I am so happy and excited – a friend, a real friend, someone to talk to and share things with other than those meaningless conversations I have been conducting on the cocktail circuit. I start counting the days.

Tuesday, March 4 The American Embassy has been girding up for the past few months for the Bicentennial celebrations. The new American Ambassador arrived a little while ago and rather blotted his copybook by ill-advised remarks on India-Pakistan relations, and also by allowing himself to be caught by a photographer in a pink gingham golf outfit. India still likes its visiting ambassadors attired as for the Court of St James. The poor man has been working on buffing up his image ever since, and all sorts of events have been planned, with flag-waving and goodwill in mind. Today there is a couturier fashion show, featuring top American designers.

Said fashion show is being held in the gardens of the American Residence. It has been beautifully organized, with charming tables set up around the pool, so arranged that everyone has a view of the latest in New York fashions. They are, of course, to drool over (a far cry from Enid's last-of-the-Empire creations) and the lunch is straight out of the pages of *Good Housekeeping*.

Friday, March 7 Today is the day, and Sheila's room (with a new Indian bedspread) awaits. I lay in a supply of books on Delhi and environs, culled from the American Library, and at the appointed hour we are off to Palam Airport to pick up our much-anticipated guest. Sheila is looking wonderfully well, and full of tales of her adventures in the subcontinent. Despite being prepared for it, Bombay was still a shocker, and her first look at the expatriate India is both a contrast and a relief. Mildred and John come for dinner and, like Heraclitus, we "tire the sun with talking, and send him down the sky."

Sunday, March 9 Eager to show Sheila the sights, we make the obligatory trip to the Red Fort, and the levitation artistes do their thing to Sheila's delight. From here we go for the first time to Gandhi's Memorial. It is *so* right – a solid block of black marble, set in a quiet garden. Its very simplicity is somehow strangely powerful, and bespeaks the man. There is a worshipful procession, and the atmosphere is like that of a cathedral. We remove our shoes and silently parade past the one, who in death, has become as a god.

Monday, March 10 I take Sheila to the Golf Club, and look on with admiration as she whacks the ball with a sure and unerring swing. She is the first person who seems to see what I see in this miracle of green fairways, flame-coloured trees, parrots and Mogul tombs. However, she also sees the ball and where it is supposed to go. After golf we go for lunch at the Cabana, and for a swim. It is lovely to have a friend with me, and I don't really care whether anybody else talks to me or not.

I still find a sort of barrier exists, which is strange as Canadians are essentially very friendly, and I have never really had trouble making friends. Doug reiterates it is the old army game, and its social pecking order, which seems incredibly silly. I obviously have a lot to learn, and Mildred is on hand to set me straight. She tells me that while I may not be asked to hobnob with Ambassadors, I can certainly snub the lower orders. I decide to digest all this, and then go my own way and be my own me, and the chips can fall wherever they jolly well want to.

Sunday, March 16 A malaise has struck our household. Doug felt distinctly seedy at a party last night, and sank into bed, from which he has yet to rise this morning. Sheila also has retreated after frequent trips to the loo. Having survived Bombay, can she possibly be suffering from 'Delhi Belly' in our carefully controlled ménage? As a result, our Sunday expedition is off, and I spend the day in Tony's kitchen (*sans* Tony, of course) and have a field day with leftover turkey – whomping up turkey soup and something I choose to call turkey fricassee. It does not tempt the invalids, alas, and Hilary and I dine alone.

Thursday, March 20 Sheila has fallen into the Delhi life with ease, and she joins me in golf. She is so much better than I, though I seem to be hacking and hewing a little more skilfully of late. We have hired a driver, Solomon by name, who is proving to be an absolute godsend, dropping us off and picking us up, just like real Memsahibs. He has also shown us hitherto unexplored areas of Delhi, as well as being on hand to take us to Sheila's list of 'musts'.

One such is a visit to a Professor Chandra, with whom Sheila corresponded in connection with the 'Mystic Circle' exhibition at the Burnaby Art Gallery. By way of an introductory step, one of the locals at the High Commission arranges for us to meet an associate of the professor's, a German lady *d'un certain age* by the name of Elisabeth Brummer. She has, we are told, lived in India for more than 30 years and has painted every noteworthy citizen from both the Raj and post-Raj period.

We are naturally agog to meet her, and she does not disappoint. She is a thin, bright-eyed lady, with a misplaced topknot and a mildly distrait air. She greets us warmly and sweeps a few canvasses off a much-used chesterfield so that we can sit down. Her rooms are unbelievably cluttered, a bit as though some giant rummage sale had run away with itself.

...as though some giant rummage sale had run away with itself

Moving across to the proffered seating, I feel ever so slightly like a giraffe, taking careful steps over the hills of clothing, paints and memorabilia. She carries on a relentless line of chatter: yes, she will be delighted to introduce us to Professor Chandra; no she is not engaged this evening; and yes, she would be more than happy to join us for dinner at Vasant Vihar. Solomon is summoned, we are gathered up and a highly diverting evening follows.

Friday, March 21 We are getting ready for our trip to south India. It is my first real bit of travel outside of Delhi, and I am mustard keen about the whole thing. One of the major pluses about Doug's position is that the Doctor probably has to do more travelling than any other officer, except perhaps 'HE'. And, as I told Doug at the very beginning, "Whither thou goest..." there too goest I.

This particular trip coincides with the Spring Break at school, so Hilary is to come with us, as well as Sheila. However, getting outfitted for this safari is not without its complications.

Sheila went in pursuit of a bathing suit yesterday, and returned with something from a Mack Sennett comedy, pure 1920s and hideous as to hue and style. I tangle with the tailor, who has "with all faith" promised my raw silk pant suit for today. Hilary's cotton skirt, also promised for today, has yet to see scissors or thread. We soothe ourselves with a trip to the American library where I pick up four books on southern India.

After lunch, Solomon picks us up and we drive out to the Qutb Minar. I have been dying to show it to Sheila, and am delighted that she is suitably entranced. I try to write out the text on the iron pillar in the hope that Professor Chandra may be able to translate it for me. We then drive out to the Institute for Indian Culture and our appointment with Professor C. He is totally charming and a scholar of vast erudition. He smiles ruefully at my text from the iron pillar, and says he will work on it, but at the moment it looks like the "scratchings of a paralyzed chicken."

In addition to answering Sheila's questions, he gives us a tour of the Institute. We see Tibetan scrolls, wonderfully scripted writings in Sanskrit and ancient Hindi on pressed palm leaves and a rubbing of a Chinese stone from 67AD. This latter is a recording of the interview two Indian travellers to Cathay had with the Emperor of China. Professor Chandra shows us all these and many other wonders, pausing only to offer us tea and introduce us to his wife. We both feel we have just scratched the surface, but have to rush home to change for yet another evening party.

CHAPTER 9

Sunday, March 23 Having spent Saturday picking up a few necessities we are as ready as we can be for our trip. Mind you, there was a lot of wasted effort in pursuit of sun lotion for Sheila's fair complexion, until we realized that this is just not a big seller in the Indian market.

However, we are up at 5.30am and packed, booted and spurred. The High Commission driver arrives at 6.15am and we board the flight to Hyderabad without incident. Delhi was cloudy and damp after a storm the night before, but we reach Hyderabad, the capital city of Andhra Pradesh, in brilliant sunshine.

It is, in all respects, a pleasant surprise. Signs of civic pride are in evidence, with billboards reminding the citizenry that "Ours is a beautiful city – keep it clean!" Most of the public buildings are dazzlingly white, while the streets are swept and lined with palms and flowering trees.

We have a nice drive along the Esplanade to our hotel. The Ritz is actually an old castle that once belonged to the Nizam of Hyderabad. It has been whitewashed recently, from its turrets to its dungeons, and looks very spiff. There is a most attractive entrance, with a gazebo and lily pond, flanked by a gate-keeper's cottage. We go through a delightful inner courtyard, full of tropical plants and flowers. Our room is a suite with a sitting room, bedroom and bathroom.

This being my first excursion away from India's capital, the tourist adrenalin is in over-drive. There is not a moment to be lost, and after bolting down a light lunch, we take a cab to the much-touted Nehru Zoological Gardens.

The drive there reveals a city, inescapably Indian, crowded with all manner of conveyances: bicycles, bicycle-rickshaws, honking taxis, oxen carts, to say nothing of phalanxes of pedestrians. Yet somehow, there is a sense of order, a pattern to the mass movements. Perhaps it is only because I am eager to see it, but the city even seems to have made an attempt at maintenance (a word critics claim is not in the Indian lexicon).

Definitely the taxis are cleaner, the houses are painted and the beggars fewer.

We reach the Zoological Gardens and are pleased to find few animals in cages. Instead they are isolated in a natural environment, surrounded by unobtrusive protection. The fauna is varied – white Bengal tigers, lions, rhinos and a group of mandrills, with their agonizingly blistered bottoms. We wander beside a lovely mangrove lagoon, which is inhabited by storks and flamingos. Nearby a brick wall is being built, and I am fascinated to see it being constructed with the advanced technology of 2,000 years ago. Women in brilliant saris, carrying water jugs on their head, walk like queens to the site. Others bear bricks in the same fashion. Apparently some engineer and a time-study expert came to the remarkable conclusion that from a time-and-cost accounting perspective, this age-old method wins out over 20th century mechanization.

We return to the hotel, have a siesta, Happy Hour and dinner. The evening – "quiet as a nun" – beckons and I walk alone in the garden, intoxicated by the night and the scent of frangipani.

Monday, March 24 One of the things that delights me about this trip is how much Hilary is getting out of it. I found her this morning, totally engaged with the gold-fish in the lily pond and building a small pebble bridge in the pool. Unlike a European hotel where she would have been scurried away, the Indian doormen smile, clap and look on indulgently at her efforts. She has an early morning swim with Sheila and me, and only reluctantly leaves her diving practice to come in for breakfast.

Doug arranges an appointment at 4.00pm with the DMP (Designated Medical Practitioner) he has come to see, so until then we have the whole golden day. We take a cab around Hyderabad and feast on all the vignettes of city life in India, to wit: a gentleman strolling absolutely starkers across the street, with nobody turning a hair or a glance; a beggar to whom Sheila offers baksheesh if he will pose for her. Pose for her? He practically turns hand-springs with delight, straightens his rags, pushes back his oily hair and punches the air with the stump of his right hand.

We do the tourist thing, snapping pictures of the Char

Minar, built in 1559 to commemorate the cessation of the plague. (It is funny, but I thought the plague was strictly European.) Nearby is an enormous mosque, capable of accommodating 10,000 with elbow room. It's unusual in that it has a long Venetian-style arcade at the approach.

The Hyderabad Museum is more than a trifle tacky and seems dedicated to apple-polishing for the current Nizam. There is a whole section devoted to his nursery exercise books, and we gaze upon coloured alphabets, verses that don't rhyme and arithmetic efforts where two and two do not always add up to four.

One might well think that the history of Hyderabad began and ended with the incumbent Nizam, but I do find a modest corner that gives a brief outline of the history of Andhra Pradesh. It was founded as a princely state sometime around the mid-16th century, and came under the suzerainty of the Mogul emperors until the French and British tossed it back and forth during the battles for power. The dynasty of the Nizams of Hyderabad eventually came under British protection, while still maintaining administrative control over the inner workings of the state. After the transfer of power in 1947, Hyderabad was declared an independent state, but only briefly, as Indian forces absorbed it into the new India. The religious schism that devastated and divided post-Raj India left Andhra Pradesh strangely undisturbed. It remained, as it had been for centuries, a predominantly Hindu state headed by a Muslim ruler.

Doug goes off for his appointment, leaving us free for a little uninhibited shopping at the local Handicraft Emporium. Hands are rubbed, smiles are bestowed, money changes hands and we return to the hotel with a lovely collection of bedspreads, sari lengths and carved miniature elephants.

Over dinner in a Chinese restaurant, we become aware of the incredible adaptability of Chinese cuisine. Just as 'chop-suey burgers' appear on North American menus, here everything has the distinct flavour of curry.

Tuesday, March 25 I can't remember the name of the film travelogue man who always wore his hat backwards and always left with his camera turning and with regret. But this morning we leave "storied" Hyderabad with regret, and fly on to Bangalore.

We are booked into a quite grand hotel, another Ashoka. Doug arranges an appointment for 9.00am the next day, so after lunch we set out to explore the sights and sounds of Bangalore.

At the hotel's recommendation, we get ourselves a driver for the day – a chubby, jovial Dravidian who looks surprisingly like Hilary's bosom chum, Claire, in West Vancouver. We promptly dub him Claire, to which name he responds as though he had just been christened.

Sheila tends to be a rather earnest tourist at times, and is keen that we really *see* the life and culture of the city. One of the tour books states that porcelain is a local industry, and we all nod approval of this as a starting point.

Claire is consulted and waggles his head, then drives some distance out of the town. Visions of delicate china, hand painted with the flowers of Shalimar, dance pleasantly through my head. Claire eventually draws up in front of an enormous gate, which has obviously not been thrown wide to welcome hordes of porcelain fanciers. As a matter of fact, Claire has to go and rouse a sleeping chowkidar (do chowkidars ever do anything but sleep, I ask myself?) who, after a great deal of conversation, goes off to rout out the manager.

There ensues a long, hot interval, until a small, obsequious man appears, rubbing his hands and bowing as he spots a car full of Europeans. A confab with Claire produces a mildly puzzled look, followed by a 'wot-the-hell' toss of the head (which I now know equates with agreement), and he flings the gate wide. He speaks a little English and, choosing his words carefully, announces: "It is a great honour to welcome you, Sahib and Memsahibs to my factory. I have never, no never, had visitors interested in my toilet bowls. Plis, plis to excuse any disorder you may find."

Toilet bowls!! Dear God, what have we done! Doug rather gracefully extricates us, saying there has been a misunderstanding. It is we who are honoured by his welcome, but if he will forgive us, we will not visit his factory today, perhaps another time.

Claire is obviously worried sick that his plans for a

lucrative day are slipping away from him, and hastens us back into the car with salaams and apologies and splutterings that he had only been following orders – "Oh yes, oh my goodness, oh yes."

We reassure him, and after a few more scrapings, he drives us back into Bangalore for what he describes as a "very great tour". It is. With some aplomb he conducts us up to an official-looking sentry box. A policeman emerges, examines the car and its passengers, speaks to Claire and then, satisfied that we are harmless, he puts a 'checked' sticker on the windshield. Beaming, Claire proceeds up to a building that looks for all the world like a giant cup-cake, lavishly iced. It is surrounded by lawns and flowers. Claire, positively bursting with local pride, announces that this is the Legislative House of Bangalore.

Someone dressed like a three-star general confiscates our bags and cameras, and writes out a chit that we are to be directed to the 'Distinguished Visitors Gallery'. I am beginning to feel that this whole scenario is unfolding inexorably and will continue to do so, with no motivating direction from us.

On the floor of the House, 28 of the Assembly's 280 members are gathered, and I wonder if this is a break period. Only a few seemed to be seated, others wander around, chatting, hawking up betel-juice stained sputum, blowing their noses Indian fashion (ie with the aid of two fingers), scratching at their dhotis and generally appearing at ease. Every once in awhile, someone will declaim something in Tamil, which may or may not deal with the business of the state.

Observing all this, we turn at the sound of a cleared throat. An usher, frowning, points at Sheila and me, who are sitting with our legs crossed. We cannot think what we have done wrong, but it is obvious that we are to un-cross, *vite, vite*. We do, and he nods his approval. I find this bizarre in the extreme, having seen the totally uninhibited behaviour of the legislators. It is not until later that we learn that it is not the length of bare leg that is offensive, it is because pointing one's feet or showing the soles of your shoes is one of Asia's worst insults, and we are lucky that a couple of 'distinguished visitors' had not been ejected, or worse, for lese-majesty.

We drift out after about ten minutes, and find Claire

Pointing one's feet ... is one of Asia's worst insults

waiting for us and eager to reveal more wonders. He takes us around the colonial verandah and into the Members' Lounge to see some very bad paintings, and from there into the rotunda. The ceilings are indescribable – elaborate squares of scalloped plaster, all painted in supermarket icing colours of pinks and greens and blues. Having given as many gasps of admiration as possible, we leave the Legislature and continue on our "very great tour".

We enter into an emporium with simply fantastic silks – shimmering cascades of gold, purple, silver and deep, glorious reds. Next stop is an open-air market, where Claire is received with smiles and salaams. He informs us the market is the largest in South India, and I have no reason to doubt him. It is vast and spectacular, the flower stalls dazzling. There are garlands and beautiful pyramids of fruit and vegetables, trinkets and ribbons and clothes – but blessedly no clutching hawkers and no beggars.

Our guide is everywhere, pinching things for us to taste; he is renewing acquaintances, and bit by bit we gather a following. Hilary is given some flowers, which Claire insists on fastening in her hair. Much embarrassed, she finds herself trailed by a coterie of smiling, admiring marketers. When we finally depart, flower-bedecked, we do so with an air of royalty, being tucked into our waiting carriage by friendly hands and waving gracious farewells. It was, all in all, a "very great tour".

Wednesday, March 26 It is the twins' birthday, and I feel sad that they are there and we are here. Shades of other birthdays haunt me. There was the one with both of them down with the measles; the one with the hired pony and the coincidental rainstorm; the one at age nine, with an equal mixture of boys and girls being boys and girls, the games ignored in the fascination of filching hair ribbons and hiding in laundry baskets.

I resolutely pack memories away, and join hands with today. Doug has gone off to inspect his DMP, and we await his return to start our planned day trip to Mysore.

Claire arrives full of enthusiasm, but informs us that "Alas, I cannot take you all the way, oh my goodness." However, we are assured that his 'cousin' (everybody's a cousin) will meet us with his automobile (which is apparently of a "supreme splendour") and that the cousin is of the purest character, has much knowledge and it is most fortuitous that he, Claire, has arranged "a very great outing".

It is a marvellous drive – the flat countryside gradually changing into hills and rocks and thick jungly areas of palms, eucalyptus and rubber trees. The villages and their mode of life cannot have changed much in a thousand years, and I feel, as I so often do in India, that I am in a time warp. Women still wash their clothes in the river and still scoop water from the well, carrying it on their heads. Oxen still pull the ploughs, and village residences are still constructed out of whatever materials are to hand – straw, thatch, bamboo, cow dung and, here and there, clay. The colours entrance me – the brilliant green of rice paddies, offset by the vivid saris that dot the fields like exotic birds. We glimpse an elaborately carved temple cart at a wayside shrine. The whole scene is like watching a film of Indian country life.

Halfway to Mysore, we stop by a coconut grove and change drivers. A small boy with enormous liquid eyes solemnly opens a coconut with a machete and from some unknown source produces a straw. Claire leaves us with his usual salaams and assurances, and it is only after he is gone that we find out that the cousin speaks no English and, for that matter, is none too familiar with his 'supreme' auto. He insists on changing a wheel at the coconut stand, then stops a little farther down the road to find water, as the radiator bubbles over with steam.

We finally reach Mysore, and now find that not only does the cousin not know English, nor the crotchets of the car, he also does not know Mysore. Fortunately, the ever-helpful *Fodor's Guide* gives us a clue, and we drive up into the hills in search of the Hoysala Temple. It is very hot, and we are beset by postcard peddlers and endless pleas for baksheesh. We find the temple interesting, but not really an architectural wonder, nor worth the dodging of the curious populace and the mopping of our collective brows.

As a result we travel on to see the giant bronze Nandi, the Great Bull of Mysore. It looms over the landscape, golden and glittering in the blaze of noon. It is awesome and strangely intimidating. I can understand why it is due and receives

60

reverence. Doug takes a picture of Hilary, dwarfed by the titanic proportions.

By now, it seems a long time between draughts of coconut milk and we drive down to the Lalith Mahal Palace, former guest palace of the Maharajah of Mysore and now a hotel, which is cool and still quite grand. We have a pleasant luncheon in a cavernous and echoing dining room (the kind where the slightest whisper carries like an amplified shriek), then leave to see the City Palace. This, to put it kindly, is *very* disappointing. To put it accurately, it is just awful. Access, we discover, is down a back lane full of evil odours, past the gent's loo, to a crude booth where, after payment of 75 paisa per head, we are allowed to enter.

If we thought the Hyderabad Museum was a tad sycophantic, this one is a pure ego trip for the Maharajah of Mysore. There are innumerable ancestral portraits and some ghastly Victorian-era furniture, including some bizarre chairs shaped like peacocks (the backs being the extended tails). Not only do they appear anatomically impossible to sit on, but at a swift glance they seem to be made of papier-mâché and shells.

The adjoining Art Gallery is even worse and its façade is as garish as that of the museum. The tacky-looking grounds are presented as a 'sculpture garden', and consist mainly of a hideous wooden couple, ferociously painted and clutching each other under an umbrella.

The artistically sensitive Sheila feels she cannot take any more and, as it is now after 5.00pm, we request the driver to start back to Bangalore. While the return is not as absorbing as the going, it is still pleasant, and we watch the sun set behind the ranks of palms and flowering trees. A good dinner at the Sapphire grill and then, as Mr Pepys was wont to say, "so to bed."

Thursday, March 27 Leave the hotel early for the airport, and after saying goodbye to the faithful Claire, we board the plane for Cochin in the state of Kerala. Cochin is so rich in history, so varied in its ethnic background and so picturesque in its architecture that I am really disappointed that we have only three and a half hours here.

Doug's DMP not only picks him up, but takes him to the

Cochin Hospital, leaving Sheila, Hilary and me to the shops. Sheila generously buys me a carved ivory necklace, and we all enjoy a prowl through the handicraft fair, but sadly one of India's most fabled cities lies unexplored.

We return to the airport in due time, and make the short flight over the palm-fringed shores of Trivandrum. We are driven to Kovalum through endless banana plantations, jungle villages and thick, beautiful coconut groves. Doug adds a medical note, by telling us that Trivandrum has the highest death rate from early heart attacks in India: "All due to the heavy consumption of coconut."

This sombre information is immediately forgotten, however, when we reach our beach-shore hotel. It consists of a number of little thatched cottages, set in groves of coconut and banana palms. The cottage is charming and contains everything we need – bedrooms, sitting room, bathroom and refrigerator, with a little shaded patio facing the sea.

It is fiercely hot, and we rush into our bathing suits and down to the sea. It is wonderful – divinely warm, with huge breakers. Hilary is beside herself. Quite a number of native boys are swimming, but there's not a woman to be seen. We are the object of a great deal of staring, but it is so lovely we don't really care if we are *de trop.*

After our romp in the sea, we round off the afternoon, and remove the salt with a swim in the pool.

A very happy 'Happy Hour', then off for dinner in the Big Thatch dining room. The dinner tends to be faithful to the stodge of colonial days. When we are offered roly-poly for dessert, Sheila inquires if they don't have any fresh fruit. There is a sorrowful shaking of the head – "No, no Memsahib, no fresh fruit."

"Well, you must have bananas," she counters, thinking of the endless plantations we had passed, each one bursting with a bumper crop. The answer lies in that ambiguous shaking of the head, which in this case could mean, "It is written" or "It is all a very great mystery."

Friday, March 28 Good Friday and, unlike the wife of the forsaken merman, I am quite content to lose my soul in this green-gold paradise. We rush down to the beach for a swim –

the breakers are literally and figuratively breathtaking. Hilary elects to spend the entire day by the pool, reappearing only for brunch. We finally drag a painfully sunburned child away for a walk up to the Halycon Palace, a new project at the hotel. They are building on to the old summer palace of the Maharajah, preparing it for a conference centre. Judging from the really weird concrete chairs on the parapets, there are going to be a lot of numb bottoms among the conferees, or I miss my guess.

There is a full moon tonight at dinner, and more than that. Beaming with pride and shyness, our waiter arrives at our table with a full basket of fresh fruit and a bouquet of tropical flowers. Nothing like a nudge in the right direction.

Sunday, March 30 Sheila and I run down for a last swim in the ocean. Hilary's hours in the sun have produced blistered and painful shoulders, and Doug forbids swimming. As consolation, he suggests they walk along the beach to take pictures of the local fishermen. Their enormous open rope net, weighted at intervals with wooden blocks, terminates in large meshed squares that are also weighted and placed alongside the nearest dhow, which begins to "chase the fish". After a suitable time, a diver checks the catch and, when it's sufficient, gives the signal to bring it ashore. A note (unheard by us) is sounded somewhere along the line, and those on the beach begin the arduous business of hauling in the net. They chant a repetitive sort of dirge that grows faster and faster until the catch is finally landed.

By and large the Indians are a handsome people and, regardless of what coconuts may be doing to their health, these fishermen are superb specimens. The men of the South favour the short, tight dhoti, worn with or without a loose shirt, or the even more attractive lungi found in Sri Lanka and Burma. In any event, the whole performance is so rhythmical and beautifully balanced that it is like watching a first-class bit of theatre, staged against a picture-poster background of sea, sand and sky.

Walking back along the shore, Hilary does her best to get wet by wading deeper and deeper into the sea. This is all in the hope that she can persuade her father that, as she is wet anyway, she might as well go swimming. To no avail, her

Spartan papa will have none of it.

We indulge in a special Easter Sunday buffet of Indian food (Sheila loves it, I don't mind it and Doug hates it). We give a large and sincere financial thank-you to our waiter, and prepare to leave. I don't want to go – it has been a little bit of tropical Eden, wherein the "gift to be simple" has been bestowed with warmth and grace.

We drive to the airport along the winding tropical road, thick with palms and flowers. Here and there are glimpses of slumberous, golden lagoons, shadow-dappled and so very beautiful.

I hold that last mental snapshot in my heart as we board the plane for the brief flight to Bombay. We say goodbye to Sheila here, who still carries scars of her time in that city. She is heading back to Delhi and to the air-conditioned comfort of the house in Vasant Vihar.

It is 7.00pm by the time we arrive in Bombay, and it is getting dark, but not dark enough to soften or disguise an appalling scene. The airport road is an endless slum, 'juggies' (the ubiquitous Indian shanties) are everywhere, and appear to have been created from compressed garbage; ragged figures huddle around street fires and scramble for scraps of food.

The guilt of privilege becomes even sharper as we drive on to the Oberoi Hotel and enter into an opulence designed for the pleasure of princes. It is a scene of more than Oriental splendour. A glittering waterfall cascades down into a huge reflecting pool, elaborate and richly embroidered tapestries fall from the ceiling and gilded chairs decorate the lobby. We are ushered up, with all due ceremony, to an equally elegant suite, and once again I ponder the injustices of life, and the inequalities of the class (and caste) system. I ponder, true, but not to the extent that I turn down the culinary delights being offered by the hotel's French restaurant.

Monday March 31 Breakfast in the poolside Garden Room, well-screened from the squalor of the street life below. Mildred had told me that she had never left the hotel when she was in Bombay, because venturing forth was "too horrible, and besides the shops in the hotel's arcade have *everything*."

Not exactly the point, but we do inspect the Oberoi shops,

64

which are truly beautiful. Still armoured against the 'real' India, we take a taxi to the Taj Hotel, inspect *their* shops and have a *nimbo panni* (lime water) beside *their* pool.

The Taj is quite close to the Gateway to India, the massive arch built to welcome King George V and Queen Mary to India. I suggest we walk and see something of the city. Hilary turns pale.

The clutching beggars still terrify her after her first experience in Old Delhi. She says she will just wait for us in the lobby, adding firmly, "Don't worry I'm not going *anywhere*!"

Away from the cool shaded verandahs and the poolside umbrellas, Bombay steams and sweats; the crowded streets seem to be sinking into a kind of invisible ghee and even the ever-present hawkers seek our custom in an exhausted sort of way.

At the end of the road, the Gateway looms large and impressive. I try to envision the scene when the royal pair stepped ashore. Not then as it is now, I am sure. Then, it was new and bedecked with all pomp and circumstance for so great an occasion. It is still massive, but somehow diminished by the detritus under its soaring arch. The walls are stained with urine and betel juice, and everywhere we are surrounded by a pungent portside smell. It is all a little *sic transit gloria*, like the time in Rome when we saw a small kitten on a lone prowl through ruins where once the lions roared.

We branch off into the heart of the teeming city, and then opt for a walk along Marine Drive. We catch a little of the mood of the metropolis, over-populated, steaming and with a kind of sullen spirit. Taking a taxi back to the Oberoi, the driver harangues us with a 'come the revolution' speech. I don't blame him, but I cannot help but contrast him to our beaming Claire of Bangalore, and his pride and happiness in showing us his town.

CHAPTER 10

Tuesday, April 1 Back in Delhi, but briefly. School break is over. Hilary goes back to classes, Doug to the office, and Sheila and I ready ourselves for our planned excursion to Kashmir. There is a bit of a mad scramble to re-arrange wardrobes, pack and rush off to the airport.

Kashmir is a name to be conjured with, and very much part of my childhood memories: my mother sweeping her fingers over the keys of our living room piano and singing soulfully of the "pale hands" being loved beside the Shalimar. There was also a notable picture of Uncle Jack and little girl-cousins in white dresses, floating along in a wondrous houseboat. They were doing something every expat did at some time, and Sheila and I are equally keen. However, the season is early Spring; Kashmir is on the edge of the snows, and many experienced heads were shaken at the wisdom of two ladies alone on a houseboat. Rather reluctantly we gave in, and instead booked into one of Srinagar's few hostelries – the Neddous Hotel.

A number of people I know have a 'hate' relationship with India; a few a 'love' relationship, and the rest a 'love-hate' relationship. For the most part, I really like the Indians – maddening, evasive and implausible though they may be – but today is a 'hate' day. Sheila and I arrive and join the queue to check in. It is almost boarding time when we finally reach the counter and I place my bag on the weighing machine. To my utter astonishment, a hand appears from behind me and removes my bag, replacing it with another. A dapper little form darts in front of me, smiling and bowing.

"I am very sorry, but you see I have a plane to catch. It is very important."

For a moment, I am rendered speechless, but finally splutter, "Well so do I." It is all to no avail because what is even more incredible is that the check-in clerk does not even blink, let alone send him back to his place. He processes his ticket, and I am left with my mouth open and, as it turns out, a seat

66

over the wing.

It is late afternoon by the time we reach Srinagar, and are duly taken to the Neddous. One look, and we wonder from which comic opera it has escaped. From what dusty attic have these creaking relics, this faded upholstery, these fly-specked paintings been extracted?

To add to the illusion of a stage set, we appear to be the only guests. Dinner will be served at 6.00pm. We barely have time to wash away the travel dust before descending for the evening meal. The place echoes with our footsteps as we make our way to the dining room. We are the sole occupants of the dining room and there is an unearthly silence – every munch sounds like the snapping of alligator jaws, every whispered scrap of conversation comes across as though shouted from the stage to a deaf audience.

Dinner is a dismal affair, an experience one is not too keen to repeat. The emptiness of the dining room may be because it is off-season, or it may be that once eaten, twice gone, but in any event, we are the only interest and diversion for the waiters. They are three in number, two very elderly and very, very doddery; the third appears to be a mildly defective adolescent. They are all rigged out in baggy pants, dreary maroon Nehru jackets, and really quite silly-looking turbans that seem to tip over on their foreheads when they are serving. One takes our order, and the other two, dissatisfied with every detail of the table setting, rearrange everything – moving the salt cellar a centimetre to the left, then back again. When the food arrives, they watch us with hawk-like attention, and I feel it is only with superhuman control that they resist pushing the forks toward our mouths. They content themselves by hovering on the periphery, wheeling and circling like dingy birds of prey, waiting to pounce when the last crumb disappears.

As a matter of fact, the whole hotel appears to have stopped in an invisible time machine. It is pure *fin de siècle*, and all the hotel's personnel seem to be dressed and ready to perform in a sort of period farce.

There is no cheery fire in the echoing lounge, so we drink our coffee and retire to our room, where we meet our 'chamber boy'. A misnomer if ever there was one, as he has obviously toiled at the Neddous for many a long year. He looks

When the food arrives, they watch us with hawk-like attention

remarkably like Harry Truman. He shuffles with agonizing slowness, and we both feel we should help him in his chores. He is accompanied by our 'coal boy' who is even more ancient. His Herculean efforts to feed and light the Franklin stove in the corner smite my conscience.

At last they go, bent over and backing out the door. We sink into our beds, warmed in one spot by hot-water bottles (alas imperfectly sealed) and equipped with a Jacob-style pillow of stone, plus a crushing weight of blankets. Weariness wins out, however, and the ravelled sleeve is duly knitted.

Wednesday, April 2 We venture into Srinagar on a chill, grey day. A first impression is of a dreary town, with narrow, twisting lanes of shacks and broken-down shops. The populace definitely lacks the colour seen in other Indian towns – there are no brilliant saris, only the black of the women's burkas. The men are in charcoal grey or brown kaftans, with dull-looking jackets and astrakhan caps. They may look drab, but their salesmen's smiles are relentless – we no sooner step into a street than shawls, carpets and cushion covers are thrust under our noses, and we are begged "only to look, only to look." We make vague promises to stop on our way back (from where? – we have no idea) and continue on our walk.

Just ahead is a park, which more than makes up for the sad, cluttered streets we have just left. It is like a smaller version of Vancouver's Stanley Park, with an Eastern accent. There are daffodils, narcissi and flowering almond trees a-shimmer with blossoms. Around some huge magnificent chinari trees are lawns carpeted with daisies and bluebells. This is more like the Kashmir of legend, and we have a good look around before moving to the nearby Government Emporium, which is part of the whole park complex. This is quite an impressive, three-storey building, featuring a feast of local wares and crafts. Although we don't ask for it, a Government man is assigned to us, and he tags along, engaged in endless explanations of everything on display. He now tells us we must attend the Production Centre to observe the embroiderers, weavers and carpet makers at their task. It is, he tells us, "most interesting and formidable". He will, of course, accompany us. There is a lot of demurring on our part, that this is most kind but not necessary. We also know that this kindness will not be extended for nothing. Nonetheless he walks us over to a taxi and steps in after us.

As we cross over Srinagar's third bridge, we begin to feel glad of the Government man. The roads become streets, and the streets lanes, congested with shacks, carts and people. At one point, a group of horsemen, attired in boots and hats of fur and looking as though they had come from the set of a Genghis Khan film, ride down from a hilly pass.

We continue on down increasingly mean, twisting little alleys, until we reach what appears to be a dead end. The taxi stops at a sort of open dirt square, and our driver and our guide get out. I am absolutely convinced that this is the end, and our battered bodies will be found on some friendly neighbourhood dung heap. Instead they both unroll prayer rugs, face Mecca and chant their required noon-day devotions. They are obviously not bent on murder.

The prayers don't last long, and then the G-man rises and points out the building at the end of the square. It is a typical Kashmiri construction, with broken windows, fretwork balconies and a general air of dusty decay. Dirty children in rags rush out to greet us as we are ushered inside.

First we are trotted off to visit the rug room. It is long and narrow and full of huge looms. Depending on the size of the rug, each loom has between three and five men or boys working at it – a paper pattern is under the warp of each loom, and a worker sings out the pattern changes in a monotone chant.

At one loom, there is a tiny little boy, no older than five or six, working on a border. The knots here are so fine that very small fingers are required. The poor lamb will work for at least nine or ten hours, and receive something like 10 cents an hour. It is his karma, and his life will probably be spent in this same building, graduating slowly up the ladder to bigger, fancier rugs.

We are then led up some wooden steps, a filthy curtain is pulled back and we enter a room that looks exactly like Fagin's hideout in *Oliver Twist*. A group of men and boys are sitting on a floor, thick with the grime of ages, and working on 'couching' – fine embroidery worked with a hook. The pieces vary in

70

intricacy, the patterns being stamped, and one colour worked in at a time. The men vary in age, some very old. The boys seem to be around ten or eleven.

We then go into the fine needlework room. This is the type of embroidery seen on the exquisite Kashmiri shawls, and is worked mainly by young or middle-aged men, since sharp eyesight and a steady hand are needed. The craftsmanship is incredible, and one fantastically beautiful piece has already been worked on for more than a year.

Down another set of stairs, past a flapping bit of cardboard and into the crochet room, where they make a type of crewel work. Using a crochet hook, the wool or cotton is brought through the material, forming a sort of chain stitch. Most of the men are working on rugs, wall hangings, cholas and so on.

In all the workshops, the conditions are primitive in the extreme, with very little light coming through the small and filthy window panes. Usually a hookah pipe and coffee maker can be found among the clutter. We ask about wages. All workers are paid on a piece-work basis, the amount being based on the skill involved. The material is weighed at the beginning of the work day, then weighed again at the end, the worker being paid according to the weight of the work done. If any imperfections are noted, the foreman is entitled to refuse payment. A man at his peak, and with a high level of skill, might earn as much as 85 rupees (approximately $8). Boys and apprentices may work all day and make perhaps 85 paisa ($1) or nothing at all for that matter, being trainees.

It has been all very fascinating, including the hair-raising ride through the back lanes of Srinagar. We battle our way back through the congested, dilapidated streets and part from the G-man, with a profusion of thanks and over-tipping, on our return to the hotel.

One of those inexplicable Indian situations awaits us back at the Neddous. A swarthy Kashmiri, in the obligatory cap and an ill-fitting hairy tweed jacket, is standing beside an ancient car and looking more than a bit miffed. He had apparently been waiting for us with his auto "to be your guide and to show you many fine things." He has, he complains, been waiting for many hours.

I bite back my "Bad luck, we didn't request your services,"

and instead opt for the more civil retort that we had no idea he had been engaged and perhaps the hotel has made a mistake.

We both know that the whole thing is a ploy, but after a quick consultation between ourselves, we agree that we would be pleased to have him as our guide for the afternoon. He is pacified, presents us with a distinctly grubby card that proclaims him to be Mustapha something-or-other. He's going to have to wait a little longer, as we brace ourselves for a Neddous lunch.

Mustapha appears promptly after the meal, and we spend the rest of the day driving into the lovely countryside of the Vale of Kashmir. There are fields of saffron crocuses, and vistas of almond blossoms against the blue of the distant Himalayas. It is entrancing. We go up to the old Mogul Gardens, and past the Maharajah's flowering orchards of almond trees – heavenly drifts of pink and white blossoms. Sheila observes that everything produced in Kashmir seems a luxury – expensive almonds, even more expensive saffron (one must pick 75,000 crocuses to get one pound of saffron); Kashmiri shawls, pricey to begin with but even more so if one gets into Pashmini or Shah Tush. I felt one of the latter once, and it was a totally sensual experience – like holding a cloud and discovering it feels the way you always imagined a cloud ought to feel.

We finally reach the fabled Shalimar Gardens, which are pure poetry and delightfully empty in early spring. They are built in a series of terraces, the stone steps lined with flower beds, still empty of colour at this time of year. However, the forsythia is golden, the almond trees in full bloom and the sycamore just coming in to leaf. It is all quite idyllic, and I am touched when a charming young girl offers me a spray of forsythia. I am getting all warm and fuzzy about the symbolism of the gesture – East welcoming West and so on – until she asks me for five rupees. Oh well, "Life is earnest, life is real" and also full of small disillusionments.

Thursday, April 3 Elaborate arrangements were made last night to spend the day on Dal Lake. The Neddous management is thrown into a tizzy in booking a shikara (a kind of lake gondola) and boatman, arranging a lunch from the kitchen, and having Mustapha transport us.

After breakfast, armed with picnic basket, cameras and everything necessary for "a very fine boating experience", we are whisked off to the docks, where we are gently and reverently handed into a vessel that would have done Cleopatra proud. Approximately 18 feet in length, it has a sun roof supported by posts wrapped in cloths embroidered in bright oranges and reds; a great cushion bed with matching pillows features the same ornate design. This splendid craft is called *Dal Pariz*, and our boatman Raman is beside himself to give us every comfort and announces with pride that we also have "best spring seats".

It is absolutely blissful, relaxing like potentates and drifting along the waters of the mountain lake while the tender green branches of willows droop idyllically over the water. The shores of the lake are lined with houseboats, bearing names such as *Little Sunflower, Star of Kashmir, Golden Gate* and the like. They are all empty at this time of year, which gives our journey the richness of solitude, or so we think.

In actual fact, to the ever-persistent Kashmiri salesmen we must seem like the first tasty titbit of spring to bears just out of hibernation. We gradually become aware that a flotilla of shikari is moving relentlessly in our direction. First to reach us is a pharmaceutical peddler, offering us panaceas for every conceivable ailment. His nostrums are covered with the dust of long winters and yellowed by the sun of departed summers. He is rebuffed, and we turn to the next arrival who is peddling saffron. We haggle amiably over a few grams, and get him down to 30 rupees, which we are innocent enough to consider a bargain. He is followed by a fruiterer with a boatload of green oranges, another selling fur hats, a woodcarver and a knife sharpener.

Just when we are getting to the shouting stage of rejection, Raman, our boatman, turns away from the houseboat area. We leave the hawkers behind, and are paddled under an ancient Mogul bridge and onto the broad expanse of Dal Lake. No hawkers, TG, but a number of fishermen who have as yet nothing to sell.

Raman takes us over to Char Chinar (the four sycamores), an island popular in the summer for picnics and the sale of drinks. In spring, however, it presents a less than attractive face. The litter of past *al fresco* meals is everywhere, there is a reeking, horrible bathroom of sorts and even the beautiful chinar trees appear glum and skeletal.

Back in the boat, we are paddled in princely splendour. It is now almost time for lunch, and we spot a small, seemingly deserted island. For some reason, Raman seems reluctant to include this in his tour, but we direct him there nonetheless, and are rewarded with a really delightful picnic spot – infinitely more attractive than Char Chinar. There is a soft stretch of grass, green with spring and dotted with trees just coming into bud. It has four little Mogul pavilions, with stone steps coming down into the water, easing our ascents and descents to and from the boat.

We lunch on Neddous finest – chicken, hard-boiled eggs, cold potatoes, bread and jam tartlets. We signal to Raman that we are going for a walk and set out to explore. On the far side of the island, we come across a group of fishermen who are preparing bait that looks strangely like cookie dough. They roll this between their palms into a long string, then break it into tiny pieces and bait their hooks. We all smile and bow to each other in a great show of goodwill.

Returning to our pavilions, and ready to leave, we hear the spine-tingling sound of the Muezzin calling the faithful to prayer. Islam dominates the Kashmiri religious life. The converse of Hyderabad with a Muslim Nizam and a Hindu populace, Kashmir is a Muslim state with a Hindu Maharajah. In my digging into 19th- and 20th-century Indian history, I find it curious that these states remain so, considering the bloody Muslim-Hindu clashes at the time of Partition.

Across the glimmering water of the lake, a new shrine and mosque are in the process of being built. Along the waterfront stretches a white marble wall, inset with latticed marble arches in the classic Islamic style. Behind the wall, the mosque and minaret are protected by scaffolding. Even in its incomplete state, the place is thronged. Raman explains that on holy days or during Ramadan thousands of the faithful come by bus, on foot or by boat.

As we approach the far side, I am whisked inside one of my very favourite childhood books. It is E Nesbitt's *The Story of the*

Amulet, the part where the five children find themselves in Atlantis and, with the rest of the populace, await on the water's edge for the cataclysmic wave that will sweep them and their world away. It is as though the book's illustrator had drawn it from life as it now lay before us. Broad stone steps lead down from the shrine, maybe three or four hundred of them. People in kaftans, burkas and Arabic robes group themselves with unconscious symmetry on the steps, their water jugs gleaming in the sunshine, clothes baskets on their heads. As it was for Atlantis, the water is their source of life.

Raman lets us out at the foot of the steps, and we make our way into the square where hundreds are rolling up their prayer rugs after worship. We approach the mosque and remove our shoes so that we may enter. We are obviously the first tourists of the season, and the stares are relentless.

Back in the *Dal Pariz* once more, we return by a different route to Srinagar – through narrow inlets and bayous. It is indescribable. Fretwork hovels and tottering shacks line the shore. Women in gypsy scarves and Kashmiri pantaloons are washing clothes in water of unbelievable scuzziness. Yet somehow, despite the squalor and the poverty, there is a strange beauty about the scene, like a intricately dark painting, splashed with unexpected and joyous colour.

We return to Srinagar and Raman guides us gently back to the hotel, dodging the now-familiar salesmen. We manage to wave them all aside, and thank Raman with a generous tip, which he richly deserved. He was a wonderful guide and what, I believe, is frequently called one of "nature's gentlemen".

Dinner is the usual dreary affair, but we are diverted by a star turn in the guise of Another Guest. A young Delhi businessman breaks the monotony by engaging us in conversation. He is with the Department of Agriculture, and is in Kashmir to help fight apple-tree scab. True, he tells us more about apple-tree scab than we really want to know, but it is a change from our usual *sotto voce* table talk.

Friday, April 4 Arrangements have been made with Mustapha for a trip to Gulmarg, which boasts the world's highest golf course. As said golf course is now covered with the Himalayan snows, there is no thought of teeing off into the depthless yonder. Mustapha appears on the stroke of nine, and we are ready. For some reason or another there are a number of conferences being held, heads are nodded, hands are waved, and we do not leave until 40 minutes later. When we finally pull out, Mustapha tells us he would advise that we alter course and go instead to Palagam. There are all sorts of logical reasons given for this change – the depth of the snow, the dullness of the road, etc – but I have a nasty suspicion, it is because the road to Palagam adds another 30 rupees to the cost. But it is his car and his country, so we set off for Palagam, past almond orchards and fields of mustard – carpets of gold, bordered with the pale green of willows. It is a springtime pastel and really lovely.

We reach Pompou, which is an unpleasant little huddle, and then drive on to Avante Pur. Here there is a ruin of a Hindu Temple, dedicated to Vishnu. It was built in the 9th century, and destroyed in the 14th century by Alexander, the iconoclast of Afghanistan.

I find the temple rather fascinating with its recurring themes in stone elephants, parrots and lotus flowers, plus a distinct nod toward the goddess Lakshmi. It is now run by the Department of Archaeology, which has been reviewing the ruins for study.

A wandering functionary tells us, "It is a temple," which we can certainly see for ourselves. Sheila is incensed when Mustapha tells us to give him a rupee for this superfluous information.

"Besides," she splutters, "Government guides are supposed to be *free*." She is right, of course, but it doesn't seem worth the hassle to argue.

At the next stop, there is another ancient Hindu temple, with a tankful of fish. Mustapha, probably to make up to Sheila for the scam of the guide, cautions us not to go in. He has no such cautionary suggestions, however, about all the temple hangers-on, like the man who feeds the fish, the man who cleans the tank, the man who serves the High Priest and the High Priest himself, who seems to be prowling about aimlessly in search of a likely sucker. We pay up in each case, and then proceed on our way.

We drive higher and higher and deeper into the mountains.

A few miles from Palagam, we stop in a beautiful pine forest beside a little mountain stream and open up our lunch. This turns out to be a re-hash of yesterday, but with the added attraction of a cheese sandwich. It is really quite delightful, sitting on the mossy forest floor and munching on cold potatoes. The fitful sun appears for a time to warm us, and the scent of pines evokes memories of home.

In Palagam, which is just emerging from the sullied snows of winter, we find little to intrigue us. We stop for tea, and then begin our return journey. The scenery really is magical, with muted and subtle tones in the deep valleys, highlighted by the gypsy colour of the women working in the fields.

We return to the hotel, then Sheila sets forth to deal with Mr Samad Shah and his kaftans. On one of our earlier expeditions, Mustapha had directed us (always on the kick-back trail) to Mr Shah's boutique ("finest in all Asia") where Sheila made inquiries of an underling for an embroidered kaftan. She said she would think it over, but feared the price was too high, perhaps Mr Shah might.... Having sown a small seed of hope, she is now prepared for the nitty gritty of negotiations.

Reaching the shop, we find Mr Shah is not in, but the staff is crazy mad to keep us, salaaming and scraping and rushing out to see if "He cometh." We say we will return in ten minutes, then run the gauntlet of other shops, and are just about to check out some luncheon cloths when a young salesman from Mr Shah's establishment comes rushing in.

"He is come, Mr Shah has come." With such a grandiose introduction, I fully expected to find a saintly figure with a hovering halo and a hand raised in benediction, but Mr Shah is simply a tall, handsome Kashmiri, with negotiating skills that belong in the United Nations. Sheila gives him her top price. Mr Shah shakes his elegant grey head and begs her to come back tomorrow when some glorious garments are due to arrive. Dusk is falling and we return to the Neddous for our last ghastly evening meal and bed.

Saturday, April 5 Up to pack and organize our departure from this dreadful hostelry. We find a long line-up of staff at our door. First is the chowkidar whom we have never clapped

77

eyes on before this instant; the same for the mali and the dhobi. Sheila considers the whole thing a fat lot of cheek, as a service charge has been added to our bill. Still, they are so poor, and I slip Harry an extra tip and another for the stove man. Leaving the dining room after breakfast, we are followed by the gloomy gaze of the smallest of the terrible trio of waiters. So there is nothing for it but to hand out another few tips. Sheila strikes on the happy thought of giving them a bonus of the bottle return, worth a rupee each. They seem quite depressed and tell us they don't know where to go. Sheila is all for telling them, but I restrain her. We settle our bill, and everyone seems satisfied; then it is off to Mr Shah's for the Grandfather of all Haggles.

The ever-present Mustapha accompanies us to Samad Shah and Sons. On the way Sheila spots a striking black kaftan with white embroidery for 250 rupees. She is all for going in, but Mustapha, with an undoubted rake-off in mind, tugs her off to SS&S.

Mr Shah is waiting for us. He has spent the night in inner conflict, but is now prepared to make a very good deal because "Madame [me] lives in Delhi." First, however, he must show us his new stock. He assures us these rare items are for inspection only, "just to see the quality". Among the lot is a glorious gown of a rich, luscious purple, with a pattern of gold grape leaves. The colour, embroidery and material are exquisite. Sheila is dazzled, and all thoughts of black kaftans are dismissed forever. At Mr Shah's urgings she tries it on – it is magnificent.

Sheila takes a deep breath: "How much?"

Mr S is beyond such commercial musings. "Madam, you are a queen – a Lakshmi!"

Sheila: "How much?"

Further raptures from Mr S, followed by a barely audible response of "750 rupees."

Sheila: "Out of the question." Some hurried arithmetic – "My top price is 450 rupees."

Mr S turns a tragic face and shakes his handsome head.

"There is no profit – it is a piece beyond price, and for 500 rupees it is a gift, but I will make the sacrifice, but not a paisa less."

Sheila suggests splitting the difference, but Mr Shah is immovable – already he has gone beyond the limits of reason in his price. I am fascinated, knowing Sheila wants it and will not lose it for 25 rupees, but I reckon without her own bargaining skill.

Still resplendent in her purple and gold, she draws herself up to her full height: "Then, Mr Shah, I am afraid we cannot do business."

Protestations from Mr S with bleats about postage and alterations. Sheila pauses and offers to pay the postage, but realizing this will probably come to Mr S's original 500, says with great dignity that 475 is her final offer, or no deal. Mr S. sorrowfully shakes his head.

Sheila, slowly and deliberately, shrugs out of the shimmering garment, and opens the door. A hand descends and shuts the door, and with infinite and studied sadness a voice announces:

"Sold, Madam."

CHAPTER 11

Sunday, April 6 Doug goes off to play golf, and Hilary is at a loose end, so we decide to have a tour of Safdarjung's Tomb – one of Delhi's most impressive Mogul monuments and one that we have yet to visit. It is oppressively hot, but Hilary is in her element, showing off her Hindi to Sheila and protecting her from the ever-present beggars. All this makes us a little late for Mildred's dinner and she is very narky. We fail to woo her back to good humour, even though we make it to the American cinema in loads of time. Movie is *Catherine the Great* with Elisabeth Bergner – a golden oldie, but we all enjoy it.

Monday, April 14 After the adventures in southern India and Kashmir, the past week slipped into a familiar routine – a bit of golf, French lessons, diplomatic lunches, dinners, discussions with tailors over ill-fitting slacks, swimming and today my first stint as a volunteer in the American School library's reference department.

On the slender strength of my familiarity with the Dewey Decimal and Library of Congress systems, they conclude I am a professional librarian. I try to disabuse them but nobody seems to pay much attention. I meet a very charming lady, Ruth Etzel, the wife of Doug's opposite number at the American Embassy, and Miss Sen, the chief librarian. The work is not hard, but I am rather appalled to find that Grade 11 and 12 students coming in to research a project seem to have little clue as to how to go about it. Somebody was doing a piece on Hemingway, and asked what I had. I directed him to the catalogue, which he did not know how to use, and he asked if I could get information out for him. Another said that all he needed for his project were pictures: "Like you could do it with just visuals." I begin to wonder about the educational system at the Delhi American School, but tell myself not to be hasty, as these are but two students.

This afternoon, Doug is leaving for Islamabad, Lahore and Karachi – magical names from a hundred stories. Wish I were going with him, but I do not want to leave Hilary, nor do I want to take her out of school.

Tuesday, April 15 Tim McCarthy, an old classmate of Doug's from Queen's University, arrives in Delhi with his wife Bonnie. He is with the World Health Organization and is scheduled to go to Burma shortly. Mildred organizes a lunch at the Imperial with Bonnie, who is a quick, bird-like woman with a crisp, no-nonsense manner. We take her shopping and, like Mildred, nobody is going to put one over on Bonnie. As a result I am the only one to buy anything.

Wednesday, April 16 First visit to the Delhi Art Gallery and Museum. Absolutely fascinating, and I must get some books out of the library on Alexander and his passage through northern India.

Hilary's birthday is less than a week away, and I shop for presents – find her a gorgeous big mirror-work horse with an elaborately embroidered saddle. Work in the library all afternoon.

Thursday, April 17 Doug returns from his adventures and recounts some of the more interesting incidents at dinner tonight. These included a visit to a snake farm where he watched them milk cobras to remove the venom for serum. Definitely not the sort of thing one would see in the average suburban practice. Nor was his overnight stay in a leprosarium in northern India. This remarkable institution was founded by the Japanese, who continue to maintain it faultlessly and run it with enormous efficiency.

I have always associated leprosy with the Bible and *Ben-Hur*, and as a thing of the distant past. So I am really surprised and shocked when Doug tells me it is on the increase in India. It apparently flourishes where there is filth and malnutrition, the twin ills of this impoverished land. The leprosarium is supported, in part, by a number of volunteer organizations in Japan. However, it may not be for much longer because of an incident that occurred recently.

One of these volunteer bodies had raised money and sent to India a particularly valuable and much-needed piece of hospital equipment. Indian Customs imposed such an exorbitantly high duty that the society, either could not, or would not, pay it, and the gift had to be returned to Japan. Why do they do it? This story produces the same sense of frustration I felt over hearing about the shipment of Canadian wheat allowed to rot in a steaming harbour while guns were unloaded. The ways of man are indeed hard to fathom.

CHAPTER 12

Saturday, April 19 Hilary's tenth birthday is still three days off, but convenience dictates we have her party today. She is itching to have a sleepover in best Canadian tradition. With Tony to arrange everything, it does not require my normal down-to-the-wire preparations.

I take Hilary into the Ashoka for a haircut and we accompany Mildred over to the jewellery repair place to pick up her watch. One of the fascinating things about India is that stores are seldom single-purpose affairs. Mildred's jewellery establishment is also a livestock merchant-cum-butcher – Birks it ain't, and the stench is terrible.

Home for lunch and a quiet afternoon until 4.00pm when the children begin to arrive. Presents are opened, much hilarity over games and prizes, followed by a wonderful meal prepared by Tony – delicious pizza, masses of child-friendly munches like salt and vinegar potato chips, and a masterpiece of a baked Alaska with meringue lettering spelling out "Happy Birthday".

Dinner over, we take them off to the American Cinema, and ourselves off to a National Film Board party. We arrive back at the theatre at 9.20pm just as the show ends. Once home there is wild excitement about sleeping under the stars on the roof terrace that leads off Hilary's bedroom. Alas for mice and men and the best-laid plans, around about 2.00am a wild dust and wind storm comes out of nowhere and the children are blown back into the house. Much re-arranging of sleeping accommodation, and finally the night is silent.

Sunday, April 20 After the horde has breakfasted, Doug takes them all down to the Commission pool. The day is frightfully hot, and they are reluctant to leave the water, but finally all are safely delivered to their respective homes, except for Sue and another friend, Kitty, who have stayed to play. The peace of the afternoon is shattered by a scream from Hilary who, while playing on the fence, has pierced her thigh on a spike. She is more frightened than anything else with all this blood, but it is a nasty gash and I am glad Doug is on hand with his sulpha powder and expertise. Hilary is more than miffed when I scoop her onto the marble in the hall to save the powder-blue rugs from being bloodied. (Lo, the careful housewife, who is only too aware of what the Commission could charge us for damage.) It being Sunday, we later dine with the Grahams, and go to see *Topaz* at the American Cinema. Hilary, not too surprisingly, sleeps through the whole thing.

Tuesday, April 22 Birthday celebrations continue, although personally I feel this birthday has gone on for weeks. Tony makes a lovely birthday dinner and a cake with colourful icing; he even finds candles. We watch slides and play charades – a nice family party – and Hilary is wildly appreciative of her mirror-work horse.

Thursday, April 24 The Queen's birthday celebrations were postponed from the 21st because of the state funeral for the ex-President who died several days ago. They (ie the QBC) are on for today at the British High Commission Residence, and a very elegant affair it is – Gurkha guards in full fig at the gate, the garden paths lined with torches, a band-box band and servants, spiffed up in scarlet and white. (They all had shoes on – Tony, please note.)

Everyone is in full dress – military uniform, national dress or lounge suit – a very swanky-looking group all round. I was quite happy with my yellow chiffon and had a perfectly lovely time. In theory, it should just have been the upper echelons who were invited, but with my bridge career launched, I had played with Enid Walker (the Commissioner's wife) and we have become friends. Playing bridge really has been the greatest ice-breaker and door-opener that ever was. We meet the Khoslas at the party and ask them out to dine with us. We pick up Sheila from home en route, and we all go off to the Golden Dragon restaurant for curry-flavoured Chinese food.

Tuesday, April 29 The days are slipping by, and with bridge, swimming, French and a companion in Sheila, I have ceased to mark the calendar off as for a prison sentence. My acquaintance is widening – mostly with Brits (thanks to Monica, the lady from the Chartered Bank) and I have been asked to join a little bridge group – more bank people, a Sheila Brown whose husband is with the Mercantile Bank, a Mrs Gorman from Barclays, plus an English lady whose husband gathers? breeds? captures? Rhesus monkeys. I don't inquire too deeply.

John has decided to retire and he and Mildred are planning to leave in the near future. Who will replace him, I ask myself? Mildred never ceases to tell me that Doug is much too junior, so I am not to get any ideas. Doug may be junior, but he is also as sharp as a tack and popular with everyone. Still, I wisely keep these opinions to myself.

Today, I am picking up Saroj Khosla and she is taking me to Chandni Chowk, Old Delhi's market street. My first visit is still fresh in my mind, and I am not sure this morning is going to be a winner. However, it turns out to be fascinating. I organize a driver who drops us off at the entrance. The street is crowded, but Saroj's presence seems to keep the hawkers at bay. She takes me to a jeweller with whom her family has dealt for years. She mentions a few things she might be interested in, including diamond dress studs for Harish. A black velvet cloth is produced and a king's ransom in diamonds is spilled out like stars on a midnight sky. I am absolutely dazzled, particularly when the dealer lets Saroj walk out with 10,000 rupees worth of gems, with not so much as a receipt or a signed chit. I feel very small fry when I can only rise to the purchase of three silver charms for the girls. However, I do experience a certain amount of reflected glory when one shopkeeper tells us he made all the silver for Roland Michener's term in Rideau Hall as Governor-General of Canada. Mr M had, after all, been High Commissioner in India, and had not just picked Mr Gupta from Chandni Chowk out of a hat.

The whole morning is highly entertaining and very informative. From Saroj and the various shopkeepers, I learn that Indian ladies wear elaborate key-rings at their waist, usually set with precious or semi-precious jewels, and that bangles are an absolute *must* for married women – you are not

85

quite respectable without them. Women are also in charge of the purchase of the silver ornaments for temple offerings and if any temple statue is broken or defaced, it must be removed and thrown into the water, and fresh offerings made.

After pausing for a *nimbo panni*, the driver takes us to the Ashoka for lunch. Saroj is a lovely person, and we are totally comfortable with one another. Over lunch, we have a long talk about religion and east-west ideologies. In many respects, and like a number of our Indian friends, Saroj is very westernized, yet essentially a woman of her own culture. Hinduism, she tells me, is a kind of 'do-your-own-thing' religion. One tends to choose one's own god – her personal favourite is Krishna - "He is so naughty." Belief in karma and as the gods will it is at the heart of Hinduism – if you draw a short straw this time, in your next reincarnation you may do better.

She tells me, for instance, that you will never see an unhappy villager. They know this is their karma – the wretched hovels in which they live, the dung they gather, the back-breaking loads they carry, the babies that are drugged so the mothers can work uninterrupted – all is accepted and cherished as what the gods have given them. I am flabbergasted. Here is this delightful, kind, educated and cultured woman with 10,000 rupees worth of jewels in her purse, telling me that life is Jim Dandy for the lower castes, and they are all just as happy as little clams. It seems like a pure cop-out to me, but then everything western in me looks for change, improvement, a way out to something better. Perhaps she is right – perhaps an acceptance of life as it is gives a kind of happiness of which constant striving robs us. In any event she believes it – and is at peace with herself. She is happy with her karma, and the woman in the fields happy with hers.

It has been an enlightening and stimulating morning, and I know I have found a new friend, which is more to me, at this point, than all the diamonds tucked into Saroj's handbag.

Wednesday, April 30 A full day of volunteer toil and trivial pleasures. At home, there is a certain amount of sadness all around, as Sheila leaves tomorrow to continue her Indian adventures. It has been a really great visit, and through her being with us, I seem to have found my place in the local scene. She is, taken for all and all, a remarkable person, with so much warmth and generosity of spirit. She has spent two months with us, and we shall miss her acutely.

Friday, May 2 Fresh departures are in the offing. I go into the Commission with Doug and have an early swim. Nobody much around at that hour, and I am surprised to see Doug coming down to the pool. He tells me he has just had a signal from Ottawa to ask that he go to Bangkok and then Hong Kong to process refugees from Vietnam. I feel quite desolate – first Sheila and now Doug. He will be gone for almost a month, leaving me to handle the brooding and temperamental Tony without the Sahib's firm hand on the helm. Nothing for it but to bite on the bullet, but the weeks ahead seem like a year.

Saturday, May 3 Hilary has friend to stay overnight, and Doug and I take off for a party given in honour of a departmental doctor and his wife, visiting dignitaries from Health and Welfare. They are probably the most unresponsive pair I have ever met – worse than the gentleman on my left at the Municipal Appreciation Dinner in Burnaby; worse even than the deadly dentist who was my luncheon companion back in my PR days.

I have gone to this reception blithely enough, knowing that the visitors are not really my responsibility. Perhaps not, but where are the H&W staff who are supposed to be engaging them in sprightly conversation? Not only does it all seem to rest on me, but when Doug does appear, it is to let me know that he is in the process of arranging for me to accompany the VIPs to Agra tomorrow. It seems they want company. Why, in God's name, I ask myself? And why me?

The answer to this latter question is a series of muttered dodges. Well, it appears that Mildred has a bad shoulder, John's asthma is acting up and Doug has to pack. All pretty feeble excuses if you ask me. I fight back with, "What do you mean you have to pack? You're not going for another three days."

I am shattered. The thought of my precious Sunday (to say nothing of my first sight of the Taj Mahal) being spent with this

silent pair is absolutely dismal, with a six-hour drive to boot –
it is too much. However, I am trapped and there is no way out.
I try a last desperate tack. Gulping a little, I make a
suggestion:

"Wouldn't it be really special and something that you
would never forget, if you saw it together, just the two of
you...." The words trickle away, as I almost disgrace myself by
adding, "like young lovers."

I glance at their solemn faces and wonder if they were *ever*
young lovers – glad I asked myself this before asking them.
Their response is simply a confirmation that they would like
company.

After the party, we take our distinguished guests to an up-
scale restaurant for dinner. It is full, and in a mad moment I
suggest they all come back to our house. They do. Tony, of
course, has long since chucked out for the night, and I have
some nightmarish moments as I ransack the kitchen in search
of basics such as eggs and milk. I manage to put together one
of my cheese soufflés, unearth some sliced ham and make
heaps of toast. Like Lamb's dog standing on its hind legs, it is
not so much that it is done well, but that it is done at all that
is remarkable. It goes without saying that Doug and I carry the
bulk of the conversation. Although it is hard to tell, they seem
to enjoy it.

Sunday, May 4 They are back again at 7.30am. Happily Doug
is either conscience-stricken or aware of my acute displeasure,
and he decides to come along. We pack a thermos full of
Gimlets, another with boiled water, a cold pack full of ice and a
blanket, and off we go. The Commission has supplied us with a
splendid big air-conditioned car, plus driver, but oh dear, our
passengers! We try every imaginable conversational gambit –
even hit on her hobby, which is coin collecting – but cannot
strike a spark. The old college try also fizzles. Doug recounts a
story of his orals at Queen's, and asks if the doctor was also at
Queen's.

"No." Just "no". The normal response of any red-blooded
medical grad would have rung out with conviction. "Hell, no,
I'm a McGill man," or whatever.

She is reserved, but he is impossible. Considering they

88

The Taj Mahal ...dazzles both eye and mind

insisted on company, they make no effort to create a comfortable social atmosphere. The best that can be said is that they suit each other. "Dry" is the word I associate with them – they both impart an impression of being utterly juiceless. Physically they are parchment pale, and mentally, they seem used up and husk-like, giving no response to the stimuli of cultural idiom or the landscape through which we pass. Even the Taj Mahal is viewed with a kind of dutiful, dreary detachment.

This is as pitiful as it is astonishing, for the Taj is a miracle. Too much has been said of it and written about it for me to attempt to describe my reaction, but all I can say is that next to the tiger, there can be no more exquisite symmetry in the works of God or man. It stops the heart and dazzles both eye and mind.

One look at the poor doctor dragging himself and his weighty camera along the edge of the reflecting pool, and my better self comes to the fore. I suggest we return to the car. His relief is palpable. We get out the ice and the Gimlets and turn on the air conditioner. This should get the roses back in the cheek, think I. Not a bit of it. Both the doctor and his lady politely decline the offered Gimlets. Doug barely nods at me, and I reach out for the offered glass like a drowning man clutching at a passing spar.

Now with Doug and I nicely fortified, and our guests cooled and rested, we take them to the marble factory and the Kohinoor jewellers, then to lunch at the Clark-Shiraz, Agra's poshest hotel. Even the ever-obliging and friendly staff cannot melt the weary chill of our companions.

We head for home and another three hours of driving. A few desultory attempts at conversation.

"How have you found your first trip to India, Doctor?"
"Hot."

A simile (mine, or did I read it somewhere?) occurs to me: "He was like a very dry funeral pyre waiting for the match."

CHAPTER 13

Tuesday, May 6 Doug has to leave by 6.00am and is away at the first honk of the horn. I feel miserable, but what to do? The day passes and I go solo to a party hosted by Don McGillivray (an Immigration officer) and his wife. I meet a nice French couple. There is an odd number for bridge after dinner, so I end up playing chess, first with Don and then with the French gentleman. I can't believe that I beat them both – or was it gallantry?

Wednesday, May 7 Only one day gone, and I really miss Doug. Work at the library, which I normally enjoy, but today I am mentally kicking stones. Take Hilary and a friend to the pool for a swim. There is a kaffee-klatch in full swing, and they all seem so matey that I descend to the level of a snake's navel.

To top it all off I get into a real confrontation with a scooter driver, who does not put on his meter. I have been warned about this and normally I would not care, but today I do. I even threaten to report him, and there follows a haggle over the price. Do I really begrudge this poor man an extra rupee or two? I am instantly ashamed and, of course, end up by not only paying him but adding a too-big tip. I am hopeless.

Thursday, May 8 Went to an amateur performance of *Stage Door* featuring a few Canadians – not exactly West End standards, but entertaining. Western cultural events are few and far between, and even those of the amateur variety always receive a kindly assessment.

Friday, May 9 Have made a friend of Kitty's mother, Patty Patterson, who is a petite, sprightly woman, with whom I find I have a number of things in common. She has invited me to a film and lecture on Ananda K Coomaraswamy. The fact that I have never heard of him I sensibly keep to myself, and determine to bone up on the man later at the American School Library.

We are to have coffee and accompanying calories

All in all the film is quite fascinating and I learn that Coomaraswamy was born in Ceylon, the son of a Tamil father and an English mother. After the death of his father, he left Colombo for England, attending University College, London. He then took up a prolonged study of Asian Art in Ceylon and India. He completed over 500 volumes relating art to all aspects of life. In 1917 he took a post in the Boston Museum, and remained there until his death in 1947.

After the showing, we all troop over to the home of a Mrs Simons, whose husband is a correspondent for the *Washington Post*. Here we are to have coffee and accompanying calories while we dissect Coomaraswamy's book *The Dance of Shiva*.

At least, Patty's group of American ladies is going to discuss it. I will keep my ignorance under my hat, although I did pick up some clues as to Mr Coomaraswamy's philosophy and attitudes from the film.

Mrs Simons leads things off by reading the introduction to *The Dance of Shiva*, and then asking for comments. Everyone looks rather shiftily at everyone else, and I begin to wonder just how many of the ladies have actually read their assignment. Mrs S is definitely batting at a sticky wicket, as not a soul is advancing a single opinion. She gamely ploughs on, and then strikes the mother lode. It is in a passage in which Mr Coomaraswamy expresses his view that women, being a lesser breed, can never reach true nobility except perhaps in the act of suttee (throwing oneself on the funeral pyre of a deceased husband). I just about choke on my coffee because I thought she had read 'settee', and it all seemed a bit down to earth for so lofty a scholar.

However, the reaction of the ladies is instantaneous – with comments ranging from "Why, the old poop!" to "What does he mean, never reaching a point of nobility?" The floodgates have been opened and the clamour is deafening. Finally, above all the indignation, a strong Southern accent can be heard:

"Lay-dies, lay-dies, surely y'all must ree-alize, Mr Coomaraswamy w-a-a-s simply a man int-a-lectually ay-lienated from his ti-yum."

It is the most interesting remark of the morning, but her Miss Lulu-Bell accent makes her sound like the bubble-head of all time.

93

In any event, the discussion is now in full spate, and a really fascinating and enlightening morning it turns out to be. I hope I will be asked to go to the book circle again. In appreciation I take Patty for lunch at the Imperial, where we proceed to dissect both Mr C and his critics.

CHAPTER 14

Tuesday, May 13 After almost five months in India, I find myself assessing the pluses and minuses of our life. It has probably been the most mind-stretching experience I have ever known. I am fascinated by Indian history, philosophy and architecture, and am eager to uncover as much as I can of this exotic country.

On a less lofty plain, there are definitely problems in bringing up an 'only' child in a household where kind brown hands pick up after her, where drivers take her here and there, where her parents bend over backward to compensate for an imposed separation from her siblings. I can understand only too well her indignation over the broken promises of local tradesmen, but can I allow her to speak so dictatorially to grown-ups, regardless of their roles in her life?

Keeping track of Hilary is a full-time job, as she has gathered such a coterie of friends, and they all seem to go in for sleeping over. I have laid down the law that I must first talk to the parents, to find out if they will be home and all the other questions that politeness will allow. Even so, I fear there are times when I feel she is marching to a different drummer. I wonder if this is because we are here, or would it be the same in West Vancouver? Ah well, I suppose I should be happy that she does have lots of friends, and that she is getting so much out of her life here. It is up to me to see that she respects promises made, and that she be where and when she says she will be.

I am also struggling to adjust to not being totally at home in my own home. I am particularly aware of this feeling with Doug away. John and Mildred have been kind and thoughtful in inviting me over for Happy Hour, or dropping in on me. Still, I cannot shake this feeling of displacement and of having but a slender control over my domain. This is obvious in the ladies' luncheon I've organized for today. I am unaccountably nervous, although it is no big deal – I have had far bigger affairs at home. But I am not *in charge*, and I guess that is the difference.

I have given Tony the menu, and received the usual head-shake, which is open to so much interpretation. I glance into the dining room and he hasn't set the table – the flowers look tacky, and I don't smell delectable things from the kitchen. I trust that all will be well, but my cook's soul cries out to go in there and see to it.

They all arrive and the 'Sleeve-Clutcher' grabs me by the arm and talks in conspiratorial whispers while I try to welcome the others. The day goes well enough, except for the fact that the power goes off and, without the air-conditioner, the room becomes unbearably hot. Brows are mopped, handkerchiefs are fanned and exits are noticeably premature.

Friday, May 16 I have never liked this house from the word go – all new and modern, but with a weird configuration of rooms: the vast go-down, the lesser upper area, and the tortured lighting fixtures. At some party or other, I probably muttered something to this effect to the person in charge of staff quarters. Anyway it now it appears that the housing man is leaving, and as a favour to the "Doc" he is making arrangements for us to have his house.

Oh dear, be careful where one casts one's seeds of discontent. I don't want the housing man's house, which I don't particularly like. I am holding out for the Grahams', which I do like. With their planned departure in June, Mildred has been at pains to point out that their house will go to the incoming Medical Officer in Charge, which is, of course, as it should be, even if I don't want to hear it.

I am thinking all this over in the middle of a rather frantic afternoon, when the housing officer phones to tell me his house is ready for us whenever we want to move. What to do? I stall by saying I can't to do anything until Doug comes back.

Then Patty phones to ask if Hilary may join Kitty at the American pool for a swim. I am reluctant because she has a birthday party later on at 3.30pm, but I let her go. She faithfully promises she will be back at 3.15pm. I get her clothes ready and wrap the birthday present.

While brushing past the living room curtains, the whole valance falls on my head and the air-conditioner goes off at the same time. It is shaping up to being *that* kind of a day.

3.15 comes and goes, then 3.30 and no sign of Hilary. Dare I take a taxi up to the American compound? But what if Hilary is on her way home. It is now 4.00pm and Jenny, her hostess, phones. I waffle an apology and say she has been held up and will be a little late. I try the Pattersons' home, just as Hilary strolls through the gate. Something erupts, and I pull her into the house and upstairs, scolding furiously all the way. I don't like myself, but I don't stop either. She tells me that Mrs Patterson had been looking at the wrong clock, and when they got the right time it was 3.40. But I'm not to be mollified, and by the time the taxi arrives, Hilary, with tear-stained face and I, glowering, make our way to Baghwanda Road. We are now more than an hour late. We both go in to make our apologies and Hilary, to her credit, rises to the occasion, and all is once more serene.

I don't think I would have been so angry if it had not been for the fact that this sort of thing is becoming a habit. She considers time something for her own personal convenience, with little thought for the resulting chaos for others. Even as I rationalize away my fit of temper, I am haunted by the behaviour of those pain-in-the-neck mothers, who remain unfailingly sweet and understanding while their sons burn down the schoolhouse and their daughters earn pocket money at a strip-joint.

Saturday, May 17 Hilary, silent and pouting, is in a 'then-you'll-be-sorry' mood. I apologize for being so cross, but tell her she really must become more responsible and understand how worried I am when she doesn't return when she says she will. Particularly with her father away.

The big issue of moving into the other house comes up – the Administrator is quite justifiably miffed when I say I won't sign anything until Doug returns. The truth of the matter is that I am not sure that moving from our place to the housing man's is that much of an improvement. I make up a list of pluses and minuses, and the end result is that I really don't want to move into it. I guess I am hoping against hope for the Grahams'. I don't know why I am, but I just have a feeling it is *meant.*

Sunday, May 18 My birthday, and a funny sort of day it is – Hilary is back to her usual sunny self, but there is a cloud somewhere. Doug phones and that cheers me up. Then John and Mildred have Hilary and me over for dinner, and Mildred has a birthday cake. She really can be so thoughtful.

Friday, May 23 Today Doug returns – calloo-callay. It's a busy day, but Hilary and I manage to get to the airport just before the plane comes in. We are so glad to see him. Once home, he spills out a positive cornucopia of treasures. There are several lengths of silk for me, plus an exotic necklace and some temple rubbings. Hilary gets a charm for her bracelet – the King of Siam's barge in silver.

Saturday, May 24 I realize how much I have missed Doug when we walk over to look at the house in question. This problem had been gnawing away at my vitals, and I had almost made up my mind that, to save any embarrassment, we would just move in. However, after looking it over, Doug decides it is not for him. To my acute distress, I find our name is already on the door. Doug, in his usual confident manner, tells me not to worry – they will just have to take it off the door. He will handle it, and I am not to give it another thought.

I feel as though a great weight has rolled off my shoulders, but determine to reform. I realize that I must not say things to be polite, and I must not let others push me into things. I remember a friend, one of my long-ago room-mates, who used to say "Each man is where he wants to be," and I used to think "No, he is not." But it is true – I did not want to be in the offered house, but I would rather have been in it than have people think badly of me for turning it down. I know the only way to solve problems is to face them, but I have always found this difficult to do, which is probably why I am not successful with Tony and Doug is. He tells him what he wants firmly, but politely. I hesitate to sound like an imperious Memsahib, and just stew away until, when I do confront him, I sound petulant and surly.

After all this self-analysis and breast-beating, I feel the need for a little diversion. We take off for the Janpath and go into the Cottage Industries to have the temple rubbings framed, and then amble over to the Ashoka for tea.

Thursday, May 29   Register Barbara at the British School, and send off the school prospectus for her perusal.

The days are full of all the usual activities, plus the recent role of playing the ogre in the social drama of my youngest child's life.

A lot of her friends from school 'hang out' at the American Commissary on their own. Square old me finds this unacceptable, as these children are only nine and ten. I put my foot down, and the expected sulks follow.

Doug comes home for lunch with a telex from Ottawa saying that the twins will be arriving on June 6!!! We are flabbergasted because school in Canada does not end until well after that date, and they have exams to write. Doug says he will send a telex back and straighten this out.

Sunday, June 1   Only two weeks and a bit until the twins will be here. I can't believe six months have gone by.

I do love Sundays, when the house is mine. Have a lovely lazy morning, then we go out to look at the Nehru Memorial House. It always astonishes me how much you can tell about a person from a house. The public Nehru is one thing; the human-at-home Nehru is another; his glasses and a book are on his bedside table. His house is simple and tasteful, and the garden lovely. I have learned a lot about Nehru from the political histories on India I have been reading, and know he came from a wealthy high-caste family, was educated at Harrow and Trinity College, Cambridge, and was accused by his political rivals of being a "sunburned Englishman". Perhaps, but his written instructions to have his ashes scattered and mingled with the earth of India – "which I love above all else" – are the words of a true Hindu.

Tuesday, June 3   A little domestic crisis that I probably handled badly – I wonder how Victorian ladies managed the upstairs-downstairs scenario?

Tony is out, and Muni, still clutching his duster, begs for an audience. I am in the den, and he rushes in and

99

immediately kneels down and touches my foot. I just hate this kind of abasement. To me it is demeaning for both of us. He has a garbled tale to tell, and between the lines I get the impression his nose is out of joint. Gopi Chand, our dhobi, is young and rather 'pretty', and travels on a great status symbol – a motorcycle!!

As Muni's story unfolds, it becomes a saga of hurt feelings, outrage and for-your-ears only. It seems that Tony treats Gopi "like a big sahib." He (Tony) has allowed Gopi to use our bathroom (apparently absolutely against servant protocol); he has also been allowed to do other people's laundry in our washing machine, and heaven knows what further excesses. I really don't know what Muni wants me to do about all this, but obviously something is required. I thank Muni for telling me and I let him know that I will speak to Tony. I can speak to him all right, but what *will* I say? "What ho, Tony, the Sahib's bathroom is sacrosanct." It all seems so small-minded somehow.

However, as I think things through, a few incidents begin to fall into place. When we have been away the odd time, we notice the gas tank is very low when we come back – even once when I distinctly remember filling it up. Come to think of it, how does Gopi manage to afford gas for his motorcycle?

There was another little occurrence that left me with a vaguely uneasy feeling. One day when Hilary came home from school, she left her bicycle outside instead of putting it away in the garage as she is supposed to. When I asked her about it, she said she would have put it away, but when she looked in the garage, Tony and Gopi Chand were having a "rest" on a charpoy (bed) and she didn't like to disturb them. I may have to be hit on the head in matters of this sort but, as Poirot would say, all the little grey cells go into action and the pieces of the puzzle fall into place.

Did Gopi acquire his motorcycle through 'services rendered'? Does the gas go from the Sahib's tank into the dhobi's? Do Tony and Gopi always 'rest' on laundry days? I have no wish to control Tony's personal life or question his sexual proclivities, but I owe it to Muni to let Tony know his favours to Gopi must not compromise his role as our bearer.

I rehearse a calm, understanding and tactful speech to

He rushes in and immediately kneels down and touches my foot

Tony several times over, and then put it off – tomorrow is another day, Scarlett. However, I do recognize this cowardly deferment for what it is and stiffen the spine.

When Tony returns, I call him into the den and approach the matter all too obliquely and we get nowhere.

Perhaps he was not aware that the bathrooms were private and off-limits....

This bit of superfluous info is received with the all-too-familiar wagging of the head. Obviously I must get down to the nitty-gritty and tell him (firmly, I hope) that I have been informed that on laundry days, Gopi Chand has been given certain liberties; that the bathrooms (all four of them) are for our use only; that the washing machine can only be used for our washing; and does he have any suspicions about anyone siphoning off gas from our car? If not, would he mind keeping his eyes open and we will do our best to keep a close check on the mileage. By the time I have wound all this up, I am feeling like a worm of the deepest dye, and Tony goes off whistling, at least figuratively, a merry tune.

Friday, June 6 A boomer day, as huge parcels arrive from home, with birthday gifts for Hilary and me. The two of us have a lovely time digging things out and reading the cards and letters from the family.

We go to a farewell lunch at Claridge's Hotel for the Grahams. The office staff has arranged this with Dr Kapur (another of the Designated Medical Practioners), and together they present him with a charming statue of Shiva and Parvati, and a very elegant tie pin. I give Mildred a small ivory Buddha, very serene and peaceful. I don't tell her this, but I rather hope it might help her find her way to becoming both.

It is a very pleasant occasion, but I can hardly wait to get home to the delicious prospect of a free afternoon of reading. I am deep into my third book on the period in Indian history from Curzon to Nehru. The first was by an Indian journalist, the second by a Hindu scholar and this third by a British historian. Studying the same period from three different perspectives is so fascinating. I hope I am not prejudiced, but it seems to me that this last one, which incidentally is called from *Curzon to Nehru and After*, is the most objective.

I had not realized that, up until the incident of the Black Hole of Calcutta in 1756, the British (in the presence of the East India Company) had been in India purely as traders, among others including the French and the Dutch. The Indians seemed to give preference to the British, who gradually gained a degree of dominance. The political fall-out from the Seven Years War in Europe also played a role in establishing British authority, as did the machinations of Clive, Hastings et al. Although later historians have tended to downplay the horrors of the Black Hole, it became a *cause célèbre* at the time and led to the East India Company petitioning the British government for permission to form a standing army for purposes of protection.

It was not until after the Indian Mutiny of 1857 that British power in India transferred from the East India Company to the British government. The princely states continued to be run more or less independently.

In November of 1858, a proclamation from Queen Victoria declared "perpetual support for the native princes, and non-intervention in matters of religious beliefs or worship within British India." Under the East India Company's mandate, the act of suttee, infanticide and the denial of remarriage for widows had all been banned, and whether this new policy permitted these practices, I have not been able to find.

The part I am up to now is the establishment of the Indian Congress in 1885, and the time the first White Paper on Imperial Evolution was presented. Voting was based on the British principle of electoral ridings, and it soon became distressingly obvious that the Congress was heavily Hindu, despite the vast Muslim population. A representation from the Muslim League appealed to the Viceroy, Charles John Canning, stating that the Muslims would never have a representative because the Hindus were in the majority in every riding.

At this point, Canning, in an honest attempt to be fair, made the historic decision that within the Congress there should be a number of Muslim seats. As the author sums it up, "and so the first seeds of division were sown."

I don't really know why I am confiding all this to my diary, but it is such a fascinating bit of history, and may illustrate why historians have stated that if the Roman Empire's greatest contribution to civilization was law, the British one was justice.

I came across this quote from John Kenneth Galbraith at the school library the other day: "India, in the 19th century, was by anybody's standards a superbly governed country, but it did not make the governed any happier to be so." And maybe that is the whole case against imperialism in a nutshell, no matter how benignly administered.

Saturday, June 7 Decide to assert my rights as the chatelaine of this establishment, and give Tony specific instructions as to dinner tonight. We have gathered up some of the grass widowers and invited them over for the evening. I ask Tony what we are having for dinner. He rhymes off the stodgiest of all possible British meals: roast mutton and roly-poly for dessert.

It is a blazing hot day and the menu sounds so leaden that the proverbial iron enters my soul. I inform him that I think not. We shall have chicken, a salad and Zabaglione for dessert. He is not best pleased, but I march off before he can show too much disapproval.

His revenge comes in spades, however, when he produces a hopelessly dry chicken that is well nigh inseparable from the baking dish, which he uses as a serving platter. The consommé is like tepid dishwater and the Zabaglione is unrecognizable as such, or anything else for that matter.

The men are polite, but the rotten meal, the heat and the fact that Tony takes forever to produce the coffee has a dampening effect on the assembly. The conversation becomes desultory, and the constant drone of the air-conditioner acts as psychological depressant. I have a feeling everyone is tired and bored (maybe because I am) and give some thought to suggesting a game of poker from which I can gracefully absent myself. It is at this juncture that the lights go out. Candles are produced, but merely to light the guests on their merciful way out.

Sunday, June 8 The heat is suffocating, but around noon a storm hits. High winds sweep up dust and foliage, swirling it about like dervishes, and this is followed by a torrential rain.

The temperature drops by 13 degrees and all Delhi turns its face to this blessing from heaven.

When it stops we venture forth for our Sunday exploration and have a ramble through Old Delhi. I have become quite interested in the Indian Mutiny of 1857, and we climb the hill where the British civilians held out during the siege of Delhi. A monument has been erected as a memorial to the event. What is interesting is the role-casting apparent in the inscription. The rebelling sepoys are the "enemy" on the monument, and I am surprised that in the three decades since the transfer of power nobody has chiselled in another version. The inscription remains inviolate and honours "those who fell defending the government they served so well." Go figure.

Friday, June 13 A letter from Miss Barrow at Upper Canada College in Ontario. She was the school nurse when Doug was there, and was a general favourite with the boys, known by one and all there as 'Barrow'. I do not feel I should be allowed such familiarity. She is very keen to have a trip to India, and as she has always kept in touch knows we are here. Could she come and stay? I whip her off a letter to say by all means. Guests are such a welcome diversion, and I don't really have to do anything except be incredibly gracious at Tony's expense.

We take John and Mildred for a farewell dinner at the Oberoi. It is blisteringly hot, but we have splurged on the roof restaurant, the Café Chinoise, which is an elegantly appointed terrace and relatively cool. Lounge suit is a must, and I feel for the men. I am in my faithful yellow chiffon, which wafts slightly in the almost imperceptible breeze. Too late, I remember that John is not big on Chinese food. It is excellent, however, and we personally enjoy it – as for the Grahams, they are polite.

Saturday, June 14 It is a stiflingly hot day, and every movement is an effort. Looking out the window, I observe a merciless scorching of the outdoor scene. The garden shimmers and dances in the heat haze – a lizard stirs in the dust-dry air and the bougainvillea droops along the garden wall.

Hilary is restless and we take Hermione for a walk to a Mogul tomb. No sensible person is about in this heat, and we are alone on silent deserted lanes and empty parks. I have had it when we return and drink two bottles of mineral water. Hilary and I have a game of Monopoly, then we both go off for a zizz. John and Mildred come over for a drink before we take them to the airport.

We leave in bags of time (they are both anxious travellers), which is as well, since Mildred finds she has not had her smallpox record updated. Doug 'fixes' that and we say goodbye when the flight is announced. We shall miss them as bridge and golf partners, as old friends and as good neighbours, but they are obviously not reluctant to leave and are happy to be going home. I surprise myself to discover that with each passing month, I am becoming more firmly entrenched, and choose not to think of our own eventual departure.

CHAPTER 15

Sunday, June 15 All is serene and a lovely, lazy Sunday stretches ahead. There will be no rushing off to the Grahams for our usual dinner, and I don't mind – we will go to the Commissary or to the Ashoka or, wonder of wonders, I will cook something myself. All this changes in an instant when Dinker telephones and I invite him to come for dinner.

Doug receives an urgent message that a telex demanding attention has come from Ottawa, so he dashes off to the High Commission and returns an hour later with a Canadian doctor and his wife from Nairobi. Hereby hangs a tale.

Another H&W doctor was originally slated to take over as Medical Officer in Charge in Delhi. However, he declined on the basis of having just gone through a messy divorce and its disturbing aftermath for him and for his family.

We now suspect that this arrival from Kenya may well be the next possibility, although nothing has actually been said. Dr B is a small, neat man and his wife is blonde and very fair (or normally would be, but at the moment both of them are beet-like of complexion and perspiring with the heat). They hover in the doorway, silent and anxious.

Doug found them looking around the High Commission, after having walked over from the Ashoka in the blazing sun. They are overwhelmed by the all-pervasive heat that seeps into one's very pores. I soothe them with some iced tea and turn on the air-conditioner full blast. They are French-Canadians and she has little English, but we muddle along with 'Franglais' and what comes through with crystal clarity is that she would rather freeze at the North Pole; exist on a diet of raw fish in Japan or be teetotal in Saudi Arabia than come to such a hell-hole as Delhi. Is this prospect Number 2 down the tube?

Dr B offers to take us out to dinner (someplace air-conditioned is the proviso) and I am now in a dilemma: a) what of Dinker; and b) what of Hilary? The situation is explained and Dr B, all bonhomie and largesse, stretches his invitation. The charming Dinker arrives; we have a happy Happy Hour and then take off in the air-conditioned car to the air-conditioned restaurant.

Monday, June 16 Oh happy, happy day – the twins are due to arrive at the crack of dawn, and I set the alarm for 5.00am. Doug sensibly phones the airport before we go to bed to find that the plane is now due to come in at 3.45am and we reset the alarm. Take a bleary-eyed ride to the airport, and arrive about 3.35am. We wait in that awful lounge – airport regulations do not allow us to go down and greet arrivals – and we don't know whether we have missed them or not, as the plane arrives almost half an hour late. Two hours later Barbara and Martin are through customs, and fall into our waiting arms.

I cannot begin to describe how happy I am to see them – it is the first time in months that I feel totally me again. The children are an extension of us, and even with the still-missing two, I know we are close to being a unit once more. Despite the long journey, fatigue and the ungodly hour they look marvellous. Barbara has a nice haircut and is her picture-pretty self. Martin has grown and looks muscular and bony at the same time. He could have done with a trip to Barbara's hairdresser, but would still look enormously attractive to me, even if he had grown two heads.

Once home, and the house and grounds inspected, they opine that they are not a bit tired, and would love to have a drive down the Rajpath. However, while waiting for Barbara to unpack something cool to wear, Martin falls asleep and is out for the rest of the day. Barbara has a brief tour, then we are back for lunch, and this time we all fall asleep.

At dinner, they tell the hair-raising story of their Ottawa-organized trip. Their passports arrived a brief three days before they were due to leave; then, when they got to the airport departure desk, there were no tickets (as promised) and a telex had to be sent off to Ottawa. A wired OK was instantly returned and the tickets were confirmed a mere five minutes before flight time – whew!

We also get their accounts of the respective households that have been their home for the last six months. The Boothroyds made for an inspired match of boarder and

108

boarded. Barbara fitted right in – she adored paterfamilias Boots (his own children being more objective in their affection) and Boots lapped it up. The combination of Martin and his guardians was not an unalloyed joy perhaps, but there was mutual respect, and I am not too sure of any place that would have been better.

My reasoning for choosing the homes of acquaintances rather than close friends was a little convoluted but not without some logic. First of all, I wanted to have a clear financial understanding about room and board, which is not always easy with really close friends. Also if there had been friction or major teenage problems, I did not want either friends or children pretending everything was hotsy-totsy if it was not.

I was pretty sure Barbara would be okay wherever she went, but Martin, the perennial free spirit, might prove difficult. All in all, the arrangements were successful, and besides I now find that Martin seems to have made the remarkable discovery that his parents are not really all that bad after all.

Tuesday, June 17 Once caught up on their slumber, I take the children to the Tibetan Market and the Cottage Industries. They enjoy it, particularly Martin, who takes to haggling like an Arab hawker to his mark. He buys two knives, a bull whip and a birthday present for Hilary – a nice little wrap-around skirt. I buy another for Barbara plus a top. We go to the Imperial for lunch, and Martin rejoices in its echoes of the Raj. I take them to the Commission pool for a swim, and then Barbara is whisked off to Captain Singh's for her first riding lesson. Hilary is, by now, an old hand and cannot be stopped from imparting all sorts of equestrian tips and letting her big sister know she is one up on her.

Sunday, June 22 We head for Old Delhi to introduce the twins to the city outside the Diplomatic Enclave. I find the street Saroj showed me that leads to the Street of the Silversmiths. It lies at the foot of the Jama Masjid mosque. In the grey mood of the monsoons, the wet and muddy passage is indescribable. The street, narrow and filthy, is lined with open shack-like shops. Men, their faces grey with fatigue or beard stubble, sit cross-legged playing cards or chess. Some sell sodden wares, others wash themselves with water scooped from the gutters, while others urinate into the same gutters. The streets are where they live, so their life is a public thing.

The ever-present cows wander through the crowds, pinching vegetables from the pavement displays. In the shadow of the mosque, we come across perhaps 30 people sleeping, or just lying down, on the pavement. One woman, naked except for a slipping sari (no sari top) ceaselessly adjusts it over her bare brown breasts; children, flies crawling in their noses and over their eyelids, sleep in the filth; wandering gurus, pilgrims and beggars rest on the steps of the mosque. Martin is keen to go into the Jama Masjid, but we decide against it for today. Barbara, Hilary and I are not wearing socks, and Doug is opposed, on medical grounds, to walking in our bare feet.

We find the street of the silversmiths, and walk along to the wider and main branch of Chandni Chowk. The smells are appalling, and we decide not to take the long way around, but return by the same street to the car, dodging bicycles, rickshaws, hand-drawn carts and cows along the way. In leaving, Doug drives forward past the mosque, hoping to drive into main Chandni Chowk. It doesn't work that way, and there follows 20 minutes of hair-raising insinuation down clogged streets until we finally reach the exit street and find the main road to home.

We all scrub up – very, very thoroughly – and go over to ACSA for dinner.

Monday, June 23 The rains continue, and we look out upon a drenched garden. This is a day for the three 'Rs' of a privileged life – rest, relaxation and reading. I am still deep into *The Great Divide*. The author, as a historian and scholar, has tried to be objective, but still puts quite a different slant on the division of India in 1947 than do many of our Indian friends.

He brings up that White Paper I had encountered before. It outlines the British policy on India, the "Principle of Imperial Evolution". I am still not sure whether this principle was meant to apply to all the outposts of Empire, or just India.

In any event, the core of the policy was expressed in the

following heavily paternal terms: "To rule well is to govern well; and it must be our goal to educate and raise a subject people so that they might evolve into a people whose submission would no longer be necessary and self-government desirable."

I could just imagine some pundit in Whitehall putting down his pen, as pleased as punch with himself for coining such a magnanimous and nicely balanced sentence. Nonetheless it does indicate that the transfer of power that took place in 1947 had been in the cards all the time.

What had not been considered was the demography of India, and the predominance of Hindus over Muslims. With the founding of the Muslim League, and the drive for the placement of Muslims in positions of importance, the triangle – Britain at the peak and the Hindus and Muslims at either side of the base – made the subsequent partition inevitable. With the British withdrawal, and dominion status for India in the offing, the Muslims feared a potential drastic change in their position within the new country. As descendants of the great Mogul emperors, India's Muslims thought of themselves as the subjectors rather than the subjected, and considered it unthinkable that an alien authority be replaced by a Hindu one. The incompatibility of religions, particularly the "there-is-but-one-God" dogma of Islam, was already a divisive force.

Having stuffed myself with all this information, you can't imagine how thrilled I am to find, in my younger son, a willing ear. Martin has always loved history and he proves only too keen to discuss the entire subject. As all my other efforts to interest the family have been greeted with yawns, Martin's undivided attention is like receiving a particularly nice present.

Tuesday, June 24 With the two potential doctors – both senior to Doug – turning down India as a posting, Doug has been coping extremely well on his own. Indications are that the powers-that-be in Ottawa are beginning to realize that Doug would be perfectly capable of handling the post's medical department himself.

Nothing further has been heard about a replacement, and Doug has spoken to Administration about getting the Grahams' house, which remains empty. Doug comes home today with the news that the move has been blocked by the

Head of Chancery (HE's second-in-command). Nobody knows why, including the High Commissioner. I don't *really* care that much as moving could be a bore, and I have sort of got used to this house – although it is definitely not my dream of domestic splendour. Still I find myself resenting the petty officiousness of some of the officers at the post, and the seniority they use to exercise it.

Herein lies one of those strange little paradoxes that keep popping up in this Stephen Potter world of one-upmanship. As I have noted before, doctors are not top of the rung on the diplomatic ladder but for a lot of reasons, they are certainly among the most highly paid. While the Administration at the High Commission locates quarters for incoming staff, a rental is charged based on salary and family configuration. Therefore, a doctor with one child may well pay a much higher rent than a senior officer with three, although said First Secretary or whatever may have much grander accommodation. This situation is often the cause for a certain amount of good-natured raillery about medical 'fat cats' with most, but with the odd person it seems to occasion a degree of resentment. Who knows – thwarting our move to better quarters might have given some sort of inner satisfaction.

Thursday, June 26   Two items to report today: one of national, the other of wildlife, interest. With regard to the latter, we are enjoying a nice laze around the pool, when we hear blood-curdling shrieks from the other side nearer the cabana. The teenage Reynolds girls (daughters of the Immigration chief) are clutching at bikinis and lashing out with towels, trying unsuccessfully to stand upright on sun cots. Needless to say the Denny girls (and their equally curious mother) go over to investigate.

What we find is the biggest, fattest bug that I, or anyone else, has ever seen. It is at least six inches in length and a good 2 inches thick. The pool attendant comes running up with a net and captures it. A jar is procured and the thing is put inside and borne indoors to be oohed and aahed at. There is no resident entymologist at the High Commission, unfortunately, but there is a general agreement that the creature be taken to the requisite government department to be examined and defined if possible.

The second news item of the day is perhaps less exhilarating, but undeniably more important. A State of Emergency has been declared this morning. More than one thousand people have been arrested. Most of these are opposition leaders, such as J P Narain and other shadow cabinet members, but also many of Mrs Gandhi's own party have been rounded up for expressing anti-government views. Newspapers have been shut down, and heavy censorship imposed in general. It seems incredible that this could be happening. When I take the girls to the polo grounds for riding, soldiers are everywhere.

Doug tells me he has explained the whole situation to Tony; but when Tony reports to me there will be no paper tomorrow because the "papers are on strike," I realize how easy it is for Mrs Gandhi to move in the direction she has, without being accountable to the vast millions of the Indian populace.

Sunday, June 29 After a lovely lazy morning, we finally bestir ourselves, We decide a trip to the Qutb Minar will be fun, and all pile into the car. I always love taking people there, and so am disappointed to find on our arrival that it is raining. I suggest that we perhaps have a little Sunday drive in the country and return to the Qutb later.

We soon find ourselves in a fantastically congested village. Its one street is so clogged that it is almost impossible to navigate a way through – a little like driving through a dense but pliable hedge that closes up behind you.

The crowds stare with intense and unfeigned interest as we inch our way along – the best thing seems to be to smile, and I can scarce contain myself from digging out a white glove and doing the royal twirl wave. Our snail-like progress is maddening, and when we spot a temple, we decide we might as well get out and take some pictures. Closer inspection shows it to be crawling with people – the women in their brilliant saris look like exotic tropical birds in a forest of stone. One old man with a hookah pipe follows Doug demanding first ten rupees; then five and settles for one if the Sahib wishes to take his picture. The Sahib feels the subject falls far short of the mark, but gives him a rupee anyway. It is fatal – the crowds press in on us, gesticulating, hands out for baksheesh, touching our arms and hair. It is all quite awful, and we manoeuvre our way back to the car. No sooner do we fall into that refuge than the throng flatten their collective faces against the window like a swarm of relentless and threatening insects. I have a sudden terrified vision (straight out of the movies) of the car being turned over.

Thank God, Doug finds a spot to turn around, and we inch our way out. There is a great view of the Qutb Minar from across the valley, and Doug is all for stopping, but the distaff side has had enough of the Sunday drive in the country, and begs him to go on. The car moves at the pace of someone just learning to walk, and we make our way inch by careful inch. A few minutes later there is a slight bump. A woman with a baby, not noticing the car, swings her child around, bumping his head against the fender. Within seconds someone places a rock under the front tire and three others stand directly in front of the car. Pearl Buck once wrote: "The cold, grey snake of fear coiled and uncoiled itself in the pit of my stomach." Nothing could better describe the emotions I am feeling.

Doug calls out to lock the doors, and moves the car very, very slowly over the rock – the three men in front of the car, finding it moving towards them, instinctively step aside, and we slowly gather speed as the crowd parts. I don't think either of the girls in the back seat realized what was happening, or what could have happened. Doug is cucumber cool, but obviously knew that we had just escaped a very nasty situation. If the baby had been hurt – even though it hit us rather than the other way around – there would have been no way out. We were fortunate to have got that one moment of surprise as the car moved and, once clear of the village, all ideas of further exploration are gone as we flee for the shelter of Vasant Vihar.

CHAPTER 16

Saturday, July 5 We are awakened at 1.30am with a telegram received at the High Commission that Miss Barrow will be arriving at 4.30am at the Delhi airport. Doesn't seem much point in trying to get back to sleep, and we make some tea, get dressed and arrive at Palam a few minutes after the plane has landed.

Strangely enough, and don't ask me how, we manage to get through to customs and greet Miss B who is looking around in amazement at the swathed and recumbent bodies on the floor and the flights of birds in the rafters. We wait with her until her luggage is cleared, then whisk her off, amid much chatter and a good deal of gawking on her part, to Vasant Vihar. After breakfast we break the news that we will have to leave her for a while in the care of the children, and dash upstairs to change.

We have been invited to attend Brian Springay's wedding. He is a young Immigration officer who has been courting a lovely Chinese girl, and today is the day. The church service is to be held at 10.00am and the reception will be later on in the evening. We scurry into suitable attire and head for the church. Like so many other things in India, the church is decaying, and smells slightly of mould and dripping candles. The heat is extreme and we begin to shift restlessly as 15 minutes, then half an hour, go by with no bride.

Finally, close to three-quarters of an hour late, the bride arrives, looking a tad flustered with her gorgeous black hair not quite dry from the hairdresser's ministrations. The head of Immigration and his wife act *in loco parentis*, and the service is duly completed. We return home, and take Miss B for a brief drive down the Rajpath. Not too surprisingly she falls asleep afterwards. Since she is still slumbering when it is time for us to leave, we direct Tony as to dinner, and once more depart to continue the festivities.

The reception is being held at the Rajdoot Hotel, an impressive Mogul-style edifice. Drinks are served in the gardens around the pool, then we troop inside for supper – a magnificent buffet. It is all very decorative with splendid fish and roast suckling pig. We leave about midnight, having had a marvellous time.

Tuesday, July 8   Take Barbara to the British School for her first day. I run into an American friend en route, and introduce her to Barbara. She remarks that both girls seem well suited for their respective schools. Barbara, she feels, looks very 'English' somehow and Hilary – well, "Hilary is the all-American kid."

I am not sure I am all that thrilled with this summation of two young Canadians, but all in all, I don't think she is that far off the mark. I just keep my fingers crossed that we have made the right choice for Barbara.

Wednesday, July 9   Miss B has yet to be blooded by a trip to Old Delhi, but is avid to venture thereto. I have yet to apply for my Indian driver's license, so I hire Francis for the day, and ask that he take me to the Licensing Bureau.

I have been coasting along on my Canadian license for the past six months, postponing the inevitable and fearful of being tested in the horrors of Delhi traffic. Hah! I simply cannot believe the speed with which I am in and out, a certified Indian driver. Officialdom shows a distinct lack of interest in my driving skills, and Francis confides that it is all "very normal," adding that he, himself, has never taken a driving test.

With this gruelling task out of the way, we head for the Janpath and the wonders of the Tibetan Market. Hilary – "the Bitsy" as Miss B has decided to call her – is intent on giving the novitiate a tutorial on the art of bargaining. Poor Miss B. Every time she closes in on a treasure, Hilary shakes her head and only gives an approving nod when the price comes down to what she considers a reasonable sum.

All this, of course, takes time, but we finally make it to Old Delhi. We go to the Maiden's Hotel for lunch. I love it. It is pure Raj, with a wide verandah, fans, palms and Empire-style wicker furniture. I can see in my mind's eye long departed 'Mems', clapping their hands for service and lording it over the underlings.

116

It is pure Raj, with … palms and Empire-style wicker furniture

After lunch, Francis is summoned, and we are taken over to the Jama Masjid. Thousands of pilgrims have come for a holy festival of some ilk. Francis is not forthcoming as to its nature. He probably does not know, but it is beneath his dignity to admit it.

There are bodies strewn across the steps, many with bundles of clothing and cooking gear. Francis, unbidden, finds us a guide. I am about to remonstrate, but decide it is probably for the best.

It is. We are led past the waiting faithful right into the mosque, and up to see the holy relics. These include the hair of the prophet, his shoe and the impression of his foot in the stone. I am assailed by irreverent thoughts. Why would his barber keep a hair? What happened to his other shoe? How did his foot make an impression in the stone? Oh me of little faith!

We are also shown pages from the Koran, written on skin. What kind of skin, I am about to ask, but think better of it. After we have viewed all these wonders then, and only then, are the patient masses permitted in to gaze. It all seems wrong somehow. They are the true worshippers, and have come with faith and piety; I come as a curious tourist, with no little cynicism. But in their case, palms have not been crossed with silver, and even Allah cannot change that.

After our tour of the mosque, we go into the Ivory Palace, a 300-year-old shop, and the Ivory Market. We watch them embroider glorious wall-hangings and carve ivory into miracles of delicate flowers, screens and deities. The carvers work in tiny little marble alcoves in impossibly poor light, and I wonder again at the exquisite precision of their work. I look covetously at some chess sets, but the price has been set for a higher market, alas.

Sunday, July 13 I luxuriate in rising at my leisure, and potter around preparing brunch. I mess up one end of the kitchen and Hilary the other, she being engaged in producing a batch of sticky brownies.

Dinker phones to say he is in town, which is always a pleasure. I invite him over for a drink later on. After hanging up, I am immediately conscience-stricken. I cannot really send him out into the night, unfed. He will have to stay for dinner. I conduct a mad scurry through the kitchen to see what Tony might have on hand. A frantic scramble reveals there is enough for three; we will be seven. There are precisely three potatoes, three tomatoes and five pieces of chicken. Some rapid calculations. Can I divvy up the chicken between six, and I will eat the left-over sliced meat from last night's dinner? No, I cannot – the meat has disappeared and I suspect Hilary and Hermione.

I set the table, mentally mulling over how I can pretend to be on a diet, while quietly salivating. At this juncture Dinker arrives and apologizes after I ask him to dinner to say he is already booked. What a pity! Maybe next time? The inner me is busy punching the air, and doing the athlete's 'y-e-e-s'. As it turns out, the twins take Hilary over to the ACSA lounge for dinner, and Doug, Miss B and I end up having a very pleasant candlelit supper for three.

Tuesday, July 15 A phone call from Sheila brings the news that she will be arriving on the 'Punjab Mail' between 7.00 and 8.00 tonight. Leaving in good time for the Northern Railway to meet her, we drive down narrow back streets that are unusually dark – there are no lights, due to the State of Emergency power cuts. As the streets are crowded with tongas (horse-drawn carts), people and cattle, the journey is stomach-clutchingly frightening. Finally reach the station, and I begin to believe that the drive was like an Irish spring compared to the Northern Railway station. We find an open concourse strewn with bodies. I am constantly amazed at the Indian's ability to sleep anywhere, but it isn't just the sleeping bodies, it is the filth on which they repose – the wretched bundles, the rags, the stenches. Heaven knows, I am no fanatic for sterility, nor unduly fastidious, but the thought of touching anything or anyone at the station is repellent.

I find Sheila at the gate by the No.5 Punjab Down, but lose Doug who has wandered off to find Sheila. We finally all stop trying to find each other, and get together for the drive home. Sheila and I stay up later talking. She tells of some of her adventures in the Himalayas, and we talk of John, her late husband. It is the fifth anniversary of his death, and if I still miss him for his wit, his kindness and for just being John, how much more must Sheila.

As usual, she has come laden with gifts – books and tea for me, a bird sculpture for Hilary, a hookah-pipe for Martin, a carved elephant for Barbara, a small Tibetan prayer rug for Doug and even an embroidered change purse for Miss B. I am so happy to have her back.

Saturday, July 19   Today everyone is mad keen for our proposed trip to Agra. Francis has been organized and arrives at 8.00am and with a gathering up of sun lotions, hats, cameras, sunglasses and our super picnic, we are away by 8.30. We see elephants and camels en route; great vultures perch in the trees, waiting for the rewards of death like rival undertakers around the upturned sod. A wild peacock walks majestically across the road. We stop at a little tea house and Barbara and Hilary take pictures of the entertainers – snake charmers, monkey wallahs and a dancing bear.

We reach Agra around noon and check into the hotel. Our room has a rather nice balcony and we gorge on Tony's picnic, while Francis goes in search of a guide. I am not big on guides but this one is rather scholarly and seems to love his subject. First stop is Akbar's Tomb. This was planned by Akbar in 1602. I wonder if he had a premonition or physical warnings as he died in 1605, and the tomb was only finished by his son Jahangir in 1613. Decided not to inquire too deeply into what they did with Akbar in the intervening eight years.

Akbar was the son of Humayan and was one of the less obsessive Moguls. He tried to create a society of religious tolerance in India, and constructed buildings that blended Buddhist, Hindu and Islamic styles in a happy enough architectural marriage. His tomb is playing host to a crowd of monkeys – females with babies, leaping and scratching and parting the infants' fur with maternal concern. Barbara is enchanted, and we get rather a charming picture of her offering them some monkey-type goodie. The grounds are lovely and the heavy clouds give the gardens a completely different dimension.

From the tomb we go on to the Agra Fort. This, too, was built by Akbar and is magnificent, and to my mind much more impressive than the Red Fort in Delhi. Built in the shape of a giant 'D' it was excessively well fortified. Personally I would have given up at Hazard No.1 – a moat stocked with crocodiles. Beyond this was the castle wall, and another area, wherein lay a jungle full of slavering wildlife – Bengal tigers and the like. Then came the thick, thick castle gate and drawbridge and an inner courtyard surrounded by a gated wall with defensive peepholes for the pouring of boiling oil or water. Not all that hospitable, perhaps, but discouraging to the enemy.

Once admitted as non-enemies, we are ushered in, hazard-free. The inner courtyards and pavilions are beautiful and, for India, well preserved. We are shown the room in which Shah Jehan was imprisoned and where he died. There is a narrow window that looks out toward the Taj Mahal. Experts say this window reveals the finest view of this incomparable building. They may be right – it seems to float in an ethereal glow, other-worldly and mystical.

It is easy to imagine the ageing and bitter Shah gazing out – sunrise and sunset – on the glorious structure that he created as testimony for his great love, Mumtaz. I am yanked from these mental Elysian fields to inspect the fort's extravagant features: the beautiful fountains in the courtyards; the huge chessboard on which dancing girls were human pawns; the harem baths; the Hall of Mirrors; and the great Hall of Audience – stripped now of its lush carpets, wall-hangings and its magnificence of gilded thrones.

For all this wonder, we have a price to pay as the guide insists on taking us to the shops offering inlaid marble items and carved ivory – no tourists, no kick-back.

Sunday, July 20 We check out of the hotel by 9.45am with a bill for 482 rupees (approximately $50) for the five of us, including breakfast and dinner. *La dolce vita*! Francis is waiting for us and we drive over to the Taj. It is pouring with rain and windy and the Muslim pilgrims are there in the thousands.

Somehow neither the weather nor worshipful pilgrims lessen the effect of the Taj Mahal. Rather the rain turns the dome to misty pearl, and the faithful turn a building into a shrine. The tombs are lit by candles and are hauntingly beautiful. I find myself glad to have seen it this way, and make an inner promise for the "must-see" visit by moonlight.

All this wandering about in the rain has left us sodden, and we slip back into the hotel restrooms to change into dry clothes before taking off for Fatehpur Sikri. It is still pouring when we reach this architectural jewel in the Mogul crown, and nobody wants to get out. Francis is clearly disappointed, but we drive on to the Bharatpur Bird Sanctuary, stopping first at the Indian Travel rest house where Francis (our man for all seasons) assists in whomping up omelettes, pakora, tea, bread and butter – a true feast.

Reaching the cool, lovely woods of the bird sanctuary, we find them awash with rain and with a minimum of birds, most of which seem to be sensibly holed up in their nests. A few gigantic deer droop through the rain forests and the odd heron swoops over the flooded fields.

Return home to find Delhi dry.

Monday, July 21   Sheila and Miss B leave for fresh adventures and what Sheila calls "Jolly Indian Surprises", ie have they been sold several pigs in several pokes? Examples: $200 tickets to "anywhere you wish, Memsahib." "What about being bumped?" "Oh no, Memsahib, this ticket will go before rajahs, ambassadors and presidents." "My God, all for $200?" The affirmative Indian shake of the head, which could mean that it as holy writ, or "Wot-the-hell, it is as the gods will it."

Saturday, August 2 Doug's birthday – all the presents are wrapped and ready. He plays golf in the morning and on his return we have a pre-luncheon sherry while he opens his presents – the jacket-of-his-choice chit, the posh cufflinks, a papier mâché box and lunch at the Peacock Lounge. Sheila and the children go off to the market, Doug snoozes and I review my diary for the last few days, and realize I am in the doldrums. The days have gone by with a certain predictability: swimming, dinners, lunches, letter-writing; trips to and from the airport, picking up and dropping off house guests.

I am glad of Sheila and Miss B as I have yet to find a kindred spirit at the Commission. Many, many spirits, but no really kindred one. I almost long for the days when I was left alone to read my book. Now I seem to be everyone's confidante.

I must be the best listener in Delhi.

I hear all about Mrs C's daughter's fiancé's accident – intimate details of his bladder and bowel problems; I hear all about the Clutcher's pre-husband romances and the chances she let slip by; I hear all about everybody, but nobody ever asks me about me. I'm glad in a way, as I don't particularly want to create an intimacy, but at least the odd question would display a flicker of interest in me and mine.

However, for now, what do I really have to complain about? Doug is happy here, more than half our family is with us, and the other two are due to arrive soon. My life is easy: I sleep when I'm sleepy, my hands have scarce seen a dishpan in months and, best of all, there is still no sign of another doctor coming. Doug much prefers to be his own boss, even if it means a lot more work. The Administrator has told Doug he will check out the situation with Ottawa, with regard to the possibility of a Medical Officer in Charge coming, and the subsequent disposal of the Grahams' house. So if I find myself in occasional doldrums, I have to admit they are still very comfortable doldrums.

Sunday, August 3 Doug's friends, Dr T F McCarthy and his unsinkable wife Bonnie have returned from their tour of duty in Burma for the World Health Organization. They come for dinner, and I realize all over again what a wimp I am for whinging about anything when I hear the saga of 'How Bonnie Faced Life in Darkest Burma'. Apparently they had been put up in a hotel that may or may not have been Burma's best but, either way, it was plagued with rats. In addition to being verminous, the hotel also served execrable food and provided the sketchiest of housekeeping.

Did Bonnie sit down by the waters of Babylon and weep? Not a bit of it. She went out into the market, found a bottle of Jeyes liquid, scoured the bathroom from top to bottom and bought a two-burner hot plate on which she could do her own cooking. She boarded up the rodent entry holes, added a touch of poison for good measure and then, as she concluded:

"We were in business." I am lost in admiration.

When they were last in Delhi, they had little time so we had strongly recommended a trip to the Taj Mahal. I had gone into my usual raptures and Bonnie said she supposed they *should* see it, and TF nodded, obviously used to a lifetime of acquiescence. We hadn't seen them since, so I asked what they had thought of it. Bonnie's brow furrowed in an attempt to recall her reactions:

"Well," she finally admitted, "I thought it was kind of pretty, but TF didn't care for it much."

So much for 20 years of unceasing labour by 20,000 workmen and an emperor's ransom in marble and precious stones, to say nothing of countless poets hymning paeans of praise. "TF didn't care for it much."

Monday, August 4 Take Sheila over to the Janpath to the Qantas Airlines for her ticket to Australia. This is the next lap of her journey – a prolonged stay with son Peter and his wife, Diana, in Sydney. Have tea while Sheila goes into Qantas. She returns beaming, with about five miles of tickets. All this business having been accomplished, we shop for the Aussies in the Tibetan Market, then return home for Sheila to organize herself for tomorrow's dawn departure. Word from Lufthansa brings the news that Kilmeny and Peter are on the flight arriving at 3.00am tomorrow morning. Sheila, a light sleeper and with her own early plane to catch, is given the alarm and we all go to bed.

I wake up with an uneasy feeling and take my watch into the bathroom. It is 2.40am and panic stations all round as I rouse Doug and Sheila and we dash off to Palam. We are barely in time, and the children have already de-planed, if not yet through customs. Kilmeny looks lovely in a blue t-shirt and matching slacks. 'Little' Peter has gone, replaced by a muscular young man with sideburns. We gather them up and then rush off to the departure lounge to say goodbye to Sheila. It is a case of hail and farewell to one of their favourite people.

We return to the car and drive through the dark of a Delhi morning to home. It is beyond happiness to see them. I want to hug them until they squeal, but am fearful of an "Oh Mum," so content myself with beaming on them and at the world in general.

Once home there is endless talk, a brief orientation drive along the Rajpath; a visit from the barber (raised eyebrows

124

from the newcomers), followed by a traditional welcome dinner and a collapse into bed.

CHAPTER 17

Thursday, August 7 Kilmeny anxious for some Indian clothes, so a morning of shopping produces a lovely peach-coloured sari, chappels (sandals) and what we have come to call a "swirly-girly" Indian skirt.

We pick up Barbara and her friend Arni at the British school, then on to my much-loved Qutb Minar. We first stop at the Qutb Hotel – very tasteful, with gorgeous crewelwork chesterfields and drapes. We have lunch and watch a performance of Indian dancers. Arni instructs us on the meaning of the movements, which adds no end to our enjoyment.

Everyone has a great time at the Qutb – climbing the tower and encircling the iron pillar. I am left on my own to discover new delights as I do each time we visit. Walking through the avenue of square, rather Grecian columns, I wonder if this is a legacy of the conquering Alexander. He was in India in the 3rd century BC, but how far back do these ruins go? There is so much I don't know. The Romans never reached India, or at least, I don't think so. But, according to Jacob Bronowski in *The Ascent of Man*, "one of man's great leaps forward was in the development of the Roman arch". As the Qutb abounds with the lovely scalloped arches of the Mogul Period (16th-17th century AD), did the Mogul architects study in Europe, or were arches simply old hat by the time they reached Delhi?

Later, we gather up Hilary, and Barbara, Arni, Peter and Martin all go riding. I strongly suspect that Kilmeny bows out until she can get herself fashionably kitted out.

Saturday, August 9 Yet another planned trip to Agra, with Francis once more at the helm. Does one tire of the Taj Mahal? As with Samuel Johnson and London, only if one is tired of life.

The day is pleasant, promising heat as the sun reaches its zenith. Stop en route, and Hilary rides a camel. She loves to act the Old Indian Hand with her older siblings, and mounts the camel as to the desert born.

At Akbar's tomb, I am commandingly encyclopaedic with all the facts and figures gleaned from our previous visit. At the Taj, the heat is stifling – Kilmeny looks lovely in a soft yellow dress, but is beginning to 'glow' and we elect to lunch at the air-conditioned Holiday Inn. The day is waning, and rather than go on to Fatehpur Sikri, we allow ourselves to be taken to the marble shop where several marble plates are purchased, plus an inlaid box and a replica of the Taj. This last is of highly dubious quality, but passionately desired by Hilary.

We return to the hotel for baths, rest and Happy Hour, then go down for dinner. Tonight's cabaret entertainment includes a strip-tease performed by a dancer, who has obviously been into the chapatis and is more than somewhat voluptuous. Hilary is agog and Peter embarrassed but intensely interested. An Indian gentleman at the next table applauds vigorously and inquires if we have anything this splendid in our country.

Sunday, August 10 Francis is waiting for us at the car, as we gather up our possessions, pay the bill and wipe off the breakfast crumbs. We are heading for Fatehpur Sikri, and I cannot be restrained from telling my captive audience the romantic tale.

The great Akbar had three wives – one Muslim, one Hindu and one Christian, to say nothing of countless concubines and the odd passing slave girl. Despite all this earnest effort, he still had no children. In despair he made a pilgrimage to seek the services of a highly renowned holy man, Sheikh Salim Chisti. For the gift of a son, Akbar was ready to offer just about anything, but restricted himself to the relatively modest promise to build a wonder of a palace, "of surpassing splendour and opulence".

To sweeten the pot, he even threw in a magnificent shrine that would be dedicated to Chisti himself. Well, this was enough for the holy man, and within nine months, trumpets blared and proclamations announced the birth of a son, Jahangir.

Faithful to his word, Akbar created a pleasure dome to outdo the fabled Kublai Khan, a miracle of gardens, fountains and pavilions straight out of the tales of Sheharazade. Its fame spread to the capitals of Europe and travellers returned with tales of pyramids of sapphires and curtains of emerald. Hyperbole, no doubt, but few there were to contradict them. It became Akbar's capital, and a supreme example of Mogul architecture.

Today it lies among the cobwebs of history, waiting for a Prince's kiss to waken it to its former glory. It is deserted by all but for tourists like us, who wander at will through this beautiful and haunting ghost town.

Deserted it may be, and its treasures lost or destroyed, but it is still a many-faceted gem. Within the palace itself, each wife had her own apartments, plus a common room where they probably got together to compare notes and pick up decorating hints.

In a central courtyard, there is another massive chessboard in black and white marble, where the Emperor and his guests played with dancing girls as pawns. I try to imagine exactly how the pieces were moved, or whether there was a lot of dancing from square to square, or leaping over knights, but my fantasizing bogs down at the checkmate stage.

The sun is high and burning hot as we stroll into the Musicians' Gardens, which are a cool and shaded oasis. The nearby Pearl Mosque shimmers and dances in the sun. This latter is the shrine dedicated to Chisti, and I have to admit that Akbar didn't have a chintzy bone in his body when it came to keeping promises. The shrine is mother of pearl, and breathes an opalescent fusion of colour in the sunlight. The carved screen that faces it is a poem in lacy marble, as delicate as a veil.

Nearby, we spot a huge pile of strips of silk, and a receptacle for change, which is, of course, a dead give-away that something is on offer. It is all part of the Chisti legend. It is foretold that if a visitor ties one of the silk pieces around a lattice in the screen and makes a wish, it will be granted. It also means that the believer will one day come again to Fatehpur Sikri. Needless to say we all tie knots like mad and make fervent wishes.

By now the heat is of a wilting intensity, and even hatted and sun-glassed as we are, I have had enough. Still Francis persuades me I have seen nothing if I have not seen the Diver.

"You've seen one diver..," I think to myself but I hate to be a wimp, so follow Francis along an open pathway.

High above the palace is a massive cliff overlooking a small, shallow water tank. At the top of the cliff stands a magnificent bronzed figure, posed for a dive from this staggering height. He spreads his arms like an eagle, turns to the right and to the left, and leaves his aerie to pierce through space into the water below leaving scarce a ripple. He more than deserves the burst of applause, and we willingly bestow rupees into the waiting hands.

We stop again at the Government Rest House for lunch, and follow the same path to the Bharatpur Bird Sanctuary. This time it is bathed in sunlight that glitters on the flooded fields. White birds, like huge beautiful blossoms, perch in the drowned trees. We are about to exclaim when Francis turns with his finger to his lips. Near the left side of the car, quite close to us, are two enormous crane-like birds – a species of stork from Jerusalem according to Francis. One, the feathered comb on his grey-black head raised in a semi-circle, is going through a precise and rhythmic dance – he two-steps, he sways, he does what Doug calls the "Upper Canada Dip" and back again swooping before his coy partner. I feel as though we are in a David Attenborough nature documentary, with this mesmerizing mating ritual so close.

After this hugely successful outing we drive home in time to send Francis to pick up Miss B at the airport. Dinker pops in for a drink, just as Miss B comes in, flushed with excitement over her marvellous trip and as thrilled with its economy as with its wonders.

CHAPTER 18

Wednesday, August 13 The days are filled with riding, shopping, swimming and general enjoyment. It is like the summer holidays of yore, when the children were home from school, and life was a thing of lazing and lemonade.

Peter has been pining for a chess set, but his between-classes-earnings do not run to the splendid ivory or Agra marble ones we have been viewing. Today, on an excursion to the shopping district of Yashwant, he finds exactly what he wants. The opposing teams are all are beautifully carved in sandalwood and rosewood, figures from the classic epic, the *Ramayana*. The bishops are camels, the knights winged horses and the castles are elephants. He is absolutely delighted and wants to rush home for a game.

Thursday, August 14 Twenty-eight years ago today, the Union Jack came down for the last time on the jewel in the Imperial crown. Independence Day, however, does not seem to engender the same whoop-de-do as does Republic Day. It is a holiday, but there is no parade, and no special events.

The heat has been excessive and Doug feels we should take advantage of the long weekend and take the children into the Himalayas. After some thought, we decide upon Mussoorie, one of the Raj hill stations. Miss B elects not to come, as she has just returned from her trip and is quite content to be left in the cool marble halls of Vasant Vihar, with a slew of servants and a driver to hand.

'Goldie' Singh, one of the Commission drivers, has been organized as our chauffeur and guide. I learn just in the nick of time that Goldie is not his name to anyone but Doug. He is a Punjabi and a Sikh (all of whom take the surname Singh which means 'lion') and his first name is Anwar, the translation of which is 'Golden'. He had been at some pains to explain all this to Doug, who promptly dubbed him 'Goldie'. I am not sure I should take the same liberty, although he beams away at Doug, regardless.

He is an older man, handsome, with a grey beard, and looks exactly like the faithful native batman in all the Bengal-Lancer-King-of-the-Khyber-Pass films. The one you just know will end up dying, as he throws himself in front of Errol Flynn or Gary Cooper to save them from the Pathans' bullets.

We have not driven north before, and I am eager to see all. We drive into Madhav Nagar, a company town, owned and run by India Industries. It is pretty dull, but Meerut is not.

As previously recorded, I have become fascinated by the Indian Mutiny, and Meerut is where it all began on a Sunday morning in May of 1857. Goldie takes us past *the* church, and the scene unfolds before my inner eye. The officers and men of John Company and their families are attending early services, all spiff plus and serenely secure in their English superiority, unaware that their world and, in most cases, their lives are about to come to an end.

Outraged by the rumoured use of cow fat on the bullets they are forced to bite before loading in their rifles, the sepoys (native Indian soldiers) have mutinied and burst through the barracks and into the Sabbath quiet of the church square, just as the congregation is emerging. Screaming women are torn from their carriages, blood spills over, blending with the scarlet jackets of the soldiers, as the carnage continues. Shooting, pillaging and raping, the sepoys finally leave, shrieking "on to Delhi" where they will enact the next bloody scene in this evolving tragic drama.

We drive on through bleached, bone-dry countryside, and spot a massive collection of vultures, fighting for a place at the table of a dead cow. It is not a landscape conducive to stopping, even though there have been mutterings about getting out our picnic.

Not too far along, however, we come suddenly upon a small green oasis in a grove of trees, with a little brook thrown in for good measure. Goldie stops, spreads a blanket and we have a Canadian-style picnic with nobody about until the arrival of a passing cowherd, who is fascinated by the bizarre sight of a family munching away in the middle of nowhere.

Ahead of us lies the vast Delhi plain, which we traverse, air-conditioner going full blast. Suddenly, almost like a towering, forbidding wall, the hills are there. We climb into

131

... almost like a towering, forbidding wall, the hills are there

wooded slopes, burrowing into an intensity of green like sinking into a vast and verdant bosom. We climb and climb, until finally at around 6,500 feet, we see Mussoorie, an aerie of a town in the Himalayan mists, perched on the edge of lush, green terraces.

Goldie delivers us to the Savoy, where we have booked three suites. It is an ancient and decaying Victorian heap, a hotel equivalent of Miss Haversham's mouldy mansion in *Great Expectations*. Despite this, it has a certain *je ne sais quoi*. I can see why the Grahams would be repelled (as Mildred told me they were) but in some indefinable way, I like it. Each suite has a sitting room with fireplace, a bedroom and bathroom. Not all 'mod con' perhaps – water is available only from 6.00 to 10.30 in the morning and from 5.00 to 10.30 in the evening. Everything is damp: towels, bedding and linens cling like poultices – still, I like it.

While the children are sorting out their bedrooms, Doug and I wander for two hours along the esplanade that curves around the edge of the town. It is a magnificent panorama of terraces and foothills, and all very Tibetan in flavour. We are only one mile from the border, and I have one of those 'pinch-me' moments. Is it really possible that I, born on the distant Canadian prairies, am now standing on the edge of Tibet, and perhaps only a dream away from Shangri-la?

We return to the hotel, have Happy Hour in the lounge, and then dinner. The food, while stubbornly adhering to the tastes of the departed Raj, is hot and surprisingly good. We even go all out in a replay of a vanished lifestyle and finish off the evening with a game of billiards – minus the brandy and cigars.

Friday, August 15 After breakfast we leave for a day's exploration. It is very hot, and I shudder to think what the temperature might be on the Delhi plain. We follow the Camel's Back Road, and Hilary spots a man with a horse who is hawking rides to the tourists. Hilary is all gung-ho for a ride, but encounters a clash of wills. The elderly horseman's usual procedure is to walk sedately beside "baby" while holding firmly onto the reins; hers is to ride full-tilt like a Mongol warrior. When we see the poor old man, almost horizontal at the end of the reins, we intervene and come to a compromise. He won't hold on, and she won't gallop.

The boys buy beautiful hand-carved walking sticks and ask to go off on a hike by themselves. The rest of us take a rickshaw. This is a totally immoral sort of indulgence and utterly undemocratic. The rickshaw is a carriage-like affair, with a canopy; two men yoked like oxen pull us up the steep lanes, while a third man acts as a brake.

It really is rather splendid being bounced around in this Mandarin fashion, although all my principles are against it. Doug can never understand why I fret about these inequities. He has an almost Hindu attitude of predestination. It is his karma to be a Sahib; it is the rickshaw men's karma to be the puller of Sahibs, and what could be fairer than that.

After lunch, Goldie drives us up to the Kempty Falls, a famed waterfall on a remote mountain trail. The water cascades down into a deep basin, which can be reached by a long descent through a thick forest. We gamely plunge our way down and watch people run in and out of a curtain of water.

It has become sort of a family game finding people in our travels who look like someone we knew at home. There was 'Claire' in Bangalore and here we spot someone who is a doppelgänger for Boots Boothroyd – in sepia.

We divert ourselves poking around the Falls, although it has become terribly hot. However, as we start the trudge back up the hill, the rain begins and it is like a gift from heaven. Goldie is waiting for us and drives us back, approaching the town from a different angle and climbing into the mountain mists. Why is it that dancing mists and fugitive fogs always impart a deliciously sinister atmosphere to even the most pedestrian scene? Mussoorie is hardly commonplace at any time, but now, wrapped in its rain-filled shroud, it appears like the opening scene of a suspense film.

Back at the Savoy I dress for dinner in my swishy new skirt, and we have a pleasant family evening.

Saturday, August 16 We leave Mussoorie around 11.30am fortified with a picnic lunch provided by the Savoy. There seems to be a marked similarity in Indian hotel picnics, and memories of the Neddous come flooding back as we open up a

134

lunch of chicken, hard-boiled eggs, cold potatoes and cake. The food is not inspired, but the spot we find to eat it in is lovely – a cool woodland, complete with babbling brook and the song of mountain birds.

The drive back lacks the anticipation of the outward journey but we receive a rapturous welcome from Hermione, and a warm, but slightly less effusive one from Miss B.

CHAPTER 19

Friday, August 22 Time's winged chariot has gone thumping by, and I can't bear to think it is Peter's last day. He goes out to buy a few last minute things and I stay home with Hilary. She has picked up some bug in Mussoorie, and has developed a nasty cough and a bit of a fever. It has not been easy to keep her away from the pool. She has spent the last couple of days in bed, but the antibiotics Doug brought home seem to be working. She swears rather anxiously that she is sure she will be well enough to go to Jaipur tomorrow. We are taking a smaller car than for our trip to Mussoorie, so are restricted as to numbers. As Martin has yet to see the wonders thereof, he is definitely going, along with Kilmeny.

The twins have been invited to go to Wheels, Delhi's major (perhaps only) disco, with some of the youngsters from the High Commission. Martin seems unduly worried as to when Tony will be serving dinner. Barbara keeps telling him that the disco does not open until 9.00pm, but he is still in a bit of a stew and confesses that one of the guard's sons has asked that he come early. In any event he scurries off the second dinner is over.

Saturday, August 23 I am up at 4.30am and take Peter to the airport. I hate to see him go, but console myself that it won't be too long before Christmas. By 7.00am. I'm getting ready for our jaunt.

Doug has roused Martin, who immediately retreats into the den, announcing that he does not want any breakfast. For Martin not to want breakfast is akin to Winnie the Pooh not wanting honey. Something is obviously amiss, and I go in to check on him. He looks positively green, and I wonder if he has picked up Hilary's bug. I come over all motherly concern and suggest he lie down for awhile and see how he is feeling by the time we are ready to leave.

When Doug comes down for breakfast, I ask him to take a look at his son. He disappears into the den and is back in a trice.

"The kid's hung-over," he announces, munching on a piece of a toast.

I am shocked, although I am beginning to see a point to last night's hurried exit after dinner.

"Don't be ridiculous," I say defensively. "He is only 16."

Doug fails to find any logic in this statement: "Believe me I know a hangover when I see one, and that is what he has. I've told him we have bounced someone else from the Jaipur trip, so he is going, hung-over or not."

I return once again to the den – no longer the solicitous mother hen. It is obvious to the sufferer that I have been told the reason for his misery. He looks up at me with his beautiful, blood-shot eyes.

"If it's any consolation to you, Mum, never again! I feel just awful. I've let you down, and Dad down," pausing for a moment, he adds, "and Canada down."

The acknowledgement of this last betrayal is obviously a harking back to my lecture when the twins arrived in India. I had made the point that their behaviour and how they conducted themselves would determine how the host country viewed Canadian teenagers. I cannot conceal a slight twitching of the lip at Martin's conviction that his nation's international reputation has been irreparably damaged.

His contrition has won back my sympathy. I offer the consoling prognosis that by the afternoon he will be surprised by how much better he will feel, and say I will bring him a cup of tea. Poor boy, not only does he feel physically dreadful, but he is also convinced he made an ass of himself, which is worse.

Francis arrives on the dot and we set out. Hilary, sadly, is still too ill to join us. The drive is interesting – all sorts of camels, peacocks, elephants, etc. We reach a spot where there must be at least a mile of trucks waiting. It seems the road has been washed out and in the enforced wait we become the star attraction. They all stare at us, and it is difficult to know whether to feign indifference or to smile inanely. Francis warns us not to put down the windows, as we will be 'baksheeshed' forever.

After a half hour's delay, Francis decides to risk the flooded road. It is dicey, but we make it by diverting our course over a patch of hard-packed sand. Not long after, we arrive in Jaipur – the fabled 'Rose-Pink City'. In my imagination, I saw shimmering towers of rose quartz rising against an amber mountain. Not quite. Our entry is not auspicious. The monsoons make everything look worse. The red sandstone is stained with the legacy of past floods; drains, if there are any, are blocked and a lot of unspeakable things come up with the rising water. It is indescribably filthy and squalid. We drive past stalls selling fruit, vegetables and meat, the produce almost totally obscured by flies.

Kilmeny, as usual impeccably clad, stares gloomily out the window. If this is the city, she begins to despair of our country-house hotel and what lies ahead. Is her father sure he knows where Francis is going? Has the hotel been recommended? She cheers up perceptibly as we leave the horrors of the crowded streets behind, drive past open fields and up to a large, impressive white building, which Francis announces is our destination.

It was once a country lodge for the Maharajahs of Jaipur and is a very attractive house, with a wide, shaded verandah, and set in a lush garden of trees, flowers and fountains. We are welcomed in by the owner (a scion of the princely family) and ushered into a very nicely furnished suite of rooms off the courtyard.

Our host is a handsome man, wearing a faultlessly tailored safari suit, and speaking with a plummy public school accent. He has had lunch prepared for us, which is served in a cool green and white room. It is lovely and quiet, with only the slight whirr of the ceiling fan and the off-stage cry of a peacock to disturb us.

After lunch we go to the City Palace and museum. Jaipur was built in the early 1600s and derived its nickname, the 'Rose-Pink City', from the deep pink sandstone of its buildings. These were covered with elaborately painted facades and must have been quite spectacular in their hey-day. It is all in a pretty parlous state at the moment, with the once splendid buildings crumbling into decay.

The City Palace, however, is not. Perhaps it is because until very recently (two weeks ago to be exact), it was occupied by the widow of the late maharajah, who died three years ago "by a heart attack of a polo game into England," as we are told by our guide. The maharajah's gorgeous widow, it seems, was arrested two weeks ago under the Economics Offences Act, charged with possessing three and a half million tons of gold. Where, I ask myself, would one store such an impossible quantity of gold? Are there perhaps wheels within wheels in this State of Emergency, and is all not what it seems?

We now move over to the Royal Museum. This has a series of exhibitions, a little dusty and turning up slightly at the edges, so to speak, but nonetheless fascinating. There are incredibly beautiful saris, gowns and princely raiment of the royal family, and a breathtaking display of Rajasthani textiles.

The guide, inspired by our oohs and aahs, scurries us into a tour of the Armoury. Talk about weapons of mass destruction – there are camel guns and tiger guns, some lethal-looking things called 'tiger claws' used in hand-to-hand combat, and a singularly nasty collection of torture instruments.

From the 'wasting' material in the armoury, we move to the Art Gallery, filled with Rajput and Mogul art. We find ancient but still lush carpets, and quite beautiful paper-cuttings done by one of the past maharajahs. Then it's on to the palace itself.

It is very illuminating to see a palace as a contemporary residence, when so many of the ones we have been visiting call upon the imagination to re-create the lavish thrones, draperies, and ankle-deep rugs that once were there. This one shows every sign of being a home. There is even a portrait gallery (shades of England's stately homes) with space for ten maharajahs and ten there are.

In the vast Hall of Public Audience, we see two enormous brass pots – over six feet in height and almost four feet across. They could have come straight out of Ali Baba's tale and are just the right size for a couple of thieves. Actually they were designed for a travelling maharajah who had been invited to England for a visit. Fearful of what poisoned food and tainted water he might encounter in a foreign land, he insisted on bringing his own supply.

The whole thing has been quite fascinating and rather personal somehow – a bit like being on a very grand house tour or simply having a chummy visit with the Maharani.

As we leave the palace, we are accosted by a man who

claims to own an emerald-cutting factory, and who would be "honoured to welcome us." Doug is mad keen, I am less so, Martin is game and Kilmeny is downright convinced of a sinister purpose behind the invitation. This suspicion grows apace as we are led down reeking back lanes, through crowded alleys, awash with the flotsam of the monsoons, and finally to a decrepit building and up a filthy stairwell into a bedroom of sorts. Three men are sitting at shaping wheels doing something with a fortune in green stones. It looks like the classic den of thieves at its worst.

Martin (a Humphrey Bogart fan) turns to Kilmeny and mutters: "If the ice is hot, swedehart, I'll hold them off while you get the cops."

It is all Kilmeny needs. She has not exactly left a trail of bread crumbs, but followed every turn of our passage, and elects not to stay, but darts down the stairs and is standing beside the car and our driver by the time we make our way back. When she chooses to look at emeralds, apparently, it will be in an air-conditioned glass-fronted store, with a splash of brilliant green against a white satin cloth. A true Memsahib.

We return down the cluttered streets and crowded markets, and finally through the iron gates and into the lovely garden and courtyard of our sanctuary. Have a delicious long soak in the tub, enjoy Happy Hour, and then go down for dinner. It is not quite ready, but our host, that suave and urbane gentleman in the George Sanders style, joins us in the lounge and regales us with tales of other times.

In what many of the princely families still refer to as the Great Days of the Raj, he recalls, Rajasthan was a thick, impenetrable jungle. The British protected the forests, but after they left, the woods were cut down and, as could be expected, the land turned into the khaki-hued desert hills we now look out on. He tells of the day a favourite family greyhound was carried off by a tiger – "Just over that ridge." He also recounts the story of his father's racing camel, which wandered away and was lost for three days, "so thick was the jungle."

Again, post-Raj, hundreds of tigers, including females and cubs, were killed – "It was the high price of tiger skins, you see." He is a superb raconteur and has us, figuratively, at his feet.

He is also encyclopaedic on the subject of subcontinental fauna and imparts some surprising facts on the sex life of the rhino. Females come into heat only once every 12 years, which undoubtedly accounts for a decline in the rhino population. When it comes to camels, he waxes quite lyrical and claims they are much-maligned beasts. Did we realize that a top breeder can charge anywhere between $300 and $3,000 for a good camel? Of course, we confess ignorance of this statistic, but eagerly wait for more.

Whatever we do, he insists, we must not miss one of India's truly great events, the Pushkar Camel Fair – a religious pilgrimage and vast camel market held annually near the village of the same name in Rajasthan. There is, he continues, a celebrated breeder, whose specialty is racing camels, and whose performance at the Fair is a must-see. His camels are noted for the almost unimaginable smoothness of their gait. As part of his demonstration, he spreads a wide carpet over the sand, then mounts his camel. A servant hands him up a full hookah pipe which he places in his mouth, then taking the reins in his hand, he races the beast over the rug. At this point in the story, our host pauses, leans forward in a confidential manner, and whispers: *"Not a single crease appears in the carpet, and not a drop of water is spilled from the pipe."*

Sunday, August 24 Up by 8.30am for breakfast. A nice hot omelette, but when I pour my tea it is full of ants. At first I thought they were just violently active tea leaves, but when the manager is summoned, he is abject in his apologies and approaching apoplexy as he bears the offending tea pot off to the kitchen. We take our leave after breakfast, and thank our remarkable host for the warmth of his welcome, and his gracious hospitality, waving aside his repeated regrets concerning the ant invasion.

Francis is waiting for us with the car and takes us off to meet the emerald man, who has extracted a promise from us before we fled his workplace to visit his father's shop. As expected, the shop is the ultimate in tackiness, but ablaze with the green fire of hundreds of emeralds. They are gorgeous and we dutifully gasp on cue but decline to buy any. Martin, however, spots a brilliant 'royal' topaz and decides to buy it for

141

The famous Amber Palace ... lies at the top of a high hill

Kilmeny for her birthday. It is a relatively good size and quite a glorious colour – best of all it is affordable on a schoolboy's summer earnings. Kilmeny is thrilled, Martin is proud of his purchase and the 'papa' beams on all as though he had just sold the Kohinoor.

The famous Amber Palace is next on our agenda, and lies at the top of a high hill, surrounded by a stone wall that snakes its way up the contours of the rising land. Who would want to do anything as mundane as drive, when a beaming mahout awaits with his elephants? Steps up a wall allow passengers to get easily into the howdah when the elephants are brought alongside. We are instructed to sit with our backs to the centre and legs over the side of the elephant; an iron bar is secured across the length of the howdah. The beast is then turned around, and the other two passengers go through the same procedure. So Doug and Martin sit back to back to Kilmeny and me.

The elephant is surprisingly hairy, and the hair is surprisingly rough – I have on slacks but am still aware of the bristles through the cloth. Not only is he hairy, but ponderous in his amble, and we sway along with him as he begins the steep climb along the cobblestone road to the Palace. I have a fugitive thought about people subject to seasickness, but am much too absorbed in the security quotient of the iron bar to worry about petty details.

As we climb, I even cease to worry about security. Kilmeny and I are on the view side, swaying gently above the wall. Below lies the glittering blue of the lake, and the ancient gardens of the City Palace, with its Mogul pavilions and rose-pink gazebos. The far-off hills show signs of ancient, crumbling walls. Apparently centuries ago, when the Amber Palace and Fort were built, the maharajah had the entire area surrounded by walls and watch-towers to warn of any approaching foes.

We reach the inner courtyard of the palace, and dismount in the same fashion we mounted. The Amber Palace is similar in design to most Indian palaces, with a Hall of Private Audience and a Hall of Public Audience as you enter. The Maharajahs of Jaipur are (and were) Hindus, but with Mogul associations, and this shows in the architecture. The builder-king had 12 wives, and each wife had a small house within the palace. No wife could visit another's quarters, but they could all meet in a sort of common room. My mind's eye conjures up an image a lot of sari-clad women all getting together in the common room and discussing the maharajah's qualities and talents (or lack of them).

There are some fascinating features – the Hall of Mirrors (a sort of Asian Versailles) and the Star Room, where the mirrors give the illusion of twinkling stars. Everywhere is stunning marble inlay, as fine as anything we have ever seen.

The day is wearing on, and we make the descent on Jumbo again – the whole return fare for the four of us is 50 rupees ($5) so we could scarcely turn down the mahout's pleas for baksheesh.

The faithful Francis is at his post, and we reach home at 6.00pm. Barbara had a great time at a pool party, Hilary has recovered from her malaise, and it is time for our Sunday dose of Americana at the ACSA lounge.

CHAPTER 20

Monday, August 25 Doug comes home with glad tidings. It seems no other doctor will be coming after all. Doug has been appointed Medical Officer in Charge, promoted to an MO2 grade with retroactive pay, and we can now, if we so wish, move into the Grahams' house. We so wish.

Wednesday, August 27 After two days of shopping with Kilmeny and Martin for presents for them to take back to Canada, after farewell teas at Claridge's and in the shaded gardens of the Imperial, I have to face the inevitable. Summer is over, and they will be leaving.

Every time something comes to an end, I find myself harking back to the way we were in what I still call "real life". Today it is the nostalgia of other summers: the annual Labour Day picnic in Lighthouse Park; the cycle around Stanley Park and lunch at Ferguson Tea House; the day out at Spanish Banks; and, of course the 'One-Child-Day'. This was a day greeted with rapture by each child in turn. "Just you and me, Mum," whether it was a special lunch, a day of shopping, a solid afternoon of sci-fi or cowboy movies – it was a day of individual choice and cherished as such.

However, *carpe diem* and all that. That was then and this is now. I spend the day working at the library, pick up the family at the pool, and return home to dress for Kilmeny's birthday dinner. How strange it seems to have nothing to do but dress! Everybody looks spiff plus – Kilmeny in her gorgeous new peach-coloured sari; Barbara in her lovely meadow green, and Hilary actually in a dress. Doug takes pictures and Tony outdoes himself in the cuisine. We drink champagne and gorge on the birthday Baked Alaska. Later, watch the Boothroyds' film of the twins' birthday party back in March. The film is hilarious, mildly manic and faintly reminiscent of the Marx Brothers, thus ending the evening on a high note.

Thursday, August 28 Kilmeny's real birthday – a young lady!

Where has she gone, that little curly-haired, pink-cheeked cherub? Little time to ponder on time and tide, as we drive her to the airport to see her off. She is so dear to us, and although we are not of the school that signs off every conversation with "love you," we do.

Friday, August 29 With Kilmeny and Peter gone, and Hilary and Barbara at school, Martin and I are left to indulge ourselves as we will. He heads for the Commission and the pool, while I elect to stay home and start sorting out things preparatory to our move next week to the Grahams' house, just around the corner. I would like to get one room done at a time. Manage to catalogue and pack all books and papers, and then, puffed with virtue, retire early.

Monday, September 1 It's a holiday at the American school (Labour Day) but not for the Canadian High Commission because they already had Indian Independence Day. So no Doug for the big move, but Hilary and Martin help pack and at 2.00pm a Commission driver arrives with a truck. We move boxes over and I start to unpack in the new house. By the time I pick up the girls for riding and collect Doug, I am almost too tired for dinner – well, *almost*.

Tuesday, September 2 The second day of The Move – I tell Tony to pack up things from the kitchen and, when ready, Martin will take them over. Explain that I want him, together with Muni, to clean up our house as we leave. I sometimes think Tony listens to his own drummer, or does not understand my instructions, because he promptly disappears to set up the kitchen in the new house, and proceeds to rearrange all the glasses I had put up the day before. I am a bit miffed about this, but realize, in all fairness, that he is the one who has to work in the kitchen and things should be convenient for him.

The truck arrives at 2.30pm and I ask Martin to go with the movers. Tony takes off, too. I repeat (rather ineffectually) that I want our house cleaned. At the Grahams' house I find that Salamat, the Grahams' cook-bearer, has used all the gas and taken most of the light bulbs, so tell Tony not to worry

146

about dinner; we will go out, but add yet another reminder that he must see to the clean-up at the old house.

Wednesday, September 3 With instructions to Tony that Martin will take him, Muni and their pails back to the old house, I leave to put in my stint at the library and work all afternoon. I pick everyone up from school, pool and workplace, and we stop at the old house to check up on the cleaning. I am surprised to find it locked up. We climb over the gates, only to find all the doors to the house are locked, but we can see through the window that the kitchen has not been touched. I am furious. Heaven knows I am not a queen among housekeepers, but pride or shame or whatever has always led me to keep this a secret from the world. Consequently, I have always left every house uncharacteristically spotless – far more scrubbed than when we lived in it. I now feel horribly embarrassed to think of anyone in Administration seeing it in this state, and my anger increases by the minute.

Barely wait to get in the door before I confront Tony with his domestic infamy. He says he decided to work on the new house. I tell him that it is *my* orders he is to follow, not his. I didn't think I had it in me. He has been bullying and ignoring me for months, and I guess I had to get mad enough to tell him off. And I did, in spades. Doug says he will arrange for re-entry into the house, and I tell (*tell*, not ask) Tony that he and Muni are to go there, and not come back until it is spotless. Finally simmer down and begin to feel the weight of guilt at having gone all Victorian Memsahib, treating the servants like less than the dust. Still the guilt comes a distant second to the inner satisfaction of having finally done what I was told to do on my very first day: "Show who is boss."

Thursday, September 4 There is nothing as effective, I rather sadly find, as the occasional kicking of the derrière. Tony and Muni take off for their task, and when I inspect everything hours later, the place positively shines. Muni, saluting with a much-used sponge, has obviously scrubbed like mad. I am sure Tony has not actively participated, but then I didn't really expect him to; being the bearer, his role would be largely supervisory. It doesn't matter – the work has been done, and I express approval.

With my new sense of authority I even manage to ignore Gopi Chand's bitter complaints about the laundry facilities at the new house. I don't care if he doesn't like them – it is better than beating clothes out on a rock.

This evening an old friend from Vancouver is in Delhi on business, and hosts a reception at the High Commission. It is quite fun, and later on we three exiles go out for dinner and engage in a conversational wallow of home and mutual friends.

Friday, September 5 Tonight we are invited to dinner at the home of Dr Etzel, Doug's opposite number at the American Embassy. Despite an unfortunate beginning, with Doug being held up and our arriving more than fashionably late, it is a delightful evening.

I have come to know Ruth Etzel through the American School, as she, too, works in the library. The other guests are people from the Swedish Embassy and a couple from the Australian High Commission. It is quite a glittering assemblage and incredibly elegant. Comparisons, as always, are odious, but I cannot help but feel that the American Embassy has done a tad better by their doctor than the CHC. The drawing room is vast and beautifully furnished. Mind you, I am prepared to accept that a few little refinements have been added by the occupants, such as lush Persian carpets and some rather splendid 19th-century oil paintings. When dinner is announced by a turbaned bearer (*with* shoes), I expect something quite grand and am not disappointed. The table is aglow with candlelight, shining on baroque silver goblets and wine glasses, silver serving plates and fine white and gold china. Ah me, dare I ask them back?

Monday, September 8 Martin's last day, and we spend it together, sorting things out for Martin to take back with him and overseeing the writing of social notes. One particular thank-you goes to Brigadier Sen, the husband of one of the High Commission secretaries, who had arranged a tour of the Presidential Palace. Martin was dazzled, and is rather smug about the fact that none of the rest of us has stepped across the threshold. He has been such a help in the move, and such a good companion that I try not to think of how much I will miss him.

Tuesday, September 9 Up half the night because of Martin's dawn-patrol departure. He is so anxious not to miss his plane that he telephones the airport at 3.00am to check on the departure time, scheduled for 6.30am. So we are up again at 5.00 and reach the airport to find it awash in a torrential downpour. Because of the rain, Doug ignores orders about parking and, sure enough, when we return there is an official taking down his number. The ensuing ticket adds to the general gloom of the day.

After school, I take Barbara for a driving lesson – she does very well, considering the monsoon conditions of the road; snakes are continually popping out of their drowned holes, for one thing. Then, a near disaster as she almost careens into two cars. I automatically yell at her. I am sorry, and say so, but it is still discouraging for her. All in all, not a really great day.

Thursday, September 11 I have paved innumerable roads to hell with good intentions never fulfilled, but today I decide to do the 'right thing' and find my way to the East-West Clinic to see the 'Clutcher' who has been a patient there for the past week. The diagnosis is that she has a manic-depressive disorder but she thinks she is in for a rest. She is quite heavily medicated, her conversation is desperately difficult to follow, and, although I did my best, I don't think I was the cheerer-upper I had hoped to be.

Hers is an extreme case, but I am beginning to learn that Foreign Service life can be really difficult for many women. It is rather sad that here, in a society where we live a life of almost Edwardian privilege with marble halls and servants to do our bidding, so many women seem to be oddly out of place, suffering from depression, alcoholism or boredom. Doug brought me home notes from a lecture he had attended on culture shock. In my innocence, I rather assumed culture shock was simply the road bumps of dealing with a culture completely alien to one's own. It is in a way, but it can also produce a destructive disorientation through the loss of all one's familiar social cues: have I said the right thing, done the right thing, served the right thing?

Personally, I alternate between enjoying the fascinating experience of a lifetime and longing for the green woods of home. Still, I have found that throwing myself into the pursuit of Indian history, going to lectures at the Museum, working at the library and studying French have kept me from going through the 'what-am-I-doing-here-am-I-measuring-my-life-in-coffee-spoons' syndrome to any great extent. I also have to remind myself that unlike a lot of the wives, I have not had to give up a lucrative job using hard-earned skills. I can fully understand the discontent, and am just grateful I don't feel that way.

Friday, September 12   Barbara is off school today, and we have a really nice afternoon. We pick up her new dress from Enid, and she is convinced it is pure Paris original.

Then we go over and see if we can re-organize the bank draft for Barbara's 'O' levels, which has to be made out to the University of London, adding to Barbara's growing image of herself as an International. This is my first introduction to the British educational system of 'O' and 'A' levels, and I really am quite impressed.

The 'O' levels are roughly equivalent to Grade 11 in Canada, but much more demanding according to Kilmeny and Peter, who checked out Barbara's papers. Barbara is working toward nine 'O' levels and, if she passes them, will start on her 'A' exams, which we equate with Canadian first-year university.

The difference is that the student usually chooses only three subjects for 'A' levels, with an eye to what he or she will pursue at University. These three subjects, however, are studied in depth. The North American system maintains that this limits the student in his scope of subjects, but most educators admit that the 'O' levels really cover all the subjects that the Grade 12 student takes in Canada.

There is, I suppose, a good deal to be said for the American system of letting the students determine their own levels, but I cannot help but compare the degree of sophistication in the programme at the British school to that in the American 'plant'. I have had the opportunity of observing the methods of research in the American School library, and have had

150

occasion to wonder. This is probably not entirely fair, as there are not only a lot of very bright students at the American School, but also a lot of originality of thought. It is just that, in my opinion, their educational bars are set too low.

Saturday, September 13   The Delhi social scene is moving into high gear after the summer lull, and I order a couple of dresses from Enid at a total cost of $28. Vancouver's Granville Street boutiques were never like this. I also order invitations for a large cocktail party we are planning for October. We have to do it, but does anybody really enjoy these things, I ask myself? The hosts sweat through it, while the guests sneak glances at their watches and wonder when is a decent time to leave.

Sunday, September 14   Forget TGIF, for me it is always TGIS. This day restores my soul. No servants, no social demands – nothing to do but what I feel like doing. The whole of me stretches in the warmth of the Delhi sun. I pick up my book, I lay it down again; I consider the wiggle of my bare, brown toes; there is a contemplation of the navel, and some sipping of wine under the Kashmiri tree. I link hands across the centuries with Omar Khayyam – "...were paradise enow."

Monday, September 15   Ouch! Doug gets a request from Ottawa to send them the other half of Barbara's airline ticket for a refund. I hadn't really thought about it, but they must have purchased a return ticket and, not too surprisingly, want to collect on the unused half. If, they add censoriously, we do not return said ticket, they will expect a cheque for $1,000.50.

An inquiry in Barbara's direction produces a look of dismay that reveals all too clearly that she does not have a clue. In the general joy of seeing her, neither Doug nor I had given one second's thought to pesky things like return tickets

With the midden of books, papers and essays in Barbara's room it will take a miracle to unearth it. I am downcast to put it mildly. Then a brilliant thought lights up the gloom. I ask Barbara if it could possibly be in her passport. She looks stricken, and my heart sinks. Where is her passport? A ticket could disappear in the house move, but not a passport – it must be here.

Tuesday, September 16   Following yesterday's fruitless search, I begin to wonder if there is any possible defence. We did say Barbara would be staying, and requested a one-way ticket, but it is obvious that they must have sent a return, else why the refund? This is not going to wash, I think to myself, if it were indeed a return fare, they are entitled to their wretched $1,000 *and* 50 cents. Could there possibly be a reference number somewhere?

I plod back upstairs, and find an irregular wad of papers, secured with an elastic band. What a relief! There it lies – waiting, as it were, for obscurity or to be discovered. It *was* a two-way ticket, and it *would* have cost $1,000.50. Doug is overjoyed when I give him the ticket at lunch, but less so when I have to report that the search for the passport goes on.

Having been given this extraordinary piece of good luck, I am moved to balance the gods' accounting sheet, and my conscience directs me to visit the 'Clutcher' again at the East-West Clinic. She seems glad to see me, but also appears a little distrait. As opposed to the rather frenzied nature of her usual conversation, she seems a bit like a tinker toy that is slowly winding down. Everything, including her speech is in slow motion.

We chat about this and that, then the doctors (all of whom know Doug, of course) insist on giving me a tour of the clinic. I am not all that keen, but politeness dictates and I dutifully follow along making interested noises as required. It is not a pretty sight, with one poor old man tearing away at his sheets and a distressed lady staring fixedly at the wall, as though trying to find a way out into a saner and dimly-remembered world. I thank my tour guides, but am only too grateful that I am on the outside rather than dwelling therein.

Friday, September 19   Barbara and I attend a teacher's meeting at the British School, and the whole thing is one long bask of reflected glory. Nothing to do with me, but Barbara has been blessed with a sweet disposition, an honest desire to please and brains to boot. I try to look appropriately modest, as her reports are excellent, and the teaching staff feels that,

152

despite the fact that she has only had one year to work on her 'O' levels (the normal is two), she should be ready to sit them in the coming June.

This could present a bit of a problem for next year when we will have home leave, but we shall have to work that out.

Saturday, September 20 More morale boosting for Barbara, as the Little Theatre group has given her a part in their upcoming production. This should compensate for our leaving tomorrow on our Pakistan trip. I always feel guilty about deserting the girls, although I know they will be well looked after, well fed and driven to school, riding and swimming. Also, if I were honest, I might have to admit that in all probability, they enjoy being in charge of the ménage.

Doug and I pack, take Hermione for an evening walk and then retire to bed.

CHAPTER 21

Sunday, September 21 True to form, our departure is at a pre-dawn hour, so we are up at 3.30 and leave for Pakistan aboard a Pan-Am flight by 5.00am. We are grateful that we have been spared another trip aboard Indian Airlines, with their dubious-looking smelly loos. Here, all is American efficiency, and we are offered a plate of quite delicious sandwiches.

We arrive in Pakistan two hours later and are driven to the hotel, which, quite naturally, is not ready for us at this hour. We saunter around the shops, find a place for tea and toast, and eventually get into our room. After a much-needed snooze and a bite of lunch, I am mad keen to go adventuring.

Doug was in Karachi in April, and knows the ropes. A cab trip reveals a city that seems cleaner, more modern and generally more prosperous than some of the Indian ones we have visited. We drive down to Clifton Beach and then visit the aquarium, which is quite good and well presented.

Next stop is a camel ride – I am a bit leery as I look at this rather seedy beast. It is sitting on its knees, and I get on with a hand from the camel's owner and settle into a rock-hard saddle affair behind the hump. It rises back feet first and then the front. For such an ungainly creature the movement is surprisingly smooth. My camel really is quite tatty looking, but Doug's is splendid (nothing but the best for the Sahib) with chenille balls and tiny bells swinging from its saddle.

We wander across fields and through sand dunes, a rather roundabout route, until we find ourselves on the shores of the Arabian Sea. It is definitely a 'pinch-me' moment. I feel exactly like Lady Hester Stanhope – minus the veils, the solar-tope and the superior air. Heaven knows my camel's profile displays enough hauteur for both of us.

We are alone on the beach, riding across the hard-packed sand in a mystical twilight. The sea gleams like beaten silver in the fading light. I want to trap the moment and keep it safe, to be savoured over and over again.

My camel's profile displays enough hauteur for both of us

However, our driver has more goodies up his ragged sleeve and is anxious to get them in before dark. He drives us to a new mosque, which is quite lovely and set in a pleasant garden. We wander through it, pausing to bathe our feet in the foot pool (or rather I did – the medico would have none of it). Then on to Jinnah's tomb.

This has to be one of the finest pieces of modern architecture I have seen on the subcontinent, creating a traditional design in a modern idiom. Its spare, simple lines somehow capture the spirit of the austere, ascetic man it honours. I am really impressed, even more so when we enter the tomb itself, which is classic and uncluttered. Then the guide points upwards, and the prevailing purity of the whole is shattered. We are looking at the most monstrous chandelier – a horror of green glass, festooned with glass grapes and with gilt shooting stars above a sparkling crescent of Islam. I cannot believe the architect of so superb a building could have countenanced such a feature; I just know he must have done the right thing, and gone off to a nearby billiard room and shot himself like a gentleman.

Back in the hotel, I sink contentedly into a nice hot bath in the marble tub, and almost instantly leap out again. Lady Hester Stanhope never once mentioned what happens to one's bottom after a camel ride. An inspection reveals two raw red spots just waiting for a hot bubble bath to send the victim into orbit. I sleep on my face.

Monday, September 22 The nation's business calls, and Doug arranges an appointment with the Designated Medical Practitioner. This is done through an emissary, a Mr Banajee, who brings the doctor's greetings and welcome, bows with a very respectful "Nameste" and sets the appointment for 3.30pm.

This suits me perfectly, as we now have the best of the day free. We go down to check out the cushion covers I saw in the hotel shop window when we arrived yesterday. The price seems a little steep, and we latch on to a driver to take us to the Karachi Cloth Market and Bazaar. It is a law of the East that once you attach yourself to a driver, it is his sacred obligation to take you to as many other places he can think of before you

156

reach your intended destination. As a consequence we inspect at least two mosques and an odoriferous camel-cum-donkey market.

When we finally reach the fabled cloth market, I am made aware once again of the old adage, "You get what you pay for." While it is true that the cushion covers are one-fifth the price of those in the hotel, they are also of very dubious quality and of lurid colour. However, I do buy some lovely white silk for a blouse and convince myself that I have got a bargain.

The afternoon passes with Doug keeping his appointment and me swimming, lazing and reading at the hotel pool. In the evening we take a fiacre and clop down the road to The Village, a tiny and charming garden restaurant where we dine on Tikka Chicken and watch the full moon rise above the jacaranda trees.

Tuesday, September 23 We leave for Islamabad at 7.30am and arrive at nearby Rawalpindi at around 9.30am. We are met by two members of the Embassy staff, who tell us our reservations at the hotel have been cancelled, and we are to stay with the Administrator and his wife at their home. My heart sinks. I am never quite at ease staying with people I know, and to be imposed upon people I don't know is a forbidding prospect. We are driven up to a pleasant house at the end of a lane, and a very pleasant young woman leads us into a very pleasant drawing room, proffers tea and bids us welcome. Did I mention that it is very pleasant? Why then do I feel uncomfortable? Our hostess is socially easy and intelligent, and our conversation is neither stilted nor difficult.

Our hosts are giving a cocktail party for the new Military Attaché at 5.00 and I go up to our room to "rest" (translation: get out of the way). My watch is on the fritz and I can only guess at the time. I don't guess correctly and do not descend until 5.30 by which time the guests are in the garden and the party in full swing. I work the room as required, and then am told we are all going over to Peter's place for a barbecue. Peter is in Trade, and has a house on the compound. I never do pin down exactly which one is Peter, but it really doesn't matter because everyone seems to be kissing everyone else between bites of rather untidy hamburgers, and I am just swept along on this tide of camaraderie.

Wednesday, September 24 We arrange a car and pick up another lady, the wife of an Embassy clerk. We head for Rawalpindi, stopping at a jewellery store that displays some truly hideous designs. We poke in several other shops and then I take the ladies to lunch at a hotel. On the way back we find some excellent shops. I buy a beautiful mirror work 'kurta' (over-blouse) for Barbara, and look for a thank-you present for our hostess. The solution comes in the form of a copper chafing dish, which she has been admiring and debating whether to buy.

Plans for the evening involve dinner with a Dr Habib (a DMP). An American doctor and his wife from the Embassy are joining us for drinks, as are Dr and Mrs Habib. The Americans are a rather startling couple – he is in his sixties, and I would probably put her a few years younger. She is quite striking, almost six feet tall, with the blackest of black hair and huge eyes that she constantly rolls.

To add to the drama of her appearance, the rolling eyes have been further emphasized by excessive kohl. Her voice is emphatic, slow and drawling, and she keeps referring to "Mother's Continental" and "Brother's Continental". I can only assume she is talking about cars, but it might be some mysterious allusion beyond my ken.

Around 8.30pm we all go out to the Golden Dragon Restaurant for dinner. We munch through a series of strange and pungent dishes. The result of trying to make conversation with the silent Mrs Habib while being loudly talked over by "Our American Cousin" gives me a rip-snorting headache, and I passionately long for release.

Thursday, September 25 Feeling distinctly unwell but, fearful of being clucked over, I fall in with the plans for the day. We do the shops again, and I find a beautiful old brass bowl, very simple but distinctive. We have a very light lunch at home which I manage to down, only to throw up in the privacy of our bathroom. Doug comes back and I pull myself together and we go out and get the chafing dish. There are the expected protests, but our hostess *is* pleased. By now I have a distinct pain in my tum, and retire to our room for the rest of the afternoon.

I get up to further distress, but realize I have to appear for the Ambassador's party, which is, in part, to honour our visit. Right at the moment, I would do anything rather than be honoured, but I do a lot of bathing of forehead, apply make-up, assume a sickly smile and we are off. Greeted by HE and his wife. I drink nothing but orange juice, and talk none too brightly to a few people. The Residence is attractive enough, but the interior rooms are a bit small for so large a party, and I seek the 'coolth' of the patio. But even the soft autumn breezes fail to soothe and, after a minimum of polite conversation, I give up the unequal struggle. I get the key from our hostess, and gather up Doug. Absolutely positive that I will throw up all over the ambassadorial lawn, and everyone will think I have had too much to drink. Fortunately, pride fights against nausea and with a lot of deep breathing I make it back to our temporary home and bed.

Friday, September 26 Up early and say a grateful goodbye to our hosts. They have been kind, gracious and generous, and now commiserate over what they are sure is a case of Delhi Belly. As Delhi has never produced this belly for me, we counter with perhaps "Rawal Bowel"?

We leave for the airport and catch the plane to Lahore and arrive at 10.00am. We've barely checked into the hotel when a Dr Ichbat arrives for Doug. I am left to entertain him briefly, while Doug gets his business papers together. Just so we won't sit and smile at one another, I show him the writing on my treasured brass bowl. He is politely interested, but claims it is neither Arabic nor Urdu. I wonder if it might be Greek, he guesses Sanskrit, and there is much conjecture as to its antiquity and source. It is all interesting, but irrelevant as I love it anyway, even if it was just beaten out by a local craftsman the day before yesterday.

When Doug is ready, the doctors depart, and I am left to rest, to laze by the pool and to treat my malaise. I am not hungry but definitely feel better.

Saturday, September 27 Plans for the day are to have a

sight-seeing tour of Lahore, and then take the car to the border to return to India. We drive past the museum, but despite the driver's entreaties, forego a trip inside. The big feature of the museum for me is Kim's "great gun" that still stands outside the "house of wonders" as it did in Kipling's time. For a moment, I am a child again, reading that marvellous book for the first time.

Lahore Fort is next – a large complex of buildings, including a rather spectacular mosque. The fort follows the prescribed Mogul pattern with a long hall of mirrors that don't really reflect all that well as they are made of coloured glass. We climb a few steps and find ourselves in the Art Gallery of Ranjit Singh (a much-loved 19th-century king of the Punjab) – not all that distinguished, as the art is mainly family portraits, but here and there are a few excellent paintings.

On to the Mosque, which is enormous and very impressive. It is surrounded by a park containing, among other things, a large columnar monument erected to celebrate the creation of Pakistan in 1947 – the founding of a new nation. The base is very rough stone, strong and unyielding, followed by smaller and smoother tiers, all representing the progress of this new society, with the last addition being an elaborate design in silver. This latter is explained (or as much as I could make out) as "great advances but not yet gold."

In our wanderings around India and delving into the Mogul legacy, we have frequently detected the hand of the great Shah Jehan. Never has it been more evident than in the beauty of Lahore's Shalimar Gardens. They are absolutely unparalleled with their terraces, fountains, waterfalls and ornamental pools. Like the gardens in Kashmir, they follow the classic Mogul design, but on a grander scale.

Lahore has more than lived up to its positive advance notices, and we rather reluctantly leave for the border. I don't quite know what I expected, but it certainly is not the palaver we encounter.

The driver stops about a quarter mile from the border, and we are ushered into a building to fill out forms and hand over our passports. They are returned and we are directed to the opposite side of the room, where we show our passports once more, make a written currency declaration and are asked to wait. We wait and we wait until finally, at a nod from an official, a bearer comes to take up our luggage. Once more I watch in awe at the burdens a small, thin man can carry – straps slung over shoulders, suitcases under each arm and cholas twined around forehead, like a Sherpa guide. We obediently follow him the quarter of a mile to the actual Indian border where we are requested to show our passports and health certificates three times more.

India is finally before us behind an invisible line. Our bearer stops; another approaches him from the other side, the luggage is transferred and we cross Jordan into the promised land.

The procedure begins again. More forms are filled out; passports are shown, re-shown and carefully scrutinized by unsmiling officials. Then comes the acid test, as we are directed into Customs.

This is not one of those 'anything-to-declare-no-okay-have-a-good-trip' Canada–US crossings. The place is full of open suitcases, their contents spread out and examined minutely. My heart sinks – what of my precious antique bowl? I begin to practice a look of innocence – a tale to tell – a sobbing confession.

We wait and wait and wait as the room fills up with young back-packers. After what seems an eternity, we are directed to appear before an inspector, who asks for our passports (what, again?) and inquires about Doug's 'special' passport. Doug explains it is diplomatic. The magic word. There are salaams and respectful namestes – no checks of luggage, no further red tape. Our bearer is summoned and delivers us, with all due deference, to a taxi, and we drive into Amritsar, stopping for tea at Mrs Bendhari's Guest House. It's very charming, as is Mrs B.

We make the plane just in time. There is a fearful cock-up with a tour, and all is chaos. The plane runs into clouds and wind, and the trip is bumpy, but no matter, we reach Delhi and find Sonny, one of the Commission drivers, waiting for us. Both the girls give us a great welcome, increasing in enthusiasm when they receive their presents. It is good to be home, and Tony's dinner tastes especially delicious in our own familiar surroundings.

CHAPTER 22

Sunday, September 28 Wake up to the pleasant sensation of Sunday. There's a swim meet this afternoon at the High Commission, with hamburgers and hot dogs served at the cabana. The girls acquit themselves well, and more than uphold the honour of the Dennys, which is not too surprising considering they spend every possible recreational hour at the pool.

There is a sour note to the day, however, as we barely make it to the filling station for gas. We had made a point of topping the tank up with 58 litres before we left on our Pakistan trip, and now it is bone dry. The natural suspect is Gopi Chand with his thirsty motorbike. What to do?

Monday, September 29 Have a little talk with Tony about the mystery of the gas. He gives me the all-purpose shake of the head, and advances the theory that some felon crept in and siphoned off the gas while the household slept. I counter with raised eyebrows, pointing out that with a chowkidar on duty that was highly unlikely, and trust this will be enough to forestall any further sorties into the gas tank in the near future. When it comes right down to it, there is little we can do without proof.

Saturday October 4 Our big cocktail party, and the easiest I have ever given. The last time we had people in for drinks, I elected to make my famed curry puffs, and asked Tony to leave out the curry powder before he retired. I suppose I had never really given much thought to curry powder, apart from the fact that it came in a neat little bottle labelled 'Spice Island's Best Curry Powder'. Did I imagine there was a curry bush somewhere, spewing out ochre-coloured powder? In any event, when I went into the kitchen, there was no friendly bottle, but a series of little mounds of varied and highly coloured spices. I could not fault Tony. I had asked for curry and curry was what I got.

Today I have left everything up to Him Who Knows, and I must say it is a breeze. When I emerge from being coiffed, massaged and generally tarted up, the shamiana (a decorated tent) has been erected in the garden, the bar is set up, the music plugged in, and the kitchen full of canapés. The last mentioned bear a startling resemblance to everyone else's tab nabs (squares of pizza and miniature sawdust sausages) but Tony's carved squash centrepiece is an original. It is a very successful evening, and a hefty repayment of social debts.

Sunday, October 3 I have a friend who always says there is a special feel to a house after a party. I know what she means: it is a combination of accomplishment, relief that it has gone well and an uninhibited gorge on leftovers. If I had expected the latter, I would have been disappointed. A prowl through the Tony-less kitchen reveals nothing but a few bitter-tasting peanuts. I am not surprised, as everything would have been scooped up by the help, and welcome to it they are.

The 'chikan' work man from Lucknow arrives with the tablemats I ordered. I really like chikan, which is very fine outline stitching on delicate material, and these are particularly nice, I think, in a lovely soft yellow. I succumb to his sales pitch as he offers another set of rectangular white mats with matching coasters. He bows his smiling way out, and will undoubtedly return, knowing a mark when he sees one.

This evening the Commissioner and his wife invite us to a theatre party with two other couples. The play is not all that great, but it has its diverting moments, and is followed by a nice dinner at the Residence.

Tuesday, October 7 I go for a swim, and am immediately pounced on by the guard's wife who has tagged me as a listening post. Some months ago, I had been treated to an account of her daughter's engagement, and now she is waiting for me with a ton of pictures of the wedding. These are accompanied by a running commentary on the inadequacies of the groom. She is keenly disappointed in his manners, his grammar and his coldness towards his new mother-in-law. She wonders if her daughter really knows what she is doing? As she's 37, I don't think she has exactly rushed into anything, but who am I to say?

I have a stab at establishing a conversational beachhead: "Er – speaking of weddings - today is our anniversary..." but to no avail. My anniversary and I are swept away on the tide of her own confidences.

Not on the home front, however. Doug has planned a dinner at the ACSA Lounge, in the superior dining room. We linger over a bottle of wine, go to the American Cinema for a so-so picture and return home to toast each other with another bottle of wine. Our mutual present – being happy with one another.

Thursday, October 8 An invitation to a reception at the home of the Peruvian Ambassador. My departed mentor, Mildred, would have told me that we would never have been invited to this type of party, as only Heads of Mission and/or their '2 I/Cs' (second-in-commands) are ever asked. However, it seems that Mrs Peruvian HE fell prey to some miserable bug and, through what set of circumstances I know not, Doug was called in to treat her. She greets us warmly and tells us how grateful she is for Doug's ministrations.

We are led out into the frangipani-scented garden. It is all quite magical – fairy lights in the trees, turbaned servitors gliding in and out. It doesn't matter that we don't know anyone – I find myself floating around in my new chiffon, waiting for a Bengal Lancer to waltz me around the moonlit garden. We meet up with our own High Commissioner, his opposite number at the British HC and our friends, the Milnes, from the Australian one. It is a case of hail and farewell to them all. It seems they have put in the brief, but requisite appearance, which is all that is required on these occasions. I suppose it is the only way Ambassadors can survive, as they may well have several more such dos to attend the same evening. There is obviously no point in settling in as the party is over almost as soon as it has begun. Besides, the bar offered only beer and scotch, neither one my tipple, so Bengal Lancer not withstanding, I am pleased enough to return home for a G&T and grilled cheese sandwich.

Sunday, October 12 A couple of weeks ago, Jeannette Ronke from the Dutch Embassy phoned to ask if Barbara could go with them on a trip they were planning to take at mid-term. The Ronkes' daughter Marion has become Barbara's best friend and is keen to have her join them.

Barbara is her mother's daughter inasmuch as she believes the last minute is the ideal time to start preparations. The expedition is to set off early tomorrow morning, and Barbara has been asked to spend tonight at the Ronkes. She now discovers she has a pile of clothes to be washed. Having not put hand to laundry soap for ten months, we tackle the washing machine with little knowledge of its crotchets, and it is slow-going. She is due at the Ronkes at 4.00pm and at 3.00 we are still ironing, with no packing done. A great flurry as all hands pitch in, and we finally get the traveller underway relatively close to the appointed time.

Monday, October 13 Dussehra is upon us, and we get passes for the Festival to be held tomorrow in Old Delhi. This is one of India's major festivals, celebrating the triumph of good over evil, as embodied by the Rama's rescue of Sita from the clutches of her abductors, the evil demons from Sri Lanka. Ravana and his accomplices are burned in effigy, everybody is happy as all get out, and the audience departs through the vengeful smoke.

Today is an official holiday, and Doug is persuaded to go riding with some people from the High Commission. I have been told on innumerable occasions that Doug has an excellent 'seat'. That well may be, but said seat was more than somewhat sore on his return. Nevertheless, I press him to come with Hilary and me into Old Delhi to take pictures of the effigies before they are burned. All is a-bustle, and we watch the enormous effigies being raised – no mean task as they are more than 50 feet in height. A huge platform has been erected to seat the VIPs. We stroll about among the crowd, and a lady who seems to be in some position of authority accosts Hilary, who is wearing her favoured garb of bibbed shorts. This, together with her cropped hair, has obviously led the lady astray.

"Little boy, little boy, do you understand everything – I will

165

be happy to explain."

To her credit, and despite resenting being taken for a male child, Hilary listens politely as the story unfolds.

Tuesday, October 14 Still a holiday for Hilary, and Doug gets off work at 3.00pm. We leave for the Festival at 3.30pm, nice and early, although the card states 4.30pm. Thank goodness we do, as the crowds are intense, even then. Our seats in the VIP section are excellent, and to our surprise we find ourselves next to the Barkers of the Chartered Bank.

The crowd begins to gather, but it is 6.00pm before anything happens. Monica Barker points out a couple of red plush seats a level above us. These have been reserved for the President of India and for Mrs Gandhi, the Prime Minister. She does not show. He does, and stays for maybe 15 minutes. Have they seen this before, do you suppose?

First sign of activity is a large chariot making its way through the crowd. We cannot see a thing from our supposedly prime position, except a few arrows being shot. The chariot makes the rounds three times and then, at last, the *raison d'être* for our vantage point becomes clear, as the battle between Rama and Ravana takes place directly in front of us. The costumes are dramatic, and the ensuing struggle surprisingly realistic. As Good begins to conquer Evil, flaming arrows are shot into the effigies, the fireworks inside ignite and suddenly the sky is alight with exploding stars and spectacular rockets.

We are impressed; our companions, the Barkers, less so. She, the Old India Hand, pronounces it to be the "same old thing," and he adds that his tongue is hanging out for a whisky, and why don't we join them at the Chartered Bank House for a noggin. Doug doesn't need to be asked twice, so Hamish goes off with the driver, while Monica stays with us as our guide.

We go past The Ridge (of Mutiny fame) down Underhill Lane and to the Bank House. It is straight out of a Somerset Maugham novel, lying in an Indian garden with a wide Colonial verandah, slightly sagging steps and the general air of a place with a past. We go through a vine-covered entrance and inside.

It is charming, with enormous high ceilings, fans twirling

166

Flaming arrows are shot into the effigies, the fireworks inside ignite

and lots of rattan furniture and crewelwork upholstery. I love it.

We learn a little bit more about Hamish and Monica. They have two sons in England: Christopher, 21, and Ewan, almost 18. They also have, in residence, a somnolent Great Dane called Cleo, who barely manages to twitch an eye at our arrival. I suppose her size is enough to perform chowkidar duties. We pass a pleasant hour and then leave for home. Tony has already told us he is going to a wedding, so we forage happily enough for ourselves and eat *al fresco* under a full moon.

Wednesday, October 15 My first meeting at the International Women's Club. I am not sure how I got in (maybe because I applied), as I was told (by guess who?) that it was very restrictive. The limit is 200, with 100 from the host country and 100 from the international community. Anyway, here I am. The feature of the morning is an interesting film on Indian wildlife.

Saturday, October 18 Today is the YWCA Sale, and I am manning a table with a friend from the High Commission. We find ourselves under the authority of a rather fearsome lady, who is in charge of our table. I am not particularly impressed with the offerings we have to sell and neither, I feel, is the general populace, as trade is not brisk.

A young Indian comes and inspects a knitted baby outfit. Personally I think the colours are more than a touch lurid, but he is in raptures. What is the price? 39 rupees. Is the price fixed? Yes. He is crushed and walks sadly away. In about ten minutes he is back to see if it is still there. While he continues to stare longingly, I find myself weaving an entire scenario: Picture it... his wife has just had a baby and is not very well... he wants desperately to get something special for this child, this amazing little creature, who is perfect and who is his....

I am shaken out of my reverie when the hero of my script asks timidly if we might come down in price. I say I will consult with my colleague. When approached, said colleague, Clare, is of a similar mind. Together we agree that we will tell him it has been reduced to 29 rupees, and we will put in the other 10 rupees ourselves, so the YWCA will not be cheated. I return to the counter and tell him we can let him have it for 29 rupees. His smile says heaven has just dropped into his lap. He opens a creased, grubby envelope and extracts 30 rupees, receives change and, clutching his treasure, floats out on a cloud. Clare and I beam at each other. We both feel as pleased as the papa to think that a little baby will be terribly grand in purple and gold.

Alas, we have been spotted and hanky-panky is suspected. The 'CO' appears and asks just what is going on. We confess all, and she is definitely not caught up in the general bonhomie of the moment. It is not sufficient that the YWCA will lose nothing; this sort of arbitrary decision-making can set a terrible precedent. Who knows how many appealing new fathers, new mothers, new grandparents will think they can just march in and expect a discount? We stand, chastened like two schoolgirls caught smoking in the loo, and skulk back to our posts. Then we look at one another and grin, knowing we have written our own ending, and it is a happy one.

Sunday, October 19 Glorious Sunday. Hilary has been invited to a friend's for the day, and with Barbara away, the day lies ahead like an unopened gift. I have been reading a lot about the Mutiny and we decide to go into old Delhi and go for a walk along The Ridge. We take Herm with us and have lunch at Maiden's Hotel, a relic of the Raj. The food tends to be British stodge with an Indian accent, but I love the surroundings. After lunch we hike up to The Ridge and let Hermione off the leash. She is in dog heaven and disappears to return what seems like hours later, covered with burrs and a tangle of twigs.

We take the long way home, and while Doug has an orgy of burr-picking, I prepare Chicken Kiev, and chill a bottle of wine. It could almost be our old Sunday-Night-Special-No-Children dinner, and feel I could look out the window and see Point Grey across Vancouver's harbour.

Monday, October 20 Canadian author Margaret Laurence once wrote that she went to Africa with a benign "woolly-muffler-cosy-missionary" approach and that it took her some time to realize how insufferable this attitude must have been for the locals. I suspect I did the same, coming to India. Now after almost ten months, I am still not sure where I stand.

At the Central Post Office this morning, I ask for 15 air letters, and carefully check the financial end of the transaction only to find, I have once again been short-changed. It happens too often to be an accident. I know that and, if I were home, I would have no hesitation in calling someone to task. Why do I feel it is an act of racial discrimination when a native sets out to cheat? They have so little – we, comparatively, have so much – but it goes beyond that. Tony's fudging of the accounts; lying about my bicycle; swearing up and down that the worm crawling out of the creamed cauliflower is "a leaf – only a leaf." All that, to say nothing of the suspected pilfering of the gas, seems as natural to him as pinching from the rich did to Robin Hood. Do I accept this as a way of life, or do I demand justice, and do a hatchet job on the staff?

Rod, a young CIDA officer, often cycles over to our place on a Sunday for tea and sympathy and Oreo cookies. A while ago he stamped in, muttering fiercely, "They lie, they lie, they always lie." Still in the woolly-muffler vein, I philosophize away.

"I don't know, Rod," I say, "perhaps they are just following another truth. Hinduism is a do-your-own-thing-and-pick-your-own-god-type of polytheistic religion, after all. What do you think?"

There is a long and pregnant silence before he utters the ultimate truth: "I think they're lying."

Thursday, October 23 Doug has always said that a bloodcurdling shriek presages yet another of my attempts at sewing. Said shriek means I have cut the wrong edge of the pattern, or cut a calf-length skirt as a mini, or some other horror. Sewing is just not my thing, as I learn once again while struggling with Hilary's costume for Halloween. She is a ghost, for heaven's sake! Surely any moron can create a ghost costume. Hilary, ever the perfectionist, however, is full of clever little suggestions, and we eventually resort to Barbara's kaftan pattern.

Friday, October 24 The Denny family seems constantly in a state of flux. Barbara returns today. Hilary leaves for her school trip to Mussoorie tomorrow, and we take off for Madras and Sri Lanka on Sunday. So it is a busy day dashing hither and yon.

We pick Barbara up at the airport, and she looks sunburnt and happy, having had a great time, and thanking the Ronkes profusely for taking her. Rush home to sort out sleeping bags and clothes, not just for Hilary, but also for a goodly number of her classmates. I'll worry about our wardrobe tomorrow.

CHAPTER 23

Sunday, October 26 Up at 5.45am and make it to the airport without incident, but suddenly realize I have forgotten my book. However, *The Times of India* and its crossword puzzle will have to do, and who knows, if I am sufficiently dense it might last the journey.

We reach Madras, and are driven to our hotel. Once again the early departure catches up with us, and a zizz is called for. The zizz continues through lunch hour, and half the afternoon. It is not until 4.00pm that we venture out into pouring, blinding rain.

The streets are a-wash, and visibility well nigh nil, but in all optimism we ask the driver to take us along the sea shore. The rain decreases slightly but the wind rises, and the sea is absolutely splendid, pounding across the esplanade and frothing over the sea wall. Despite the miserable weather there still seem to be masses of people about. There is a variation of costume, differing slightly from that of Northern India. Most of the men sport a short, cotton sarong (no shoes) and the women favour a slightly different version of the traditional sari.

Our driver is surprisingly well informed, and thinks we might be interested in the Government Fishermen's Project. We are driven past row upon row of identical houses. These are owned by the Government, and rented out to the fishermen for the nominal sum of three rupees a day, which is simply deducted from their income, all the fishermen being under government contract. In about 20 years this accumulated rent will have paid for the house, the ownership then reverting to the erstwhile lessee.

The houses were built by the Tamil Nadu government, after a major slum clearance when hundreds of unsightly and desperately unhealthy mud huts were razed. I am really impressed by such an enlightened project, socially commendable and economically viable, and so am astonished when the driver concludes his story. Despite the vastly improved living conditions, and the status of owning their own homes, many of the fishermen have sub-let the new accommodation and gone back to the mud-hut life.

Much and all as I have come to love India, its social ills still seem insurmountable, even with all the well-meaning international agencies striving to help. The answer, I suppose, lies deep within the Indian psyche and the country's ageless philosophy. Apropos of which is an article I read before we came to India. The Ford Foundation had sponsored lengthy research into India's most basic problems: over-population and low agricultural productivity. As India has operated for centuries on a kind of loosely-knit internal welfare system; large families are a form of social security, with the children becoming responsible for their parents, so birth control is not an easy concept to sell. Making the land more productive, however, the Foundation decided, was a possibility.

After years of expensive research it hit upon a truly remarkable solution. Increasing fertilization of the soil was absolutely essential, but terribly expensive. True, countless cows wandered across the Indian fields, leaving ample evidence of their passing. But the wisdom of their ancestors dictates that cow dung be used for a multiplicity of domestic purposes, including fires for cooking. It was not to be wasted on the soil. After constant experimentation, the Foundation scientists came up with a method of extracting gas from fresh cow dung for cooking, while retaining essential nutrients for fertilization of the soil. One can only imagine the shouts of "Eureka" and the general rejoicing in the labs at this giant leap forward. However, imagining was as far as it went. Eastern tradition and Western initiative clashed and the twain did not meet. The people refused to countenance any relinquishing of the ancient uses of cow dung. The gods had ordained the pattern of life, and bunging cow dung on the kitchen fire was part and parcel of that pattern. So there we have it, and it does rather make one wonder about aid programmes.

We finish off our sodden tour with a visit to the Annie Besant Theosophical Centre, named for the woman who had such a great influence on Nehru in his early years. By now, dripping and rather chilly, we return to the hotel, but find no message from Dr Rao, Doug's DMP in Madras.

Monday, October 27 The elusive Dr Rao is contacted and arrangements made. Doug will see to business and then the Raos have offered to take us to lunch at their club, and subsequently to the airport.

The Raos pick me up in the lobby. She is absolutely beautiful, very poised and charming, as are so many Indian women. We are taken to the Madras Club, which is an elegant white colonial building – high ceilings, magnificent rotunda with black and white marble floor. Have drinks on the patio overlooking vast green lawns sloping down to the river. The lunch is the best I have had in India, and the conversation lively. I would love to stay just where I am, and hear more of Mrs Rao's ideas, but Doug is looking at his watch.

Alas, the rain begins again as we leave for the airport, and the roads are flooded. The airport is an absolute quagmire, but there is nothing for it but to wade through water to the main terminal. The Raos kindly press an umbrella on me, but it is impossible to handle it, hold up my skirt and clutch my purse all at the same time. I dash ahead, step in a submerged pot-hole, twist my ankle and fall flat on my face in a small lake in front of the terminal steps. It must have been a diverting sight for the onlookers for falling flat on my face was literal as well as figurative. Inside it is not much better. I am absolutely soaked, and Doug is standing ankle-deep in a puddle as he hands in the tickets. It is one unholy mess.

We manage to stop the luggage long enough for me to extract a clean pair of slacks and t-shirt. I struggle into the 'Ladies', which is predictably filthy and revoltingly smelly, but somehow I manage to do the needful and at least am dry here and there. Emerging into the main concourse, I find the plane is now not leaving until 3.15pm instead of 2.00. I ponder on another trip to the loo with dry footwear in mind, but even this flitting thought is traumatic and besides, it seems we are to be summoned into Customs and Immigration.

I am constantly amazed at the intensity of officialdom in Asia. An unsmiling Immigration officer asks for our passports and scrutinizes every inch. He asks why there is no indication that we have left Delhi. (Our standing before him in squishing shoes is not proof enough that we have left Delhi?) I sensibly keep this a silent question. He then requests our embarkation cards, which clearly state the nature of our travel, and answer all the questions that he proceeds to ask us anyway.

The next gauntlet we have to run is at the Customs end of the office. Here an official asks for our passports and embarkation cards, all of which he gives the same demanding attention a mother gorilla gives her baby's scalp. Not content with the information contained in the documents, he then proceeds to ask us all the same questions asked by the Immigration man, adding a few queries of his own. Why do we leave Delhi? Why do we leave Madras? He looks in Doug's suitcase (fortunately not in mine or he would have found some disagreeably wet underwear). I am sure he tries hard, but cannot think up any further questions, and summons a porter to whom he hands our passports. The porter disappears into the crowd, and I am convinced we will never see him, his drooping turban or our passports again. I see a future in which generations will be born and die, and I will be here forever, in sopping shoes and bedraggled hair.

Despite my concerns about the above scenario, my curiosity is piqued. Forms have been signed and re-signed, cards filled out, passports checked *ad nauseam*. To which bureaucratic branch could our documents possibly have gone now? We never do find out, but it is with great relief that I see our raggle-taggle porter return with our passports, and even greater relief when they are firmly restored to where they ought to be.

An hour later we arrive in the Sri Lanka capital, Colombo. An official car and a Canadian government communicator meet us, and we are driven off in style, behind a fluttering maple leaf, to the Galle Face Hotel.

We gasp. We stare. We are overcome. It is absolutely magnificent. Set off by itself at the end of a vast park, with the sea on its doorstep, it looms like some other-world castle in a romance novel. It is grey stone, and slightly Aztec in style, with an enormous verandah, rough stone columns and an open foyer, through which a wind from the sea sweeps and swirls. The reception desk is flanked by titanic carved wooden figures, and backed by a stone wall, sculpted in bas relief. A great, grey stone staircase curves to an upper landing, and I fully expect someone bearing a sharp resemblance to Count Dracula to

175

descend with a "Good e-ven-ing."

Little wonder, this inescapable feeling of being on a film set, as the Galle Face was used as a location for several films. Anyway it is all as dramatic as the raising of a theatre curtain, except for one thing. We are the only audience. Apart from the staff we do not see another human being. Forget about the romantic film set, my all too vivid imagination now takes me to a very grand version of the Bates Motel.

As I already observed, the hotel lies directly on the beach and in the twilight we catch glimpses of phosphorescent waves, and hear the roar of the surf. With all this atmosphere, why is it so empty? I begin to have doubts as to its creature comforts. With good reason, alas. As we are escorted to our room, the mood changes. Our accommodation is quite pedestrian, and while the space is there, it is sparsely furnished and there is no hot water. My dreams of a long soak in a warm bath depart.

Things pick up with the applied recuperative powers of a good stiff drink before we get changed and go down to dinner. We are the only guests and are shown to a table by a splendid looking maître d' who is sporting a handsome red mess jacket and a spotless white lungi. The dining room is on an inner arcade, but open to a wonderful ocean vista, the thunder of the surf and a magnificent avenue of tossing palm trees. We just get started on our meal when the wind, which had been blowing but with some degree of decorum, goes suddenly mad. Ocean spray splashes across the table, soaking the back of my navy chiffon (will I ever be dry?). Dishes scuttle across the table like agitated crabs, the napkins fall off our laps and are blown out on to a verandah now swept by driving rain. It doesn't take a weatherman to decide it is time to move elsewhere. Servitors appear and lead us into the indoor dining room, make attempts to mop us up and re-arrange our table. The manager comes out all apologetic, but cannot be deterred from telling us of other famous and noble guests who have also experienced the whims of weather at the Galle Face – the Queen, for one, and the Prince of Wales, our own Mr Trudeau and film stars beyond reckoning. If misery likes company, does august company make it even better?

Tuesday, October 28   The hot water situation has not

remedied itself and Doug decides, against enormous picturesque odds mind you, that enough is enough and that we should check out. Unfortunately, departure time is 11.00am, and Doug must leave for the office in half an hour. Things become too complicated, so the Galle Face is ours for another night.

Doug returns at noon, and we go over to the Sri Lanka Oberoi for lunch. Like all the Oberoi hostelries it is the ultimate in luxurious living, albeit lacking the haunting atmosphere of the Galle Face. The central rotunda is enormous, with a raised dais covering the better part of the expanse. There are abnormally high ceilings, from which are suspended three huge, colourful and stunningly designed batiks. Furniture is rattan, in a contemporary style, and all most attractive. We investigate the hotel shops, which are full of chic and exotic items; the bar is expansive, and we sample its wares before lunch.

That night we decide to check out the Intercontinental for dinner. It is not quite as flossy as the Oberoi, but it is right on the seafront. We walk along the esplanade before dinner, about two miles, and enjoy the astonishing versatility of the kites that are being sold, and being flown. Dinner is quite good – 'Poulet Granmere' or, as they would have said in simpler hostelries, roast chicken.

Wednesday, October 29 We elect to move to the Intercontinental because of the sea view, and when Doug returns from an early appointment, we leave the Galle Face and its fascinating ghosts, and settle in at the Intercontinental.

We have a nice room overlooking the sea and the hotel has a swimming pool. When Doug returns to his duties, I go down for a swim. The pool is not busy (I suspect because it is none too warm) but I enjoy it in a chilly sort of way, then return for a heavenly soak in a *hot* bath. We go to the Cat's Eye Supper Club for dinner, where, wonder of wonders, they serve *real* French bread.

Thursday, October 30 The Canadian High Commissioner (female) is 'out of station' (I love that foreign service expression – it always sounds as if they are 'out of sorts' or 'out of kilter'), and we have been invited by her 2 I/C to dinner that evening.

One of the pitfalls of travel, with social sidelines, is that you never know what will happen to you in the local beauty salon. I get myself badly coiffed in the hotel, and spend some time this afternoon trying to control a madly curled hair-do, but I still come out looking like Charles II.

HE's secretary picks us up, and takes us to our host's home. He is a nice young man, and definitely on his way up. The house is attractive, the dinner good and the company interesting – two doctors working for the Canadians and their wives. I must be getting more expert in table talk with the distaff side, as I actually get a conversation of sorts going.

Friday, October 31 Halloween in the western world, but not an event celebrated in the East, so there is not a ghoulie or ghostie in sight. Doug managed to wind up his business yesterday, and we are free for the weekend. In our stroll the other evening, we passed the offices of an enterprising business called Safari Sights, which is run by a group of young Australians. They have a fleet of jeeps and, according to their brochure, a vast knowledge of Sri Lanka and its flora and fauna. We booked in for a three-day tour starting this very morning, at 6.00am to be exact.

With admirable punctuality our driver arrives on the dot. We had expected a jeep and at least four other travelling companions, but not so. It seems we are going solo (for reasons not fully explained) and in a comfortable small van. Our driver is one Stuart Delamotte. He is a very light *café au lait*, speaks perfect English and seems really nice. He tells us he was born in Sri Lanka (or Ceylon as he still calls it) and, while he can speak Tamil, he can't read or write it. He produces a map, shows us today's route and we are off.

The drive is beautiful, following the curving coastline, thick with palm trees and coconut groves. We can see stretches of golden beaches beyond a fringe of green, and the sea beyond that. We stop to walk along one totally empty strand, and approach it through springy bright green foliage that is dotted with the loveliest of lavender-blue flowers.

In one of the coconut groves, we watch the locals gathering coconuts. When they have a reasonable number, they are put in sort of small holding basins in the lagoon, and weighted with something heavy to keep them immersed. Stuart tells us that when they are ready, they are brought out and the women beat them with a mallet to get the fibre ready for spinning. I shudder to think of the prickly garments the fibre will produce, but am assured that this coconut offshoot is used solely for spinning rope.

Doug stops to take a picture of a pretty girl pounding for all she is worth. Most of the village women wear a variation of the sarong, or a lungi with a white blouse. Almost all the men wear lungis topped with an over-shirt. By and large they are a handsome people and seem in superb physical shape.

Farther along still, we come across a seaside village, and see a series of stakes, perched in the surf. Stuart stops the car, and we walk onto the beach to see what is going on. All the stakes are made from the branch of a tree, and don't appear to be either thick or particularly strong. They are topped with a cross bar, and it is on these precarious structures that the anglers sit and fish by surf casting. This dicey method is apparently the only way they are allowed to fish, other than by boat. As not too many can afford one, and those boats that are available are pretty primitive and none too safe, it seems a bit of a Hobson's choice to me.

I am lapping it all up and savouring each new sight. The only flaw are the pestering children who pop up every time we stop. They all have their hands out, asking for baksheesh or cigarettes. Stuart warns us not to give them anything or we will be mobbed. I know this is true from past experience, but it is not easy to turn away from the appeal of all those liquid brown eyes. Stuart, on the other hand, is inured and shoos them off without a backward glance.

We next reach the village of Ambalangoda, famous for the carving of masks and 'devil dancing'. Most of the masks are made from kaduruwood, and then painted in lurid and terrifying colours. I am not sure they are exactly *the* thing for the average living room, but they are fascinating just the same, and superbly carved. I am buttonholed by a venerable and toothless carver, who tries to sell me a 'heritage' piece carved by his great-grandfather. My suspicions are aroused by the fact that the paint is barely dry, but I do succumb to the charm of a little 'fire devil', and receive a suspect tale of its significance.

Next stop is at the seashore village of Hikkaduwa, where you can have a ride in a glass-bottom boat. I am madly keen, but a) they won't take the boat out unless they have four people, and b) it is too cloudy, meaning I suppose that we wouldn't see anything.

Around 10.00am, having been on the road for four hours, we stop at a Government Rest House for morning tea. We look out on the sea and spot a rocky island fairly near the shore. We have seen nothing but the simplest type of housing so far, and are rather surprised to find the island contains a quite splendid mansion, partially concealed by a wealth of tropical vegetation.

Stuart tells us that at low tide you can wade there through the shallows from the shore. The official name of the Island is Taprobane, but locally it is still called the Ile de Mauny, after the original owner, a French Count de Mauny. He died sometime in the 1940s, and the present owner has rented it to a number of celebrities, including Arthur C Clarke of sci-fi fame.

We pass through the little towns of Galle and Matara, and through a series of small villages, most of which boast Buddha shrines beneath a boa tree.

Every turn in the road is a delight. We see a brilliant kingfisher darting in and out of the rice paddies, golden orioles, emerald parakeets, and groups of monks in their bright saffron robes. The land is an artist's palette of exuberant colour. As we drive on, the hills begin to deepen and overshadow the quiet valleys.

After some time, we turn off the road and follow a narrow lane down to the Ibis Lodge, where we are to spend the night. Stuart has obviously given advance notice of our coming, as three handsome and smiling boys rush out to meet us, taking our luggage almost before the car stops and announcing that lunch is ready.

The lodge has a wide shaded verandah on which a table has been set up for two. First, however, they take us to our room, which is simple but spotless. After washing off the travel dust, we move out onto the verandah for a drink and take stock of our surroundings.

There is a wide expanse of what appears to be a deep green marsh, and beyond that a small lake. A herd of water buffalo is grazing near the edge of the lake, but from the distance of the verandah, they could be just about anything – wildebeest, I think, has a nice ring, and sounds more Hemingway-ish somehow.

We are served an excellent lunch of tomato rice and lamb curry, with all the required accompaniments of mango, coconut and fresh pineapple. The boys don't speak much English, but we all smile back and forth and mime our appreciation of their efforts.

Around 2.30pm, Stuart reappears to take us into the village where we will transfer to a jeep for a tour of a wildlife park. On the way there, we watch a crocodile slithering through the marsh to disappear into the waters of the lake.

When we reach the village, Stuart turns us over to the driver of the jeep, who is clad in a lungi and a flimsy hat of sorts, and he seems a trifle overwhelmed by his responsibility for us. He is very shy and uncommunicative, probably because his English is almost non-existent. We seem to drive for some distance before reaching a large building, which is the park office and museum. Here, another handsome boy gets into the rear of the jeep with us – our safari guide. Then an unexplained youth with a load of coconuts also hops in, settles beside the driver and thus equipped and staffed we set off.

Our guide points out the "fascinating" fauna as we go along. It is not all that fascinating, being a flock of peahens and herds of wild water buffalo, of which we have seen many in India, and then a herd of spotted deer, of which we have seen many at home. The park itself is 57 square miles, very wild, with lots of winding trails into the forest. I am all for getting out and following one or two, but our safari guide practically faints at the thought. He hastens to tell us of two people who went adventuring on their own, and who were "trampled to death, Memsahib". It would have been all right just to be "trampled", I suppose but not "to death".

Anyway, we proceed slowly along with me peering hopefully into the jungle. I am just about to despair of ever seeing any wildlife other than the ever-present water buffalo, when I hear a crackling in the bushes, and spot the enormous feet of an elephant. First one, then another and another. It is impossible to get a picture – they are too close and it is too dangerous according to our guide. He suggests that we make for a nearby watering hole where the elephants may be headed. We wait for a short while – not long enough, in my opinion, but they don't show. Still in our jeep, we circle around the hole, and are finally allowed out under the watchful eye of our guide. We see flocks of wild peacocks – a brilliant blue blur against the fading light – and several painted (or Maribou) storks. I am busy admiring how stately and haughty these latter look, when I spot a crocodile slink into the water on the far bank. I am absolutely positive he has his eye on one of these gorgeous storks; rather the way you always want to warn the stupid people in horror movies *not* to go down the dark basement stairs, I find myself calling to the storks to get out of the water *now!* The guide reassures me. This particular crocodile is a swamp crocodile, and he and his kin are not carnivorous (unlike the river crocodile) but subsist for nourishment on whatever they can find in the clay on the banks of the swamp.

Back in the jeep, we are just about to start off once more, when a crashing in the jungle signals the arrival of a mother elephant accompanied by her baby. We wait very, very quietly, and the jeep does not budge. Slowly, cautiously, the mother edges forward, munching as she goes, and trampling down the underbrush. Now she is in full view, and heads toward us. We stay perfectly still, as they have been known to charge. Not this mamma. As a matter of fact as she comes closer it is almost as though she has come to pose for the pictures that we are snapping like mad. Once she has done her "close-up, Mr De Mille," she saunters across the road followed by junior. A few minutes later another female appears, with a very *baby* baby elephant in tow. She strides purposefully across the road, and the poor infant has to trot as fast as his new little legs will carry him to keep up with her. We sit back and let out our breath. It has been all quite thrilling, more so, I feel, in following them with cameras than it would have been with guns.

We continue our tour, stopping by a jungle river and watching a family of monkeys playing in the kubo trees. We also see herds of spotted deer, wild pigs and masses of water buffalo. We finally leave the park in a brilliant sunset that bathes the jungle in a strange saffron light before it disappears into the swift tropical darkness.

It seems to take forever to get to the village where faithful Stuart is waiting. We return to the Ibis Lodge and watch the fireflies in the dusk as we sip our drinks on the verandah before dinner.

Saturday, November 1   A knock on the door at 6.00am, breakfast at 6.30 and away by 7.00. A beautiful morning, with the early sunlight gradually rising over the acres of palms and flaming into its full force as we ascend the hills and into a rubber plantation. This had been privately owned up to a month ago, when it was taken over (with all the others) by the government. I ask Stuart about compensation, as most of the owners had been foreign. He says it will all be determined by an international court.

The rubber trees are tall and straight and evenly spaced. They make a beautiful woodland, dappled with sunlight. Suddenly we are in a blinding intensity of green as we pass acres of rice paddies. I begin to wonder about the phrase "paddy green." If I thought about it at all, I always assumed it was of Irish derivation, but perhaps not, because green these paddies are. We are in luck, as many of the fields are in the process of being harvested. We watch as they spread the rice out onto the intersecting roads to dry, after which it is pounded to remove the outer husks.

We drive for some time into the interior – the sun rising high in a cloudless sky – before turning down a narrow side-road to the village of the Veddhas. Hereby hangs what seems an almost improbable tale.

The Veddhas, according to the encyclopaedic Stuart, are people of a totally different race and language, the original Aboriginal inhabitants of Sri Lanka. Theirs is a primitive tribal society, living off what they can hunt. Many of the young Veddhas have learned Tamil and left the community to intermingle with the Sinhalese. Those who remain continue to live a slightly up-dated version of their old existence.

Armed with all this background, we proceed on foot into Veddha territory. After a few feet, a raggle-taggle of dirty,

183

tattered children crowd around us, hands out-stretched for "rupees, more rupees" – these simple people are certainly wise to the ways of the world, thinks I, as I dodge the clutching little fingers. We stop in front of a hut, primitive, but no more so than the grass shacks we have been passing en route. An ancient emerges from the hut opening. He is small, seamed, and bent, bearing a bow and arrow on his back. He reaches out with both hands and shakes our upper arms in greeting. Another elder – this one with a stone axe – does the same. There is a lot of hanky-panky with the bow and arrow and the axe, all the time pointing at Doug's camera. He obligingly snaps away, and they snatch at the ten rupees for each picture taken. It's all kind of a jungle Petticoat Lane. We dutifully trail after the tribe as they lead us deeper into the forest, until we reach the chief's residence. It doesn't look all that grand – more of a lean-to, actually. It has a roof of palm leaves resting on four bamboo poles, which forms a sort of hanging rack featuring several unpleasant looking things, including the skin of a civet cat and a lot of clumps that I don't like to guess at.

We are absolutely surrounded by bodies, all whining for baksheesh. Stuart tells us these are the chief's family – children and grandchildren, and a pretty seedy lot they are. Things get a bit out of hand when Doug pulls out a cigarette, and these simple nature's children practically snatch it out of his hand, along with the box. I have a slight shiver of impending menace when I realize that the village is sufficiently remote and the trail to the chief's 'summer palace' sufficiently far off the road that it wouldn't be too difficult for them to take the cigarettes, our money and chop us up into little pieces with their 'alley-oop' axes. I reason that this would be very bad for business, but it is an unpleasant thought nonetheless. With very little reluctance we retrace our steps – after rewarding the chief handsomely for his hospitality – pursued to the end by keening children.

We motor on for a brief distance and then turn off the road once more, driving up to another rest house for lunch. The efficient Stuart finds to his consternation that the boys from the Ibis have failed to fill the ice chest with the sandwiches he ordered, so he rushes in to order up a curry lunch.

Doug digs out a bottle of gin, and we take our ease on the

verandah, sipping on a preprandial while we wait. The rest house is built high above the road on a rise of land overlooking a ravine and a turbulent stream. It is very pretty, lush and tropical with palms, hibiscus, temple flowers and jasmine.

Lunch, when it comes, is delicious: rice, mango curry, dried fish and bananas. I really like Sinhalese food, and find it much more pleasant to my taste than Indian cuisine, or at least that of Northern India. I don't mind how hot it is, it is the flavour of the Indian spices I dislike.

After lunch we drive on through intermittent rain into the ever-rising hills toward Kandy. Stuart is marvellous and a veritable fount of information on the local flora. The terraced hills offer us vistas of rice paddies, cocoa trees and pepper and spice trees. We get out of the car to rub the leaves, and the aromas of pepper, nutmeg and cinnamon are a delight to the senses. Still climbing, we come to a tea plantation – acres and acres of plants stretching across the hillside. I cannot believe how verdant and productive the land is.

I am loving every minute, and am almost disappointed when we finally reach Kandy around 4.00pm. Before we enter the town itself, Stuart heads toward Kandy Lake, and turns the car into the hills and up toward The Chalet, a delightful guest house with beautiful gardens looking out on a tropical hillside and the adjacent lake.

Our room is very clean and pleasant with a big balcony. It is raining, so we unpack and then, rain or no rain, go for a walk along the dripping hill road. The rain comes down in earnest, so we return to a nice hot soak in the tub, and a western-style dinner, which is all very pukka, down to coffee served in the lounge.

Sunday, November 2 Up at 7.00am. We breakfast and go out into a rainy morning to explore Kandy. First stop is the Temple of the Tooth, a Buddhist shrine that incorporates the old palace of the King of Kandy and contains the sacred relic of the tooth of Buddha. Needless to say I internally toss around a lot of theories about the tooth, Buddha's dentist and how the tooth found its way to Sri Lanka.

The temple is an offbeat bit of architecture, although all the usual Buddhist symbols are in evidence. By now the rain is really coming down, and we hurry inside. First into the main shrine, and in front of us is a garish altar with enormous elephant tusks, temple lions and a draped cloth. (The Tooth, perhaps?)

The building is in the pagoda style, with open spaces between the roofs. The ceiling is brightly painted, and flowers are strewn across the steps leading up to the altar. To the left of the shrine, a very old lady is sitting and reading aloud from what I imagine is a holy book. We find a side altar with bas-relief figures of lesser gods, dragons and other mythical creatures, all painted in the same strident tones of pink, green and yellow.

We are suddenly aware that off to the left of the altar a heavy wooden door is being shaken and then pushed by an unseen hand. It opens, and a robed monk emerges, smiling and beckoning us to follow. We trail after him up a flight of stairs and come face to face with another door. The monk digs out a ring of keys from the depths of his robe, opens at least six locks and leads us into a circular room that is obviously the library. There are not only books, but also all sorts of those pressed leaf scripts like the ones Professor Chandra had shown us in Delhi. Information is scanty due to language barriers, but I gather this collection of ola leaf manuscripts is very precious and rare.

We then follow our guide up another flight of stairs to another altar. This one is hung with flowers, and the tiny strips of cloth we have been seeing everywhere in Sri Lanka. Stuart has told us each strip represents a prayer, usually a request for a favour from Buddha. Atop the altar is a special casket containing something ancient and sacred. (Perhaps The Tooth?) All this conjecturing is rather frustrating, so I think it is time to bring charades into play. I point to one of my own molars, then to the casket, and look inquiringly. The monk is delighted and nods away excitedly.

When we rejoin Stuart, I ask him to confirm the whereabouts of the tooth. It seems a dentist had nothing to do with it; the tooth had been rescued from Buddha's crematory ashes in 543 BC and brought to Sri Lanka in the 4th century AD. The relic itself is never seen, but is kept inside the casket we just saw, which, in turns, contains six other golden caskets,

186

all heavily bejewelled. It is also never, ever, taken outside the temple. A replica is paraded in the streets of Kandy during the Perahera festivities in August.

Doug has developed a sudden passion for having a shirt made from the saffron-coloured cloth the monks wear. Why, I ask myself? Still, after the temple, we drive into Kandy in search thereof. I am rather relieved to find that there are complications to fulfilling Doug's wish. The first shop sold the robes in a gift package containing the robe, razor, handkerchief etc, ready to present to the monk-in-training by his loving family. The second contained unpackaged material, but it was already stitched into a robe pattern, and even a Delhi tailor would have trouble eking out a shirt. Doug recognizes a lost cause when he sees one, and we give up the project.

A trip to the Central Market is fun, offering as it does splendid cones of tropical fruit and vegetables. We check the prices, and decide India is cheaper. It is pouring, so we don't dally, although we do drive along by the elephant 'baths' and view them from the car. It is too wet for pictures, but a little later we get a shot of a working elephant clearing underbrush, and a charming one of two little girls sheltering under a banana leaf. A little shopping for souvenirs, and then back to the hotel for lunch, before starting on the road once more.

First stop is the Peradeniya Botanical Gardens. They were started by the British 150 years ago, and are absolutely spectacular. Located on the shores of the river, the banks are lined with giant bamboo, reputed to grow two feet a night. There are enormous banyan trees, and others with spreading gnarled roots. Nearby is the International Tree Plantation. This contains trees planted by visiting foreign dignitaries. There is one for Trudeau, but we cannot locate it.

The *pièce de résistance*, however, is the orchid house with 500 varieties of exotic blooms. I hadn't realized that all orchids are actually parasitical plants. They are cultivated in moss-growing bark, in pots filled with stone and charcoal. The colours are exquisite and the plants beautiful: spider orchids, scorpions, tiger-face – some with heavenly scent, some with no fragrance at all. We spot a lovely lavender-blue blossom, and are nationalistically proud to find it is an 'Olive Diefenbaker'.

Out into the spice garden. Most spices come from trees, I

find. Just as Stuart did for us, the guide crushes the leaves, and the wonderful smells of cloves, camphor, bayberry, citronella and nutmeg fill the wet garden air. Something like allspice brings back memories of hot apple pie. I am thoroughly enjoying the whole thing, until it is tinged with the usual embarrassment of being offered a flower or some leaves, smiling graciously on receipt, only to find there is a price tag.

We drive on through the rain and pass the high point of the Hautane Range – 4,380 feet. It was once the site of human sacrifice. Maidens (they were *always* maidens) were thrown from the peak to appease some god or other. Personally I could never see the point of this type of sacrifice. Fat lot of good a battered maiden was going to do anyone, even a god. We go through the village of Kegalle where a notorious outlaw and his band were captured. Then it's on to see the family home and the tomb of the Prime Minister's late husband, Solomon Bandaranaike, who was assassinated in 1959.

Having driven past a number of tea plantations, Stuart stops at one that has an adjoining processing plant. The manager takes us through the whole 'tea experience' which I really find quite interesting, viz: tea was discovered by the Chinese 2000 years ago, but it was not introduced into Ceylon until the British did so about 150 years ago. The manager graciously acknowledges Sri Lanka's debt to the Raj for this financially rewarding legacy.

The soil proved ideal for the production of a very high grade of tea. As we had seen elsewhere the tea plant is large, but only the two top leaves and bud contain the tannin necessary to produce the tea – the rest is waste. The Ceylon tea was given the name 'Orange Pekoe' and in the trade, 'Broken Orange Pekoe'. 'Pekoe' means black and is also the word for the tiny little shoot inside the bud. 'Orange' indicates that it is a refreshing drink, while 'broken' means that the plant must be snapped to take the valuable top shoot. Hence the famous Ceylon BOP.

I think this is probably the end of the tale, but not a bit. The harvest is every 14 days, and the plants pruned on a regular basis. When the leaves are picked they are spread out on a tray and left in a dry, warm room to wither for 18 hours. They are then sent down a chute into a rolling machine; the leaves are not actually cut but are rolled and re-rolled going through a sort of dull blade. After rolling they are taken over to a large tray table where they ferment in water held between two screens. From here they are removed to the roasting machine (at temperatures between 130° and 150°F) where a conveyor belt ensures they are in constant movement and roasted evenly. A huge sieve then removes any tough fibres and impurities. The tea is now ready for grading – high, low and medium. All teas sold are a blend, otherwise masses of tea would be wasted. The government, however, allows companies to produce limited editions of high-grade tea. Our host brews us a pot. He recommends one teaspoon per person and one for the pot. A bit strong for my liking, but still a lovely tea, and we leave – far more informed than we ever thought of being – clutching three one-half pound packages of special edition 'high' tea. I am really not sure why I made all these meticulous notes to record in my diary, but then I would hate to find myself, at some future date, on a quiz programme, about to win a million, and unable to answer a question on tea.

This is the last lap of our journey, and we reach Colombo and the Intercontinental at around 6.00pm. It has been an unparalleled few days, largely due to the incomparable Stuart, who has been a guide among guides, unfailingly courteous, informative and protective. We tip him handsomely, but it is in no way enough, and say goodbye to someone who has become a friend.

Monday, November 3 Up comparatively late, breakfast and then head out for the Mariposa – lovely batik shop in the Oberoi. It is not open yet, so we go to its sister shop down the road. It is owned and run by Ena da Silva, who made the magnificent batiks in the Oberoi lobby. We buy some attractive boxes, but find it is later than we think and there is no more time to poke. This is a pity, as Ena's things are of a very high quality and totally original.

Leaving Sri Lanka is a cinch compared to the trauma of leaving Madras. Indian Airlines, however, remains faithful to its predictable menu. Lunch is identical to the one we had flying in: a curry pastry, a greenish sandwich with an indeterminate filling, a limp salad and a very tired piece of fruit

189

cake. Arrive in Madras and, after a few hours wait in the airport, catch a plane to Delhi. It leaves on time, and after an identical supper to the aforementioned lunch, we reach Palam at 9.00pm and are met with a full barrage of Diwali fireworks, and two excited daughters. They rush to meet us, we exchange news and they receive their gifts with their usual gratifying enthusiasm.

CHAPTER 24

Tuesday, November 4 We are out of just about everything and I shop lavishly at the Commissary. Doug comes home for lunch and tells me that Jack and Doris Shadbolt came into his office this morning, and he invited them for dinner tomorrow night.

I am delighted at the thought of seeing two delightful people and getting news of the Vancouver art scene. Jack's painting is gaining national recognition, and Doris, as the doyenne of curators from the Vancouver Art Gallery, was incredibly generous with her time in helping us with the formation of the Burnaby one.

I rush back to the Commissary determined to give them a good meal tomorrow. I can't believe my luck – they have Rock Cornish Game hens, just flown in from the US. I buy four and some quite decent shrimp.

Back home, I call Tony in for a consultation on tomorrow's menu. He rhymes off what he had in mind. It is pure British army stodge, and I shake my head in what I hope is an authoritarian manner, and reel off the *table d'hôte* I have in mind. We will have shrimp-filled crepes to begin, roasted game hens and a light meringue for dessert. He is none too pleased, but I am surprised and chuffed with my bold stand and march off before he can argue.

Wednesday, November 5 It should have been a memorable evening on a soft autumnal night, hosting two notable Canadians to a modestly gourmet meal. Doug picks them up at their hotel, and we usher them out to the patio, Jack stopping to comment on how odd it seems to be a world away in India, and to come across a Don Jarvis above the fireplace. Said Don Jarvis being our very first purchase from the Vancouver Art Gallery's 'Do You Own a Canadian Painting' project.

Outside, the fireflies are twinkling in the garden, a pale moon is rising above a lyrical tree, and Tony appears with drinks and wonderful roasted cashew nuts. When dinner is announced, we are ushered into the candlelit dining room. It is at this point that the gilt crumbles off the gingerbread and my role as gracious hostess comes apart. Instead of tender shrimp resting in rich velouté sauce – tough little pellets of cold beastliness are hidden in dry curling pancakes. A chew through these, and then we are presented with four little white rubber corpses that bounce beneath the thrust of a fork, and a meringue that is a gooey blob.

I had gone over everything in detail, backed up written recipes with verbal instructions, and I cannot understand how this lovely menu has strayed so far. I say nothing in front of the guests when we return to the patio for coffee, but remember back to the last time I had interfered in Tony's domain. I realize I am being taught a lesson. Stay out of my kitchen, and keep your pinkies off my menus, or this will be the result. I am furious, and although the Shadbolts have probably expected nothing more, I find myself stewing, and the magic of the Indian night has gone.

The Shadbolts themselves are "mixed" on the subject of India. In the course of the evening, they recount how they had fallen victim to three basic Indian no-nos. They had paid the Maiden's Hotel, where they were booked for three days, in advance. After one uncomfortable night, they decide to move, and request a rebate. Hah! Lesson 1: never pay in advance in India. Then Jack was relieved of 500 rupees during a walk through Chandni Chowk. Lesson 2: never show your wallet. Lastly, having passed up a shoeshine boy, he is horrified to find a large betel-juice splatter on his shoe. Lesson 3: step lively in the presence of those you reject among the shiners of shoes. We commiserate with them, but also console them with the reminder that thrice bitten, thrice shy. They are now blooded and armed with experience for the next lap of their journey to Nepal.

Monday, November 10 I have promised to take a visiting widow out shopping today. She is an Immigration officer's brother's mother-in-law, which is a lot of apostrophes and a relatively remote connection, but they feel obligated and are grateful for a hand in entertaining.

She is a keen shopper, and happily has the lolly to indulge

this pursuit, so we have a really fun time. Actually, it is one of life's great vicarious pleasures helping spend someone else's money. In two hours, she manages to buy several souvenir spoons, two mirror-work elephants, one Kashmiri shawl, one skirt length of fabric and one wrap-around skirt.

I have parked the car at the Imperial, and we load the loot into it, then have a leisurely lunch in the hotel gardens before heading out once more, this time for Sundar Nagar. Here, she tots up a gold elephant charm, one dozen brass coasters and a couple of carved ivory elephants. She is on a roll, and pausing only for tea at Claridge's, she continues to spread goodwill and rupees at the Kahn Market. She is ecstatic over her day, and is as rapturous in her gratitude as a gourmet who has just been dropped off at Julia Child's for dinner.

Thursday, November 13 Well in with my British bridge group, thanks to Monica, and I really like them all. I used to think it was rather decadent to play bridge in the afternoon, now here I am with bridge beginning at 9.00am ("before the heat of the day saps our strength"). Any possible sapped strength is revived with a round of Bloody Marys at 10.00am. I draw the line here. Decadent I may be to play at 9.00am, but not that decadent – *yet!*

I have to rush away at noon to attend a parent-teacher interview at the American School. Hilary may be a bit of a handful, but the marbles are certainly all in place. She gets straight As and glowing comments. Like many a mother before me, I want to ask, "Are you sure we are talking about *my* child?" Anyway it is all gratifying, and I take this academic paragon along with me to pick up Barbara, and the three of us head over to the offices of the President's Bodyguard.

Captain Singh at the riding school has told us that the official outfitter not only makes all the uniforms and boots for the bodyguards, but also has a sideline making jodhpurs for the Captain's students. This has been the dearest wish of both the girls for their Christmas presents, so they are duly measured and we order riding boots and jodhpurs.

Friday, November 14 I have joined just about everything the International Women's Club has to offer, and have been named their corresponding secretary. They already have a recording secretary, and maybe they are just trying to give people titles. However, I do have to write a number of letters, and I do have a typewriter, so perhaps that explains a lot. I am also required to become the editor of the monthly club newsletter. "Full participation" is expected of the Executive, I have been told, so as a consequence I am now in the French Club, on the Museum Course and in the Book Club. It is to this latter that I now dash, having dashed to have my hair done, and will probably have to dash off to the Residence for lunch. We discuss Indian poetry – quite interesting really – and then, sure enough, I dash to the Residence.

Lunch is a small and pleasant group – Mrs HE's brother and sister-in-law and a local doctor are the other guests. We have sherry on the patio, then lunch in the arbour. It is very charming, with echoes of a privileged past gone in most parts of the world. Once home, I turn my energies to organizing things for our trip to the Pushkar Camel Fair tomorrow.

Saturday, November 15 Unprepared as we are, we are still ready to leave at 9.30am. A number of people from the High Commission are also going to the Camel Fair, and we draw lots for drivers. We end up with Ram Singh, whom we have had before, and who is an expert at car games, such as camel counting, or how many vultures will we see around the next deceased cow.

Passing the Amber Fort we spot another High Commission officer's car, and also Goldie Singh driving the Moultons. I love the approach to Jaipur. First the gradual rise of the mountains, and the long wall of fortifications, then the Palace on the hill, with the Fort above and the lake below.

We drive through the narrow pass and take the now-familiar turn where we look down on the Rose-Pink City of Jaipur. This 'rose-pink' business is the queen of euphemisms, but I have to confess Jaipur looks better than it did in the monsoons. We veer off on the road down to the Maharajah's Guest Lodge, where we stayed in the summer. We don't get quite the same personal attention as we did then, probably because our host has other guests and business is brisk.

We spend the afternoon sight-seeing, with a visit to the

Rambagh Palace and the Jamal Palace hotels. Both are now in the tourist business, but far and away the more interesting is the Rambagh – a beautiful old palace with vast, Versailles-style staircases, open terrace and patio, squash courts and indoor swimming pool. The Maharajah did not stint on creature comforts. We also chase down the Gem Arts that we visited with Kilmeny and Martin. KJ had admired a necklace that we decide to get her for Christmas. The price has gone up, but after a bit of haggling we make our purchase.

The light is beginning to fade, as we return to the Lodge, and we are just settling in when Ron and Dianne Hartling appear. This young couple, still in a honeymoon glow, arrived at the High Commission a short while ago. They bring in beer and peanuts, and we have a jolly Happy Hour, and then join forces for dinner. They are on the return trip from the Fair, and fill us in on what to expect.

Sunday, November 16 Away by 10.00am and discover that Ajmer is a lot farther than we had anticipated (80 miles) and that Pushkar, where the Camel Fair is held, is another 15 miles beyond that. Still, we set out happily enough – the countryside is interesting and full of delightful things.

As we near Ajmer, we are aware of being in a desert land, with stretches of sand dunes and withered grasses. Beyond the town is a distant lake and rising ochre hills. It is a sepia landscape, until we suddenly become aware of a brilliant coil of colour that is snaking across the brown curve of the valley and climbing the rocky wall of the hills. The reds, saffrons, blues and greens are dazzling. Only when we draw closer do we realize that we are looking at a procession of hundreds and hundreds of people en route by foot to Pushkar. The Camel Fair, which is our main reason for the trip, is only a part of what is essentially a religious pilgrimage for the devout. Pushkar's lake and main temple are dedicated to Brahma, and to many Hindus, Pushkar is as Mecca is to the Muslims.

We drive alongside the hill path that the procession is following, and get a good look at the pilgrims. They have already walked countless miles, and are now heading through the pass – a steady stream, most of them carrying supplies on their heads. A few are accompanied by donkeys, with charpoys (cots) strapped to their backs. The women are wearing elaborately embroidered bodices above their trailing skirts, and the distinctive flowing headdresses of Rajasthan. The family wealth they carry on their person, in the form of large gold nose rings, ivory bangles and silver ankle bracelets. The men are almost equally festive in their distinctive Rajput turbans. These are large, set squarely on the head, and woven like twisted rope. The rest of their costume includes the strange flaring Rajput over-blouse, almost always in white, and worn with the heavy silver necklaces we have seen in the bazaars.

The mountain road is narrow and hazardous, and policemen are stationed at numerous junctures and curves to direct the mass of vehicular, pedestrian and animal traffic. We finally ascend to the peak of the pass, and begin our descent. The coloured line does likewise and can be seen dipping over the valley floor. We follow the crowd into Pushkar and on to the fairgrounds.

It is an incredible sight. The fair is set on a narrow flat piece of land, between two almost identical pyramid-shaped hills, each topped with a temple. Fanning out from the centre of the site are lines of stalls and bazaars, shamianas and other trappings of the fair. They all surround the great ring where the camels, horses and cattle are shown to buyers.

On the periphery, the ground curves into hillocks, which are literally covered, as far as the eye can see, with camels, tents and campfires. It is an utterly astonishing spectacle. Amazingly enough we spot Goldie Singh and one of the Moultons as we wander through the crowds, stopping here and there at the various bazaars. The stall wares are mainly camel trappings – saddles, blankets, etc. I buy a brass camel bell, and the girls get a camel ride.

After a couple of hours, we go into a filthy little stall for an equally filthy cup of coffee. The coffee is my undoing – I desperately need a loo. The girls tell me there is a 'comfort station' they have already used behind one of the food tents. They accompany me down a crowded little sideway and there, in full view of half of Rajasthan, is a dirty pocket-handkerchief of canvas on a shaky pole. A lifetime of shiny bathrooms, scented soap and total privacy revolts. Despite my need, despite the girls spreading themselves across the inadequate

196

Camels, horses and cattle are shown to buyers

197

canvas, my bladder goes completely coy, and I cannot do it.

I prefer to draw a veil over any conjectures about what might have ensued, because fortunately luck intervenes. We are all keen to see the camel races, even if I have to agonize and squirm my way through them, but as we emerge back into the centre ring, it is announced that the races have been postponed until tomorrow. There is no reason for us to dally, and with fingers (and legs) crossed, we head for Ajmer and – oh bliss, oh rapture – a proper loo.

It is a long drive back, but we arrive at the hotel around 6.00pm. We are just settling down for a drink, when the Canadian contingent of fair-goers joins us. We have a very jolly little party, exchanging anecdotes and impressions of the day. We decline to join them for dinner, as we have promised the girls an evening at the Rambagh Palace.

The dining room is opulent, as expected, but the big surprise is the quality of the dinner. It is great – a delicious soup, roast suckling pig and a marvellously light marmalade steamed pudding – all beautifully cooked and presented. We are just finishing when who should walk in but the Shadbolts. After exchanges of pleasantries, we join them with our coffee, as they eat their dinner. They have had some interesting adventures, and have been bewildered and thrilled by the diversity of the land and its people.

Monday, November 17 After talking to a fair official who assured us that there *would* be races today, I look at the programme, and it quite clearly states November 18, the final day, is set for racing. We are, therefore, torn as to what to do. It is a long, long drive to see the same things we saw yesterday, but Barbara is keen, and we hate to miss anything, so we decide to go regardless. As we have to leave tomorrow, we will not see the hookah-pipe camel rider do his thing, and everyone is disappointed, but who knows what other wonder we may catch. In any case, what is on the programme seems to bear little resemblance to what actually happens.

The hotel packs us a lunch, which we feel will be better than driving all over Ajmer in search of a decent restaurant. It's rather nice actually having a picnic just beyond the fairgrounds, and watching the whole colourful scene unfold, as if for our personal pleasure.

Back at the fair, we find almost half again as many people as yesterday, and the atmosphere is electric. However, not too surprisingly, there are no races. Ram Singh digs around and finds out that the selection of camels for the final race will take place at 3.30pm. This turns out to be almost as good as a proper race, being a series of elimination heats. We also see a display of camel control and judging, which is rather interesting, although as far as the judging of the camels' finer points, they all look much the same to me.

We leave to return to Jaipur around 5.00pm and enjoy the sight of camel caravans returning from the Fair. It is growing dark, and as we drive on, the moon rises over the fields. It is difficult to imagine a more romantic setting– swathed, turbaned figures riding their camels toward the fire-lit campsites in the fields.

Tuesday, November 18 The last day of the fair, but we must return to Delhi. En route we plan to stop at the Amber Fort. As neither Hilary nor Barbara had been with us on our previous visit, they are anxious to do the Jaipur 'must', namely the elephant ride to the top. It is a beautiful morning, and the girls are itching for a tour of the palace. I join them, but Doug says he wants to sit this one out on the grounds that he does not need to see one more Mogul arch, nor one more marble screen. Of course, we all insist, he doesn't *need* to see them, but there are bound to be some heretofore missed camera opportunities. Enough said. He tags along after us snapping for all he is worth.

Along the way, we pick up one of the ever-present guides who attaches himself to us like a leech. The girls are properly thrilled with all the exotica of the Fort, although the guide keeps calling Hilary "baby", which annoys her no end. Still they make appropriate appreciative noises as he points out the hidden images of bees, snakes, monkeys and butterflies in one intricately carved marble panel, and are suitably shocked at the tale of the Shah's 17 wives.

Having exhausted the delights of the Amber Palace, we reluctantly descend and start back for Delhi, reaching home around 2.00pm. Barbara, the disciplined scholar, throws herself into her books, and then begins her mock exam, with me invigilating. It is a three-hour paper, and throughout she shows every sign of frustration: sighs, gasps, running of fingers through her hair. On the stroke of 6.00 I stop her, which she accepts with no attempt to prolong, although she still has two more questions to answer. I am proud of her for that. She says she had trouble with her précis, which was a real stinker loaded with a lot of fulsome facts she felt she just could not leave out.

CHAPTER 25

Wednesday, November 19 There is something of a shadow on the household, although nobody mentions it on the principle that if we don't say anything maybe it will go away. A few days ago, when Hermione was sitting as usual with her head under Hilary's hand, Hilary felt some lumps on her neck. Doug was consulted, and although he didn't say anything, his expression spoke volumes.

I know all dogs are special to their owners, but Hermione *really* is. She was a present to Hilary on her sixth birthday, and they have been the closest of companions every since, with that special bond that is supposed to exist between a child and an animal, but seldom does. Herm is small for an English Springer Spaniel, but beautiful and intelligent, with a heart that beats just for us. She seems to be getting thinner by the day, although she gamely comes for walks and waits for Hilary by the gate every day at 4.00pm. Today after golf, I take her to a vet, a Sikh who lives just down the street and who was recommended by one of the British bridge players. He's pleasant man with an excessively tight turban, and I swear he doesn't hear half what I say. His diagnosis is that Herm is just "run down" and suggests vitamins starting on Friday.

Saturday, November 22 Herm started on her vitamin shots yesterday, and I anxiously (but not too hopefully) look for signs of improvement. In kind of a blue mood, I glance at the calendar, and realize it is 12 years to the day since President Kennedy was shot, and that "one shining moment" became history. I guess we all look for a little magic, a touch of glamour in our world leaders. It is an indefinable something that none of Kennedy's successors seems to have. Certainly it has been notably absent in our own grey prime ministers, men like stout little Mackenzie-King and the be-jowled Diefenbaker. However, despite criticisms of his arrogance and overbearing authority, even his enemies have to admit that Pierre Eliot Trudeau has it in spades.

Sunday, November 23 Doug walks Herm down for her third shot and discovers the vet has added calcium to the vitamins. Whether this has anything to do with a distinct swelling around the eyes is doubtful, but Doug hasn't much faith in the efficacy of the vitamins nor, for that matter, in the vet's diagnosis of "just run down".

Monday, November 24 Peter's 18th birthday, and the young-man-about-campus is zillions of miles away, geographically and emotionally, from his mother's angel cake. I come over all nostalgic, with memories of a sweet little boy, hair slicked down, excitedly waiting for his birthday party guests.

An American friend has not been well, and I take her some flowers. She tells me her staff problems – her cook has stolen 5,000 rupees, and this has stirred up a hornet's nest of troubles with accusations and counter-accusations. I guess Tony's peccadilloes are but petty irritations after all.

Thursday, November 27 A three-table bridge luncheon at the Chartered Bank House, with a United Nations guest list – the British banking crew, a couple of Canadians, two Americans, a Chinese, a Korean and an Indian. The horizons widen.

Friday, November 28 A teacher's conference at the American School, so Hilary is home, and I bow out of bridge to spend the day with her. She has been hovering over Hermione, and trying to tempt her with special little titbits. I know she is desperately worried, and I feel a diversion is called for. We have fun shopping for Christmas presents, and then go out to the Qutb Hotel for lunch. It is really nice to have her all to myself again.

Saturday, November 29 For some weeks we have been avoiding rehearsals for the St Andrews Night Ceilidh to be held at the Barkers' in Old Delhi. I have told Monica we know nothing about Scottish country dancing, and she assures me that it doesn't matter – they are just having rehearsals for fun, and nobody is that serious about it.

It is a black-tie affair and we arrive at the Bank House at the appointed hour. It looks like the beginning of a 1930s

I am caught up in the Dashing White Sergeant

movie. There are torches in the garden lighting up the palm trees, the verandah is ablaze and elegant people, glasses in hand, are assembled. Moreover, and to my horror, they are all wearing laced-up dancing slippers – what does Monica mean, they don't take it seriously?

A lot of the guests I know, and a lot I don't. The British High Commissioner and his wife are there. Through the sisterhood of bridge we have become friends, and as she has told me, rather proudly, she has a Canadian connection. A lot of the ladies are wearing clan tartan sashes across their shoulders, and Lady Walker has one in the Duncan tartan. She was born a Duncan, and her grandfather explored the Canadian West, founding the little town that bears his name, Duncan, BC.

Hamish has a bad back and declines to dance. He is, instead, presiding at the bar. Despite all the turbaned help, Doug decides Hamish needs a hand and places himself beside his host, "out of harm's way" as he says. Not so me. Before I know it I am caught up in the Dashing White Sergeant, the Gay Gordons, et al. I haven't a clue as to what to do and wish I had attended the rehearsals after all. Strangely enough, I find myself swept around in the correct twirls by a lot of gallant gentlemen and have an absolutely marvellous time. The evening concludes with haggis and magnums of champagne and, like everyone else, I am sorry to see it end. Hamish tells me Monica absolutely forbad him to go all traditional and plunge his dirk into the steaming haggis and pitch the glasses into the fireplace. A pity!

Sunday, November 30 Do a little Christmas baking and go to the finals of the Polo Match – very exciting, with Delhi's darling, VP Singh, in great form.

Tuesday, December 2 Tony comes to tell me that Muni has a received word that his father is gravely ill and our sweeper must leave for Madras immediately. The corollary, unspoken, but clear from the outstretched palm, is that Muni will require money for the trip. I come across with the needful, and agree that Tony may engage temporary help. I was all for gathering flowers for Muni to take to his mother until Tony says he can get Muni's brother as a replacement. Hold on! If Muni has to rush to his father's side, why does his brother not have to do likewise? I query Tony on this point and he gives me that non-committal Indian nod, so I am not one whit the wiser. This afternoon, however, the ladies at today's luncheon tell me that the Indian use of the word 'brother' is a loose one. It does not necessarily mean a blood relative, but simply someone, possibly from the same village. One learns.

Wednesday, December 3 A lot of running around today, and by mid-afternoon at the library, my head is aching, my throat is sore and I feel unduly hot and then unduly cold. I get home as soon as is reasonable, crawl under my feather tick, and indulge in the luxury of feeling extremely sorry for myself.

Thursday, December 4 I hate the thought of having servants dust around me while I recline in bed, hence I struggle up and spend the morning writing letters in the den. My usual comforting little slogan at times of distress – "poor me, this calls for a chocolate bon-bon" – produces only waves of nausea and lunch has zilch appeal. If anything, I feel worse, and retreat back to bed, the faithful Hermione at my heels, to sleep away the afternoon.

Friday, December 5 Still feeling and looking like the proverbial five miles of bad road, I nevertheless convince myself I must go to bridge, even if for no other reason than to unload some of the invitations to our Boxing Day 'Punch 'n' Brunch' party. Invitations are not only an absolute must in Delhi society, but they must also follow a set formula – a snowy white card engraved with Park Lane script that imparts information on the date, the nature of the entertainment and one's name, rank and serial number. Well, not quite, but titles are *de rigueur* in order, I suppose, to allow the recipient to weigh the prestige of the inviter. It also appears to be important that one's invitations be delivered by hand, either by one's bearer, through the office or, as in this case, at another social event. There seems to be some taboo against using the Post Office. Whether it is the fear that your invitations will be pinched and you will find yourself hosting a party of mail sorters and carriers, I cannot be sure.

After bridge, I stop by the Commissary and spend most of our boodle on liquor for the party. Gratefully tumble into bed after lunch, and Doug starts me on antibiotics when he comes home.

Saturday, December 6 "Stern daughter of the voice of God" demands that, as promised, I work at the Canadian booth at the Annual Chrysanthemum Sale. However, I feel distinctly better, probably the pills.

CHAPTER 26

Monday, December 8 Yet another journey, this time into the depths of the Punjab to visit Doug's DMPs. A Commission driver arrives at 8.00am, lunch is organized and we are away by 9.00. We drive through Old Delhi on the way out of town, and stop at The Whistling Teal, a Haryana rest house for tea. It is quite pretty, on a nice little lake, and surprisingly clean. Around noon, we find a pleasant treed area and stop for lunch, which is vastly improved by the sipping of wine.

We reach Ludhiana about 3.00pm. It is a terrible, crowded, filthy place. The hotel is not good, but better than expected. Doug had warned me that this hostelry doesn't provide sheets, so we open up our sleeping bags over the dubious mattress.

Doug goes out to meet his doctor and on his return brings the news that a dinner has been planned for this evening, and we are both expected, although at an indeterminate time. We hazard a guess, and drive through the dark of the Punjab night, reaching our destination at 7.00pm for one of the most disconcerting evenings of my life.

As I learned earlier, sociologists analyzing culture shock have expressed the opinion that it occurs when one is thrown off base. Europeans, for example are used to shaking hands every five minutes, and are often left wondering what to do with a dangling and unaccepted paw. As we discovered in the Bangalore Legislature, an innocent crossing of the legs, so displaying the soles of one's feet, is the deepest of insults to an Asian, and so it goes. With regard to tonight, I am totally unprepared for, and unguided into, the niceties required of me in Ludhiana.

Our arrival is the occasion for what seems a massive gathering. Even in the darkness of the Punjabi night, I can distinguish a mixed crowd descending on the car. A tall figure in a shepherd's check jacket and a vivid yellow turban opens the car door almost before we have come to a full stop.

"Welcome, welcome," he proclaims, and with a wide sweep of his arm encompasses the pack behind him. "These are my colleagues," he beams.

I am ushered out like the Queen and graciously start shaking all the outstretched hands, which, as it turns out, are attached to camel herders, curious villagers and general hangers-on.

"No, no," he protests, swirling me around, "*these* are my colleagues," and indicates a group, sartorially a cut above those whose hands have just been so warmly shaken. First major goof.

I am then escorted by a greatly reduced contingent up a set of very chilly stairs into an even chillier room. The wife of our host shyly comes to greet me, eyes cast down, and does not seem to notice my extended hand. A younger woman is standing nearby, and a muttered introduction is made. It turns out she is the wife of one of the colleagues and is herself a doctor. I begin to have hope, which fades as she remains as quiet as her hostess. Other wives drift over, all silent as the tomb.

Doug is led off to the other end of the room, and is quickly surrounded by the colleagues, all bowing and beaming. In addition to our host, there is a radiologist, an ophthalmologist and a few more GPs. One appoints himself as the bartender and produces a bottle of Scotch for the men.

I find myself isolated with the women, in a kind of social ultima Thule, and imprisoned behind my own fixed smile. A servant appears with an enormous platter of hors d'oeuvres – cheeses, tandoori chicken and fish sticks. I see a conversational opening.

"These looks delicious – are they Punjabi specialties?" A nodding of the heads. I have another stab.

"I understand the cooking of Northern India is less spicy than that of the South."

Several more nods. I grow desperate and glance down the room at the medical profession swilling it down and think dark thoughts. A wind from the open door sweeps up the stairs and I settle my Kashmiri shawl around me for warmth. It is then that I am assailed by a stroke of genius.

"I just bought this shawl and I love it, but I don't seem to be able to fold it as cleverly as you do. Perhaps you could demonstrate, Mrs Singh?"

208

I'm off the hook. They all leap up and start draping shawls this way and that amid much chatter and giggles. Just when I am thinking that perhaps we can be chums after all, a bearer comes in to announce (I think) that food is ready. What have we been eating, I ask myself, having consumed several very large pieces of chicken, and heaven knows how many fish sticks.

The table is set and I am handed a plate. Ah, a clue, it is buffet! Then I notice the table is set with surrounding chairs – am I to sit? Not sit? Help myself? Help!! Where is Emily Post when I need her? The table is laden with sandwiches, tomatoes, curd and replenished mountains of chicken. I begin to get the impression that whatever decision I make will be as a royal edict. Sit down or buffet? The thought of a non-existent round-table discussion casts the vote for me, and I begin to fill my plate and lead the way into the other room, which by now is colder than ever.

Throughout the evening my hostess keeps looking at me for signs of approval of her efforts, and I do my very best – praising everything lavishly. She is such a nice gentle sort of person, with a lovely kind face, and I feel she has put her heart and soul into the preparations for this soirée. I really want her to know that I appreciate it, but find communication more than somewhat sticky.

Finally the evening draws to a merciful close. In parting, Mrs D presents us with a vividly hued bedspread, and a guard of honour is arranged on the wind-swept steps to bid farewell. Thanks are expressed, hands are shaken (the right ones this time) and from the happy smiles on the faces of the doctor and his colleagues, I detect a general mood of satisfaction that it has all been a splendid affair indeed.

Tuesday, December 9 We get away by 10.00am after some hassle with travellers' cheques, the Ludhiana Hotel not having an international clientele. We reach Jullunder around 11.00am and Dr S, our second DMP, and his cohorts are lined up, delegation style, to meet us. We once again ascend a chilly staircase and enter a cold, bare room.

Dr S's daughter, a very pretty girl, is on hand to bring us coffee. She is a graduate doctor, and preparing for a specialty in obstetrics. A brother-in-law, a professor of physics, and Mrs S are also on hand. Mrs S must have been a beauty in her day, and in many respects still is. Sadly, she suffered an accident a year or so ago and was unconscious for three days. While physically recovered, she is just a trifle distrait. There is the usual anxious flutter to assure our comfort, and the usual uneasy lulls in conversation. Not for the first time, I think what a pity it is that all these attractive, well-educated and bright people are gathered in this icy room for the sole purpose of pandering to us. What do they really think about it all, I wonder?

I choke down the coffee, which has floating grounds and has been made with milk, and then we all troop over to see the new clinic and house Dr S is building (thanks, he says, to the Canadian business). We all exclaim appreciatively, and then take our leave.

We head out for Amritsar, and after some difficulty locate Mrs Bendhari's Guest House, despite the fact that it is where we had tea a couple of months ago. It has been highly recommended by other HC personnel and rightly so. It is a pleasant house set in an attractive garden. We are given a nice lunch, then take off for the Golden Temple.

This remarkable structure is almost the *raison d'être* of Amritsar. Physically, it dominates the town; spiritually it is the soul of Sikhism. Coming upon it as we do, in the pale sunlight of a winter afternoon, it has an otherworldly aura, a white and gold monument to a passionate belief.

It is set in a huge quadrangle of marble and fronted by a lake, which reflects a shimmering image of the golden-domed building. We cross the lake by way of a long marble causeway into the heart of the temple itself. Once inside, there is that special feeling of serenity one finds in most holy places, cathedrals, mosques, synagogues. Something strikes me quite forcibly – there are no 'money changers' in this temple. Admission is free and donations are neither asked for nor accepted. Furthermore no one need ever leave hungry. A huge pot of food, constantly replenished, is always there and is available to all who come, regardless of faith or race.

I have only a hazy notion of Sikh ideology, but the faithful hold to a belief that through knowledge of the cosmic 'prana' of

210

The Golden Temple… a monument to a passionate belief

211

the universe an ideal state may be achieved. Inside the temple there is a canopied platform that contains the Guru Granth Sahib – the Sikh bible or book of wisdom. Usually there is some one reading from it to enlighten strangers and comfort Sikhs.

Having had my own wayward soul warmed by the quiet, peace and charity of the Temple, it is a bit of a shock to go into the nearby Sikh Museum, which is a testament to man's inhumanity to man. Every imaginable weapon of destruction, every form of torture is featured in song, story and pictures. It is a relief to leave and return to Mrs B's comfy establishment.

Our room is cold, but a fire has been laid and is now lit. The bed is turned down showing clean sheets, and pretty embroidered pillowcases – a far cry from the bare mattresses of the Hotel Ludhiana. We draw our chairs up to the fire for our Happy Hour. Dinner is good, and we enjoy conversations with the two other guests – a businessman from Bombay and an American lady living in Rawalpindi.

Wednesday, December 10 Breakfast under a jacaranda tree in Mrs B's garden. The sun is shining, and I am enjoying the tranquillity, when the plates begin a slow and stately slide off the table and, like the girl in *For Whom the Bell Tolls*, I feel the earth move. It is a minor earthquake but nobody gets unduly alarmed and the bearer simply dusts off our plates (and the toast) and returns them to the table.

We leave Amritsar and arrive back in Jullunder in time for our appointment with our third DMP, a Dr M. Jullunder appears, over all, a larger centre than Ludhiana, and Dr M's home reflects this. It is considerably more up-market than the draughty corridors of the past two visits. Gathered for lunch is a much larger group than we had expected. In addition to Mrs M we are joined by the couple's two sons (16 and 11) and Mrs M's parents. Mrs M and her mamma are faithful to the 'silent partner' role of Indian wives, but the conversation is infinitely easier than the stilted ordeal of the other night. Dr M and Mrs M's father are interesting conversationalists and things go along smoothly. The lunch has been prepared with western tastes in mind, which is both thoughtful and appreciated.

Before we leave I present Mrs M with a small 'hostess' gift, and she rushes off and returns with a quilt for me and a brass lamp for Doug. We make the usual demurs about not accepting gifts (a no-no, lest it be conceived as a bribe) but the crestfallen expressions and the insistence that these are "personal welcomes" would make it an insult to refuse. We thank them warmly and leave in a flurry of handshakes, with promises to return.

We head out for Chandigarh, the specially created state capital. Never having been in a purpose-built town, particularly one designed by the great Le Corbusier, I am dying to see it.

When Jinnah announced in that terrible summer of 1947—"I will have India divided or I will have India in blood," could he possibly have known not only that he would have both, but also of the long-reaching and history-changing effect separation would have?

When Mountbatten's appointee, Sir Cyril Radcliffe, isolated himself in a small, shuttered bungalow in Delhi, and began the impossible task of carving up India, one of his greatest problems was the Punjab. The Sikhs were almost a nation unto themselves, but ancient ties to the North dictated that the greater portion of the state should be ceded to Pakistan. With this went the ancient capital of Lahore.

The new state, Harayana, must have a capital, but choices were made and discarded, until Nehru, always an internationalist in thought, decreed that this, the newest Indian state, would have a totally new capital. Still another startling departure was the appointment of the famous French architect and town planner, Le Corbusier.

The spot chosen was at the foot of the lovely Siwalik Hills, which provided a dramatic backdrop for the new city. Some may love it, others hate it, but all acknowledge it as unique.

This is no ancient city, lost in time and past cultures. Instead it rises, a symbol of 20th-century thought and a defiant step forward for a new nation. As we drive along the wide and impressive central avenue toward the administrative core, we find boulevards and promenades reaching out on either side. It has been designed with people in mind, unlike Sir Edward Luytens graceful, elegant treatment in New Delhi, which breathes grandeur and selective privilege.

To my eye, it all looks quite splendid, a balance of unity

and innovation that is both fluid and exciting. Closer up, however, the "centre cannot hold", at least in my view. The Secretariat, so commanding from a distance, shows up with a lot of fussy distractions on the facade. Discolouration and water streaks stain the buildings, and crumbling concrete attests to the lack of maintenance. I feel mildly betrayed that this remarkable concept and imaginative plan fall apart on closer inspection. This, of course, could just be me, as people come from all over the world to see the city, ever since its inauguration in 1966.

After our quick tour of Chandigarh, we head for home. We have to fight our way past a Sikh procession en route, and return home an hour later than anticipated. The girls are still out riding, and I take a peak at the wrapped lamp. It is sculpted metal, inset with coloured stones, and the shade is scalloped in lace, and composed of red and black georgette in agitated swirls. At this point the girls come in the door, and Hilary gazes at our treasure.

"Come and see our gift from the Punjab, Hilary," I call out.

There is a long look at the lamp and a longer look at me before she replies.

"Personally, I think it's a barf." Out of the mouths of babes....

CHAPTER 27

Saturday, December 13 Christmas is coming and somewhere in the world geese are getting fat, snow is falling and choirs are singing in the malls. Here in Delhi, only the calendar tells me it is mid-December, and I had better see to yuletide matters.

The American Women's Club are having a fund-raising "Go-Down", and we go over to have a look. It is really quite good, with an interesting assortment of things. I buy a lot of stocking stuffers – Chinese embroidery, silver anklets and quite a pretty silver and moonstone bracelet for one of the girls.

Sunday, December 14 The silly season is every bit as silly in Delhi as it is in West Vancouver. Gay apparel is constantly being donned, and we seem to be going from one groaning board to another. Today we have an invitation from a hostess whose name I do not recognize and I am in a complete fog as to why we have been invited. Fortunately, as it turns out, the face is familiar – I just never knew her last name.

Monday December 15 Just on our way out for dinner, when Tony runs in with a telegram from Martin – he has received no travel arrangements. Complete panic on my part. Doug phones the on-duty staff to send a telex to Ottawa. I fret through dinner, but word is there on our return – Martin *will* be arriving with Kilmeny and Peter on December 24. Whew!

Tuesday, December 16 Another changeless tradition of Christmas is the School Concert, as predictable as Santa and his army of elves. Or so I thought. Tonight's concert at the American School is refreshingly different and rather touching. It is not just an American presentation; other schools have been invited to participate – British, Japanese, Russian and Indian, among others. Looking around the audience at the beaming parents snapping innumerable photographs, I am aware, once again, of being part of a universal body that shares the common emotions we all find in just being parents.

Wednesday, December 17 Poor Barbara sprained her ankle and limps onto the stage for the British School concert. While there are no outside participants, the school's student body consists of children from 45 different nations, so the programme is both varied and international. Barbara is really happy here, and has a positive United Nations assortment of friends. Most of the Canadian teenagers from the Commission attend the American School, but Barbara is also part of that scene, more socially active than she has ever been and loving every moment.

Saturday, December 20 Today is the Christmas party for the children of the locally-engaged staff at the Commission. Santa makes a dramatic appearance into the compound on a richly caparisoned elephant, and a sea of rapt little brown faces look on in wonder. True to tradition, he comes complete with a heavily laden sack, and dispenses largesse to every child. This is followed by a feast of wonderfully indigestible goodies, and all that is left is to count the days until the same delirious occasion next year.

Sunday, December 21 The kitchen is mine, so I bake Christmas cake and shortbread. Hermione sits close to the stove watching me, as I am sadly watching her. She is, I know, going slowly downhill. There never was a sweeter dog, and to see her try to wag her tail is so heart-rending. Hilary is devastated and holds her paw by the hour. I continue to take her down to Dr Singh, but Doug has no faith in him and is sure he doesn't know what he is doing. Hermione's glands are swollen and she has ceased to eat.

Tonight is the party at the Residence and it is lovely. The teenagers are invited, and Hilary is only a little miffed that she can't go. She has to admit that her heart would not be in it with Herm so sick.

It really is quite delightful, with old-fashioned games and the singing of English and French carols, plus a quite remarkable magician. For a little while we exiles become a special kind of family, diverse in interests and even language, but a family just the same.

Wednesday December 24   Christmas Eve, and this the day and this the happy hour – our children are arriving at worse than the usual ungodly hour – 1.40am. There seemed little point in going to bed last night, but we did set the alarm, and the joy of having the family together makes up for any lack of sleep. The travellers look tired (and are) but we still sit up and talk until about 4.30am. A couple of hours of sleep, then up to head for the Ashoka to have my hair done.

Some instinct tells me to check with Tony about Christmas dinner tomorrow. "Fish," says he. *Fish? Fish?* I completely flip – what on earth did he think I got the turkey for? With this monumental goof over Christmas dinner, what jolly Indian surprises does he have for our Boxing Day party?

I try not to sound cross, and go over every detail of tomorrow's meal. I would happily make some things tonight, but he would lose face, and I really don't want to hurt him.

We are all exhausted, but dutifully set the alarm and go off to the Cathedral for midnight mass. The church is almost empty and we find, almost too late, that everyone is squeezed into an enormous shamiana set up in the churchyard.

It is sardine-packed; there are flickering candles everywhere and several open braziers – a tragedy waiting to happen. All these floating saris, one errant candle and... disaster. Doug insinuates us into a position beside a flap in the tent, which we hope may provide a safe exit. Neither church nor service is what they should be. I do not experience one iota of spiritual feeling, and I am sure neither does anyone else. We are freezing, bored and uncomfortable, and after what seems an eternity, we stumble out at 2.00pm.

It is so still beyond the clamour and crush of the shamiana. The stars are out and provide the only light apart from the glow of the odd campfire. Here we are, on the edge of the Delhi plain; there could be shepherds keeping watch by night, and for the first time I begin to feel what one is supposed to feel on Christmas Eve, as our whole family, together again, walk out into that "hushed and holy night".

Thursday, December 25   The snow should be falling and the

217

carol ships should be in the harbour, but we exiles wake up to a bright December sun. Nobody is up all that early, and when I come down Tony has the doors to the living room and dining room closed, and is preparing breakfast.

The family slowly filters down, and we call Tony in to give him his Christmas bonus, a present for Mary, his wife, and financial bonuses for Muni and Gopi Chand. Doug has managed to get a type of eggnog at the American Commissary (with the addition of rum, who cares if it is not quite the real thing) and we all open our presents.

Peter gives me *Canajan, eh?* (a glossary of Canadianisms, English version) and Kilmeny's gift is *French-Canajan, eh?* (a glossary of French Canadianisms); Hilary's is three ceramic wise men she made herself, and Barbara's is a lovely sketch of our house in West Vancouver. Doug has come up with a silver punch bowl and 12 matching cups, just in time for tomorrow's do. All in all there is a feeling of flowing blessings. This is now the time when I customarily go into the kitchen to make breakfast, and stuff the turkey. Not in this privileged set up, I don't. Tony comes in with leis of marigolds for each of us and, pulling back the dining room door, leads us into a breakfast of pancakes, sausages and bacon.

We have barely finished breakfast when the first 'Christmas wallah' appears. He and his dancing bear await us outside. We all troop out onto the patio, and the performance begins. The bear is a trifle mangy, but extremely agreeable, proffering the odd paw and lumbering into a waltz or jig depending on the tempo of his master's music. Both are rewarded handsomely for their efforts, and the wallah salaams and we wish him a Merry Christmas (form only – he speaks no English). Man and bear are followed by a snake charmer, with your friendly neighbourhood cobra. I know the cobra is under control, but I keep a sharp eye on him nonetheless.

The last visitor is the monkey wallah, and he really is a class act. He has two small monkeys who leap around to the sound of his tambourine, but really come into their own in a mock wedding. From a dilapidated bag, the master pulls out a once white, frilly dress and tiny veil. The little female joyfully gets herself outfitted. The boy monkey dons a turban, and the tambourine beats out some wedding music. It is then that the bride has second thoughts and turns all coy and virginal. The groom gets down on one furry knee, is spurned, tries a kiss, is shrieked at and finally trudges off dejectedly and sobs in the arms of his master. The bride repents, pats him on the shoulder and they end up in a Hollywood-style clinch, with wild applause from the entire Denny clan.

We have been invited for a Christmas morning noggin at the Parkers. They are Vasant Vihar neighbours and she is a member of my British bridge group. It is a pleasant and relaxed group, and we spend a convivial hour or so. Next event on this remarkably carefree Christmas day is an excursion to the Qutb Minar. We are back around 3.00pm. Doug's office nurse and her husband arrive to wish us a Merry Christmas. A couple of preprandials with them, then the family is gathered into the dining room for Christmas dinner. Tony claimed last night that this festive banquet was all new to him. A little waffle, I think. After all, he did cook for the British Army, who must have sprung for turkey and Christmas pudding in the best Anglo tradition. Whatever – he has risen to the occasion and produced a quite splendid dinner. We all thank Tony warmly and give him deserved praise for his meal.

It really has been a lovely Christmas – offbeat, untraditional and exotic perhaps – but still Christmas. The only sad note is Hermione, who seems to be slipping away. It breaks my heart to see her so thin, but still so loyal, so loving and so dear to us all.

After Tony leaves for the night, I slip into the kitchen to check on the preparations for tomorrow's brunch. The menu consists of quiches, stuffed crepes, salads, rolls and desserts. My worst fears are realized. I see the quiches have been organized with the crepe stuffing (no eggs) and the crepes with the quiche filling. What to do? As the old song goes – "let's put out the light and go to sleep."

Friday, December 26 Up at 7.00am and go straight into the kitchen (I *am* getting bold). Tell Tony to make some more pastry shells, and we begin all over again. Fortunately he had not yet stuffed the crepes. So, under my none too kindly direction – I blush to say – we pull things together.

Doug meanwhile busies himself making the punch, and

the smell that permeates the house is pure intoxication all by itself. The house looks lovely and the grounds beautiful. Tables have been set up on the lawn and under the trees. I kept assuring the children it will not rain because it is now the dry season, but nature is a great one for flukes, so I am incredibly relieved to find the day is sunny and warm with the gentlest of breezes.

The guests begin to arrive at the expected hour – the youngsters all closing ranks in a quiet spot in the garden. All in all, with the rescued menu and Doug's masterful and potent punch, the party is an enormous success. I lose track but I think about 40 to 45 people showed up.

Saturday, December 27 Two parties on the calendar for today. The first a luncheon at the Gormans, with all the children invited. Hilary, as usual, is mistaken for a small boy, and Heather promises her she will never invite the misguided offender again. Kilmeny and Peter leave early to go to a tennis party, but arrive home in time to get organized for tonight's 'Vicar and Trollop' party at the McGillvrays. They have been invited as well, being in their late teens, and we spend the rest of the afternoon organizing costumes. Peter really is a dab hand when it comes to any form of construction. He and Kilmeny decide to go as Irma La Douce *et son flic*, and Peter whips up a very professional-looking kepi out of a dark blue Eaton's box someone had brought from Canada. I have been lent a black wig, which looks properly tarty and just right for my Sadie Thompson to Doug's Reverend Davidson from W Somerset Maugham's *Rain*.

I thought we were rather effective – *but nobody had ever heard of them!!* Doesn't anybody read any more, I ask myself? Still, it is a fun party and we all tumble home around 2.30am.

Sunday, December 28 A lovely slopping-around morning – playing quizzes, drinking Bloody Marys and munching post-Christmas goodies. Duty calls in the way of an invitation to tea at the home of one of Doug's Indian doctors. Very hospitable and kind, but equally stiff – my repertoire of social opening gambits is increasing, although I wonder if a spray of fixative would help the smile.

An invitation from a couple at the American Embassy includes the children, as it is a Christmas party complete with an imported movie. They have a vast house, and we are given a drink on entering and then ushered into the screening room. The movie is ancient – Fred Astaire and Ginger Rogers in *Top Hat* – but with all the R-rated films being produced these days, I guess the hosts felt it was safe for a family party. An American-style dinner follows and we are home by 11.00pm.

Wednesday, December 31 New Year's Eve, and the days have whizzed by – I want to stop time, and keep the children here with me, and things as they are, with teas at the Oberoi and tennis parties and outings to Old Delhi. We have nothing on for tonight, and plan to have a family feast at midnight with lobster and champagne. Doug moved heaven and earth to organize the lobster from the American Commissary. Meanwhile we have to pick up the travellers' tickets at JAL, and take some of Hermione's specimen samples to the lab (such as it is). She is now being force-fed with consommé and eggnog, poor little dog. I think with sadness of how she used to bounce through the woods on our walks, or race along the beach. It is just such a shame that this beautiful little dog should be made to suffer, and in my heart of hearts, I know we must help it to end.

We have a festive lunch at Claridge's, and an orgy of shopping to take back to Canada. Tony tells me Monica Barker has phoned to ask if we will be in this evening, as they would like to call by. I am delighted, and we are playing charades when they come in. They make a big hit with the kids, and we are having such a lovely time that it is 11.00pm before they go – more than somewhat late for their party, which started at 8.30. After they leave I organize the Lobster Thermidor, the champagne is popped and we toast the New Year. I am so happy we are together, and happy that we are happy being so and in the joy of the moment even forget to worry about when we will not be.

CHAPTER 28

Thursday, January 1, 1976 The New Year dawns bright and sunny, and we all rush off for the Canadian Monkey Golf Tournament. I don't mind this at all, because nobody expects any pro golf and it is strictly for laughs. My team is the High Commissioner, somebody's visiting brother-in-law, young Chris Sen and me, This gallant little band does surprisingly well – I even sink a couple of putts. When the points are added up, through some miracle, we win. Lunch is laid on at the Cabana and after a noggin or two everyone is in such a jolly mood, you can't tell the winners from the losers.

Friday, January 2 The faithful Tony is up at 5.00am to make breakfast for the three departees, who are leaving at the customary impossible hour for home, via Bombay, Paris and London. It is a great adventure for them, but we see them off reluctantly.

Doug is convinced that Hermione has leukaemia or a carcinoma of the lymphatic system, and has spent sometime trying to arrange for a biopsy on one of the swellings on her neck. It will be done at the clinic of a local vet, then taken for a pathology test at the Holy Family hospital.

I wait in the reception for ages, and it is suggested I return in an hour. Poor little Hermione. Doug attended and said it was terrible – the vet did not seem to know what he was doing, and the dog bled profusely. She finally comes out, terribly weak and swathed in blankets.

Saturday, January 3 Look anxiously at Herm, who struggles to follow Doug downstairs. I take her to the vet for further shots, although I have little hope.

Tuesday, January 6 Barbara has her first game of golf, and after a few flubs, plays really well, and shows every sign of being a natural. I give my caddy Sampat a belated gift of a carton of cigarettes. He is delighted, and will probably always 'find' my ball in a perfect alignment with the hole.

Wednesday, January 7 The day I have been dreading. Doug phones to tell me he has received the results of the biopsy – malignant lymphoma. We discuss how to tell Hilary. Doug is for telling her tonight, but I am all for waiting until it is a *fait accompli*. The thought of her patting her little doomed dog and imagining what is ahead of her is horrible. Eileen Parker phones to ask after Herm and I tell her. Hilary is upstairs, but I wonder if she hears because she stays in her room and is very subdued at dinner.

Thursday, January 8 I hate the thought of seeing Doug go off with Herm and disappear, only to find that he hasn't taken her. Heaven knows I don't want her to suffer, but nonetheless, I feel a sense of reprieve. It is obvious, though, that she is getting more and more uncomfortable. I come downstairs, and cannot believe my eyes. Tony is bent over, stroking Herm. He has always treated dogs like carbuncles, and never gave Herm the time of day. I am touched, and will remember this the next time he does something outrageous and I want to throttle him.

Hilary is at a friend's house and asks if Doug can pick her up. He comes home early and takes Hermione off, and says he will collect Hilary after the event. Barbara and I do not want to look at one another. About 6.30pm Doug returns. Hilary does not come in to join us but goes directly up to her room. Doug, looking suspiciously close to tears himself, says she took it very hard, poor little girl. I want to go up to her, but he says it is better to leave her alone. After awhile we hit on the solution of going to the American Theatre to see *That's Entertainment*. Nobody thinks Hilary will go, but I say I will try. When I go into her room, she is lying on her bed and the sight of her tear-stained face starts me off, too. I tell her we all feel so miserable that we thought it might help us to go to see a silly movie. She wipes her eyes with the back of her hand (having abandoned a sodden handkerchief) and nods. We hug each other, and I tell her that Herm was the nicest dog I have ever known (she *was*) and that she, Hilary, is lucky to have experienced such total and unquestioning devotion – a love that is like no other.

The movie is predictably diverting, and "like a bridge over

troubled waters" helps us to the other side.

Sunday, January 11   Monica and Hamish are hosting the
United Kingdom Citizen's Association Lunch, and we are
invited. Jim Parker is away, and we offer to pick up Eileen, but
she is anxious to drive her brand new car, so we go alone. It is
a pleasant party, but a little stiff. We stay for a while after the
others leave for what Monica called "a trashing of the
departees."

Eileen asks if she can follow us home. She has to stop at a
light, and we wait for her. She starts up again, and then we see
her stopped in the middle of the road. Doug, fearful that she
has run into someone, goes back to help her. *Au contraire.*
While she was sitting at the red light, two buses on either side
started up and squeezed her, one creasing the whole side of
the spanking new car. She is all too understandably furious,
and demands that the driver stop. He has no intention of doing
so, but Doug puts his hand up (just like a traffic policeman – I
was quite impressed) and the sight of a Sahib was all that was
needed. Fortunately, or so we think, a policeman is on duty at
the intersection, and Doug calls him over. The scraped side is
displayed, Eileen sputters her indignation, and Doug asks for
the driver's license. He doesn't have one, has never had one,
and the policeman just smiles sheepishly, spreads his open
hands and shrugs apologetically. It is, to us, absolutely
incredible that the driver of a public vehicle loaded with
citizenry has no driver's licence. India never ceases to amaze
me.

Thursday, January 15   I host a bridge and luncheon, the
date of which had to be arranged and re-arranged. The expat
social calendar is becoming increasingly busy. For the first
time, I am satisfied with the results of the planned menu. Tony
did all the chopping and left the ingredients in the kitchen for
me to put together last night. This doesn't sound entirely fair,
as Tony is an excellent cook and has produced a lot of good
meals – but the operative corollary is, if I don't interfere. If I
plan the menu and try to give instructions it ends up a
culinary disaster.

Saturday, January 17 Barbara is spending almost every hour studying for her 'O' levels – she has so much to catch up on, trying as she is to do two years' work in one. Hilary is going to a birthday party and we go shopping together for a birthday present. On the way up to Vasant Vihar I stop in at the vet's to pay our bill. I feel it courteous to tell him about Herm, although it obviously hadn't bothered him that we had taken her elsewhere.

Monday, January 19 Barbara sits her 'O' level Biology, the exam taking almost four hours. I put in my stint at the American school library, but there's not a great deal to do, and I wonder if I am really needed. I would almost welcome the Grade 12s asking me to look up information for their projects for them.

Tuesday, January 20 Attend a lecture by the *Hindustani Times* cartoonist – quite interesting, but surprisingly apolitical. I suppose that with the recent censorship, he is wise to take a neutral position.

Thursday, January 22 The UK golf champion is giving lessons at the Delhi Club this morning, and Monica has asked me to join her in taking part. The pro is Roger Bacon who, after watching my death's grip on the club, tells me golf is for fun and to relax. I ask him if, in all his teaching experience, he ever lost control and found himself rolling on the ground, helpless with laughter? I swear his lips are forming "Not until now..." but he catches himself in time.

Saturday, January 24 A busy day, driving Doug to golf, Barbara to lessons and Hilary to riding. A brief relaxation when I pick up Doug, and the long-suffering Roger Bacon joins us for a drink.

A cocktail party in the evening presents me with another challenge in my ongoing struggle to become conversationally fluent in French. I am introduced to a charming French lady, with whom, wonder of wonders, I manage to chat quite well (or so I think). Who is to say? With the French it is *toujours la politesse.* I am reminded of a lovely essay I read years ago,

Confessions of a Francophile. The author, like me, had persevered through irregular verbs and even more irregular pronunciations, but lacked practice. He finally made the acquaintance of a defrocked French priest, who promised to converse with him. Our poor *Anglais* thought he was doing splendidly, but apparently reeled off stately sentences such as: "Is it not a handsome day that begins," or really obscure ones such as "I notice no insult – you merely gnaw my arm."

In any event I do not detect any twitching of the lip on the part of my companion, so I can but hope I committed no such gaucheries.

Monday January 26 Republic Day and Tony asks for time off to see the parade. I say of course, and tell him not to bother with breakfast, as everyone would probably prefer to sleep in, nor does he need to concern himself about lunch. But, I say, I would like him back for dinner. He seems mildly taken aback by this, and I realize I should have said to take the whole day off. However he has had quite a bit of time off lately – we've been out so much – so I repeat that he need not be back until dinner time.

Barbara's friend Marion joins us and we pack a picnic and head out the Jaipur Road. We stop at a government rest house, with a pretty garden and picnic area, but the young declare it is "too public", so we opt for a nearby lake. It is pretty barren, with a few wandering cattle and women beating out clothes on the lakeshore We find a bit of shade under a thorn tree and enjoy the Sunday night leftover chicken. Returning home at 4.00pm, we ask Marion to stay for dinner, but there is no Tony by 5.00, and still no Tony by 6.00. It is now obvious that he has no intention of returning. I am furious – if he had come out and asked for the whole day, I would have given it to him – but that enigmatic nod should have told me he would try this little act of rebellion on for size.

Doug and I talk it over. Is this the last straw, or do we give him another chance? Doug is all for the latter, and I, remembering his patting of Herm, soften. However, coward that I am, I ask Doug to talk to him tomorrow. For one thing, I get too emotional and my anger shows through, making me feel like a 19th-century Memsahib. Besides, Tony has much more

226

respect for Doug than he has for me. This settled, we head for the ACSA Lounge and munch on hamburgers, concluding the day with shuffleboard and bowling. God bless America!

Tuesday, January 27 Doug does the needful with Tony. As usual, he is calm, decisive and unequivocal. Tony is told he deliberately ignored my instructions, and if he ever does that again he and Muni (why Muni?) will both be fired. Period and amen, and that is that!

The High Commission has given a lot of business to Japan Air Lines, and tonight we are being wined and dined by the local representative. There is quite a number of HC staff on hand. The whole affair is extremely elegant and extremely expensive, and we all lap it up as our due.

Saturday, January 31 The Willis Trophy Polo match, and very exciting it is. See the Barkers, with son Ewan, and invite them all back for dinner. He seems a nice young man, and Barbara describes him as "dishy".

Wednesday, February 4 The Powers That Be have informed Doug that they will be sending out a young doctor, currently stationed in Rome, to be 'seasoned' by Doug. As Doug himself has only been 'seasoned' for a year, this is either a compliment, a mistake, or said doctor has been proving a pain in the neck in Rome. Doug picks him up at the usual ungodly hour of Delhi arrivals. He brings him home for breakfast and leaves him to me while he goes upstairs to shave.

The newcomer presents rather an extraordinary figure. He is wearing jeans and cowboy boots, and a bored and petulant expression. Doug has managed to drop a hint or two that I may find the doctor a bit truculent. It seems his entire conversation while driving in the dawn hours along Palam Road consisted of a series of "Oh, Gods" as he looked out at the murky fields, the huddled roadside dwellers, the cows and the filth. He carries this aura of despair into the dining room as Tony brings in breakfast. I ask him if he is enjoying the pleasures of Rome.

"It's all right," is his response. "Girls are hard to get, but not for me, of course." I gaze at his pimply face and hobbledehoy stance and wonder, but persist.

"Well, it's a great city, and the social life must be wonderful."

"Not really," he replies. "I am a realist, and they don't like my fascist views." With all the unpleasantness of 30 years ago behind us, I am not surprised, but gamely change the subject and mutter something about India being fascinating, to which he responds:

"It looks godawful to me." Pinching his skin, he adds, "You see that – that's white – and that makes me different, and nothing is going to change that."

I don't know what I could have said to this incontrovertible truth, but happily Doug comes down for breakfast, and I make my excuses and go off to ponder from what planet our guest could possibly have wandered.

Thursday, February 5 A dinner party to introduce the new MO to Delhi society and to his fellow toilers at the High Commission. A successful enough party, but Dr H endears himself to no one, including me. One parting guest hisses in Doug's ear, "Don't *ever* go away."

Saturday, February 7 One of my Christmas presents was an IOU from Doug for a new suede coat. A Kashmiri salesman, all oily smiles and salaams, has been a regular visitor, spreading out shawls and rugs and embroidered yards of material. One day he appeared with some beautiful, deep blue suede. We were both impressed and a coat was duly ordered. I rather fancied a double-breasted mid-calf job, with a slight flare. A picture was drawn, and he beamed. I have offered him the joys of paradise to be allowed to produce so beautiful a garment, and off he went, promising to return in a week. He arrived in two, with what Doug suspected was a different quality of suede, already cut and basted. Doug questioned the material, but there were so many denials and calls upon Allah to bear witness that we gave up. It seemed to fit all right except, as Doug pointed out, it appeared to be higher at the back than the front. The salesman promised to fix it, and he also re-iterated his initial promise that if I don't like it, I do not have to pay. He returned later and I tried it on once more.

He always appears at dinner, and I happened to be

"Oh yes, it is because the Memsahib is wearing shoes"

wearing a long skirt. Even so, I got the impression that the coat was shorter than before. Doug told him it was still higher at the back and may need a new panel cut, but warned him *not* to shorten the front. The salesman looked shocked at the very thought and gave Doug the look of a spaniel that has just been kicked by the 'walkies' lady. All will be well.

Tonight he returns and I try on what I can only describe as a car-coat-length jacket. Doug is convinced the suede is indeed of lesser quality, and I am sure the shade is not quite what I picked out, and a scene ensues. Suddenly the salesman's face lights up like a beacon, and you can almost see the light bulb of an idea floating above his head.

"Ah Sahib," he beams, "I know the problem. Oh yes, it is because the Memsahib is wearing shoes. If she will remove the shoes with heels, all will be well."

For one strange, frightening moment, it almost makes sense. Then logic returns, and I protest that it is a winter coat, and I will always wear shoes, or boots. Doug is all for telling him what he can do with his mini-coat and refusing to pay. I just want to be rid of him, so he is paid off, with Doug banishing him from the premises forever and sending him scooting off with a final Parthian shot: "And that goes for the entire Diplomatic Enclave."

CHAPTER 29

Monday, February 9 Today we are starting off on our journey to the heart of India's faith: Benares or Varanasi, depending on how modern you are.

I meant to make up a picnic last night, but my personal moral code (which Doug considers asinine in the extreme) dictates that if I mess up the kitchen on Sunday, I should clean it up. Ergo, I stayed up late last night after our dinner guest left, and the picnic remains unmade.

Tony's picnics are slap-dash affairs, but he pulls something together by the time the High Commission driver appears. We have drawn Ram Bahadur (known among the staff as the Chapati Kid). He is young, considered something of a wild driver, but he has a wonderful smile and enormous joy in life, so we all go off, grinning away at one another.

In an informal sort of way, I have decided to make the following of the Sepoy Mutiny of 1857 a hobby. So far, I have managed to go to Meerut, where it all began, with the rioting of the Sepoys, and the killing of the officers and their families as they emerged from church on that fateful May morning. From Meerut to The Ridge, scene of the Siege of Delhi. It was in this area that I found signs of the fortification, and saw where the heroic young officer blew up the arsenal and himself along with it, rather than let it fall into enemy hands. I have also explored St James Church, with its memories of Skinner's Horse and regimental memorabilia. St James churchyard reveals countless tragedies in its headstones, but perhaps none sadder than the story of Mr Beresford, manager of the Chartered Bank (I think it was the Chartered Bank), his wife and five little daughters.

They had just finished breakfast, and Mrs B was still in her loose morning dress, as were the little girls. Their bearer (through the jungle telegraph) was aware of the approaching rioters, and was in an agony of indecision. On the one hand was his loyalty to his own and their cause; on the other was this innocent family, whose children he adored.

The moral laws of the East are complex and to a Westerner sometimes incomprehensible – but those who have taken the King's shilling must die in his service, as the Indian ethical code has it. Perhaps, in a lesser way, that is how the bearer saw it, and the decision was already made for him. In any case, in a panic he gathers the family together, shouting and screaming them into action, and leads them up to the sanctuary of the roof of the Bank. He is only just in time, as the raging Sepoys begin a horror of looting and killing.

They rampage through the bank house, and are about to leave, when one looks back. The bearer had told everyone to lie flat on the roof, but the white muslin skirt of one of the little girls is caught by the breeze and becomes visible to the watcher below. With a shout he calls to the others. Shrieking with laughter and mad with the need to destroy, they storm up to the roof, and slaughter the terrified family, running the bearer through as he stretches his arms in front of the children. There is a memorial plaque in St James Church with the names of all the Beresfords who died on that sunlit morning for no reason they knew.

Now we are on our way to Lucknow, the scene of the 87-day siege, and the site of one of the last battles in the Mutiny. Raj, Doug's secretary, has family living here, and we barely check into the hotel, before her brother phones to ask us to his Club for dinner. He has invited another couple, and we have a very interesting evening. The wife is young, attractive and very modern in her outlook, and yet she tells us she had an arranged marriage. This surprises me, as she seems the type who would have done her own picking and choosing. Nonetheless her marriage has turned out very happily.

She recounts that she was in a convent school when her parents sent word that a suitable boy would be coming to inspect his potential future bride. She said the nuns allowed her to wear her sari, but went easy on the kohl and *bindi* (a forehead beauty spot) as they said they did not want her returned after the wedding "not as advertised".

She was so terrified she did not even look up when the young man presented himself. As a matter of fact she said she never actually saw his face until the day of the wedding, when he took her hand and she finally dared to raise her eyes.

Despite her contemporary attitude and western-style education, she still believes arranged marriages are desirable. A great deal of time and thought goes into the selection process by one's parents, and in most enlightened families the bride's wishes are considered. The similarity of background and community of interests seem to be a major part of the formula. I love her description of the difference between western and eastern marriages: "Marriage in the west is like taking a boiling pot of water off the stove and waiting for it to simmer down. Eastern marriages are like putting a cold pot of water on and waiting for it to come to a boil." Neat.

Tuesday, February 10 We had planned to get away earlier, but had reckoned without the Chapati Kid. In the exuberance and speed of our passage to Lucknow, we sustained a flat tire. However, "sweet are the uses of adversity..." Doug is able to see his DMP at leisure, and I can do what I really want to do, explore the Lucknow Residency, the site of the siege. Having read an entire book on the event, I feel I knew the people involved intimately, having suffered with them as they descended into that hell of fear, hunger and filth. It is an eerie sensation seeing it now more than a hundred years later.

The surrounding walls are still standing, as is the Residency, which has been turned into a museum. I am the sole visitor, and I wander in and out of the abandoned rooms, accompanied by the shades of Sir Henry Lawrence, the Governor, and people like the gentle, pampered Katherine Bartrum, who was reduced to killing and boiling rats to feed her child. I can almost believe I hear the bagpipe echoes of the *Campbells Are Coming*, which must have sounded like an angel choir to the besieged.

Interestingly enough, no attempt has ever been made to restore the Residency. It remains much as it was the day the relieving force marched in through the ruined gates to find several hundred starving, ragged and hysterical survivors of the original 3,000 who had refused to surrender.

Inside the Museum, things are in typical Indian shape. I enter a vast room, lined with old etchings and engravings all badly in need of re-framing and re-hanging. On a table in the centre of the room is a model of the Residency as it was in

233

1857. The whole display had obviously been set up by the British after the end of the Mutiny, with neatly printed cards indicating the positions of the defenders and the enemy. Some time in the years after 1947, attempts were made to redefine the antagonists. Nothing as fancy as having the cards reprinted, mind you, but instead there is a simple scratching out wherever the word 'enemy' appears to be replaced by 'Indians', hand-written in crayon. The accompanying legend has not been altered, but has yellowed with age and is encrusted with flies.

On the way back, Ram Bahadur stops to show me the new monument erected to the 'Indian Martyrs in the Fight for Freedom'. It is a high white tower, surrounded by scads of ghastly elephants, all painted in milk-of-magnesia white, with kohl-rimmed eyes and with their trunks pointing toward heaven. It is located on the edge of the embankment with the river in background, and the farther away you get, the better it looks, until it even begins to appear quite impressive.

Back at the hotel, Doug and I wait for Ram to return with the mended tire, and I bone up a little on what we are not going to have time to see, more's the pity. Lucknow in the 18th century was the foremost city in Oudh, a place of supreme and beautiful gardens and a centre for the arts, particularly Urdu poetry. We have only touched the surface.

When Ram returns we leave for Varanasi. I have yet to learn why Benares was changed to Varanasi, and 90 per cent of the populace are with me, as just as many people call it Benares as call it by the new name. As a matter of fact, most books I have consulted seem to feel Benares is how it is most commonly known.

The drive there is full of the most extraordinary traffic. For a devout Hindu, to be cremated on the banks of the Ganges (Holy Mother Ganga) is to have one foot in heaven, and so they come bearing their dead to the sacred flames of the ghats. The shrouded figures are brought on every imaginable type of transport – on the luggage rack of cars, the swaddlings flapping in the wind, on the running boards of mini-buses and one even being dragged along on a litter tied to a bicycle. The shrouds distinguish the sex and status of the deceased: white is for men, saffron for priests and holy men and red for women.

We follow this bizarre procession at a snail's pace, and eventually reach this holiest of cities. It is now 5.30pm, and the world is slipping from dusk to dark, so we are content to stay within the classy confines of the new Varanasi Hotel.

Wednesday, February 11 Up at 5.30am and out to greet the sunrise on Holy Mother Ganga. It is chilly and I am glad of my woollies and warm jacket. We walk down the steps to the river, accompanied by a highly suspect temple priest, who waves to an extremely eager boatman. The wide steps are dotted with platforms and bamboo umbrellas, under which the temple priests are praying devoutly with one eye out for a likely mark. Our boatman has taken no chances and is waiting at the top of steps. Just before getting into our boat, I buy a couple of candles and a marigold garland to cast out on the river. Doug raises his eyebrows, but the gesture appeals to me, and I must say it looks lovely bobbing along as the rising sun chases the dawn mists and turns the waters to gold. The sights along the river are extraordinary. Temples line the banks, and at the first of the ghats hundreds of pilgrims bathe, wash their clothes and brush their hair (and, dear God, their teeth) in the filthy river.

We spot a number of Sadhus (holy men), still as the dawn, praying on the riverbank. Higher up even some young and not-so-young westerners are doing likewise. Most of this latter group are robed in Hindu dress, sitting in the lotus position with hands clasped together in prayer. Personally, I find them (perhaps unfairly) more than somewhat pretentious. Maybe they are, indeed, seekers after truth and spiritual wisdom, but I have a feeling that this is the 'in' thing for today's youth, just as mooning around Montmartre was What One Did in Hemingway's generation.

Our guide, anxious to please, gives a running commentary as we drift along the river. He explains about the purification of fire, and tells us that some of those who have died cannot be cremated. These are babies, who have had no time to be corrupted; priests and holy men, who presumably are incorruptible; and victims of cholera and leprosy. This last lot requires some inner pondering on my part, which gives voice in a stream of questions to our guide. He waffles and inclines his

235

The sights along the river are extraordinary

236

head in the all-too-familiar gesture and I never really do get clear answers. However, I figure out that it probably has something to do with not wanting to come back in that particular body when one reaches Nirvana. In any event the custom is to weight these bodies (however imperfectly) and throw them into the river. I find myself looking with some degree of anxiety at the surface of the water for any unseemly blips. With the sun now fully risen, the boatman takes us back to the main ghat, where a body is in the process of being burned. Our guide tells us that it takes between three and four hours for a "normal, healthy body" to burn. How healthy can a dead body be, I ask myself? The cost of cremation ranges from 45 to 400 rupees, depending on the quality and dryness of the wood. Top price is for sandalwood. There is a snag, however, and our guide shakes his grey head at the infamy of man.

The etiquette of ghat cremation is that the eldest son (or senior male) lights the funeral pyre; the family members make their farewells and depart. As soon as they are safely away, the unscrupulous attendant has been known to remove the expensive sandalwood to serve another day, and substitute some 'el cheapo' wood, with nobody any the wiser. I am sure that in all these years, somebody must have caught on to this scam. Still, I could not help but notice that in the general squalor of the riverfront, the only building that appears in the least bit grand is the home of a ghats entrepreneur, which bespeaks one who is doing a brisk and profitable trade.

The House of Widows is another riverfront property. Since the British forbade the suttee there have been no more widows immolating themselves uselessly on the funeral pyres. However, there are still certain circumstances, spiritual and secular, in which women cannot remarry. Those without means, or children to care for them, end up in this House, where they pass their days in chanting and in prayer. What a peachy life! A far cry, think I, from the glamorous widows of song and story in the western world, with their winter cruises and devoted toy boys.

Our boat docks and our guide takes us up for a closer look at the burning ghats. Doug is scientifically fascinated and intrigued but I find it more than a trifle macabre. I can't bear to see the foot sticking out of the flames, and watch the uncaring attendant poking away at it with his stick of green bamboo to aid it in burning faster. Once Doug is satisfied with the disarticulating of bones, our priest leads us up higher and higher into the heart of the city. The steps are indescribable, befouled with cow dung and human excrement, and lined with lingam (the phallic symbol of Shiva, Benares being the City of Shiva). He leads us into a maze of crowded, teeming streets and fetid alleyways, and finally into a narrow passageway where he announces we will see Benares silks and brocades being woven: "A very great sight, indeed, oh yes, a very great sight." I simply cannot imagine anything beautiful being created in this nightmarish place, but more fool me. We are led into a vast room, where we see first a loom, and then a greeter. He is a rather effeminate young man with a lisp and a hideous itch. He never stops scratching as he unrolls one fabulous and exquisite length of material after another.

Of course, we are bid "only too look" (although I always feel as though the door is being mentally locked behind us). It would not have made any difference. I forget all about the smells, the verminous salesman and the clutching guide, and succumb to a wondrous brocade, lit by subtle ambers and golds. There is a good deal of bowing and smiling (and, I am sure, a rake-off for the 'priest') after this purchase, and we leave with the blessings of Shiva being called down upon our heads.

I swear we will never make it out through this bewildering labyrinth of streets, but somehow we emerge to catch a glimpse of the golden trident of Shiva and the gold-leafed roof of the Temple. Through a miracle we find the Chapati Kid. He is engaged in a game of chance with some locals but is all smiles as he drives us back to the hotel for breakfast. Later we pick up some sandwiches for lunch and start out on the road to Patna.

It is an uninspired landscape, with low-lying marshes on either side of the road, precluding any chance of a sylvan-style picnic. Instead we find ourselves munching very dry sandwiches as we jolt along over impossibly bad roads. By the time we reach Patna and the Republic Hotel, one tire is completely flat and the car covered with bugs. The Republic Hotel, hidden behind a ramshackle garage, is pretty awful and very, very dirty. We do have a bathroom, but neither of us wants to sink into the stained and rusting tub. We tough our way through dinner, declining the proffered water and go early to bed, once again using our sleeping bags, since the beds do not come with sheets. The mosquitoes from the Patna swamps come calling in large numbers, and although the beds are equipped for mosquito netting, it is for swank only, as there are no nets. We have reason to be grateful for the Raid insect killer I had so presciently brought with us.

Thursday, February 12 Only too glad to leave the hospitality of the Republic Hotel. As we are paying our bill, a large rat runs across the hotel ledger. I stifle a scream. The clerk does not turn a hair.

Doug has an appointment at the Holy Family Hospital, and Ram and I wait for him in the car. Had I known Doug would be quite so long, I might have had a bit of a tour, although I could not really think of anything I wanted to see. Patna goes down in my book as a bit of a nothing – at least on the surface. Perhaps if we had more time or knew more about the town, it might have proved interesting. When Doug finally comes out from the hospital at 11.30am, he has an amusing little anecdote to relate that illustrates Patna's sense of priority.

A few years ago, a devastating flood hit the city. With the river rising steadily and heading toward the army encampment and its tanks, there was a hurried conference among the city elders. It would be unthinkable to allow the loss of any military property, but hold on. What they can do is to divert the course of the flood away from the military base and toward the hospital and the core of the city. It apparently was quite a spectacular sight, floating patients out on makeshift rafts, and sending intravenous machines and other hospital equipment a-bobbing on the floodwaters. Doug tells me the hospital has never been quite the same since. By dusk, we are back at the gates of Benares, and into our hotel, a palace among palaces, after Patna's infamous Republic.

Friday, February 13 We head out for a morning of sightseeing, going first to Sarnath and the Buddhist Temple. It is set in a lovely garden and the Temple itself is quite

239

fascinating, with the life of Buddha depicted in some rather splendid murals. These were done by a Japanese artist, and show all the inherent Japanese sense of design, spare and clean, with a lovely balance of colour.

Outside the main window, is a giant stupa, reputedly first built by the Emperor Ashoka in the 2nd century BC. The whole area was the heart of the Mauryan Empire and the great Ashoka was at its core. Ashoka created pillars honouring the precepts of Buddha all over India, but the most famous, the Lion Capital – familiar to all as the symbol on Indian currency – is here in the Sarnath Archaeological Museum.

It was on the site of the stupa that Buddha first started his teaching. On the other side of the temple is a Bo (Bodhi) tree under which Prince Buddha first found enlightenment in the 5th century, and as such is sacred to all Buddhists.

Ashoka, notably tolerant of all faiths, became a convert to Buddhism and adopted it as the state religion, but after his death the religion lost its hold. The story goes that Ashoka's daughter, fearful for the tree's safety, felt that Ceylon might offer it a more sympathetic home, and had it dug up and transported. In 1931, some devout Indian Buddhist took a cutting from the original tree and brought it back to its home in Sarnath, and it is this tree that now flourishes and shades the faithful.

Right at the moment it is also shading the unfaithful. Doug suspects the accuracy of this tale and, unlike me, does not get carried away with visions of the young Prince being revealed an eternal truth. As a matter of fact all visions vanish as Doug suddenly announces that he must get back to the hotel – pronto, *vite*, right away.

"Why?" I squeal. "This is historic – can you believe we are actually under the tree where Buddha found enlightenment?"

To which Doug replies, sensibly enough, that if he doesn't get back to the hotel, and quickly, any passer-by will receive a different kind of enlightenment. We flee. Because of this abrupt change of plans at Buddha's tree, we have to forego the trip to Benares University, which is rather disappointing, but that is Delhi Belly for you. Instead we start our return trip to Lucknow.

We reach there in the late afternoon, and Raj's mother

appears and takes us in tow. She finds us just the right places for all we want to buy, and then rounds up Ram to drive us to her home for dinner.

She has a few other guests, including one deliciously snobby Indian lady. Said guest sweeps into the room majestically and introduces herself with full credentials:

"Mrs Hullander Singh, wife of General H Singh, former Military Attaché at the Indian Embassy in Washington, DC."

I love the way Indians always cram in every honour (or nearly missed honour) as means of identification. A prime example is the doctor in the house across the street from us in Delhi. An engraved plaque tells the world that he is Dr Harish Gupta, F.R.C.S. (Failed), former physician to the ex-President of India.

Mrs S's lovely and charming daughter accompanies her mother, but declines to give her qualifications. Her mother, on the other hand, does not. We are consequently introduced to Asha Kumari, 28, a graduate of Georgetown University in Washington, DC, and affianced to the young Maharajah of Jaipur. This fact is very proudly announced, although Raj's mother tells us later that the Maharajah is reputedly a bit of a lad, a known lush and in the process of divorcing wife Number 2. All in all, it turns out to be a super evening. Asha is a charmer and an interesting conversationalist, and Raj's mother is a real poppet.

Saturday, February 14 Off and away by 9.00 with Ram none too sure of the back tire. As it turns out, not without cause. We keep stopping to pump it up, but finally it is totally flat. Ram changes it for the doubtful spare and we drive on, stopping briefly for lunch. We carry on, with Ram driving at what, for him, is a relatively sedate speed. Suddenly there is a horrendous bang, and the tire bursts, scattering bits of hot rubber across the road, and into the startled path of an oxen cart. Poor Ram digs out the deflated job in the trunk, and sets off for a garage, which a passing mendicant tells him is "just up the road". Which road may well have been the question, as two and a half hours later, a weary Ram returns, having left his watch for security. We redeem it on the homeward lap, but with one thing and another, we reach home in the dark of a winter night around 8.00pm, not much interested in anything but an early night.

CHAPTER 30

Sunday, February 15 Dear Barbara has made up a lunch for our Monkey Golf Tournament with the Brits at Faridabad. Ewan Barker joins Barbara, Doug and I, along with an Australian couple. I receive a real ego-soother – Mrs Aussie is worse than I. The chant of the day is: "Oh bad luck" (ladies' play) and "nice out" (men's play). Being six in our group and with all the drives into the snake-infested thicket, we are painfully slow, and by the time we emerge, most of the players have had their lunch and are ready to depart.

Monday, February 16 Hilary is leaving on a school trip today to the Jim Corbett National Park, and we arise for her dawn departure. A little sadly, I realize my "baby" is growing up. I am obviously needed to drive her to school, but once there, bags are removed and she dashes toward her friends, giving a vague wave in my direction. It has to happen.

Tuesday, February 17 Togged out in my new raw-silk pant suit, an Enid original, I leave with Eileen Parker for the arranged tour of Old Delhi. We start out from the Chartered Bank House with Monica in charge, and begin with Metcalfe House, a large and imposing yellow structure on the banks of the Jumuna River. The history of the Metcalfes runs parallel with the history of British India. Major Thomas Metcalfe built the house in 1830 when he was a Military Commander with the East India Company, his son carrying on the family tradition. It is now a government-run institution that embodies everything from Department of Defence offices to an Institute of Psychology.

From there on to St James Church, built by James Skinner in 1836. It is quite touching for me to see all the memorial plaques on the wall to the people whose fortunes I had followed in my literary journey through the Indian Mutiny. It is a lovely church, with a beautiful simple mahogany altar, flanked by two deeply coloured stained glass windows. We tour the graveyard, then go over to Hamish's handsome office. He cashes a cheque for me, and I take the ladies to lunch at Nurula's restaurant – new to me, but recommended. The lunch is so-so, but the conversation is lively and the group even seems mildly interested in my historical findings. At least they don't shake their watches.

After lunch we wander on to the Bridge of Boats – a bridge built on the palings of large and heavy dories. From there to Kashmiri Gate; Delhi Gate; the hanging bridge and one or two other sights then back to the Bank House for tea. A delightful day, doing the things I most enjoy.

Wednesday, February 18 I am really pleased that Barbara's social life is so pleasantly full, although she is really deep into her 'O' level studies, and almost begrudges the time. Today, arrangements have been made for her to join the Barkers for lunch at some friends in Old Delhi, then she and Ewan will play tennis and go swimming. As for our own social circuit, little did I think a year ago, that our calendar would be so full, that I would have trouble identifying the hosts. I suspect we have been invited to today's luncheon to meet the new British doctor and his wife, who turn out to be absolutely charming, and I really hope we will see a lot of them.

Thursday, February 19 A peril of living abroad is the delay of cheques, bills and bank statements from Canada. I spend the morning at home, sorting out my Indian research material, catching up on my diary and, horror of horrors, trying to sort out our accounts. They *are* in a mess. Certainly hope the receipt comes soon from Martin's school, so we can be reimbursed, as things are looking more than a bit thin in our account at the Bank of Nova Scotia. Also the London Life Insurance is badly muddled and there have been no family allowances received since October – mail strike???

Life here is so far removed from Burnaby and West Vancouver. It isn't just being physically on the other side of the world, it is that I am so deep into the Indian past, in a world of princes and palaces and a pantheon of alien gods that I feel culturally alienated from such things as unbalanced cheque books.

Friday, February 20 Hilary returns in the afternoon – very excited about Jim Corbett and his park and the whole adventurous outing.

Wednesday, February 25 Golf in the morning with Ruth Etzel and then a lunch and bridge at Freya Current's in the HC Compound for visiting Canadian mothers and mothers-in-laws.

I have invited dear Rod, our CIDA friend, and the horrible 'to be seasoned' doctor for dinner, so scurry home to check things out with Tony. I leave him to his own devices, more or less, so dinner is okay. I have come to the conclusion that, for the most part, this is a wise and peaceful course and only a true meanie would also call it cowardly.

Friday, February 27 Off to the American Women's Book Club, and absolutely revel in a recorded performance of *Under Milkwood*. What a genius! I recall a remark someone made about Thomas Wolfe – "a genius, but an unkempt genius" – and the same could have been said about Dylan Thomas. It matters not. I am afloat on the rhythms of his words and carry them with me for the rest of the day, which follows a little more down-to-earth course.

After the Book Club, I rush to find Hilary a present for a birthday party, then over to the British School for their sports day. I have to admit to an inner glow of maternal pride, as Barbara does herself and us proud: first in the 400m, the 800m and the high jump. There's also a first for her relay team and she is the first girl in the mixed mile. A starry showing, and I feel more than slightly emotional as I watch her collecting all these medals, particularly as the only sports thing I ever won was 'Second Prize Junior Dive' and even then I know I was pushed off the diving board.

Saturday, February 28 A madly social day with Doug at golf, tea at the Ashoka, polo game, picking up girls, dropping off girls, cocktails and finally dashing off to Old Delhi for a dinner party at the Bank House. Poor Hamish is having an awful time with his back, but rallies to become his usual charming self and, as ever, an excellent host.

Sunday, February 29 A day which comes only once ever four years. Marion, who is staying with us, and Barbara are studying; Hilary is at a friend's house, and today I set out to show Tony how bread *should* taste. He really is a good cook, but I hate his bread, which is always so dry and tasteless. One of the women at the American Club gave me a recipe for American-style white bread, and with flour from the Commissary, there is no reason why the heavenly scent of a New England bakery should not emanate from our Vasant Vihar kitchen. If I can prove to Tony that this recipe works, and he has the right flour, then we shall be on our way to thanks for our daily bread. A nasty suspicion occurs to me, re the flour. Could he possibly have been siphoning off my Commissary flour and substituting the Indian variety? Unworthy of me to be sure, but also all too likely. I really like to cook, but I have an unblemished record of failure when it comes to making bread. Not this time, I say confidently. I mix and knead and knead again. Cover and wait for it to rise. Everything according to plan, until they emerge from the oven – two little lead pellets. I just do not have it in me, I guess, and I would have dismissed the failure as a genetic flaw, but for the crucial matter of disposing of the evidence. I cannot put them in the garbage for Tony to get rid of, because it is his wont on a Monday morning to uncover any mishaps in the kitchen from Sunday, and has been known to indulge in the odd taunt – "Oh, Memsahib, there were weevils in your cake, ha ha."

I will never be able to criticize his bread again if I let him find these unseemly little lumps. If I pitch them over the wall (which I strongly suspect is one method of garbage disposal employed by Tony) then he will observe them being munched by passing cows at our back gate.

What to do? Perhaps I could hide them among my smalls, and dispose of them on Tuesday when the girls go riding at the Polo Club. No good. Gopi Chand, the dobhi, comes on Monday, and Tony always puts my things away. I can see his joy in finding a couple of rock-hard loaves in the lingerie drawer. Finally, in desperation, I put them in a little zippered travelling bag in the closet and will get rid of them at the first opportunity. Once again the shade of the second Mrs De

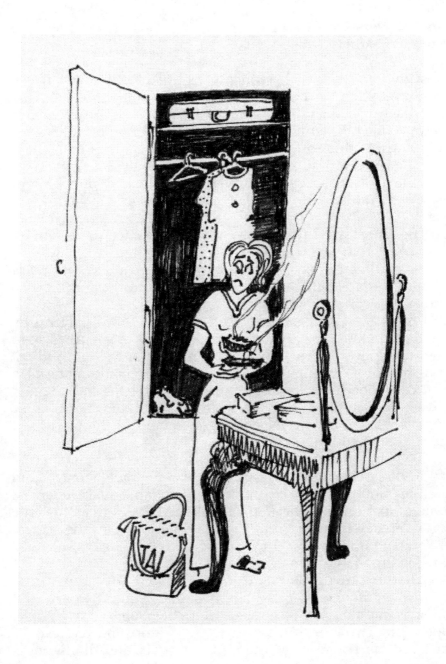

What to do? Perhaps I could hide them among my smalls

Winter hovers, and I realize I run her a close second when it comes to dealing with servants.

Tuesday, March 2 Have lunch with Ruth Etzel after our golf game, and she tells me that one of their people, an American Embassy driver, has died as the result of one of those horrible Indian traffic accidents. I don't mean that Indian accidents are more horrible than any other, but it is the complete disregard for basic rules of the road that causes so many of them. That, plus the fact that driver's licenses are handed out without tests, or in return for a package of cigarettes or a few bottles of beer.

The American driver apparently had an encounter with an army truck that was on the wrong side of the road. It was all terribly sad, as the poor man was really hard up and had five children. No one will be held responsible and there will be no redress in a court of appeal.

Ruth's story makes me recall my own traffic adventure, and how lucky I was. I was driving down a quiet, treed road when suddenly a man jumped out in front of the car and fell down, writhing in apparent agony. I was creeping along at a snail's pace because I wasn't sure of the street numbers, and so was able to stop a good few feet in front of him. Fortunately for me someone saw it all, and could vouch for the fact that I had not touched him.

It is an oft-repeated scam. The 'victim' frequents some well-to-do neighbourhood, recognizes a foreign car, and carefully plots his 'fall'. He manages to collapse just under the bumper, and feigns a broken leg, arm or both, agrees to settle for a predetermined number of rupees, and the driver (preferably a woman) who wants no hassle, pays up and watches the 'victim' run off with the loot.

When I related this tale to Doug, he said if it happened to him, he would insist on examining the "injured" man, and transporting him to the hospital before he coughed up a single rupee. But then he is a natural-born Sahib and a doctor. I can't see me rummaging among the shawls and dhotis for a pulse or heaven knows what.

Monday, March 8 Doug leaves for a business trip to Goa and

Bombay, and won't be back until Saturday. I would love to go, too, but have got myself so committed that it would involve endless apologies and backtracking.

Wednesday, March 10 Today is my first bridge session with a new group I have been asked to join. This one is principally American, and now makes my third ongoing group, and I thoroughly enjoy both the bridge and the participants. As a matter of fact, I really don't know how I would ever have made my bow into Delhi society without bridge. It has been great, but not without its hazards.

After my first few games with the British banking wives, I decide to pass on the mid-morning Bloody Marys as I do not want to fall into the abyss of the chronically tipsy Memsahib. Without too much difficulty I could find myself having a couple of Bloody Marys in the morning; a martini at lunch, and a G&T before dinner. So I have set the inner rule (except on special occasions) of nothing alcoholic before sundown. At receptions – bottled water for the first drink, and a gin for the second. The first party I attended, it was so hot and I was so thirsty that I drank the gin like a glass of water and was promptly poured another. Hereby lies a downward path, and all too soon it would be, as Eliza Doolittle put it: "Gin was mother's milk to her."

Having found a place in the expat community, the International Women's Club has given me the matchless opportunity of making friends with women of the host country. The Executive meets on a regular basis, and it is amazing the breadth of our various interests. If I say the Indian women in the Association are very westernized, it sounds as if this were a virtue in itself, and besides it isn't really true. They are products of their own culture, but have not lost themselves in ancient customs or accepted precepts of the past. In other words, like the rest of us, they are women of their time with roles to play in a larger society beyond the home.

Saturday, March 13 Barbara busy with homework and social life, so Hilary and I spend the day together. Take in a polo game, and Hilary is a bit scornful of two spills and what she considers, in her infinite 10-year-old wisdom, some sloppy playing. We leave before the second game and do some shopping at the Kahn Market. Barbara goes out for the evening, Hilary falls asleep and Doug returns from Goa, where he had run into Monica and Ewan, and had walked the beaches with them. I feel a little jealous that I was not there, particularly when he tells me of the stretching coastline of glorious sand and sea.

It is rather nice, though, to hear that in Goa, after all the bloodshed in the sectarian strife at the time of Partition, Hindus, Muslims and Christians live side by side, completely tolerant of each other's religion. It was, of course, all due to Father Francis Xavier who taught peace, brotherhood and acceptance of differences. He was a European, but showed great respect for the Hindu way of life. He was so loved that when he died on the borders of China, they brought his body back to Goa where he lies in a glass coffin in the Bom Jesus Basilica. There are endless pilgrimages, and on prescribed days of the year his mummified remains are displayed. It is considered something of a miracle that his body has been so well preserved, but can he really look that well, all things considered?

Sunday, March 14 *A* rare treat – the Parkers take us to a Symphony performance organized by the British Council. The programme features a Grieg Concerto, played by an excellent pianist, and Mozart's Symphony No 35 – a little uneven perhaps, but it is so lovely to be at a concert without a single sitar, and I enjoy it enormously. We go back to the Parkers for a light supper and a rubber of bridge.

Monday, March 15 At first, I thought it was my imagination that the meals were going downhill, but the family has begun to complain about tough, unidentifiable meat, and an increasing number of burnt offerings. I know it is time to face up to my responsibilities. I call Tony in this morning for one of those unresolved conferences. I spout away, and he gives me his enigmatic nod. I tell him that I will work out the day's menus; he is to tell me when he is going shopping and I will give him a list; anything he can't find I will bring home from the Commissary. I wait anxiously for lunch, which is to be cheese soufflé, sausages and salad. The soufflé is rather depressed and the sausages over-cooked, but all in all, not bad. The soup at dinner tonight is good, and everyone enjoys the cheese-stuffed baked potatoes. I am mildly encouraged that things will buck up. Marion stays for dinner, then all the children leave to stay overnight at the Ronkes where they will celebrate Holi. I give Tony and Muni the day off tomorrow.

Tuesday, March 16   The significance of Holi continues to elude me. It is held annually in the early spring (February or March) and I am sure it has something to do with the spring equinox. If I would only take the trouble to address myself once more to *The Golden Bough*, I might be able to trace its origin.

Its name suggests something spiritual, but it all seems a bit of a romp to me. Children (and a number of adults) make up great vats of coloured water, which they pitch on any passer-by, preferably those wearing white. Doug and I stay safely inside, but hear the shrieks of the Vasant Vihar populace as they dodge being doused in purple and gold baths. When the children return they describe a riotous morning wherein they drenched countless numbers by tossing out plastic bags full of coloured water, and whooping it up at the discomfiture of their victims. It is, I suppose, innocent enough merriment, and I can see the parallel with other cultures: the symbolic driving out of the evil or winter spirits through beating drums, weirdo dances and thrashing with brooms, rituals that are to be found in European, South American and West Indian countries.

Wednesday, March 17   From Hindu Holi to Christian St Patrick's Day, but there's little green to be seen. It is Valerie Patterson's turn for the British bridge, and this is the first time I have been to her home. Her husband is the one who is in the 'monkey business'. His company is concerned with breeding Rhesus monkeys for medical and experimental purposes. He offers to show me around while the others are hitting the Bloody Marys, and I find it absolutely fascinating. I don't inquire too deeply into the medical and experimental part, as I think it better that I not know, being rather divided on the subject.

251

They have a huge estate off the Jaipur Road, with a lovely garden and swimming pool. Their children, five boys and a girl, are charming and absolutely delightful hooligans, who love it here and don't mind about the monkeys. I won't tell Hilary.

Friday, March 19 A doctors' dinner party at home with a collection of Indian medicos and Doug's British and American counterparts. I pick up the necessary at the Commissary, arrange flowers and make the thermidor base while Tony has his rest after lunch. I try to keep close tabs on the kitchen, since I am concerned about another disastrous culinary 'misunderstanding'. All worry for nought – the dinner is excellent, with the food covering all bases for western and eastern tastes. Finish off with coffee on the patio, and watch the rising of the moon above my 'poetic' tree.

Saturday, March 20 The Delhi Commonwealth Women's Association's Spring Sale, and I am figuratively on board with the Canadian Flag. The morning is quiet, and I go home for lunch. I return just after 2.00, when it seems that the vast hordes of Delhi have all gathered around the Canadian booth. My English friend, Eileen, who is working with me, is frantic. Not only have I been assigned the bookstall, but I am to do the cashiering as well. Rapid calculation is not my thing, and Eileen says she is even worse. Happily Barbara has come back with me, and takes over the till with her usual goodwill and exuberance. We do an incredibly brisk trade and take in more than 1,000 rupees in just two and a half hours.

When I turn in my cash, I find to my surprise that for the volunteers from the host country, the day is not without its personal profit. It seems to be accepted that the sale is a great vehicle for getting rid of old clothes and bric-a-brac but the donors keep two-thirds of the amount taken in. I also learn that it is customary for the Indian ladies to have a preview of the stalls before the doors are officially opened, enabling them to obtain some handsome bargains from the British, Canadian and Anzac donations. "It is written," I guess.

Tuesday, March 23 Monica has invited me to accompany her on an errand of mercy for the British Citizens Society, an association formed to offer aid to needy British citizens living in India. Lady Walker is the head, and has asked Monica to stand in for her on a visit to an elderly couple called Thompson who live in Meerut.

Monica fills me in on the Thompsons' background en route. They are among the core of Brits who 'stayed on'. He was a brigadier in the Indian Army and, after a lot of thought, elected to take the Indian Army pension rather than return to the UK and receive a British one. Financially, this was not all that great a decision, but the main reason was that his wife Lorna had been born and brought up in India, and could not even think of 'going home' when, as far as she was concerned, she was already there.

When she was a young girl she became crippled with polio, but still insisted on riding. A disastrous fall resulted in broken legs and a severe spinal injury that left her permanently disabled. Nonetheless, with a wealthy family and an army of servants, she had only to clap her hands for dozens to come running.

Now in her eighties, I wonder how she feels, living in a tack room behind the Meerut Race Track. The place is incredibly squalid, and Mrs T sits on top of an elongated table, surrounded by uneaten scraps from heaven knows how many meals.

The Brigadier comes to greet us with old-world courtesy, and sweeps a clutter of books and clothes off a couple of chairs. I offer my shortbread, and Mrs T claps her hands and a shambling, grinning young man lopes in. She orders tea with all the aplomb of a true Memsahib. The thing that both touches and surprises me is that the Indians at the racetrack treat them both with the same deference and respect they would have been given in their glory days. Monica tells me that the boys are track employees, and they look after the Thompsons for little or no pay.

It is all rather poignant. She is clad in men's trousers and a collarless shirt, and looks pretty awful. He is a very nice old man but he, too, is dressed in bits and pieces, and wearing a pair of brown plimsolls that are falling off his feet. While we are having our tea, she asks us if we could arrange to sell some of her linens. They are beautiful pieces, hand-embroidered by local nuns, and lovingly preserved in lavender presses. We take what we can, finish our tea and make our farewells, turning a page on another chapter of the past.

CHAPTER 31

Wednesday, March 24 Today I receive two letters regarding possible accommodation for our forthcoming home leave: a house in West Vancouver for $450 a month (looking after a dog, as well) and an apartment for $500. I find it difficult to realize that in another month we will be leaving. It comes to me as a bit of shock that 'going home' was the dream of heaven a year ago. Now it is almost mildly inconvenient. I have so many things on the go, I wonder how I can manage to get away. I have to acknowledge to myself that, almost unaware, I have become a part of this community; that I have put down tendrils in this alien soil and they have taken root.

Thursday, March 25 Let's hear it for the British Council. Tonight we go to a performance of *The Merchant of Venice*. A really good production, with a superb Shylock.

Friday, March 26 The twins' birthday. I wonder what Martin is doing? Did our present arrive? Will the school have baked him a cake? Barbara's party is all organized, and she alternates between excitement and worry that it will be "right".

Doug has arranged for Barbara and her guests to have the Commission pool to themselves for an hour or so, to be followed by pizzas and hamburgers at home, and dancing on the terrace – 'carriages at 12.00'. I shop for things for the party, and take care of details. It seems to me the entire fifth form of the British School will be in attendance, and with parents and/or drivers providing transport, there is little left for father and mother to do but make themselves scarce. Consequently we gather up Hilary and go off for dinner to the ACSA Lounge and then to the American Cinema to see *Jaws*. It's pretty horrible but absorbing.

We return home to find the party in full swing. The lights in the living room are turned down, and a few tiki torches on the terrace cast a glow on the cheek-to-cheek dancing. We retreat upstairs until the drivers arrive to pick up the guests.

Considering the range of nationalities and cultures, I am impressed that there seems to be no alcohol problem, perhaps a little smooching in the garden but, by and large, the party has the sort of innocence one associates with another age. I *know* from experience that we could not have had a party like this in West Vancouver without some celebrant spiking the punch and throwing up in the rose bushes – let alone having chauffeurs arriving for the guests on the stroke of midnight.

Saturday, March 27 Barbara bubbly over the success of her party, and after a full rehash of the evening, she and I then retire to the den for a serious talk about next year's school. The British School in Delhi just goes up to the 'O' levels, and now that she's into the system Barbara is keen to continue with 'A' levels. She has to admit that, in many areas, she feels she has finally been challenged. When she came home a few months ago with one of her first essays, marked with crossings-out and written suggestions in the margins, she was surprised but pleased.

"Gee, Mum, I think they really read it. At Hillside they used to just write 'Great, Barb' across the top and that was it."

She has learned to write a précis and has been forced into the basic laws of composition, which in the *avant* world of Canadian schooling were frequently considered "restrictive of expression".

I get a book out of the Commission Library on *Les Ecoles Privées Suisse*, and would love to send Barbara, but they are terribly expensive, and besides she is set on getting her 'A' levels. It seems Marion's parents are planning to send her to a Quaker school in Pontefract in northern England, and Barbara is hinting in that direction. Marion is keen that they go together.

Dinner party tonight, and I still find it odd to be having guests and not running madly around cleaning silver and stirring pots. Maybe I should have, as the crisp little puffs to be served with the consommé turn out to be closer to flapjacks, the cauliflower has been served with mayonnaise rather than Sauce Mornay and the Cornish Game Hens are a bit pale and wan. Still, I have learned to be philosophic about these little wanderings in the cuisine, and a goodly supply of wine works

256

wonders. Besides, if I ever felt alone in my seeming inability to communicate cooking instructions, I no longer do.

Talking recently to a friend who had been posted in the Gaza strip, she told me of one occasion when they had a standing rib roast specially flown in from Beirut for some special event. Some instinct directed her toward the kitchen where she found her desert chef dicing it in preparation for some Berber stew. Overcome with remorse, he even made a fist at sewing it back together again. What was even worse (could anything be worse?) she recounted another tale of the servant who hadn't quite understood the purpose of the pass-through hatch 'twixt kitchen and dining room. He got the impression that he was supposed to accompany the food, and spent endless hours trying to crawl through the hatch himself.

Sunday, March 28 Tonight is a Pool Party at the High Commission, an evening that requires a certain amount of mental bracing. I hate all that business of being pitched into the pool fully clothed and everybody acting like juveniles. You never see His Excellency and Mrs HE at these frolics. They are really such a nice couple, but he does not have the portrait of his stern and sober antecedent the Reverend Ryerson over his mantel for nothing. It turns out to be a rather chilly evening, so we are happily spared some of the usual capers, although somebody did find an inflatable shark and placed it in the pool. With *Jaws* playing locally, it got the desired response of screams and shrieks.

Tuesday, April 6 Invite a few of my British chums, with children, over for swimming at the pool. They include Eileen and her daughter Selena, and Sheila Brown with her three pretty moppets (gorgeous English complexions). All is going along, dare I say, swimmingly, when Catherine Brown sustains a nasty cut. All the forces of the Canadian High Commission are summoned along with a car, and she is whisked off to the British Hospital where Dr Grene (forewarned by Doug) turns a blind eye to the regulations (members of the Commission staff only) and binds her wounds. Eileen and I return to our cooling libations by the pool.

Wednesday, April 7   One of the problems of guests, particularly children, is the sudden onslaught of the dreaded Delhi Belly. We have been boarding a delightful little girl, Elizabeth Burrows, daughter of a doctor with the World Health Organization. Her parents are out of town, and Hilary wants to have a party for her. Among the guests is a rather pasty-faced child by the name of Amy, who is no sooner seated at the festive board than she dissolves into tears and says she feels sick.

She does look rather green (and I mentally apologize for my criticism of her complexion). I decide I had better phone her mother, but Amy does not have the number and her mother, recently re-married to an Indian, is not in the phone book under Amy's last name. Between taking Amy on trips to the loo, I eventually find a Mrs Agarwahl, who asks that I bring Amy home to the Defence Colony, which is miles away. I mutter something about having a houseful of children but this falls on deaf ears so, leaving Barbara in charge, I none too sympathetically pack up the distressed Amy and we eventually get her into the arms of her rather indifferent mother.

Thursday, April 8   I have been invited to the Membership Tea of the International Women's Association, in my role as corresponding secretary. As I noted before, I am really pleased about this, as it gives me the chance to get to know a lot more of the Indian ladies. Doing the monthly newsletter is also stimulating. Apart from my French lessons, I feel I have been leading a rather sybaritic existence, but these activities give me a sense of purpose. While I am indulging in all these high-minded thoughts, the other 'me' cannot help but notice how very elegant Clare Moulton looks in an absolutely fabulous mauve linen dress.

Friday, April 9   As Doug is emerging from the dressing room this morning, I find him sniffing the air, and looking puzzled.

"There is a funny sort of mouldy smell in the closet," he announces. "I wonder what it could be?"

I am about to answer that I haven't a clue, when memory comes flooding back. Oh Lord, I think, it's the bread. The bread I had tucked away in the little zippered bag weeks ago, and

I am just in the act of unzipping the bag ...

forgotten all about. I waffle away about Asian damp, and determine I will despatch the offending loaves this very afternoon when I take the girls riding. The Polo Club, where Major Singh conducts his riding academy, is on the edge of an area known locally as the Jungle. There are all sorts of bridle paths and trails and no traffic hazards, making it ideal for young riders and the disposing of domestic failures (vegetable, that is, not human). Consequently, once I have seen the girls mounted, I amble off down one of the trails, armed with my little bag and every show of nonchalance.

I am just in the act of unzipping the bag, when I am startled by some horrible shrieks. I hastily zip up the bag again, only to find that it is a covey of peacocks parading across the path behind me. How such beautiful creatures came to be cursed with such frightful voices is one of the cruelties of nature. I start out once more on my disposal mission, and find a nice little clump of vegetation, when I hear the clip clop of approaching horses. It is not, as I thought, some stray riders, but the President's mounted bodyguard out on an exercise assignment. The bag goes behind me, as I stand on the edge of the path to receive their courteous salute.

I am almost on the point of accepting that these loaves, like the poor, will be always with us, when I see a little break in the trees, dart in, unzip the bag, and with a throw worthy of a football quarterback, I pitch them into the waiting underbrush. I cannot begin to describe the sense of relief – no murderer could ever have felt a greater liberation at the disposal of a body. This is not a tale I am ever likely to recount to any Memsahib of the show-them-who-is-boss school.

This evening we have a Canadian guest from Vancouver. We stay long over dinner, until the candles start to sputter. It is wonderful having first-hand news from home.

Monday, April 12 With the shift of personnel at the Commission, I find that I am now an 'Old Indian Hand' and have been selected to be in charge of the Canadian Booth at the International Chrysanthemum Fair. This is the big charity event of the year, and is under the aegis of the YWCA. From now until the event in December, we will gather clothes, toys, books and memorabilia, to repair, sort and categorize.

The Canadians have a goal in mind: to 'adopt' a village and supply a crèche or nursery where the working women may leave their children to be cared for while they toil in the fields or on building sites.

The aim is to show women that there is more for them in life than they now have, and that their children can have a different future. The cost of financing this programme for a year amounts to roughly $1,000. It seems so little, but considering the minimal resources of the fair's buying market, this means an awful lot of items to gather. I set out this morning for the YWCA to gather information on rural welfare programmes and background on financing, as the first step toward our goal.

Thursday, April 15 A lot of reassignments have come through, and the High Commission will soon have the face of a stranger, just when I have come to be at home with the face of a friend. The guard's wife with whom I have had so many cosy chats is thrilled that they are being posted to Vienna; the Smiths have been offered South Africa but, not unnaturally, "have views"; the Currents are in limbo – they can have another year, but do they want it?

All these departures and potential arrivals make me realize why I still find myself thinking, "In real life, I would be doing such and such...." There is always a sense of shipboard life about being in the Foreign Service, of something not quite real, the fleeting impermanence of a watched film or a fragmented dream.

If I feel that way after 16 months in India, I can only imagine how one of our new arrivals must feel after a weirdly surreal experience that occurred four days after she de-planed.

Cook-bearers and sweepers seem to come in matched sets. Tony is partnered with Muni, and the Grahams' Salamat, hired by the newcomers, begs to bring in his old friend, Benwari. Benwari was really past his sell-by date when he worked for the Grahams, but the new Memsahib was happy enough to have her domestic staff settled for her.

As they used to say in the Movietone News, "It was a day like any other day," and Benwari's first day on the job. Salamat set out on his bicycle to stock the house with groceries, and

261

Benwari was assigned to sweep the driveway. At 10.00am there was an agitated knock on the door by the mali, and Mrs W went out to find her new employee in extremis – gasping for breath and clearly in pain. She did her best to make him comfortable with a pillow and some water, then rushed in to phone the clinic at the Commission. When she returned, Benwari was dead.

Doug was away from the office, but his nurse came to the scene, accompanied by a host of helpers who offered suggestions, from covering the body with a sheet to phoning the police. Both suggestions were followed, but at least three hours passed before there was any sign of the constabulary. Meanwhile Salamat returned, laden with provisions. Told the news, he insisted he must go at once to Benwari's village to inform his family. The eventual arrival of the police brought a fresh flock of curious passers-by. Delhi's finest were strangely ineffectual. They had no vehicle to move the body and besides, the deceased's family should be on hand. Could the Commission perhaps..? The heat was intense and Mrs W looked anxiously at the covered corpse. For one hysterical second she wondered if she should make tea (they always seem to do it in Agatha Christie novels) but dismissed the idea as inappropriate. Eventually Salamat returned with a grief-stricken relative, and at the same time a station wagon appeared as a kind of makeshift hearse. But wait – there is a cartage charge for the van – 50 rupees, and now the relative fights back his grief long enough to claim compensation for Benwari's faithful service of an hour and a half.

As Mrs W recounted later: "Does one really bargain over the disposal of a seven-hour-old corpse?" She settled for a receipt, and shortly after 5.00pm Benwari was placed, none too reverently, in the van, while nine others squeezed in around him, receiving in his death more thought and attention than was ever given him in his life.

Friday, April 16 Good Friday. The Easter holiday has begun and like many an expat family before us, we are heading for the hills and the hill station of Simla. The hot weather began earlier, but has become increasingly uncomfortable, and the thought of the pleasant mountain 'coolth' has an irresistible appeal.

The plan is to travel in convoy with the Hartlings, the young couple who were married in Israel and haven't yet got used to the idea. It is Romeo and Juliet with every passing glance. Her parents are visiting and join the party. They have a Commission driver, and we have borrowed Bolar Singh, the Chartered Bank driver, for the weekend. It is a very hot drive to Chandigarh, but we stop at the Pinjore Gardens to picnic with the Hartlings. The Dennys look at the flowering around us and at the food; the Hartlings look at each other.

Press on in the smouldering heat to Chail, and take off into the cool of the hillside forests to the former summer home of the Maharajah of Patiala. It is a handsome old stone mansion, with echoes of a memorable past. We are sorry to be so rushed, but it is now 5.30pm, and Bolar Singh tells us it is another hour's drive to the main road, and from there another hour to Simla.

It doesn't sound too daunting until we start the climb up a mountain road – a road that consists of sliding shale, potholes like craters and construction works. We spot the odd bus, front wheels hanging over the cliff's lip, and an abandoned car or two at the bottom of a mountain chasm. I just don't want to hear what happened to the occupants. Suffice it to say that my relief is palpable when we come within sight of Simla. It is now dark, and all we can see is a jewelled hillside beckoning like Diamond Lil. As we draw nearer, the seductress appears less attractive. It is of no consequence, as long as she offers a bed and a bite.

She does all of that in the Hotel Oberoi Clark. The cuisine of the departed Raj still persists, as we were sure it would. I pass on the mutton, but wolf down the surprisingly delicious almond soufflé that follows.

Saturday, April 17 A brilliant bright mountain morning, although the light of day does not show the rather seedy hotel to advantage. It is very old, perched on the edge of a cliff, and looks dangerously inclined to give in to age and gravity. Still, it is the best hotel in Simla. Around 11.00am, armed with stout walking sticks, we set out to explore.

Simla is built like an aerie, with shops and houses

The Dennys look at the flowering ...the Hartlings look at each other

hanging like tattered eagles on the edge of the mountain tops. We walk along the main mall, which is lined with shops, mainly Tibetan in their crafts and wares. At one time, no local was allowed on the Upper Mall, it being the exclusive preserve of the Sahibs and their 'Mems'. Even today, the architectural legacy of "forever England" can be seen in the number of half-timbered, Tudor-style buildings.

Barbara, Hilary and I buy up a lot of hostess gifts and souvenirs for our projected visit home. It is great fun and it is only when we begin to flag that we realize we have been walking for almost three hours. We lunch and then leave the urban centre and hike for another couple of hours into the hills and along the forest paths.

Returning to the Hotel OC, the Hartleys call on us as does the High Commissioner's rather odd secretary. She has also come up for Easter, driven by our old friend, the Chapati Kid. She is rather bitter about both him and the Peugeot the HC lent her. Remembering our trip to Benares, I am not surprised to learn that she had four flat tires along the way, was positive she faced certain death at every hair-pin turn, and is very displeased that Ram Bahadur has not reported in to her this morning. In defence of the irresponsible Ram, we say he probably thought he would not be needed, there being essentially no vehicular traffic in Simla.

"It doesn't matter," was the response. "*I* might have needed him."

Sunday, April 18 Easter Sunday morning, and how strange it seems to be in this eagle's nest of a town in the high Himalayas. Memories of my own childhood Easters, including the totally secular excitement of getting decked out in a new outfit for church, come flooding back. I am struck once again with the enormous gap of time and space between the 'me' of then, and the 'me' of now.

After breakfast, we re-stock the ice chest, gather up the hotel picnic (which is like every other hotel picnic) and are ready to depart. The Hartlings, together with visiting parents, join us and we are all off by 10.30am. An absolutely spectacular drive through spruce and fir-thick hills, higher and higher until we finally reach Narkanda at 2,700 metres, 60 miles as the crow flies from the Chinese border. We are almost at 10,000 feet, and the view is beyond imagining – the eternal snows of the Himalayas and a panorama that stops both breath and heart.

We go a little deeper into the forest, and find a perfect spot for our picnic. Dianne's father is feeling a bit ill and is uninterested in lunch. The rest of us heartlessly munch away, and after the picnic, we leave the parents in care of the Hartlings' driver, and hike down the hillside for a trek across the saddle of the mountain. It is heaven going down in that unbelievable air, but purgatory climbing back up.

Another exercise in repressed hysteria, as we drive back along the mountain switch-backs. Stop at the Wildflower Inn for tea, and find the British High Commissioner and his wife already into the scones. Apart from the towering mountains we could be in a country tearoom in Sussex, with the velvet lawns, flowering shrubs and a very English garden.

It has been a long day, and we all opt for an early night back at the Hotel Oberoi Clark, after another tussle with the obligatory mutton chops.

Monday, April 19 The drive back to Delhi (like all drives back) lacks the excitement and anticipation of the outgoing trip. We drop Bolar Singh back at the Bank House, pick up our own car and return to Vasant Vihar.

Wednesday, April 21 Has all that French dictation and studying been worth it, I ask myself? Encounter an acid test today, when a rather worried-looking couple ask if I speak French. I give a modest and slightly Gallic wave of the hand, while I mutter "*Un peu*," hoping they just want to ask, What hour is it? How many years have I? And what do I call myself?

Much more complicated, alas, but miracle of miracles, I understand them and they understand me. It turns out they are trying to find Air France and change their ticket because of a missed trip to Kashmir. The end result is I drive Monsieur over to the Air France office, get things sorted out and return him to his anxious *femme*. You just can't believe how international I feel, and find myself thinking in French all the way to the Ashoka. I revert abruptly back into English while I

266

shop for odds and ends needed for our trip, and things for Hilary's birthday tomorrow.

Thursday, April 22 On one of our plunges into Old Delhi, we had discovered on the Street of the Silversmiths (where else?) a store that will duplicate your silver pattern, in silver, at a surprisingly good price. We decide that we want to add some place settings to our Birks silverware.

I pick up Doug and we set out at lunchtime to chase down the stinking alley and up the smelly lane until we reach the premises of G Chandi Jain's shop. He has upped his price from the last time, so we check across the street where the quote is 500 rupees lower. Back to Mr Jain, who shakes his head and sorrowfully agrees he is helpless in the face of such competition, dolefully bringing his price down while questioning whether his rival will put in the "absolute, full amount of silver". I am not one bit sure of either Mr Jain or his rival, but we finally settle on 35 pieces for 3,500 rupees – approximately $11 a piece. Hang down your head, Mr Birk! As proof of the impeccability of his status, Mr Jain shows us a letter of thanks from no less a personage than Roland Michener, who did a stint here as High Commissioner.

The rest of the day is a flurry of picking up and depositing. Barbara buys Hilary a silver ankle bracelet, and I pick up prizes for her party, then rush over to collect Hilary. The birthday girl is in tears – she has lost her chola with all her books, she is sure she flubbed her social studies test and fears she has missed riding. We tear over to the Polo Club and just make it, a sop to stretched nerves.

By the time her friends have gathered and Tony produces her dinner, as ordered, with a magnificent birthday cake – it is a case of "What books?" "What social studies test?" All is hilarity and good feeling, although I shed a silent tear that 'little Hilary' is 'little' no more and gone, without a ripple, into another phase of growing up.

CHAPTER 32

Friday, April 23 This is the day the travel plans bear fruit. Our first leave, and I am strangely reluctant to go. Still, as the ads used to say, getting there should be half the fun. We are to meet our dear friends from West Vancouver, Hector and June Perry, in Athens and spend a week cruising the Greek Isles aboard the schooner of a Greek doctor, who is on the Canadian payroll in Athens as a DMP.

It is not quite what we had planned as both Hector and Doug wanted a 'bare boat' charter. However, Doug's opposite number, the Canadian doctor in Athens, has organized this with Dr N, who will accompany us. It is a great deal cheaper this way, and we rather grudgingly admit that it is not a bad idea to have a skipper who knows the waters. A week later we will meet the girls on their flight to Athens and continue on with them to Paris for a few days before flying home.

I spend most of the day taking things out of my wardrobe, putting them back, trying to co-ordinate outfits, setting gifts and souvenirs aside to fit into crevices. When Barbara comes home, she is wonderfully helpful and we are finally organized. Doug and I sit out on the terrace and have a celebratory drink while waiting for the driver. Say a rather sad farewell to the girls, despite their father's "It's only a week for God's sake" and wave 'til they are just dots at the gate.

Indian Airlines, faithful to its traditions, serves us tea and cookies for dinner. We de-plane at Bombay, and are met by a nice young man from JAL. We had to pay 20 rupees for excess baggage at Delhi, but he pooh-poohs this and waves us into the Executive Lounge, while informing us that we have been up-graded to First Class. *Vive la différence!* We have masses of room, foam rubber foot rests, wide seats and s*ervice!!!* We are offered champagne, smoked salmon, artichoke hearts and chicken pâté, plus two little Japanese writing sets as presents. I savour every golden moment, although I had piously declared beforehand that I thought it was quite right that the government should not spend the taxpayers' money in sending its Foreign Service officers first class. All such egalitarian virtues, however, go straight out where they belong with my first sip of champagne – and besides, it isn't the government's money. We fly to Karachi, then to Cairo all through the dark of night and land in Athens at 6.10am.

We dismiss a few hotels as too expensive but finally settle on the Athens Gate, which is smack-bang in front of the Acropolis and opposite Athens Gate Park. Needless to say, we cannot book in at that dawn hour, so we go for a walk through the park and take a look at this city of the gods. I like what I see – pleasant streets, trees and rocky out-croppings – but it is *cold*!! I am grateful for my new suede coat, no matter how abbreviated. When we estimate the hour is right for admittance, we return, get into our room and sink into bed for a zizz.

Later on Doug phones the Perrys who are at the Hotel Grande Bretagne, Athen's grandest hostelry. They are not in, but he gets hold of the Canadian doctor who not only takes us out for lunch, but also gives us a little personalized tour. This includes a trip up to Athen's highest point, which, while not Olympian, gives us a god-like view of the whole city at our feet. Beyond are the mountains that have been the source of marble for the Greeks for thousands of years; and there is Mount Parnassus, the home of the muses and the arts of peace. It is scarcely necessary for our guide to point out the Acropolis, the soul of ancient Athens, but an interesting historical titbit he throws in is that the original city-state extended only from the Acropolis to Athens Gate – a postage stamp. We plan to tour the Acropolis this afternoon, and Dr C strongly recommends a senior guide. They are expensive, he warns, but worth it.

Consequently, we latch on to a bespectacled middle-aged lady, with a brusque manner and a limp. We book her for one hour, and that is exactly what we get, to the second. The cane should have warned us, as she allows no rambling to anything remotely like high ground. Furthermore she rattles off her prepared lectures like a machine gun. As she scarcely ever stops for a breath, my questions hang, half-spoken, in limbo. Looking all the time at her watch, she stops almost mid-sentence dead-on the hour. We pay her $50, and then go where we want to go with the aid of an infinitely more

269

interesting guidebook.

We go by the Perrys' hotel and leave a note for them before returning to our hotel for a nap. Sometime later Hector calls. Dr N is with them, and we arrange to meet in the bar of the Hotel Grande Bretagne.

We are so glad to see June and Hector, both of whom look well and happy. Dr N is a brawny, self-assured Greek, with a rather macho attitude. We have just started our drinks when a tall, well-built girl comes and joins us. This, apparently, is Linda, who will be joining us on our cruise. I am not quite sure of her status with regard to the boat, or her relationship to the married Dr N. Never assume. A tentative inquiry as to whether she is going to be our chef is promptly quashed. This leaves one inescapable conclusion, which is candidly confirmed. She is Dr N's mistress and, she assures us, she is on *holiday.*

It is at this juncture that June suggests a trip to the loo, where she voices serious doubts about this curvaceous addition. After all, we are paying guests, and also, I now discover, are paying for all the supplies. It all seems a bit of a cheek to throw in another mouth to feed at our expense, but is it worth making a fuss about? Neither one of us is that sure, particularly after June describes her day spent with Linda provisioning the boat. This, as June confides to me, consisted of the purchase of masses of tins of marinated grape leaves, eggplants and a goodly supply of olive oil. June's only participation in this shopping excursion was to pay the bill.

Having unburdened herself of this none-too-welcome information, we return to the bar to find that Dr N (whose first name is an elongated Greek form of John) is going to take us to his village, a drive of approximately 15 miles. First, though, he would like Doug to see his office. It turns out that the office has an apartment attached, and it is probably here that he conducts his little dalliances. In any event Mrs N is away somewhere, and the doctor is free to spread his wings. I should add, in all fairness, that I might be doing the man an injustice. For all I know, he and Mrs N may have one of those 'open' European marriages, so alien to Canadian suburbia.

After Doug has inspected his office, Dr N drives us to his village where he has invited us to attend the Greek Orthodox Easter Ceremony. This vast earth has become such a tiny and traversible place. Here we are, having just celebrated Easter on the roof of the world, and seven days later are experiencing a second one in a small Greek village on the shores of the Aegean.

We walk along to the church down the main village street, which unhappily is mined with firecrackers. As we near the church, we see a long procession of villagers carrying candles. Someone puts one in my hand, and we move slowly forward as the church bells peal that Christ Is Risen.

After the service, Dr N, whom we are asked to call Jannie (pronounced Yannie), makes reservations for a midnight feast, but first invites us to see his house. He has every reason to be proud of it. It is 140 years old and absolutely charming, with beautiful antiques and fine old rugs, but *cold!!* Where is this Aegean Spring of legend? The only occupant presently in residence is a delightful little Irish terrier, who gives us a lavish welcome and performs several tricks with enormous zeal.

We now scurry along to the restaurant for the traditional Easter midnight meal, which consists of Once-a-Year Soup made from the blood, heart and kidney of a lamb (I am glad I did not ask until I had finished it), followed by roast lamb and salad, washed down with Greek country wine. It is terribly kind and generous of our host, but it has only taken me one evening in his company to decide that Dr N is deeply in love with himself, and is not really interested in anyone else's thoughts or opinions, and may well prove the worst bore who ever clutched at a buttonhole. We return to our hotel, exhausted, at 2.30am.

Sunday, April 25 Hector calls to say they will meet us at our hotel at 11.30am. I frantically sort through our possessions and finally squeeze our boating gear into one small bag and Doug's briefcase, sailboat space being what it is. We will leave the rest of our luggage in storage at the hotel, where we will return after the cruise. We are ready at the appointed hour, but the Perrys are delayed and do not arrive until 12.15. This is all right with us; having missed breakfast, we are able to down a ham sandwich in the lobby and watch the Beautiful People of the continental jet set at play.

We had planned to take a taxi to the Acropolis, but when

We (me included) can think only of the price of strawberries

the Perrys arrive, June, looking extremely chic in well-cut cotton, is freezing, so it is back to their hotel for a coat. What do the Greeks do for transport? Dozens of taxis go by, but all are engaged. Finally we walk up the hill to the Grande Bretagne. Further and pleasurable delays, as there is a general consensus that we are all in need of fortification at the bar before we set out to scale the Acropolis.

By now, the afternoon is well launched and we are well braced, so once again we look for a taxi. Here we are, at Athens' most luxurious hostelry, and there are *no taxis!* After what seems a century-long wait, we opt to take the Number 16 bus, which is clearly marked 'Acropolis'. So we wait and we wait. Is the driver having the $50-an-hour lecture, I ask myself? Finally, and at last, we see a 16 bus approaching. It nears but does not pause in its journey, sailing by with never a friendly wave. Just when all looks hopeless a taxi stops and a lady gets in. We all climb in after her. I will never know what she thought, but I am terribly embarrassed. Nobody pays any attention to my demurring, and I am bundled in regardless.

We are dropped at the foot of the Acropolis, just beside a lovely little terrace restaurant, with a vine-covered trellis. I might have known that this would represent yet another delay in our assignation with the Ages. It never fails: when we are travelling, the merest glimpse of a bar, a tavern, bistro or restaurant presents an irresistible lure and creates a hunger or thirst that was previously unsuspected. Naturally, we opt for lunch, and everyone is appalled that our desserts of exactly four strawberries each come to $17, or more than a dollar per strawberry. This absorbs us completely, and you can scarce conceive the discussion about it. Here we are, in the shadow of the Parthenon, in the Isles of Greece, "Where Delos rose and Phoebus sprung," and we (me included) can think only of the price of strawberries.

The subject finally exhausted, we tool over to view the wonder of the Parthenon, a miracle of architecture if there ever was. Alas, this entire expedition was doomed from the start. The Acropolis is closed on Sundays. There is disappointment, but I am quite certain that no tears will be shed, and somewhere around the corner, there will be a taverna waiting to comfort and console.

CHAPTER 33

Still Sunday, April 25 Back at the Hotel Grande Bretagne we wait for the arrival of Dr N to escort us to the boat in Piraeus. I am never sure when a boat becomes a ship but there is no doubt about the *Larres* – it is most definitely a boat. Every jaw drops at the sight of the narrow and none-too-sleek tub that confronts us.

The interior is dark and cramped, with shallow seating. There is one cabin aft, and there is a toss-up for it, which (God be praised) falls to us. The narrow bunks will preclude any turning and tossing (or anything else come to that) and there is absolutely no storage space. I have a few inner congratulations on my frugality when it came to clothing and at least we have privacy, and a place to which we can retreat. I feel for June and Hector who will be sharing the main cabin with the galley, the lovers and a goodly amount of tackle.

The galley is a hole, with a minuscule stove with two burners. The head is somehow connected with the water supply, and can be entered only while in the praying position. It is not exactly what we had envisioned to sail the wine-dark seas, and I can see the storm clouds gathering on the faces of the paying guests. Pollyanna (next to Elsie Dinsmore) has to be one of the most irritating characters in children's literature, but I tell myself that I will try her philosophy on for size. After all, I muse inwardly, we will be sailing the seas Ulysses sailed, exploring the islands of Byron's love and wandering through the olive groves where Plato taught. Does it matter how we get there? I glance at the faces of my companions – it matters!

Monday, April 26 Up at 7.30am; as the ship's provisions have been geared to the Greek taste for oily grape leaves for breakfast, we walk around Piraeus in a fruitless search for bacon and eggs. We settle for bread and butter, eaten to a recital of the horrors of the sleeping accommodation.

At 1100 hours (even if it takes some figuring, I feel I should record the time in boating parlance) we are away and heading for Aegina, about 17 nautical miles away. Before we leave, however, there is a lot of mucking about with sails, first up and then down, as we try unsuccessfully to catch the wind. I say 'we' although I have completely divorced myself from all proceedings. My Greek dictionary does not contain the words I am hearing from the Captain, and Hector's *sotto voce* comments to Doug are not recordable.

Aegina turns out to be a touristy village with a lot of sidewalk cafes, shops, etc. They have calèches with bright orange, blue and yellow canopies that ply the streets and are wonderfully colourful against the white buildings. I go back on board to change my sweater for a blouse because, at last, it is beginning to feel a bit warm. When I come out the entire crew has disappeared. I feel it is a bit churlish of them to have left without me, so I wander, lonely as the proverbial cloud, until Linda finds me and takes me to a little restaurant where Jannie, Linda and I eat alone. Hector finds us, and goes to locate June and Doug; Doug returns on his own, followed by Hector who then goes once more in search of June. Every mother knows the scenario: send Kilmeny to find Peter, then Barbara to find Kilmeny and Peter, then....

Once together again, we just start to wander, when the ever-restless Jannie announces he wishes to leave to reach Epidaurus before dark. We arrive around 1900 hours and gather for a rather awkward Happy Hour. For one thing, there is simply no place to sit and the night is really chilly. For another, Jannie and Linda are drinking some heady Greek brew, which they seem only too happy to abandon in favour of Johnnie Walker, which is in limited supply.

A charter is tied up alongside, and we are invited in for a gander. Of course, we should not have gone, for what had been grumblings about our own accommodation could well erupt into a veritable volcano of discontent. There are ten staterooms, elegantly wallpapered and beautifully equipped, a gorgeous salon and proper stand-up accommodation in the head. Return rather disgruntled to the dark inner confines of the *Larres* and nibble on some pistachio nuts, until the Captain bellows out that if we wish to have dinner, we must go ashore *now*. Doug asks me (as if I would know) why we put up all that money to provision the boat, when we have yet to eat

275

one meal aboard. Oily grape leaves or not, it had to have been better than what we tucked away in a ghastly little taverna near the dock.

Tuesday, April 27   The landlubbers revolt! Hector and I are the only ones up, and while I wash up last night's glasses, he goes shopping and returns with bread straight out of the oven, bacon, eggs and the biggest, juiciest oranges I have ever seen. I whomp up a breakfast to die for, and even Jannie and Linda are wooed from the tins of oil lining the larder.

After what the New World contingent considers the first decent meal we have had, the four of us get a hired car and set off for Epidaurus. This is more like it. We have a glorious outing, and while the weather is not hot, it is sunny and warm.

Epidaurus is everything it ought to be. The Greeks believed that the god of healing, Asclepius (he to whom Socrates owed a cock) was born here. In this sanctuary are the ruins of a still impressive temple, and a museum celebrating the arts of healing, including a gorgeous stone inscription for the cure of the sick and a case of ancient surgical instruments. Doug is fascinated by it all, and has to be dragged off to the theatre.

This is fantastic and in remarkably good nick considering the centuries that have passed. It was capable of holding 14,000 and the acoustics are incredible. I try to imagine Aristophanes or Sophocles pacing in the wings, waiting for the reaction of the 'first-nighters'.

The setting for this outdoor theatre is spectacular. In the hollow of deeply forested hills, it presents a montage of varying shades of green, from the sombre dark of the cypress to the silver-green of the olive groves. It is magical, and best of all there is no one about but us. Sitting where the ancients sat I am lost in another world, another time, when I feel a tap on my shoulder and hear a voice in my ear.

"Excuse me, Madam, but my family has had season's tickets here for 2,000 years, and you are sitting in my place."

Talk about a Pavlovian response. I spring up apologizing, only to be met by Hector's devilish grin.

On the way back we buy some more of those spectacular oranges that Jannie has informed us have "no juice". We find the Captain and his lass champing at the bit and ready to go.

We take off only to find our anchor has become entangled with a metal chain from one of the large boats in the harbour. Best to draw a veil over the ensuing scene that features (as they say on TV) "violence and coarse language". Tempers are indeed frayed, until finally through what Jannie refers to as "seamanship" and Hector describes as "sheer dumb luck", we break away and are off.

In his usual high-handed fashion, Jannie directs me to the galley to make spaghetti. I am not quite sure how this delegation of responsibility has come about, but it seems I have been elected the galley slave. Why me, I wonder? I am, after all, a customer, and Linda has yet to wash a dish. June, after a stint at the wheel, is already threatening mutiny, so I suppose it is a case of natural selection.

As the captain, Jannie's word should be law, but there is a general outcry against spaghetti. Linda wants bread and cheese, and there are, of course, all those tins of eggplant and what have you. I am told we will be at our destination in half an hour, and I am left pondering what I can manage to time with our arrival. Just as well I don't attempt it, because it is a good five hours before we reach Poros. Meanwhile I manage some toasty hors d'oeuvres with cheese and chopped up (guess what) grape leaves, so the hunger pangs are somewhat assuaged.

Poros turns out to be a pretty little town, with a cluster of white box-like houses piled one on top of the other and overlapping in a delightfully higgledy-piggledy way. It's also a busy small port, with a regular ferry service, and people are coming and going at a great rate. On a rocky summit above the harbour is the town clock, apparently a must in all Greek villages. We prowl around for a while, and it is decided (once again) that we will eat out. So into another taverna, until crammed with moussaka we return to the *Larres*, to sleep tight, which is a word all too accurate in these crowded quarters.

Wednesday, April 28 I wake reluctantly at 8.00am to find June and Hector gone, and Jannie and Linda still abed. Doug unfolds his arms and legs from his cramped cot, and we, too, set out. We run into June and Hector, have a coffee and then return to the boat.

There follows an altercation in a mixture of Greek and English. Doug and Hector want their breakfast, and want it now. Something is being boiled on the inadequate stove and they are told they will have to wait.

Nobody, but nobody, tells Hector Perry he must wait. Captain or no captain, he, Hector, is the one who is paying for this boat from hell and he will not bloody well wait. There is a lot of surly muttering from the Greeks, but the boiling object is removed. I am dug out from the embarrassed hole into which I have climbed, and placed in a position of command in the galley, and that is that.

Having established who is in charge, we then set out for our day's outing to a small island, which we reach by ferry around noon. It is a delightful island of steep, terraced hillsides. I don't know how she managed it, but June is transported up the hill in a charming little cart, while Doug, Hector and I are issued donkeys.

My donkey is sweet, with rather nice long lashes and a stubborn disposition. I have never ridden on a donkey before and never experienced anything as uncomfortable as the wooden saddle with which he comes equipped. Remembering the result of my camel ride beside the Arabian Sea, I try desperately to find a comfy position. As we climb, however, the world around us is so incredibly beautiful that I cease to think about mundane concerns like chafed bottoms. The hillside is covered with hundreds and hundreds of lemon trees and their golden fruit. The scent surpasses Chanel, as we drink in the fragrance of lemon, rose and lilac. This is what I dreamed Greece would be, and all I need now is to see a curly-haired shepherd boy guarding his flock to complete the picture. The day is over too soon, as all treasurable days are. We leave reluctantly to catch the return ferry.

Linda is pretty easy going (as well she should be as I have yet to see her turn her hand to dish or sail) but Jannie always seems to be in a hurry to leave wherever we are for wherever we are going. We return to the boat about 3.00pm (I have abandoned my calculations in naval times) but with all the usual bustle of sails and petrol, it is about 4.00pm before we leave. It is bitterly cold, with dark looming clouds, so I elect to take a little nap and do not wake up until we reach Hydra around 6.30pm.

Hydra is attractive, built on a rocky promontory, with a cluster of stone houses, all whitewashed and clean-looking against the darkening sky. There is a wide esplanade with small and charming shops, full of delightful things waiting for me to buy. We are all anxious to get to shore before it is too dark, but there is a dicey berthing, as we slide between two yachts. I am holding the dinghy and am petrified that either it, or I, will be crushed. There is the usual exchange of recriminations, but finally we are secured and enjoy a walk around town.

Happy Hour is not really all that happy. The stress of our comings and goings into various ports, the inadequacy of the boat itself and, for the Perrys, the forced intimacy of the shared cabin accommodation, have taken their toll. The daytime Jannie is not all that easy to take, but a snoring or amorous Jannie must be a trial beyond bearing. June, who has nobly gone along so far, snaps. She expresses her discontent with everything – the larder full of inedible food, the unseasonably cold weather and the misjudging of her travel wardrobe. Hector, all too aware of the mutinous atmosphere, responds sharply and June wisely absents herself by stalking off to the end of the pier.

Hector gathers up Doug, and the two of them go off to suss out the town. I have either been lumped in with the general female discontent, or they just do not think of including me. Linda and Jannie have disappeared long since, so I take my book and return to the narrow confines of my bunk. When Doug returns, he regales me with tales of the taverna, the music and the men all dancing. He adds that it was really great fun, then takes a look at my face and sums up the evening with:

"You wouldn't have enjoyed it, though, sweetie."

'Sweetie' will never know.

Thursday, April 29 Doug and I get up and walk along the picturesque quay of Hydra. We run into June and Hector, who are having coffee. Hector is particularly attentive, and all appears serene.

Back at the boat, Jannie, as usual, is impatient to be off. We haul up anchor at 11.30am and spend the day at sea, reaching our next port of call, Nauplion, at 5.30pm. It is a fascinating harbour, with an equally fascinating history. After the War of Independence with Turkey in the 1820s, it briefly became the capital of the newly independent Greece. Along the ridge are the remains of the fortifications and the walls of the old city. We elect to walk up to the Hotel Xenia Palace, which is built into the wall. In order to get into the hotel, however, you must walk up the mountain to a park, and then take a mountain elevator to the top. I just can't imagine the hotel clientele, with masses of expensive luggage, going through all that palaver, but you never know.

While we are wandering the twisting streets of Nauplion, Hector confides in Doug that he is "giving Junie a break," and has booked them into a shore-side hotel, the Agamemnon, for the night. June has obviously brightened at the prospect of getting away from the infamous cabin of the *Larres* and invites us up for baths. What bliss!

Rupert Brooke in his poem, *The Great Lover*, refers to "the benison of hot water". It truly is one of life's blessings – the washing away of dirt like sin, and a sense of renewal, second only to a cup of tea when exhausted. The other great bonus offered at the Agamemnon is to be able to go to the loo without dropping into a Quasimodo crouch.

Now clean and refreshed, we return to the boat and find that, as usual, we are to eat out. I am not really hungry, but rather fancy a small slice of pink, juicy and tender lamb. Alas for dreams of something edible, the restaurateur is noncommittal as to what manner of beast we are eating, but whatever it is, it has been around for a long, long time. I, for one, retire for the night, essentially unfed.

Friday, April 30 Up early and make breakfast for Doug and me, under the ever-watchful eye of the Captain. It is more than somewhat unnerving, so I leave a half-cooked egg, wash up and escape to collect the Perrys from their overnight accommodation. I warn them that Jannie is anxious to depart – what else is new – and as a result, we do manage to get away at a reasonable hour, heading for fabled Mycenae.

One of the things that drew me to the Isles of Greece was the tale of Agamemnon. It is probably one of the greatest sagas of Greek or any other literature, and now we are on the threshold. Mycenae and its ghosts are but a cab drive away. We do not know whether Jannie and Linda are interested in accompanying us, because we do not ask them. As we start out, Jannie yells after us that an hour or so will be enough. I just turn a cold eye, but June has had enough, and tells him that we will take as long as we choose. After all, *this* is what we came to Greece for!

We arrive around 10.00am, after a scenic drive past orange and lemon groves, and field after field of scarlet poppies. We come to a bend in the road, and the driver leaves us in a large car park. He points to a hill path that leads to the ruins of Mycenae.

As I have said before, we do tend to bankrupt our language by over-spending words such as "thrilled", but that is exactly what I am. There is a tingling up the spine, a strange deep excitement about walking toward that windy acropolis of stone. Here is the Lion Gate, through which the young Electra ran; this is the home to which Agamemnon returned to find death waiting for him. I am hand-in-hand with legend, and am seeing what the ancients must have seen on a spring day thousands of years ago. The wind is blowing a scarlet montage of poppies; there are golden daisies and heliotrope defining the rocky outcroppings, and the surrounding hills are aflame with wild flowers.

I read Irving Stone's *The Greek Treasure* before we came, and we follow the path of Henry and Sophia Schliemann through the ruins. They began their explorations on the premise that Homer's tale was factual and that he was, indeed, history's first war correspondent. Many things fitted, many were assumed.

Among the outbuildings and foundations of ancient houses is the grave shaft with the bodies presumed to be those of Cassandra and her babies. There is the grand staircase and the throne room. It unfolds like a movie in my mind. I see Orestes waiting, knife in hand, to kill his mother and her lover, and so avenge the death of his father at their hands; there is his sister, poor tragic Electra, whose very name is cursed. It is better than a time machine.

But not for all. Doug and Hector, down-to-earth travellers both, declare that it is just "a bunch of rocks." Doug, observing my shocked expression, kindly consents to hearing "all about it." It is like the presentation of a gift, but I barely begin with:

"Well there was Agamemnon and Clytemnestra, and Helen and Menelaus," when Doug adds in an aside to Hector:

"And Ted and Alice and Bob and Carol." Somehow I know that I am not going to have the hushed and awed audience at my feet as Homer once had at his, so I wander off, content with my personal journey into Mycenae and its legends.

I spend more than three hours in this happy pursuit before moseying down to meet the others at the car park. I find them, not too surprisingly, in the taverna, and join them for a drink. A short walk down the road is Agamemnon's tomb, which is located between Cyclopean walls. The entrance is supported by a huge lintel of a solid slab of rock, above which looms an enormous 'beehive' structure of positively leviathan proportions.

We take a lot of pictures, then walk to the top of the hill and look down on the ruins of this lost kingdom. A very soft wind blows across the summit, bringing with it the scent of thyme and wild flowers; a lizard stirs in the sun, and the bees drone a soporific lullaby. It is utterly still and incredibly serene. Does Agamemnon sleep, at peace at last, I wonder? Is he one with the gods on clouded Olympus?

It is now 4.00pm, and rather late for lunch, so we order bread and cheese and a bottle of wine, while we wait for our driver. On the way back we go by Tiryns; June and I would like to stop, but both Doug and Hector feel we shouldn't push Jannie too far, and we return to the boat by 5.45pm. A little later, and much to our surprise, Jannie takes the boat out, and we head for Spetses in the dark of night, sailing through chilly but calm seas, and finally anchoring in the old harbour at 11.10 (this after several attempts at mooring). I am beginning to think that our Captain is not of that breed that once chased the Golden Fleece or snared the Cyclops on the Grecian seas.

Saturday, May 1 May Day is a holiday in Greece, and the majority of the shops are shut. We move from our anchorage in the old harbour to a berth in the new. I do my thing in the galley, and then Doug and I go for a walk and manage to pick up a few salad things. When we return to the *Larres* we find it in yet another berth, with only Jannie on board.

We go in search of the others, whom we find and we all take a carriage through the streets of the village to a little beach on the other side of the bay. It is quite lovely with masses of poppies, and the usual scented groves of oranges and lemons. Hector is chosen to test the water, which he declares to be too cold for swimming, much to everyone's relief I suspect, and we make our way back to the boat.

Here, the odious Jannie gives me his 'I-am-the-captain-nod' toward the galley. I put together a tuna salad, with some toasted cheese biscuits, clean up and then decide to go to our cabin for a rest. I have just begun to read when the lights go out and I fall asleep (which I probably would have done even with the lights on). I wake up some time later to the pitching, rolling, jolting of the boat – I decide to stay put until the pitching becomes increasingly violent and I have need of the head.

I stumble into that black hole, feeling more than a tad queasy. After being bashed about and frustrated in an attempt to stand up, I make my way to the deck. Hector (bless him) recognizes the symptoms and gives me his place so I can get the wind. A few deep breaths help no end, and I am able to maintain my unblemished record of being never, never sick at sea.

We put into the little bay at Poros where Jannie's son and another lad come on board. This 'unexpected' visit has obviously been carefully arranged and probably accounts for our near midnight arrival yesterday. However, they are nice boys, and it is a pleasant enough encounter. Everybody is going out for dinner, but Doug digs in his heels. He for one (and me, for two) are staying on board. As he says later, he is determined to have at least one meal of our investment in provisions. So I forage among the tins, and come up with an imaginative, if rather peculiar, meal. As it turns out, it is one of the best and most enjoyable evenings in Greece, so far. We light a candle or two, have a bottle of wine and retire before the rest of the crew return.

Sunday, May 2 It is bright and sunny in the little harbour of Poros. With the extra crew still aboard, the four paying guests take off together to explore the town. We do a tour of various coffee shops and bistros. At one we are treated to a cheese pie created by the owner's English wife; at another, we sit in a lovely little outdoor café under a cloud of orange blossoms. Hector disappears briefly and returns with a silk handkerchief for me, featuring a curly-headed little shepherd boy exactly what I had been looking for to complete my mental photograph album of the Greek landscape. We rather reluctantly return to the *Larres* and take off at 12.53pm, dropping the boys off at their campsite before heading back in the general direction of Athens.

It is a wonderful day of sailing, enough wind, but not chilly. I have a bit of a problem getting to the galley (full of gear) to make Hector a tomato sandwich, but emerge triumphantly with something to everyone's taste. If it isn't, they know better than to say so.

After lunch, June and I go ashore for a long walk. We come to a strange little clutter of new and ugly houses, and conclude that this is probably a weekend resort for Athenians. Why the inheritors of Pericles should elect to build such an ugly retreat is hard to fathom. All in all it is a pleasant, lazy sort of day. Furthermore, we are anchored in such an attractive little bay and the weather is at last benign, so we even have hopes of a swim tomorrow morning.

We are just about to retire for the night when Linda comes rushing onto the deck with the news that the radio has announced a storm warning and we must return immediately to Athens. It seems so at odds with what we can observe. There is no wind, the stars are clear and bright and we are in a sheltered anchorage.

Doug and Hector both question and protest, but it is Jannie's boat, and he says we have no idea how rough it can be. The mutinous and suspicious Canadian contingent notwithstanding, we leave at 11.30pm. I decide to absent myself and fall asleep, not waking up until the engines stop and we come into Pireas at 1.35am. Doug is just coming down

284

the steps into the cabin, and declares that the "storm" has not materialized, the night is still, the sea calm and we have been done out of a day of sailing. To the sound of his indignant mutterings, I fall asleep once more.

Monday, May 3   Absolutely no gale and no wind, but an enormous storm as Hector has what he refers to as "wee chat" with Dr N. He (Hector) is furious and delivers himself of his opinion of Jannie's seamanship, ancestry and honour in no uncertain terms. Doug, less choleric, feels cheated, both by the lack of value for his $100 worth of provisions, and for being short-changed a day on his charter agreement. Personally, I am so looking forward to space, space, space, and a comfortable bed in the hotel that I cannot get too exercised. over these infamies. Doug hits the nail on the head when he theorizes that as Dr N has another week of the Perrys' charter ahead, he manufactured the story of the storm warning in order to get back to Athens to check his office before he has to take off again. The partings from the *Larres* are cordial enough on my part, but there is still a distinct lack of warmth in the general atmosphere. June and Hector return to Athens with us and luxuriate in baths at the Athen's Gate. When Doug and Hector go off to the bank to get some cheques cashed, June and I re-hash our adventures.

She is not, repeat, *not* happy about returning for the second week, although we both agree that Hector has more than made his point and things may well be different. I ask her if there is anything I can do for her, and she replies with a "yes" – I can give her our tickets to Paris.

When the men return, we decide a cheery outing will be a visit to the Museum, which is fabled and contains such wonders as the gold mask of Agamemnon. We take a cab only to find that Monday is closing day. We seem thwarted at every turn, but, as usual, we locate that great soother, a taverna, where we have lunch and say goodbye to the Perrys. Despite everything, we have all loved being together and know there will be not-to-be-forgotten memories of thyme-scented hills, of Epidaurus and Mycenae, and sailing in the Aegean, even if it was not all as originally envisioned.

Doug and I spend the rest of the afternoon enjoying a poke

around Athens. I hope we will return some day so that we can go to Delphi and Delios and the Museum. If not, I will still go away with a feeling for the Isles of Greece that I don't think will ever leave me.

CHAPTER 34

Tuesday, May 4 We get a wake-up call at 4.00am. Ready to leave by 5.00am and reach the airport at 5.25. Whew! After all that dawn breaking, the plane is late, but finally we are on board by 7.00am, and there are the girls! They look so sweet, clean and pretty, and I glow with pride and relief that they are indeed on the flight, as organized.

The journey is uneventful and we arrive in Paris with an incredible mass of luggage. In addition to the wardrobe necessary for two and a half months at home, Barbara has brought all her 'O' level books for study. We load the luggage onto the airport bus while Doug checks with JAL and confirms our onward flight. Once at the bus terminal downtown, we get a porter who piles the bags into a taxi. Every square inch of said cab is filled, and Hilary ends up sitting on Doug's lap. We give our destination address, only to observe a look of complete incomprehension on the driver's face. He casts his eyes toward heaven, spreads his hands and mutters something that after all my French study, I recognize as meaning to eat something unspeakable. It seems our hotel, the Lafayette, is in the International Centre, which is exactly where we are. By now, of course, our porter has fled, and he must have spread the word because it is well nigh impossible to get another. Rather red-faced and unaided by the taxi driver, we unload our mountain of luggage, an 'O' level paper floating out to be lost forever in the International Centre. Doug goes over to pry a porter loose from the hotel. Centuries later and after getting stuck in the elevator, we finally are in our rooms. The great universal fixer-upper is duly mixed, and we slowly begin to relax.

Not only is JAL putting us up in this very downtown and upmarket hotel, but we discover that meals are included, so we all toddle down to L'Arc en Ciel for what turns out to be a bang-up lunch. We have four days in Paris, and our thrifty plan is to stay in the posh Lafayette for the two days JAL allows us, plus one more (our stop-over allowance from the Canadian Government), and then one night at our old friend,

Les Colonies on the Rue St Ferdinand.

After lunch we walk over to Les Colonies only to find they have no vacancies until Sunday, so return to the Lafayette and happily prepare for a second free gourmet meal. However, jet lag and fatigue take over, we fall asleep and none of us wakes up until 10.00pm, only too pleased to go back to sleep.

Wednesday, May 5   Ah Paris, City of Light, Centre of the Cultural Universe. I recall my first youthful visit, and envy the girls seeing this wondrous city for the first time. Hilary taps at our door at 7.00am. When Doug asks her what she would like to do today, she gawks at him. "Today?" She is convinced it is 7.00pm and time for last night's dinner. Absolutely flabbergasted that she has slept for 16 hours.

After breakfast we take the Metro to the Louvre. 'The Winged Victory of the Samothrace' still stands at the top of the central staircase and still fills me with awe as it did the first time I saw it. The children are very impressed, and we wander tirelessly through the Roman-Greco and Egyptian rooms, and *les salons de peinture*, gazing at the Mona Lisa with all due deference, although I conceal from my offspring the fact that I have always felt the famous smile to be more of a simper.

Despite the enjoyment of all that culture, the thought of another sumptuous lunch draws the girls back to the Lafayette. We then walk in the Tuilleries and along the Rue de Rivoli, where we shop and poke and enjoy a lemonade. The girls are loving it, and Barbara, although she won't admit it, is rather chuffed at being whistled at by *les Français* with the added corollary of "Ooh la la, cherie."

Thursday, May 6   Doug goes to make a duty call at the Canadian Embassy, and the girls and I walk along L'Avenue de la Grande Armée, and on to the Champs Elysée, where we buy Hilary a pair of canvas sandals and some new socks. The ones she had on revealed an embarrassingly enormous hole.

After a lemonade on the boulevard, we take the Metro to the Eiffel Tower, where we are to meet Doug. We arrive at 1.00pm on the dot, and Doug, predictably enough, comes along an hour later. The view of Paris is, as always, spectacular, and I am once again impressed by the inspiration that guided that long-ago town planner. Paris is doing its best to combat urban sprawl and the current trend for a forest of high-rises, but the soaring towers are beginning to appear and sadly I suppose that Paris, too, will gradually change.

We lunch in the Eiffel's restaurant, and the children are enthralled. Much to his delight, Doug at last sees Napoleon's tomb at Les Invalides. He swears that Paris sees him coming and decides to *fermer* everything the minute he comes to visit. He never has managed to get to Le Jeu de Paume.

While at the Embassy, Doug had checked in with the Health and Welfare incumbent, Dr Kubrik, who kindly invited us over to his apartment for drinks. Consequently around 6.00pm we present ourselves at 185 Rue-Faubourg-St-Honoré. Remembering my impoverished backpacking days in Paris, I find it hard to believe that I am actually calling at Paris's Nob Hill.

Mrs K greets us warmly and pours an absolutely sublime G&T. I am so thirsty and it is so deliciously cold. Not too surprisingly, considering the elite address, their apartment is superb, with nicely appointed living room, huge kitchen and pretty bedrooms.

We find we have much in common. The Kubriks had been posted in Delhi, and lived in our house, with the Grahams' Salamat as their cook. We have a really pleasant time, and after several attempts, finally leave at the shocking hour of 9.00pm. Fortunately the French eat late.

Friday, May 7 Our three free nights are up, so after a family confab, we decide to spend the next day and night in the country. Doug and I go off to arrange a car. I am needed, not for my knowledge of French cars, but for my knowledge (?) of French. We drive off with a Renault 20 – very nice and not unreasonable, and with a trunk big enough to accommodate our ever-increasing luggage.

We get out of Paris without incident, thanks to the new *périphérique*, and head straight for Fontainebleau. It is a glorious day, as only a day in May can be. We find L'Hôtel Londres, which, as advertised, is right across the road from the Chateau.

We have lunch on the terrace. Hilary, with her short hair,

and penchant for denim shorts, is frequently taken for a little boy, but I have assured her that no Frenchman would ever be guilty of such a mistake. Any Frenchman worth his salt will always know a girl from a boy. So much for maternal assurances. Sitting on the lovely terrace under a flowering arbour, we inspect the menu. Orders are placed, and the waiter turning to Hilary asks:

"Et pour le petit monsieur?"

Despite this little contretemps, the lunch is very French and very delicious, after which we walk across the road to the gates of the Chateau. It is not particularly busy, and we wander at will. The Chateau seems smaller than I remember it, but that could have been because I had seen so few palaces at the time of my first viewing. Napoleon's 'bees' are everywhere and it really is a fascinating tour. The girls are entranced. This is a real castle, the stuff of fairy tales where princesses eat off golden plates and handsome princes are around every corner.

I have recently read a biography of Napoleon and his family, *The Golden Bees*, and am able to fill in a few corroborative details and such spice as decorum allows. After a tour of the Chateau, we walk around the gardens, which are magnificent and very much in the French style. The lawns are green and of a manicured perfection; there are fountains playing, ponds with swans a-swimming and, hidden away in the shrubbery, the charming little belvederes so beloved of lovers.

We stop for tea and then decide to drive on to Barbizon. I come over all tutorial and lecture the girls on the Barbizon School of Millet and Co. Fortunately they know nothing of the subject, so any inaccuracies escape contradiction. A beautiful day in the springtime countryside, and one to remember.

Saturday, May 8 Leave Fontainbleau at 7.30am and reach Charles de Gaulle without incident and in loads of time. When we check in the car, we learn that our whole golden day yesterday – car, hotel, meals et al – is less than the cost of our room alone in Paris.

We board an Air Canada 747 for a smooth and comfortable flight and, after a brief stop in a cold and drizzly Montreal, land in Toronto. We are home, or at least our collective foot is on our native heath. "Breathes there a man...."

CHAPTER 35

Canada – Spring/Summer, 1976

Once back on home ground, my diary is more or less abandoned in the flurry of family gatherings and friendships renewed. When we left Canada more than a year ago, I was prepared to give this whole Foreign Service fling two years at the very most. Now I am not so sure. It is wonderful to be back and to see cherished friends, but although they are glad to see us, they are not truly interested in our life away. It is the return of the native, and the expectation is that we will once again pick up where we left off, and return to the 'real world'.

And in a way we do. We see Doug's relatives in Toronto, and mine in Winnipeg; we visit Martin's school in Selkirk, and have tea with the Head. This once again is Canada, "our home and native land," but 'home' is also a lovely house on a tree-lined street with a bougainvillea hedge and a poetic tree in the garden. Home is also my commitment to new associations and enterprises, and for the first time I experience the cultural schizophrenia of the returning exile.

When we finally reach Vancouver, and leave Customs to come through the main concourse of the airport, I spot people waving – a delegation of friends has come to greet us, and I am touched to tears. Peter is there, but Kilmeny is still at the university. She phones later to report that she successfully passed her ski instructor's exam – only 14 out of 50 applicants passed, and only three girls. She is totally elated, as this can lead to a lucrative job for the winter holidays. As an after-thought of little importance, she adds that she got an A+ in her essay on Sartre. That's my clever girl.

The group of greeters accompanies us back to the house we have rented in West Vancouver. Drinks are poured, and tea is made. It is a nice house, and handy to everything, although I do feel the owners, away for two months, are a bit grasping.

The rent is not all that cheap. In addition we are to pay the hydro bill (the garden lights must be on all night), the telephone bill and they even asked that we bring our own bedding. On this last point, I dug in my heels, and told her to forget the whole thing, as I was certainly not going to cart sheets, quilts and pillows half-way around the world, particularly considering we already had a good percentage of the British School library in our gear. They also threw in pet-sitting of an elderly and rather smelly dog.

Later that evening, family and a contingent of faithful friends gather at the house. The wine flows freely, as does the conversation. We get caught up on local gossip, who is where, and what is what, and for a few minutes it is as though we had never left. Nobody is particularly keen to hear any breathless account of our adventures on the subcontinent. Someone will ask that we tell them "all about India." One of us barely begins, when someone else breaks in with "Have you heard that Jim and Cynthia are getting a divorce?"

The first week or so is occupied with arranging a car, checking on the house, arranging dental appointments, etc. Eventually all is settled and there follows a time of mixed fortunes, and a balancing of pros and cons. It turns out to be one of the worst summers in living memory as far as weather is concerned – constant rain and grey skies. Balanced against this is the glory of being in this immensity of fresh and lovely green after India's dusty landscape.

All is not totally serene with some of our friends – one of Doug's closest colleagues is gravely ill with an inoperable malignancy, two neighbours are in a land dispute and a couple of old friends are on the cliff's lip of legal separation.

Against these cons is the pro of permanence in our personal relationships. These are not fleeting acquaintances about to be posted and never heard from again.

We are swept up in a flurry of social activities and outings – picnics (sodden and otherwise); boating with the Perrys, the Whitens and the Walcotts; dinners and lunches; golf (where I do not distinguish myself) and bridge (where I do). While Doug and Barbara are still with us, we have a number of great family get-togethers, but work and 'O' levels call them back, and they leave on their return journey on May 29.

There is a sense of real letdown after they go, and that night, Hilary and I stay home, listen to the rain, and snuggle under comforters to watch some mindless TV. On that subject, I had been looking forward to television after more than a year of abstinence, but now I find I haven't really missed it at all.

The social pace continues unabated. Hilary spends a great deal of time with her friend, Claire, who was her bosom buddy on Stone Crescent. I reluctantly turn my attention to our house, my house, my beautiful house. To me it is not the bricks and mortar it is to Doug, it is a place of heart and soul, into which I had poured so much of me, and leaving it was one of the hardest things I ever did.

When I phoned our lessees to ask if I might come up to see the house, I found it was no longer mine. They have been good tenants, but without our furniture, our paintings, our family, it is not the same. My garden is a tangled forest and the grass is growing up between the stones on the patio. I cannot really fault the tenants – she is pregnant and he is busy, and it is not theirs. Also, they tell me, they are 'shower' people and all the bathrooms need 'doing'. As an extra added depressant, they tell me that yesterday the oil truck broke a water main under the driveway, which will have to be repaired.

What follows is the downside of being an absentee landlord, and on my own. I hire our next-door neighbour, who has a small contracting business, to re-do the shower stall in what had been Barbara and Hilary's bathroom. He gives a rough estimate of $1,500 and asks for $500 down, which I pay him. No sooner done, than my very good friend Ruth Robinson (vastly knowledgeable when it comes to this sort of thing) tells me that there is no legal requirement to pay a cent until the job is done, and the price is outrageous. Contracting neighbour and Doug had been emotionally at sword point before we left, and I felt that in giving him the job, I was offering an olive branch. Instead, I now have to assume he is rubbing his hands at my immediate response of the $500 cheque, which indicates apparently that I am a pigeon just waiting to be plucked. After weeks of delay, he finally finishes. Our tenants have kept a time chart of the contractor's hours on the site, which totalled three; the tile people have applied the tiles I paid for and our tenant has re-hung the shower door and done the clean up.

The total bill, which happily I do not get until the day before Hilary and I are due to leave, is $1,500. Meanwhile

"Oh but you see, the trees had to be topped, oh my, yes"

The tenant has phoned the Better Business Bureau and a local bathroom firm, and both assess the job at $500. Coward that I am, I do not want a confrontation, so after consultation with our dear friend and indispensable adviser and lawyer, Glen Baker, I leave the matter with him. On his advice, I write the contractor a letter that I will mail from India.

Said letter is much mulled over, and carefully couched. Its tenor is that the bill arrived rather late, and consequently was turned over to our solicitor, together with the bill from the tile people, and the tenants' timesheet. If he, the contractor, will send any remaining receipts to Mr Baker, he will see to payment.

It goes without saying that the matter never went any further; in the end, justice was served and the correct amount was paid.

I do not get off so easily with the gardener I hire. I should have known from the singsong accent on the other line that I am in the hands of a wily *mali*. I meet him at the site, and point out the overgrown flowerbeds, the ragged lawn and the general tackiness of the garden. He promptly says the trees should be topped. Forget the trees, I respond; if the tenants want them topped, they can top them. I just want the garden cleaned up. Price: $1,000. What? I have not spent one and half years in India for nothing. We bargain back and forth, and finally settle on $480, which is about right.

When I return to view the transformation after he had been, my mouth assumes a permanent gape. Nothing, but nothing, has been tidied up, but all the trees at the bottom of the garden have been topped. I turn into a proper Memsahib and the telephone line sizzles with my indignation. Ali or whatever his name is comes, back, smiling and crawling:

"Oh but you see, the trees had to be topped, oh my, yes, and I gave you a very good price." My protestations fall on deaf ears, and I receive the all-too-familiar Indian head waggle. When the dust has settled, he magnanimously tells me he will now see to the tidying of the garden for another $160.

If I had the backbone of cooked asparagus I would have told him where to sling his backside. But it is all getting too much, and I tell him to go ahead, insisting it had better look as though it had been trimmed with nail scissors. Of course, it doesn't, but I pay the $160 anyway and long for the Sahib.

And so the time of our departure nears. Martin spends part of the time with us after school ends and he, Hilary and I do our holiday thing of cycling around Barnston Island, as well as the other summer 'musts'.

Upon request I write an article on India for *The Franciscan*, the parish paper for St Francis-in-the-Wood Anglican Church. Also on request, I am the guest speaker at a meeting of the Franciscans, the church's women's auxiliary.

It is during this meeting that the vast abyss between the 'haves' and the 'have-nots' shows up in Technicolor. During the business section, the discussion centres on how $10,000 raised at a recent event should be spent. The Franciscan's charter decrees that any money raised in the community must be spent in the community. In a neighbourhood where the norm is to have either a swimming pool or a tennis court, it is not all that easy to find a suitable charity.

The vicar comes up with a suggestion that perhaps the money might be spent in counselling those suffering from the dark side of affluence – such as alcohol abuse, drug addiction, divorce and the growing number of dysfunctional families. Listening to all this, I want to scream at them that I know where they can spend their money. I think of our ambitious hope of raising $1,000 to give a whole village a crèche programme for a full year. It is sad, but it is reality, and I have to admit that a couple of years ago I, too, would not have given a thought to India's social ills.

CHAPTER 36

Saturday, July 17   It's 'D' for 'Departure' Day, and after a major clean up of our rented house and garden, plus a flurry of farewell events, Hilary and I are on our way. It is another typically fraught exit. There are last minute business affairs, travellers' cheques to be arranged and, most important of all, Hilary to be collared before she goes blithely out the door on some lengthy and undiscussed junket.

All is organized, and we are away at 3.35pm. Just reach Dundarave, when we remember our coats, and race back to collect them. It is now 4.30pm and the Lion's Gate Bridge traffic is already beginning to pile up. Georgia Street is even worse, and we inch our way along Burrard, until it becomes blocked off. By now, I am really panicky and Hilary knows enough not to open her mouth.

We finally reach the airport, and rush to organize tickets and weigh our luggage. *Disaster!* We are 19 kilos overweight, and there's no friendly JAL representative to say "pish-tush". There is, of course, a substantial sum to pay before we can proceed. For some reason, this particular employee is not keen on a credit card, and I hesitate about using up my travellers' cheques, since we still have a long way to go, with a number of planned stops.

The original arrangement for a civilized departure (before forgotten coats and traffic tie-ups) had been to meet Kilmeny and her lifelong friend Lynn in the airport lounge for a leisurely drink, but forget that. We just have to get rid of 19 kilos. I send Hilary off to find Kilmeny in the lounge. She returns with the report that there is no sign of them. I suspect the maître d' would not let her in, so I leave Hilary with the luggage, which by now is being jettisoned in full view of a crowd of neat Orientals – several books, a large piece of driftwood, a pottery creation of dubious origin, a starter set of Gladys Wright's 'monster dough', and heaven knows what else.

I locate Kilmeny and Lynn, who have been waiting for ages for the promised drink, and gather them up to help. I give

Kilmeny the keys to the car, and she and Lynn begin removing the excess out to the car's inadequate trunk. As they retreat, I hear my eldest child mutter to her friend:

"This would never happen if Dad were here."

It's all I need. We have time only for a couple of desperate hugs, and Hilary and I check our luggage – minus 19 kilos – through to Osaka, and stumble toward the boarding gate.

We are no sooner on board, than there is an announcement that the flight will be delayed, due to the unexpected intransigence of a First Class passenger who has decided "she does not wish to go." It is too much. I shut my eyes, and dream of unfettered travels and magic carpets. Hilary glances over at me.

"Never mind, Mummy, the drinks are coming, and not a minute too soon." Her insight never fails to amaze me.

Nonetheless, with the unseemly debacle in the departure lounge still a sharp memory, I am aware that this coming expedition with Hilary is totally my responsibility. I am now far removed from the independence of my youth, and Kilmeny's cogent comment still lingers in my ears. I am now the one responsible for seeing to tickets, carrying luggage and booking into hotels. However, apart from our hand luggage, heavy and crammed with some of the 19 kilos, our bags are checked through to Osaka; our traveller's cheques and passports are firmly zipped into my purse, and all should be well. Barbara and Doug took the same route from Vancouver to India at the end of May, and Barbara wrote me a full account of where to go, what to see and what to watch for. I read it over again with interest, fall asleep and do not wake up until the plane lands in Tokyo at 8.30pm the next day.

Sunday, July 18 We de-plane and get our hand luggage through customs. I cash a traveller's cheque and then we board a bus to our hotel (pre-arranged by the indefatigable JAL). Everything goes smoothly, except for our *really* heavy hand luggage, which we must load and unload. If the Japanese provide porters, we do not see them. At the hotel, we stay awake long enough for a light supper, then fall into our beds.

I am deeply asleep when the phone rings at 1.00am and a voice on the other end of the line tells me I have "offended the

299

Emperor". I think I must be dreaming. I don't even *know* the Emperor, how could I possibly have offended him? The highest rank I ever offended was when I contradicted the Grade 7 English teacher. I think back. Did I ever draw a moustache on his portrait, or recite the story of there was a "nasty Nip in the air" when he flew to London? I am still half asleep, but I ask the caller for an explanation.

It seems that when we de-planed in Tokyo, our luggage was also taken off the plane and we did not check it through customs, upsetting the Emperor no end. Our battered bags are now in the Lost and Found at JAL, and must be processed tomorrow morning. I do not ask why, if they were booked through to Osaka, they are not in Osaka. Such a question would probably cause the Emperor to go into a fatal decline, so I toss and turn over the weight of my appalling sin for the rest of the night.

Monday, July 19 Up at the crack of dawn, but even though we are down for breakfast at 6.40am, the meal does not arrive until half an hour later, and we only have time for a bite of toast and a gulp of coffee. Dash out to the bus, and there is a real donnybrook when the driver takes us to the International Terminal instead of the Domestic. Once transferred to the Domestic, I have to return to the International because that is where the disgraced luggage is waiting to be claimed. Hilary is posted to guard the hand luggage at the Domestic Terminal while I scurry over to the International, a good two blocks away.

I address myself to the department for repentant travellers. A lot of sign language and charades, but I finally get a young man who speaks English. He bows and tells me to sign an apology to the Emperor, and pay 2,400 Yen as a penalty *or*, (and this is a monumentally important 'or') collect my luggage at Customs in Osaka. My ears prick up at the mention of "Customs in Osaka".

"Why," I query, "if there is a Customs at Osaka, and I checked my bags through direct to Osaka, are they not waiting for me there?"

A muttering and hand-waving, and the young man departs. Comes back and tells me I do not have to pay 2,400

Yen, only 100 Yen, but I must sign apology to the Emperor. I say all right, but why did my luggage not go directly through to Osaka as I was told it would? A deep bow, and he rushes off once more. Returns. Bows again. He apologizes, JAL apologizes; the Emperor's Customs apologize. I do not have to pay any yen, I do not have to sign an apology but I will have to "lun vely vely fast," to the Domestic Departure if I am to catch the flight to Osaka. The luggage will be checked through. Another bow.

Back I dash, gather up Hilary, drape myself in several layers of coats as a space-saving device, and carry our luggage, Sherpa fashion, to the waiting departure lounge.

A pleasant enough flight to Osaka, and we board the bus to the Grand Hotel in nearby Kyoto. The traffic is slow, and we reach the hotel around noon. There are no porters in evidence, so once again Hilary and I lumber around loading our luggage onto a hotel conveyance. No sooner is the last piece added to the pyramid, than a bowing, toothy-smiled porter rushes up to help.

I am rapidly coming to a decision that once I am in our room, I shall never leave it again, nor shall I ever lift another bulging bag onto another bus. However, at Hilary's urging, I bestir myself for lunch, after which we agree to treat ourselves to a 'rest' which goes on until 1.00am.

Tuesday, July 20 While in Vancouver, last year's summer visitor to Delhi, Miss Barrow, got in touch. It turned out that she, too, was planning a tour with a group, and would be in Japan at the same time as us. Through coincidence, her group is also booked into the Grand, and we have agreed to meet.

With our prolonged slumbers of last night, we are up early – organize a much-needed laundry service, have breakfast, arrange future tours, leave a note for Miss B, then set off, on foot to walk to a temple recommended in Barbara's informative letter.

It is our first Japanese temple, and it is quite lovely. Like everything else in Japan, it is very neat and tidy, with a spare and understated grace. We take pictures, then pick up a taxi, and are very impressed that the driver is wearing white gloves, as it seems they all do. He takes us to the Kyoto Handicraft

Centre. We watch artisans making damascene jewellery, painting scrolls and creating woodblocks. It is all quite fascinating. We make a few purchases, and have lunch at the Centre. After a brief rest at the hotel, we take a tour bus to Nara.

The drive there is a bit dull. The rice fields are a brilliant and beautiful green, and there is the odd little Japanese touch but, by and large, the countryside is ordered, highly industrialized and not all that interesting to drive through.

Once at Nara, however, it is a different story. We enter into a heavenly park of pines and cypress, absolutely alive with spotted deer (more than 1000 of them). In October, they organize a 'hunt' for the purpose of cutting horns. They are sold – the horns, that is – apparently very profitably.

Unfortunately, the Todai-Ji temple is being renovated, and is covered with scaffolding that makes it look like an airport hangar. However, the 1300-year-old gate, with its enormous guardian figures and its great stone lion dogs, is in full view, and quite awesome.

Inside, the huge and overwhelming figure of Buddha dominates everything. Cast in bronze, he sits upon a gigantic throne, surrounded by smaller Buddhas, each one representing a level toward enlightenment. Two gold-leaf figures are mounted on either side of the throne, one representing Peace and the other Fortune. Perfectly honed wooden pillars hold up the roof, one of which has a hole in it (the size of the leviathan Buddha's nostril, we are told). The legend goes that if you can climb through it, you will be blessed with good fortune. Personally, I cannot think of anything I would rather do less than climb up Buddha's nose, and Hilary, being mildly claustrophobic, also declines. A boy of 17 or so takes up the challenge, and we are both relieved to see him emerge at the other end.

We walk back through the deer forest to the bus, which takes us to our next stop at a Shinto shrine. I rather like the Japanese approach to religion – it is so open-minded. There is none of this "there-is-but-one-God" religious dogma. In Japan you can be a Buddhist and a Shintoist, or anything else, all at the same time, and take the best from all the different faiths.

As a matter of fact, it seems a lot of worship is largely a

matter of occasion. Buddhist shrines are usually attended for solemn events, such as funerals and services for the sick, while attendance at Shinto shrines is mainly for joyful occasions such as weddings and to celebrate a birth.

The gate is painted a brilliant 'Chinese' red, a colour that seems to have a powerful significance throughout Asia. We walk up a long flight of stone steps, past endless little Japanese stone pagoda affairs, which I am sure have a meaningful purpose, but one which eludes me.

It has been an interesting afternoon, but tiring. Back at the hotel, Hilary is keen to go swimming, and I dutifully accompany her, although the day has turned cloudy and thunderous, and not all that conducive for swimming. There follows a long discussion as to where we should go for dinner. A nearby Japanese restaurant does not appeal, and is also woefully expensive, so we select a Chinese one, which seems a bit unfair in Japan. However, it is a super meal, and Hilary has to be restrained from licking the plate.

When we return to our room, we hasten to turn on the TV to watch the Olympics, which have just opened in Montreal. We are full of nationalistic fervour to see our compatriots compete. It is our first experience of viewing an international sports event anywhere but in Canada, and it is rapidly brought home to us that we are not going to see any Canadians. The only contests we see are those in which Japanese athletes are participating. This all seems grossly unfair, until we acknowledge that we are equally selective in Canada, as they probably are in the US or England or Timbuktu.

Wednesday, July 21 Still no call from Miss B, which I can't understand. Hilary and I go down for breakfast, and book an afternoon tour, then set out to spend the morning on our own.

First to the Golden Pavilion. It is a reconstruction of a 12th-century building, attractively (rather than garishly) gilded, and located beside a charming little lake. The gardens and walks are lovely, and we enjoy it, strolling along, smelling the flowers and listening to the birds.

Next stop is the old Imperial Palace. This boasts a rather peculiar system called "Permission and Tour". We are not a tour, nor do we have permission, but we do have persistence,

303

and after a lot of unintelligible haranguing from guards, we locate the 'permission' place, only to find the next tour is not until 2.00pm. We are already booked for an afternoon tour, so we elect instead to seek out Nijo Castle.

This is of particular interest to me, having recently read James Clavell's *Shogun.* We go into a 'waiting salon', the only Caucasians in a group of Japanese. As we enter the Shogun's wing, we are aware of a strange, but not unpleasant, whistling sound. Our guide speaks only Japanese, but thanks to Mr Clavell, I recognize this as the 'Nightingale Floor'. It leads to the Shogun's quarters, and was installed to alert the guards of any possible enemy approaching the exalted chamber.

The castle is really something! The rooms are large, with clean matting and beautifully painted golden walls. We see the various attendance halls and throne rooms, and Hilary hangs gratifyingly on my every word, being unable to hang on to the guide's. We really feel we have not had enough, but reluctantly leave to get back in time for our booked tour.

We barely have a moment to wash our faces, and then dash down to lunch. We phone Miss B again – no answer – and head out for the bus, and who should be waiting there... Miss B! She is in a queue for another bus, and we fall upon each other. Apparently she had been phoning us when we were out, so we have a quick exchange of apologies and agree to meet for dinner.

First stop on our tour is the Kasuga Taisha Shrine located at the top of a very steep village street, lined with shops. The shrine itself is lovely and the weather sublime. We take pictures, then walk over to the 'lucky fountain', for a 'cup of health'. This is a communal cup and, like true North Americans, we wipe it with Kleenex. Still, it is a toss-up whether our drink will bring health or Kyoto Kinetics (the Japanese equivalent of Delhi Belly).

We walk over to watch some very slick potters at work. We would like to have dallied longer, but "Time is frying, and we have to hully along," as our guide so quaintly puts it.

Next on the agenda is Sanjusangendo, a Buddhist temple containing 1001 statues of Buddhist statues, all located in a large central hall. Hilary is all for counting them, but our guide is in full explanatory spate. With all the Ls and Rs I am not sure of the accuracy of my understanding, but as far as I can make out, Sanjusangendo means 33, which is a propitious number for Buddhists, based on the belief that Buddha saved mankind by disguising himself in 33 different forms. I miss exactly how these transformations saved mankind, but take our guide's word for it.

There are all sorts of grotesque figures in the outer halls that we have to skim by on orders from the guide. She really does her best to keep her straggling flock around her, and repeats every phrase twice, almost like the refrain of a song.

Back on the bus, we drive through a torrential downpour to another Shrine. Our guide, nonplussed by the unexpected rain, announces: "We are 21; 21, but have only 19 umblerras – only 19 umblerras."

Hilary and I rescue her, volunteering to do without 'umblerras' and walk out into what is now a mild drizzle. The Shrine is quite splendid in green, gold and amber, but the gardens are the chief delight, and an example of the highest standard of Japanese landscape design. I think nostalgically back to my plans for a Japanese garden and how dramatically short it fell of the real thing. We have a lovely saunter past clear pools, framed in fern-like shrubs, and under flowering arbours until we are recalled once again to the bus.

Back at the hotel, we change and get ready for our night out with Miss B. She had invited us to have dinner with her when we met up in Vancouver. So, as she is paying for the meal, I feel it only fair that I order up drinks and canapés before hand. Meanwhile Hilary has sussed out the hotel restaurant, and come up with the astonishing news that salmon is only 1,500 yen (I think about $8-$10). We should have suspected something was amiss, but the ever-thrifty Miss B is elated and declares that is where we shall have dinner tonight.

My worst fears are realized as we go up to an incredibly swishy restaurant and I check out the salmon on the menu outside. It is 1,500 Yen all right, but for the small smoked salmon starter. The rest of the menu is strictly for Shoguns and robber barons. Knowing how carefully Miss B organizes her finances, I suggest we go elsewhere, but scarcely have the words died upon the lip when we are swept into the grandiose dining room, and snowy napkins are tucked under our chins. As 'face' is everything in the Orient, I cannot see us skulking out at this stage. If they had had chicken feet on the menu, we would all have opted for that, but finally we settle for some sort of fowl, and I offer to split the bill.

Miss B, to her credit, thanks-but-no-thanks me. It is her treat, she insists. Whatever it is we had, it is remarkably good. The bill comes, and Miss B does not have sufficient cash – she'll have to cash a traveller's cheque. We are already running late for the cultural performance we'd booked for the evening, and the bill ends up on my credit card. Miss B promises to leave the money for me at the desk tomorrow morning. It is all rather embarrassing, and I have seldom felt less comfortable about being taken out for dinner.

It is an interesting programme, although we arrive ten minutes late and miss the tea ceremony, but we all enjoy the flower arranging and the glimpses into the performing arts of the No and Kabuki theatre.

Thursday, July 22 Up at 6.00am because the bus to Osaka and the airport arrives at 8.00am. It is not easy to get a drowsy Hilary going, but we get down to the lobby in the proverbial nick, and bump into Miss B who, faithful to her promise, has an envelope full of yen for last night's dinner. I thank her profusely and dismiss my feelings of guilt. Making our farewells, we board the bus.

Never, never again, I promise myself, will I be loaded down with luggage. I will take a leaf out of the Cartwrights' book in matter of wardrobe. The *Bonanza* family on TV appears every week in identical garb, regardless of occasion. I will not carry extraneous goods such as pressed maple leaves and blackberry jam from West Vancouver berries. All this I solemnly vow as Hilary and I struggle with our Everest of baggage. It is hot and steamy and nobody gives us a hand. I finally lasso a porter who takes us up to the desk, is richly rewarded and departs before I can load him up with hand luggage.

The nightmare continues at the airport as we drag our burdens up to the departure floor, where we find a line-up as long as the whole concourse, We join it. There is only one customs gate, and this sort of jam-up is apparently normal. We are in the queue for almost an hour, pushing our bags along. At the customs, the attendant takes every last thing out of my bag, and I have to stuff it all back in. This is followed by an absolutely interminable trek down the miles to our gate. By the time we are actually in our seats, I am the colour of a ripe tomato and hara-kiri has a distinct appeal. However, a certain amount of calm is restored after I down a walloping gin and tonic.

By the time we reach Hong Kong, I am braced for a repeat, but a JAL representative is waiting for us, with our hotel arrangements. A luggage cart is miraculously produced, we are whizzed like VIPs through customs and bundled into a hotel car for delivery to the Park Hotel. We are so relieved by this blessed service that we do not mind too much that neither one of us is particularly impressed with the hotel. It has an odd smell, unsmiling (if efficient) staff and no TV. However, it is only an overnight stay, and it is still day. We walk for a while through a tropical rainstorm, dodging in and out of shops, then return through steaming streets as the sun comes out. We munch our way through an appalling meal, and then head for bed.

Friday, July 23 Our departure from Hong Kong is a miracle of ease and efficiency compared to the nightmarish exit from Osaka. A pleasant flight and we arrive at Bangkok around 3.00pm, and are settled in the Montien Hotel half an hour later. Determined not to miss anything that Doug and Barbara had seen, we inquire about tours, then organize a taxi for 60 baht He takes us to the Wat Trimitr and we see the Golden Buddha – as impressive as only 5.5 tons of solid gold can be. It seems all that glitters was encased in plaster, and reposed for a few hundred years in a ruined temple near the docks. For some reason in the past, it was being moved and was chipped. Talk about a heart of gold! Anyway from that point on, the Golden Buddha has been the star performer in the Wat Trimitr, and gazed at with awe by all who see it. The day is fading, but the driver takes us to a shopping centre where we buy Doug a shirt, and return to the hotel for a quiet evening.

Saturday, July 24 Refreshed and ready for any sight

Bangkok has to offer. After breakfast, we poke into a few of the hotel shops, and find we were ripped off on Doug's shirt. I paid $9, and the same items are $4 everywhere else. The moral of the story is not to buy anything at a cab-directed store.

Checking Barbara's price list, we get a taxi to take us to the Oriental Hotel for 10 baht. Just before we get there, the cab is stopped by a boat owner, who offers us a trip on the River of Kings for 150 baht. I am surprised because a quick look at Barbara's invaluable document, shows that this is the price she and Doug arrived at only after a great deal of haggling.

We go along a lot of back alleys and finally arrive at the landing dock. Upon inquiry, we find that this price will only give us one hour, and no cruise into the floating market. According to those who know and the guidebooks, the floating market is an absolute 'must-see'. Urged on by my daughter, who has become a hardened negotiator in the Indian bazaars, we make our stand. Thank you, but we will not go, and prepare to depart with some hauteur. In a trice, he calls out to our departing backs that he is a poor man, and there is no profit, but he will give us a two-hour cruise, including the floating market, for the niggardly sum we are prepared to pay.

We set off, and it is marvellous, although more than somewhat smelly. We make our way through narrow channels and canals, some of which are unbelievably tropical and lush, with wild hibiscus, bougainvillea and palm trees. The famous floating market is a bit of a letdown, as we bob around moving displays of fruits and vegetables. I would not really rate it a 'must-see' but it is definitely something one doesn't experience every day.

We decide to lunch on the river terrace of the Oriental, with the rich and famous jet-setters – just as if we belong. I love it. My international image falters when it comes to taking the water taxi, as I have no idea where he will drop us off, so we decide to go by road.

Barbara's missive is getting somewhat dog-eared, but I consult it before hiring a cab. All the drivers want around 35 or 40 baht, to take us to the Wat Po, but Barbara claims 15 is the going rate for locals. We really feel like Old Asian Hands, as we dismiss the 'tourist' price with a cool chuckle and a surely-you-jest smile, and end up paying 20.

The Wat Po is probably the most notable of all Bangkok's many temples. The grounds are rather mucky, but nobody seems unduly fussed. When we arrive, there are classes going on in various areas of the compound – some for student monks, others for children. The elaborate coloured roofs with the distinctive Thai 'prow' are everywhere, most of them painted in the brilliant orange and green with which we are becoming familiar.

We make our way to the Hall of the Reclining Buddha. It seems strange to think of Buddhas being repaired. They should be 'is now and ever has been'. Still that is what is happening, and his massive, recumbent figure is shrouded in scaffolding. Even so, we can still see the immensity of this colossus. He is a little over 150 feet in length, and we slowly pace off every inch until we reach his feet. They are pressed together perfectly, and the soles are absolutely flat. They are made of ebony, flawlessly inlaid with mother of pearl. In the centre of each foot is a large circle, presumably the Buddhist wheel. Surrounding this wheel are squares, approximately four inches by four inches, roughly 84 per foot, and each square is inlaid with horses, elephants, Buddhist temples and what have you. It is truly remarkable and another example of man's search for something eternal, and his need to honour and worship his gods.

From the Wat Po, we take a cab to the Wat Phra Keo, the Royal Palace gardens and the shrine of the Emerald Buddha. The whole complex is dazzling with brilliant green, blue and orange roofs rising above the green foliage and flowers of the gardens. Each shrine has an enormous gateway and even more enormous painted guardians. We go through one of the gates and see the Golden Chedi, which contains relics of Buddha. Everything is very well preserved and it is all quite stunning.

We rather unscrupulously latch onto a tour whose conductor is speaking English, and we follow him into the Pantheon of Kings and the Hall of the Emerald Buddha. This latter is absolutely exquisite, but the Buddha is placed so high above the altar that is difficult to see him.

The guide is telling us that he has a different costume for each season, and this being the rainy season today he is wearing a simple, but beautiful gold robe. Hilary is tugging at my sleeve, and asking me why he is wearing gold for the rainy season, and if she had a golden gown she certainly wouldn't wear it in the rain, and it just doesn't make any sense to her... I can see the guide getting restive over all this chatter, and I hush Hilary up before the guide clues in that we are not paying customers. As we approach the Buddha, the guide warns us not to point a foot in his direction. We have already encountered the perils of foot-pointing through our adventures in Bangalore. To point a foot at a god would, I gather, be the ultimate sin.

It has been a long day, and Hilary and I seem a little abrasive with one another, although we both have enjoyed everything we have seen. Back at the Montien, I buy a bathing suit to match the dress and bag I had previously purchased, and we go down to the pool for a swim. This seems to ease all tensions, and we are chums again by dinnertime.

Earlier in the day, we had signed up for a hotel-sponsored outing to the Pinman, a theatre-restaurant. The bus is waiting for us, and all the pressures of haggling and tipping are eliminated. The whole expedition is very well organized – a delicious Thai dinner, and a good show with some classical Thai dancing. The Pinman is tastefully decorated and furnished.

Similar to the Japanese fashion, we sit on cushions at a long table set in a well, dangling our feet below the table. Everyone is served individually, and we have our own waitress, who offers us several small bowls containing soup, chicken, mushrooms, lemon, curry, fish, bean sprouts, delicately sautéed prawns and rice. All this is followed by a fruit bowl and tea. On the other side of the table is a very nice French couple from Paris, and once again I bless my long hours of labour over French. They charm Hilary, and monsieur assures her she does not look the least bit like a little boy.

Sunday, July 25 The last day of our Asian saga. We arrange our luggage and pay our bill. The only thing on Barbara's list that we have not done is to eat at the much-touted Baht Boat restaurant. We get directions, written out in Thai, and take off.

We locate the Baht Boat but feel it is too early for lunch, so decide to go to the Marble Temple and wander around. It is desperately hot, but we stray back and forth across the bridges

310

into the temple and the private chapel of the Thai King who became a monk. Definitely not Anna's King.

All the Sunday hawkers are out, and Hilary buys a little bird trapped in a hideously dirty cage. As soon as she has it, she opens the door and lets it fly away. The vendor is furious, although I can't see why: she sold the bird, got her money and gets the cage back. It is probably a matter of principle for her, as to free the bird is one for Hilary.

We make our way back to the Baht Boat, where we indulge in a gluttonous feast of chicken and prawns. Back at the hotel I succumb to the silk I had seen earlier, re-pack and we are delivered to the airport a good hour or so ahead of time.

CHAPTER 37

Still Sunday, July 25 We reach Delhi at approximately 9.30pm and the rain is pelting. We get through customs with hardly any hassle, but are discomfited at not seeing any sign of Barbara and Doug. After waiting a little while longer, we brace ourselves for the usual shaking of heads and parlay as to price, but finally organize porters and get a cab.

Still no sign of husband or daughter. The full force of the monsoons has caused the roads to flood, cars to stall and general chaos. I am sure our reception committee is marooned somewhere, while we, on the other hand, reach Vasant Vihar high and dry. It being Sunday there are no servants around, so we pile our luggage under the eaves, then Hilary and I crowd ourselves onto the sheltered part of the patio. It is at this point that Barbara and Doug arrive full of apologies. They had been at a movie, rushed out to the airport, arrived too late, and "well you know how it is," they add, their voices dwindling away.

I do know how it is, and I don't really mind. I am *so* glad to see them that I view them as totally without flaw. It is a wonderful, if transient state of mind, and whether it is Canada or India, I look at Doug and know where home is.

Monday, July 26 When I left Delhi back in April, the International Women's Club made me swear on a stack of Veddas that I would return for the meeting on July 26, so I am up betimes and at Pat Milne's by 10.00am. As corresponding secretary I have masses of letters to write, as well as the newsletter to get out, all of which are required *now!* They all gaze at me as though these chores, once outlined, are already accomplished. I gather up IWC stationery and address myself to the above tasks in the afternoon. This evening the Canadians are gathering at the High Commission to watch their compatriots not win at the Olympics.

Wednesday, July 28 I finished off the newsletter last night and Doug arranges to have it run off ready for distribution. I feel a distinct "whew" coming on. Now feel free to go off to Sheila Brown's for bridge. I rush home to get ready for the British doctor's dinner tonight.

It turns out to be a really nice evening, with an interesting *dramatis personae*, including a girl from the British Council who happens to be a former pupil of Queenswood, which is the school near Potter's Bar that we have in mind for Barbara. Poor Barbara – she rather hoped to go to the Quaker school in Pontefract where Marion Ronke is going, but Doug just doesn't like the look of the rather drear, red brick, functional layout and all the earnest-looking staff. Not exactly sound reasons for dismissing it out of hand, I feel.

Barbara, of course, will have the deciding choice, and she, always wanting to please, is torn between joining Marion and acceding to her father's wishes. The brochure on Queenswood, with its mile-long, tree-lined entrance, its velvet lawns and stately towers swings the vote. With good 'O' level results she should be in. The other English guests at the party all speak highly of Queenswood's academic record, and Elizabeth Grene promises to supply us with a few addresses.

Friday, July 30 We have been introduced to the new Australian doctor and his wife, Justin and Barbara Tiernan. They are our contemporaries and the parents of three daughters, two of whom are around Barbara's age. We all hit it off, and we have been invited for dinner, *en famille*, tonight. Barbara Tiernan and I find we have a universe in common. She, too, has been a journalist, and both of us have husbands who are constantly asking why we don't write bestsellers if we are 'writers'. Do they really think we can make the quantum leap from reporting on the Kildonan Flower Show to *Peyton Place*, just like that?

The oldest daughter is in Australia, but the two younger ones join us for dinner. They are delightful, but very sophisticated for their age, and I suspect a tad wild. They, too, will be going to England in September, and are destined for a very strict Catholic establishment, which, as their mother announces, has no idea of what it is in for. The girls, not unnaturally, feel this school is the ickiest thing they've ever heard of, and our Barbara, not to be outdone, tells the others

313

that Queenswood rules call for any brother or boyfriend being sent away if he arrives without advance notice. The three go off to act out the charade of dismay about their up-coming educational durance, and have a lovely time together.

Monday, August 2   It is Doug's birthday, and I achieve a minor miracle at the American Commissary in that I find a leg of lamb, which we will have for a celebratory dinner tonight. It will be such a change from goat and water buffalo, and is Doug's favourite of all time.

Wednesday, August 4   Barbara and I have lunch with Erryl Dickenson, the old Queenswoodian we met the other night. She supplies us with tons of useful information on the school, including the unwelcome news that the school blazers are purple, Barbara's least favourite colour.

Later on I join Saroj for tea at Claridge's. It is a joy to me that there is no restraint between us. We have the comfortable relationship of old friends, with none of the East-is-East-and-West-is-West feeling I used to experience with Indian women. I think being accepted into the inner circle of the International Women's Club has broken down any such hang-ups. Once again, I am in the company of friends.

Saturday, August 7   The dawn patrol is on duty to pick up Martin, arriving via Pan-Am at 4.00am. Is there any plane that arrives at Palam at noon, I ask myself.? It is all worthwhile, however, for the pleasure of seeing him in the vanguard of the de-planing passengers, looking well and not too tired. We stay up and talk for a while, have breakfast and go back to bed. Doug and Barbara, who were not part of the welcoming committee, go off to play golf.

Sunday, August 8   I suppose parents always experience a sense of guilt about what life in the foreign service does to family life. Having the twins with us for a while is great for them and for us, but Barbara has a whole new school experience ahead of her next month, and Martin will be back in his own milieu in a few weeks. Hilary, on the other hand, has hit a hiatus since her return. Almost all her friends are still away, and Barbara is busy cramming for her 'O' levels with the rest of the Upper Fifth.

We all go down to ACSA for Sunday supper, and the children play shuffleboard. There is an altercation over something or other, and Hilary stalks off in a huff. The twins tick her off as a poor sport, and she announces she will wait in the car. I take up the slack in the game, and when we start for home, Hilary is in a towering sulk. After everybody goes to bed, I call her down, and she sobs out her woes. She feels desperately lonely, and adds that before, she always had Hermione for company, and she misses her so much. I comfort her by saying she will feel so much better when her friends return and school starts. I have a fleeting (very fleeting) thought about getting another dog, but acknowledge the lunacy of such an idea at this stage of our stay in India.

Tuesday, August 10 Jeanette Ronke and I, together with children, have been invited over to Old Delhi for tea at the Chartered Bank House. Monica has arranged bridge for the ladies and a tour of Old Delhi for the young.

With the preponderance of females, Martin is a great hit with the distaff side, and I, not entirely unbiased, am not surprised. He really is very personable and, when enjoying himself, can also be quite charming. I know he will get a lot out of the Old Delhi tour, being a history buff, and he does. The evening is spent in a barrage of questions, answered and unanswerable.

Sunday, August 15 Independence Day – our second one. Now that I have read *Freedom at Midnight* its significance seems so much more real. Mountbatten's insistence on setting a date before he left for his assignment as India's last Viceroy was understandable but, in many respects, disastrous. The last frantic rush, the intransigence of Jinnah, the enormity of Sir Cyril Radcliffe's Herculean task to carve up the subcontinent in such an impossibly short time – all contributed to the appalling blood-bath of separation.

The days have sped by, filled with meetings for the IWC and getting things organized for the International Chrysanthemum Fair. As chairman (do I *have* to say

315

It is a dubious depiction of the Taj Mahal

316

chairperson?) of the Canadian booth, it is incumbent on me to host the meetings for sorting and pricing the items we are gathering for the White Elephant stall.

So far, it really is the most incredible hodgepodge of bibelots. Today Mrs HE brought an item she had unearthed from the Residence godown. Presented to some past head of Mission, it is, in its way, beyond price. Or at least beyond pricing. It is a dubious depiction of the Taj Mahal, edged in lurid sequins, with a bright purple mat and a gilded frame. The potential price tag ranges from 5 paisa to a 'you-never-know' high of 10 rupees.

A lot of work it may be, but we all enjoy these sessions. In addition to the sorting, mending and pricing, we down a great deal of coffee, and munch on a few juicy titbits of gossip.

On top of these absorbing activities, I have also been asked to take over the editorship of *The Scoop*, a Canadian High Commission newssheet started by the Activities Committee. I am happy enough to accept this assignment, as there are few restrictions imposed on the editor and, in a modest way, it becomes *your* paper. Besides, it is good to feel that, more and more, my roots are spreading in the shifting Indian soil.

Our social life, too, continues apace, and pleasantly so, with dinners, lunches, golf and bridge, plus the sheer pleasure of having family around. The monsoons continue unabated, and we wake regularly to a drenched and steaming world.

Tuesday, August 17 Doug brings mail home from the office, including a letter from Ruth Baldwin containing the joyous news that she intends to visit India. I am ecstatic, as Ruth is one of my best and dearest friends. After a European holiday with her husband, Bill, she proposes carrying on to India. Said Bill has declared himself uninterested in Asian wanderings, but is prepared to see her off with his blessing, and a handsome supply of traveller's cheques.

Wednesday, August 18 Still pouring with rain, so I stay home and work on *The Scoop*. I am almost finished and want Doug to take it up to the High Commission for printing. The office is closing early for Lord Krishna's birthday (I never really think about gods being born – they just are) but *The Scoop* is still duly printed and returned to me for collation. Barbara and Hilary pitch in and by 10.30pm, both the paper and I are in bed.

Thursday, August 19 A massive mix-up in arrangements with the car. I planned to pick up Saroj to take her shopping, while Doug had arranged to meet Raj and Martin to go to look at jewels. One car, two outings, one solution. We all join forces, starting with Doug hosting lunch at Claridge's, and concluding with Saroj and Raj proving invaluable in the jewel-shopping department.

Friday, August 20 The Walkers (the British High Commissioner and his wife) are leaving Delhi, and I shall miss Enid. Our bridge foursome, with a delightful Indian lady and the wife of the Administrator at the British High Commission has been an exceptionally pleasant association.

Sir Michael is due to retire and both the Walkers are looking forward to their home and garden in Surrey. Today, at the British Residence, Enid shows us the Post Report she has written up for her successor. It is very thorough and informative, and she signs it off with this wise poetic advice from that old Imperial sage, Rudyard Kipling, from his *Naulahka*:

Now it is not good for the Christian's health
To hustle the Aryan brown,
For the Christian riles,
And the Aryan smiles,
And he weareth the Christian down;
And the end of the fight is a tombstone white,
With the name of the late deceased,
And the epitaph drear: "A fool lies here
Who tried to hustle the East."

This is our last lunch and bridge game. I look around the beautiful garden, and take my tea from the hands of the splendidly attired bearer in his starched white coat and crimson turban. There is a little breeze that carries the scent of frangipani, and I know I will never forget this moment, which for me captures all that was India, all that was the Raj, all that will not come again.

Saturday, August 21   This evening, the Canadian High Commissioner's son is holding a dinner party at the Residence, and the twins have been invited. His mother told me he had planned the whole thing himself, and has even hired a pianist for some background music. I suggest the twins array themselves suitably for the occasion. Barbara is only too happy to do so, and dons her very best pale green evening gown. Martin rather grudgingly wears his blazer and a collar and tie. I can't help myself – I see them off with the same mixed feelings of pride and apprehension that I used to have when they were all slicked up for a childhood birthday party.

I am still up when they return, and get a full report of the party. Barbara is a-glow with the elegance of the whole scene, and excitedly describes their arrival, with the bearer, all spit and polish, opening the door, as their young host descends the circular staircase wearing a deep crimson velvet jacket and a cravat.

"It was just like the movies," Barbara proclaims dreamily. Martin has been equally impressed, but less effusive.

"It was class, Mum. It was real class."

Sunday, August 21   We have invited the Khosla family for dinner tonight. The twins and their daughter, Reba, are the same age, and both the girls are taking their 'O' levels.

I carefully check the menu with Tony, and he gives his usual shake of the head, which could mean: understanding; go away and don't bother me; a complete lack of comprehension. We all gather on the twilit patio, and I anxiously await the moment when the dining room door is drawn and we are ushered in for our meal. It is a little bit like a suspense film – what is going to happen in the next frame? It is not really good, but it is also not really bad. The dessert is terrible, but nobody seems to care.

Saroj has become a very good friend and Harish, a graduate of Edinburgh University, is international in his outlook, so it is a bit of a surprise when the conversation turns (as it so frequently seems to do) to the subject of arranged marriages. Harish is of the opinion that it is still a good thing, but believes the daughter should have the right to reject any prospective groom. Saroj agrees with him, and adds that their own totally satisfactory marriage had been arranged by her parents, with a view to similarity of upbringing and social status.

The girls are then asked for their opinions. Barbara's response is totally predictable: a) she would have to fall in love first before she ever thought of marriage, and b) falling in love is something no one but the two lovers could possibly foresee, so how could parents pick out a suitable boy?

Reba, on the other hand, says she is glad her parents agree on her right to veto, but she will always depend on their wisdom and love to choose well for her. It is a graceful and reasoned reply, but one that is still difficult for our western minds to accept. Here is this bright, modern teenager who has been, and will continue to be, well educated, falling in happily enough with a centuries-old authoritarian custom.

As this discussion continues with Martin and Hilary adding their two-paisa worth, I find myself thinking, as I have been doing frequently of late, of our unconscious western arrogance. Why do we always assume that ours is the only way, our God the only God, our faith the only faith? There is a vast wisdom in the customs of this ancient land, and who are we to presume it should be changed?

CHAPTER 38

Monday, August 23   Was there ever a time when I truly wondered how I would fill the day? I am now on a happy, if exhausting treadmill. Rush off to the IWC meeting, which runs on until after 1.00pm. Then rush like mad to fulfil my stint in the reference department of the American School library. I am in such a flap I lock the keys in the car.

When Hilary comes in, looking rather unwell, I send her off to the High Commission to get the keys from her father. When we pick up Doug later on, he sends Hilary off to bed. Needless to say I fret about everything from beriberi to rabies. I am particularly concerned because Hilary and her group have adopted a 'pi' dog, which Doug has absolutely forbidden Hilary to pet or feed, but knowing Hilary, I am aware that she will not be capable of turning her back on this poor, mangy creature who would sell its soul for a pat.

Friday, August 27   Barbara and I have been in a flurry of packing, sewing on name tags, and doing last minute things for her launching into boarding school life. She is happy and excited, but also a little nervous – understandably so.

More meetings of the YWCA Executive about the Fair; finish off the IWC newsletter, and pull together the next issue of *The Scoop*. Apropos of this last chore, a couple of weeks ago, the Activities Committee decided it would be rather fun to give *The Scoop* a new masthead, and elected to hold an open competition. Hilary submitted a rather engaging little beaver, taking a bite out of a palm tree. Other entries included an elephant with maple leaf ears, a turbaned rajah, and a camel wearing a Mountie's hat. They all went up against an independent panel, with no names showing on the submissions. Hilary's was selected, and she was terribly pleased, particularly when I explained about nepotism, and swore I had nothing to do with the final decision.

Saturday, August 28   Kilmeny's birthday, and I wonder what she is doing on the other side of the world – her first birthday outside the family circle.

It is Barbara's last day here, and we are both a little subdued. She finishes her packing and we leave for the airport at 9.30pm, meet the Ronkes and the Tullys in the concourse. Mr Tully is a correspondent for one of the British newspapers, and he and his wife are having Barbara to stay overnight, and taking her up to Queenswood. It really is terribly kind of them, and I shall have to give some thought as to how I might repay them. Barbara is all bounce now, but I feel a little sad, as she seems so young and vulnerable. On the other hand, Barbara's relentless cheerfulness has always paved the way to easy friendships so, let us hope, she will be heading up an inner coterie of the Lower Sixth before we know it.

Sunday, August 29 A quiet Sunday, and I miss Barbara acutely. Hilary goes off to a friend's, and Doug, Martin and I take in a very good photographic exhibition in Old Delhi, followed by a hike along The Ridge. Martin is keen to hear more of the defence of The Ridge, and I am gratified to have an interested audience.

Monday, August 30 Raj, Doug's secretary, and I go out to Old Delhi to pick up the reproductions of my Birks Sterling. I find it almost impossible to tell the difference. Raj says she has made sure that each piece of flatware has its full measure of silver, and I must say it looks spiff-plus. Anyway I now have another 34 pieces, and at a price to make Birks blush.

Wednesday, September 1 Have joined the French Group in the International Women's Club, which is a bit daunting. My first meeting finds me sitting next to a very elegant older lady, with a distinctly upper crust English accent. We sneak in a few minutes of chit chat *en anglais,* before business begins. She is charming and friendly, and I ask her if she can speak French, or does she sort of 'hack and hew', like me. She gives a little deprecating chuckle before she pats my arm in a kind of never-mind gesture:

"Actually, I am the French Ambassador's wife, and I really speak French quite well."

She declares that she is *un mélange*, with a French father and an English mother, and can understand my confusion. Despite her attempts to soothe, I still feel I have pulled the first of a whole series of future gaffes. This sense of being out of my depth increases when it is suggested that, for the next meeting, I deliver a speech, in French, on Quebec and its place in Canada.

Moi? Mon Dieu, zut alor, and any other phrase indicating panic. I am in the French group, and it is now clear that my role is to go beyond a *bonjour* or the occasional "*Très bien, merci.*" I foresee not only a lot of heavy research into Canada's 'two solitudes', but a great buffing of my accent and a course in how to avoid any grotesqueries of composition.

Sunday, September 5 The indispensable Raj comes over to pick up Martin. His summer earnings are burning a hole in his pocket, and he has decided to invest it in an emerald. This is not without its logic as the buzz is what you pay in rupees is what it will be worth in dollars in Canada. Consequently, we make up a small party – Raj, her aunt, Doug, Martin and me – and head for Chandni Chowk.

After a pleasant lunch at the Imperial – Martin (aided and abetted by Raj) argy-bargies his way to a perfectly beautiful emerald. Doug opines that it is a little pale, but of a very good quality: 1.70 carats, price 1,100 rupees per carat, or $225. Martin is enormously pleased with the transaction, and the only thing needed is to have Sidney Greenstreet huff and wheeze into view, with a tale of its being a special jewel beyond price.

Monday, September 6 Doug comes home for lunch, a-flush with news. Our posting has come through, and we are off to Germany as of November 15. *November 15!* This is terrible, we can't possibly go on November 15. I am in the middle of a hair-raising children's serial in *The Scoop*; I have the Chrysanthemum Fair booth to pull together; and there are my commitments to the International Women's Club. All this might be as nought, but for the incontrovertible, bottom-of-the-line truth. I just don't want to leave India. I remember the pathetic marking off of the days back in January of last year, and now

323

the very thought of departure sees me being dragged by the proverbial wild elephants to the airport.

I have re-invented myself in a useful role, and am very happy in it. Besides it will be really awkward for Hilary's school term, and I know she will not be too thrilled about leaving her friends, and starting all over again in a new school. Doug says he will try to have the departure date set for after the New Year.

Tuesday, September 7 Off to Roosevelt House to attend a morning event in honour of the American Bicentennial. They show a film of the American School Choir singing all those hand-over-the-heart songs suitable to such an occasion. I, of course, only have eyes for my own little Canadian.

Chris Barker's live-in love, Linda, is in India, and I have invited Monica to bring her for lunch. They are already into the sherry by the time I arrive, with Martin playing host with no little aplomb.

The Barkers are leaving for the UK on Thursday. Hamish is to see a specialist about his back, but the general opinion seems to be that he will need a spinal fusion. Unfortunately, some idiot told him a horror story about someone they knew who had had this operation, and who never walked again. Doug has a long talk with H and persuades him that this is probably a one-in-a-thousand case, and not to worry. Relief from pain will make it all worthwhile.

Thursday September 9 Monica, *en passant*, drops off some hand-embroidered linens, with the injunction to "flog them and give the lolly to him not to her because she will just put it all on the horses." As with many of Monica's injunctions I haven't a clue who or what she is talking about, and have to ask her to back up a bit.

It turns out that she is talking about the Thompsons of Meerut, and the family linens Mrs Thompson had asked us to try to sell. I have to confess that I haven't thought of them, and obviously neither had Monica, as they remain unsold. I look at them again, and they really are exquisite. They have become slightly yellowed with age, but Monica has had them beautifully laundered and folded with lavender sachets. It seems it is now my task to sell them. I set a few pieces aside for the girls, and then take the rest to the British bridge this afternoon. They all rally around, and by the end of the afternoon, mission is accomplished and money received. I will now have to arrange a trip out to Meerut and try to corner the General to give him the money before paying my respects to her.

Saturday, September 11 I am up at the crack to see Martin off, but dawn has more than cracked by the time I rouse Doug, and we come close to missing the plane.

A typical Saturday of delivering Hilary or delivering Hilary's guests; of shopping and suffering moments of apprehension as to what will emerge at this evening's dinner for the Tiernans. Their daughters have now left for boarding school in England, so it is just us.

Justin and Barbara really are a delightful couple. She tells me she is having a hard time adjusting to India, but adds "Although heaven knows why, after Lebanon." It would have been more than normal curiosity could bear to let this statement go unquestioned, and there follows an absorbing tale.

The Tiernans had been posted to Beirut shortly before the outbreak of the 1976 hostilities. Barbara had no sooner congratulated herself on being sent to this 'Paris of the East', than the bombing began. It was incessant, she relates, and she even made a tape of the sound of bombs and gunfire, which she heard from her kitchen window. She adds that she now plays back all this recorded mayhem to remind herself that Delhi is not so bad. The violence continued and increased, until the Australian government decided to evacuate their nationals from Beirut.

There was, however, one treasure the Tiernans felt they could not leave behind, and one whose welfare was a matter of deep concern. Before they arrived in Lebanon, Justin had bought what had long been his heart's desire – a brand-new Bedford van. This, he explained to Barbara, would be their motorized camel, transporting them in comfort on innumerable desert adventures. It was treasured; it was polished; it was buffed and smothered with love. Now, it stood in considerable

325

danger of being scratched, to say nothing of suffering possible serious damage.

It was at this point that a friend came up with the brilliant suggestion that they store it for safekeeping in the garage of the Holiday Inn. This seemed like a splendid and inspired idea, and so, as they say in the Bible, "it came to pass". Consequently that was exactly where it was when what became known as the 'Battle of the Holiday Inn' took place. One can only imagine Justin's grief. However, they have brought the van to Delhi with its scars of battle intact, preserving the bullet holes in the Bedford's chassis as sort of 'camp' souvenirs.

Monday, September 13 With all the September changes at the High Commission, Mrs HE hosts a 'getting-to-know-you' coffee morning. I meet a number of the new ladies, and once again feel I want to cling on by my fingernails.

A letter from Ruth Robinson, one of my West Vancouver friends, brings news that she, too, will be coming to Delhi. My calculations work out that she will leave just before Ruth Baldwin arrives. I wish they could have come at the beginning of our tour, when I lived in a social desert. However, it is probably for the best now that I know where everything is, and what is what.

Monday, September 20 Spend the morning at the Canadian library researching my dreaded speech. I was hoping to find something to pad out my Quebecois address, but apart from a rather macabre little film about a lot of mournful *séparatistes* bearing off a coffin containing a murdered Quebec, there really isn't anything usable.

I am excused from library duty today as there are school interviews this afternoon. I approach Hilary's teacher, with some misgivings. My fifth child seems to have received all the rebel spirit that should have been shared equally among the other four. I need not have fretted. It seems that although she is "an independent child", (teacher-speak for 'stubborn'), she is also a "quick learner, a quick spirit and quick to answer" – and quick to talk back, thinks I. She is also "a natural leader" and an asset in any class. None of this, of course, will I divulge to Hilary – simply congratulate her on doing well.

Thursday, September 23 The Museum Course, and the morning's lecture is on Mogul architecture. It is absolutely fascinating, and I am sorry when it is over. It is such a bonus to be able to take a course, in situ, so to speak. One can listen to the background and then wander almost anywhere in Delhi to experience it first-hand.

Saturday, September 25 This is the first chance to go out to Meerut with the money from Mrs Thompson's linens. It's a busy morning and we don't get away until 3.00pm, reaching Meerut just as the second race is beginning. Mindful of Monica's instructions to give the money to the General, I hang about rather than going directly to visit Mrs T. I am relieved to see him shuffle into view after the race. I give him the fruitcake I have brought, and press the envelope of money into his hand. So much for all the palaver and careful precautions.

"Oh," says he, "you must give that to Lorna – after all, they were her things!" There seems little point in spluttering away about how it will all melt away like snow in thaw on the next race, and I bow to the inevitable as gracefully as possible.

Tuesday, September 28 This afternoon, I drive to the airport to pick up Ruth Robinson, who is de-planing from Thailand at a surprisingly civilized time. I bring her back, and apologize, en route, that we must leave her to attend a dinner party. I explain that this had been arranged before we knew just when she would be arriving. I tell her she has been included in the invitation if she would care to come. I am so used to newly arrived guests falling asleep before they reach Vasant Vihar that I am surprised when she readily agrees. As she says, she is over the major jet lag, and has only come from Thailand today. I admire her spirit, as she quickly picks out something to wear and we are off.

Wednesday, September 29 It is all a bit of a baptism of fire for poor Ruth. I dash off to attend a YWCA meeting, remembering too late that I have forgotten this afternoon's bridge. I shamefacedly ask Ruth if she could possibly substitute for me. It all seems a bit thick considering she only got off the plane yesterday, but she reluctantly agrees and I

327

She barely has time to digest her tea

heave a sigh of relief.

She barely has time to digest her tea from the bridge, when I pick her up, and have to tell her she has been invited to a ·cocktail party at 6.00. Happily it is a very friendly and relaxed group, who make Ruth extremely welcome, and she enjoys herself enormously, although she admits she is more than a bit bemused by the persistence of the social whirl.

CHAPTER 39

Thursday, September 30 Our "planned" trip to Nepal begins this morning and Goldie arrives to drive Ruth and me to the airport where we are to meet Doug.

What a farce!! First off, Doug has forgotten to arrange tickets, and there is much mournful shaking of heads at the airline desk, followed by a slow, slow issuance of tickets. Then Doug faces another Indian crisis as he seeks to have his camera entered on his passport. He is held up, but Ruth and I go through the security check and wait for Doug on the other side. He does not appear, and we are urged to go ahead to the plane. No way. When he still does not show, we get an airport official to check, and he returns pointing to Doug already on the tarmac. There is a great deal of bustle, and an airport bus is hailed to take us, in solitary splendour, to the waiting plane. Once aboard, we find our seats are occupied by others. A bit of a donnybrook follows. We are hot and edgy, and the occupiers are all for exercising the possession of which nine-tenths is the law. However, reserved seats are reserved seats and the interlopers are ousted.

We think the worst is now behind us, but there is a catastrophe at Kathmandu Immigration. Ruth does not have the required visa nor the picture to identify her as her. Doug, flashing his special passport and his best Sahib manner, sorts everything out. Ruth's picture is taken, she is parted from 64 rupees, and we drive down the ramshackle main street of Kathmandu to our hotel. Barely into the lobby when we are accosted by two gibbering men from the airport.

"A terrible mistake has been made, oh my, yes, we have given the Memsahib change for pounds and not for dollars; therefore, we are owed, oh my yes, many more rupees. See here is the exchange sheet, so you will see that all is right," they conclude, now out of breath and anxiously waving the proof of their case under our noses.

Ruth pays them, and they exit bowing and smiling – their jobs, we trust, still intact.

A dinner has been arranged at the home of a Canadian nurse, Maureen Brown. She has been appointed as a sort of liaison for us, and arrives at the hotel to pick us up. She has obviously gone to some trouble to arrange her guest list, which includes a medical missionary from Calgary and his wife; Cecilia Leslie, a Canadian doctor working with the Peace Corps, and her husband, and a Larry Holbert, Director of Psychology (and a long title of extended responsibilities which I miss). It turns out to be an entertaining evening, and becomes more so when the first four guests leave shortly after dinner, and Maureen's bearer, brings on more wine. The evening then takes on a slightly bibulous note.

Friday, October 1 I am on wake-up duty, and arouse Doug at 7.00am, phone Maureen at 7.15 and Ruth at 7.30. Finally we all get together over tea and toast, then pick up Larry at the Yellow Pagoda at 8.30 and are off to explore the city and its preparations for tomorrow's Durga Puja.

I am not one bit sure this particular event is going to be my cup of tea. Once a year, the Durga Puja takes place in the Durbar Square, with the King and all the King's men in attendance. It is here, with much ceremony and solemnity, that sacrifices in blood are made to the Durga, or Kali, as she is sometimes called. She is the bloodthirsty goddess in the Hindu Pantheon, who wears a necklace of her children's skulls, and has an 'off-with-their-heads' philosophy that makes the Red Queen in *Alice* seem a veritable Portia of mercy. The theory is that if blood is offered to the Durga at this ceremony in sufficient quantities, she will be satisfied for the rest of the year. This belief is so strongly held that there are rumours of human sacrifice in some of the more remote areas of Nepal. We might tut-tut over such a primitive and pagan custom still extant in the late 20th century, but back in Delhi, our friend, Colonel Veitch (the "Sherpa Colonel") tells a tale that defies intellectual scepticism, and lends credence to the belief.

As a representative of CIDA, the Colonel had been called upon to present the Nepalese with the gift of an airplane from the people of Canada. Said plane was delivered with all due ceremony, and the Colonel was shocked, and probably offended, to see its spanking white wings immediately splashed with blood. He was told not to be outraged, because the Durga would now be satisfied.

A few days later the plane was taking off with some VIPs on board, faltered and crashed almost immediately. It was a total wreck and a really nasty mess, but by some miracle everyone on board emerged unhurt. It goes without saying that the Colonel is now a believer.

For today, however, the shrines and pagodas are the site for gentler offerings. The people, mostly women and children, approach the altars with offerings of fruit and flowers. As we near the centre of the city we park the car, and walk into the main concourse. It is an architectural revelation and a social horror. The streets are filthy, but the pagodas are a miracle of intricate fretwork and wooden carving, all created by the hands of the Newars (the valley Nepalese).

On one side of the street is a particularly ornate pagoda that is the palace of the Living Goddess, or Kumari Devi. Poor little girl. She is all rigged out in elaborate robes and must present herself at a little barred window at specified times during the day. Her story involves the theft of a life. She is not only robbed of the natural joys of childhood, but of her hopes for a happy future.

The legend goes back to the 8th century, and begins in the way all fairy stories should begin: Once upon a time, a very young girl proclaimed to the populace, or to anyone who would listen, that she was a goddess, so there! Today, she would have been hustled off to a psychiatrist, or kept under wraps by her embarrassed parents. However, the reigning monarch, not liking to think of anyone claiming to be higher than himself, had her banished.

Shortly after the exile, the queen began to exhibit some rather strange symptoms. She declared that the girl had transferred her divinity to herself, and that she, too, was now the Nepalese equivalent of a vestal virgin, and proceeded to withdraw the King's conjugal rights. At which point the King decided the girl could jolly well take back her godliness and he ordered her returned from exile, paraded her through the streets to be reverenced by the populace, and set her up in her own little pagoda. The pattern was set, and this poor deranged child has been followed by a succession of young girls who are selected to be 'Living Goddesses'.

This selection of the Kumari is done by temple priests who, in my opinion, ought to be committed. They gather together a number of female toddlers (aged somewhere between 18 months to two years) and place them in the hallway of the temple. Then, men emerge from the wings, dressed as demons. They leap about, shrieking and lunging at the infants. Any normal child would be terrified, and do a fair amount of shrieking on her own. However, the rare infant will remain undisturbed, an indication to the priests that she is predestined to be the next Living Goddess. Any psychologist worthy of his salt would probably assume that a child subjected to such terror and remaining unmoved would have to be at best slow, if not downright retarded. God willing, this is the case, for her childhood is one of constant incarceration, from which she is freed only by puberty.

When she retires, she is endowed with a small fortune, but has little chance of any kind of life ahead. After a couple of horror stories of strange accidents happening to men who married an ex-Kumari, she is considered untouchable and unlucky. So the poor girl is robbed of the fruits of maturity as she was of the freedom of childhood.

We happened to be lucky inasmuch as we did catch a glimpse of her at the window. Some people say she never appears unless you tip an attendant and, who knows, maybe somebody in the crowd did so. She is allowed out once a year when she is carried in a palanquin through the streets to the Royal Palace where the King pays his respects.

Next stop is a Hindu Temple. The only entrance is through a door within the vast carved gate. However, as today is a holy day, 'abominations' such as us meat-eating leather-wearers are forbidden entry. It doesn't really matter as life on the outside is interesting enough – the place is alive with colour, and people everywhere are clutching chickens, or leading goats, kids and water-buffalo calves to the slaughter. The plates of rice cakes and eggs women are offering as their puja are beautifully festooned with flowers. One sweet-faced woman reverently places a platter containing something black on an altar and, to my horror, I see it is a goat's head.

I avert the eyes, and we continue our walk through the

bazaars and crowded alleys, back to the Hotel Crystal where we enjoy tea on the terrace. Arrangements are made for the evening. We invite Maureen and Larry up to the hotel for Happy Hour, and then to join us for dinner at the Yak and Yeti.

This is a fabled restaurant run by an equally fabled Russian, Boris Lisssanevitch who, now in his eighties, is a legend in Kathmandu. A former dancer with the Ballet Russe, he fled from an increasingly oppressive regime in his native land, and found his personal Shangri-la in this remote mountain kingdom. After a series of adventures and misadventures, he became the proprietor of the Royal Hotel, with its famous Yak and Yeti bar. Every western visitor to Nepal need only ask for Boris to be directed to this bizarre hostelry, once the palace of a Rani. Its interior shows an abandoned indifference to continuity of style – there are marble staircases and halls lined with rhino heads, and, at one time, a resident horse that wandered amiably through the vast rooms.

With all this, Boris's fame became so widespread that correspondence addressed simply to "Boris, Kathmandu" reached him without trouble. A story, perhaps apocryphal, has a western writer asking him for his last name. He replied:

"Lissanevitch – sounds like sonofabitch, but it's spelled differently."

The Yak and Yeti cuisine is also legendary, and tonight's menu includes borscht and roast guinea fowl. At one point, an errant wing of the bird sticks in Doug's throat. He manages to croak out a request for water. When it is brought, and Doug is about to fall on it like a wanderer upon a desert oasis, Maureen puts up an imperious hand, and demands to know if it has been boiled.

"Boiled!! I don't care if it has been boiled!" Doug manages to squeak as he downs both water and impediment.

We are all having a lovely time, and a fair amount of wine has gone down a treat, when we hear the strains of the music from *The Graduate* floating into the dining room. Larry fixes Ruth with a slightly unfocused gaze, and rather dreamily inquires:

"Are you *really* Mrs Robinson?"

After dinner, we go into the ballroom – other voices, other times – which could have been a stage set for *Cinderella*. The size of a city block, it has a dais for the orchestra, royal boxes with velvet-covered chairs for visiting elite and a chandelier straight out of *The Phantom of the Opera*. With all this European grandeur, a reminder of Asia is an enormous mural, which shows a whole mass of frolicsome tigers leaping about in a vividly hued jungle.

It is a great evening, and none of us want it to end, so we wind up back at our hotel, where Larry proposes several toasts of "Here's to you, Mrs Robinson."

Saturday, October 2 Up even earlier, for today is *the* day for blood-letting and sacrifice to the insatiable Durga. I am a bit squeamish about the whole thing, although Ruth and Doug keep telling me this is a fascinating glimpse into Nepalese culture.

We make our way to the Durbar Square, and are led into the courtyard of the jail. This is mercifully empty, but already blood-bespattered. We are directed up a flight of filthy stairs to a balcony overlooking the sacrificial square. It is full of people, all peering avidly at the gory goings-on below. There is only a smattering of Europeans, and all of them, like Ruth and Doug, are armed with cameras.

A gun is fired, and I hear the swish of a kukri knife and the thud of a falling head. The various Gurkha and Nepalese regiments are lined up against the walls of the square and, in a special ceremony, present their regimental flags to be dipped in the blood from a decapitated animal.

Unlike a bullfight, where the fate of the bull is irrevocable, there is a small glimmer of hope for those who are about to die. According to custom, it is considered only courteous to ask for the consent of the victims to become a sacrifice. This is achieved by dribbling water on the beast's head, which he naturally shakes off. This shake is then classed as a sign of assent.

All the animals have obligingly given consent, until we come to a pretty little kid, who is being led before his executioner. The water is duly dribbled, and the head is not shaken. Again the same thing. I am pulling like mad for the victim, and silently pleading with him not to shake. There is a third and final spray of water, and the crowd is still. As the water dribbles down his nose, he gives a brief shake, and the kukri descends.

I declare enough is enough, and I wander off into the outer square and, some time later, am joined by Ruth and Doug. We are beset by salesmen who are all for catching white-faced tourists as they come out from the Durbar Square. We make a few purchases – I buy some postcards, a yak horn charm, some beads for Christmas stockings and some lovely rice paper; Doug and Ruth – more into the purpose of the day – buy kukri knives.

When we return to the hotel for lunch, we find a message from the Calgary doctor's wife, inviting us for coffee after dinner. The doctor, a noted surgeon, has been sent by his church as a sort of medical missionary. His wife is a very nice lady, albeit straight out of Central Casting as a 'missionary wife'. I can see her, like Rose Sayer, in *The African Queen*, thumping out *Onward, Christian Soldiers* on an inadequate organ. She is also, however, obviously very bright, very dedicated and very hospitable.

I am searching around for some common ground of interest, when the doctor suggests we might enjoy some slides he took on an expedition to Everest. I think I am one of that rare breed who actually enjoys other people's slides, and these are brilliant. Several months ago, the doctor had joined a group who planned to scale the West Col of the great mountain. His slides show the complicated preparations required and the various stages of the journey. Enormously interesting, particularly for Doug, are his notes on his own personal encounter with altitude sickness. His commentary is meticulous and, accompanied by the dramatic and breathtaking slides, I can almost feel the approach of the symptoms myself. Our thanks for such a rewarding evening are genuine, and I leave feeling an unexpected bond with the mountain.

Sunday, October 3 Up betimes, and Cece, the Canadian doctor working with the Peace Corps, arrives on the stroke of 10.00am to take us to inspect a TB sanatorium on some Himalayan mountain top. I say 'some' advisedly, as Cece has never been there, is not absolutely sure how to get there and, for that matter, whether it is open and receiving visitors. This does not faze us one iota, and the drive is fascinating. Ruth and I make ourselves comfy in the back, while Doug and Cece discuss sputum tests and gastric washings and the like in the front. The road, while not up to the Trans-Canada Highway, is not bad, and we notice that the houses, by and large, seem a little more substantial than those in the Indian villages. After approximately seven miles, we come to a village that contains the Shrine of Budhanilkantha. It is the site of a religious festival in November, and for now is almost empty, but in every respect it is an extraordinary sight.

There is a high-walled pool (or tank, as the Indians call it) inside an enclosed courtyard. In the centre of the pool lies a 30-foot statue of Vishnu reclining on what appears to be a bed of snakes, coiled into an intricate and sinuous pattern. A loose translation of the name of this statue is 'Blue-throated Narayan (Vishnu)' but in common parlance it is simply Vishnu-upon-Serpents. Considering what he is lying on, Vishnu looks remarkably tranquil and contemplative. Above him is a crown, elaborately carved as the face of Buddha emerging from a nest of cobras.

Although the worshippers are relatively few compared to the crowds for the November fête, still they keep arriving with their gifts of flowers and other offerings. We infidels are not permitted, and we watch the faithful go through the gate, down some stone steps to the feet of the god. A priest has already smeared the gigantic feet with holy red powder, and takes the flower offerings to spread over Vishnu's upper body. The sculpture dates back to the 6th century, and is reputed to be around 1500 years old. It signifies Vishnu's waiting for the re-birth of the world at the end of his ninth incarnation. He will then take the form of Buddha, satisfying both Hindus and Buddhists who claim the shrine for joint worship. The story goes that the sculpture was lost for several centuries and only surfaced by accident when a workman's spade hit a solid object. Once uncovered the statue then either bled or spouted milk (depending on which version appeals to you) and only stopped when placed in the pool.

With all this exotica on Vishnu-Buddha and lost-and-found gods, the TB sanatorium's attractions begin to dim a little. However, we resolutely press on up a muddy and rocky road. En route we meet three young men, patients at the institution. Quizzed by Cece, they say the doctor in charge is away at a wedding, and there is no one there but a chowkidar and a couple of female patients. We leave the car and hike up a steep incline to the hospital. I really cannot see much point in this, but it seems to draw Doug and Cece like a magnet.

Having out-stared the chowkidar and smiled at the ladies, there is nothing for it but to drive back down to town, where Cece leaves us at the hotel, declining our offer of lunch. We bolt down some tea and a sandwich, and barely wipe away the last crumb when the doctor from Calgary, arrives to take us on our afternoon outing. This is an excursion to Swayambhunath – a monastery or, more accurately, a lamasery – atop a hill approximately two miles above Kathmandu. It can be seen from anywhere in the town, and is probably Nepal's major identifying symbol, on a par with the Sydney Opera House, the Eiffel Tower or Edinburgh's floral clock.

It is a massive stupa, rumoured to be one of Ashoka's and dating back to the 3rd century BC. Atop the stupa is a huge golden cube (toran) on which has been painted a pair of watchful and slightly sinister Asian eyes above a question mark nose. I have no backing for my theory that this mouthless face is meant to see and smell, but not speak of any evil that may rise from the valley below. Towering above both stupa and cube is a golden spire that seems to touch the sky, soaring high above the hill itself.

The purpose of our visit is to accompany Dr H on a house call. A short while ago, the head Lama had his gall bladder removed by Dr H, who privately reported to Doug that he had never seen so many gall stones in any one human before. In any event, we are going to check up on the patient. Dr H has also brought along his little blonde daughter, her friend – a dark-eyed Belgian child – and a little Nepalese patient from the hospital who is recuperating from treatment.

When this little band arrives at the lamasery, the monkeys (which are everywhere) begin screeching and gibbering what I hope is a welcome, and go swinging from tree to tree, from Hindu arch to Buddhist lintel. Like so much else in Nepal, the monastery seems to be non-restrictive as to faith, which the

At the lamasery, the monkeys begin screeching and gibbering

architecture bears out. We are still gawking at this fascinating mish-mash of styles, when Dr H asks if we would like to meet some of "the fellows".

'The fellows', for the most part, seem to be having a lovely time chanting indoors, rather like the hum of a giant and exotic mosquito, and we hesitate to disturb them. At this point a young monk appears, bows and leads us up a flight of filthy steps to where the Lama is waiting to greet us. He is very elderly and a little bowed, but he bends his head politely and invites us, by gesture, into his private quarters. As we follow along, Doug is whispering into his tape recorder, already full of the sounds of chanting monks and chattering monkeys:

"We are now about to enter the private chambers of the Head Lama. Unfortunately the Lama speaks neither Hindi nor Urdu – only Tibetan...." The absurdity of this little confidence causes me to stifle a guffaw. It sounds so much as if Doug could rattle off Hindi, Urdu or Tamil for that matter, like a native, but dash it all, his Tibetan is just not quite up to snuff. For stubbornly monolingual Doug, the implication is all the more ridiculous.

The Lama smiles us into his apartment, where we remove our shoes, and sit down at a low table that rests atop a much-worn square of Tibetan rug. A serving monk offers us tea. After a hurried consultation with the Lama, the decision is to give us 'western' tea, as opposed to the Tibetan variety, which is heavily salted and afloat with rancid ghee. I am much relieved until I find the western type is made with tepid water, floating leaves, milk and, I swear, at least half a pound of sugar per cup. It is absolutely nauseating, but 'face' requires that I drink it down. The tea is accompanied by a biscuit and some yak cheese. In theory, I can see no reason why the milk of the yak should not produce something at least a-kin to goat cheese, but what is put before us reminds me of nothing so much as one of those old, grey school erasers, long past their sell-by date. It is rock hard, and for a while I fear that the Lama may well be treated to an ejection of foreign fillings at his tea party.

After the refreshments, Dr H takes the Lama's blood pressure and does a few other medical checks, and with a lot of bowing and salaaming and smiles we leave. One of the monks takes us up to the roof to look out at the distant peaks and the vast valley below. A wind sweeps across from Himalayan snows and despite the sun we feel a slight chill.

All in all, it has been an extraordinary experience, and we thank Dr H for including us on his house call. I also thank him again for the slide show evening. After all, not too many people of my acquaintance have vicariously scaled the West Col of Everest.

Monday, October 4 Doug is up early and out to have a tour of the Shanti Bhwan Hospital and to conclude some other bits of business. He is free after lunch and, complete with car and driver, we set out to 'do' the Kakani lookout of Everest at sunset. This is a bit of a comedown as really dedicated Everest-seekers rise while it is yet night to see the great mountain at sunrise. But as that requires the sunrise-viewer to stay overnight in Kakani at the State Bungalow, we simply haven't got the time. We might have made it if we could have managed to get Doug up before dawn, but that would have required an effort beyond my powers of persuasion, so it has to be a tea-time view or nothing.

Kakani is about 18 miles northwest of the city, and is roughly 2,000 feet higher than the Kathmandu Valley. We start off in sunshine and hope for a spectacular sunset grows. The views are awesome, but about two-thirds of the way up, the clouds begin to gather ominously, and by the time we crest the pass, it has started to rain. I look apprehensively at the road ahead, which appears to have disintegrated into a mud and rock trail etched out of the mountainside. Part of it has been washed away, and other parts, like grease, cause us to skid hideously in the direction of the cliff's lip. After a little inner conversation, I decide not to thank "whatever gods there be for my unconquerable soul." My soul is so conquerable it isn't even funny, and my relief when the driver parks is palpable. He points to what appears to be an isolated heap of wood on a pinnacle that, he proclaims proudly, is the lookout. From here, he adds, we may see the mountain peaks with Everest beyond.

We doggedly climb up through mud and sliding shale and eventually reach the lookout. By now the fog has rolled in – not on "little cat's feet" but on the claws of a tiger. We can't see Everest – we can't even see the valley below. I wonder briefly if I

341

might 'fuzzy' things up a little, and record an improvised version for my diary, complete with a flaming sunset painting the eternal snows. But the sunset does no such thing, and the nursery morals of my upbringing remind me to tell the truth always, and that is that. Somewhat disheartened, we trek back down through the clinging fog to the car and the terrors of the return drive. All I can say is that my craven heart rejoices when we are once again on blacktop.

A farewell dinner at the Yak and Yeti ends the day, and ends a not-to-be forgotten visit to the Roof of the World.

Still the world is wondrous large
Seven Seas from marge to marge –
And it holds a vast of various kinds of Man;
And the wildest dreams of Kew are the facts of Kathmandu
And the crimes of Clapham chaste at Martaban.
                    Rudyard Kipling

CHAPTER 40

Tuesday, October 5 Our flight from Kathmandu is aboard a Fokker Friendship – has it been blooded, I ask myself – and we fly low over the mountains and jungles to Calcutta. We arrive about 5.00pm and Dinker is there to meet us. His driver takes us to the Grand Hotel, which is an oasis of privilege in a desert of poverty. Getting out of the car we are surrounded by clutching beggars, despite the sturdy efforts of the turbaned porters. Dinker comes up for a drink, and outlines some of his plans for our visit before taking his leave.

Ruth treats us to dinner at the Prince's Ballroom. The décor is definitely *autrefois* but the spirit is big-hotel modern, complete with floor show. This features a pair of exotic dancers, togged out in scanty tiger skins and a grimy singer warbling dirty songs. The dinner is good.

Wednesday, October 6 Ruth and I spend the morning at the pool, which is lovely. There is a white-columned colonial terrace, palm trees and soft tropical breezes. Deferential bearers bring us cool drinks, and the swimming is strictly coincidental. Doug returns around noon to take us out to meet the local DMP for lunch.

From the haven of tranquillity of the Grand's pool terrace we are back among Calcutta's seething masses as the cab ruthlessly ploughs through a sea of pedestrians. The DMP turns out to be a real sweetie – an elderly English bachelor who has lived and practised in Calcutta most of his life. He takes us for a bang-up lunch of excellent Indian food at the Amber Lounge. He has written a book, *The Painted Pagoda*, and presents us with an autographed copy.

He is not really an example of 'staying on' as per the Paul Scott novel. I rather feel that he, like the Thompsons in Meerut, is already home.

Dinker picks us up at the appointed hour, and we are whisked off to the Museum. It is incredibly hot, and while the museum is wonderful, 'museum fatigue' sets in after a thorough tour of the archaeological and anthropological sections. We are restored by tea and 'orange blossom' at a little tea shop before we set out for our riverside walk along the Hoogley. The intense heat of the day has gone, and the river is magical in the brief Indian twilight. The lights come on and the water is silvered with their beams. I could have walked on, but time is running out, and we return to the hotel to change for tonight's dinner at the Rao home.

Dinker's nephew comes to pick us up, and we are greeted warmly by the charming Vatsala (Dinker's wife) and Mrs Rao Senior (Dinker's mother). Dinner has been carefully prepared and is an interesting mixture of Indian and western dishes, with a slight Burmese accent. We are so at home with Dinker, who is his usual urbane and charming self, but the ladies, though both gracious and welcoming, have to be wooed into conversation.

Thursday, October 7 Our 22nd wedding anniversary and an Indian holiday – Lakshmi Puja. This is fortunate for us as Dinker is free and puts himself completely at our disposal. He arrives with car and driver at 8.00am on the dot. I have managed to shush Doug's mutterings about ungodly hours and compulsive risers, with promises of an exciting day ahead.

We head for the Howrah Bridge, and I cannot believe it – it is a solid and slow-moving mass of every imaginable type of transport. Dinker tells us that it is rather empty today because of the holiday, but normally over half a million people on foot, in buses, in rickshaws, on bicycles and what have you cross the bridge from Calcutta to Howrah and back. The mind boggles. The bridge is enormous, and strangely enough was built in the early 1940s, while the war was on. I try hard to imagine how 27,000 tons of iron and steel were diverted from armaments for a bridge.

Over the Howrah we head for Shibpur, a Mecca for foresters, botanists and down-home gardeners. Back in the late 18th century, close to 300 acres were set aside as a botanical garden, and today it boasts a world-famous herbarium with more than 30,000 species. After I get past parsley, sage, rosemary and thyme, I am lost as far as a herb lexicon goes, so I am fascinated and eager to learn.

The herbarium really is a marvel, but the main event and what we are all anxious to see is the Great Banyan Tree. Back across the bridge, and when the car stops, I look around for the tree. All I can see is a forest and I am still trying to sort out which one is *the* tree, when Dinker enlightens me. The forest is the tree, and the tree is the forest. Close to 90 feet high and almost a quarter mile wide, with 600 roots – it is utterly and completely magnificent and beyond anything I could have imagined.

Next stop is the market, which again is wave upon wave of humanity, poking and prodding at mangos and green oranges, vendors expounding on the quality of their wares, beggars touching head and stomach and pleading for baksheesh. Dinker whips us through this, and directs us over to the Victoria Memorial, with its impressive statue of the impressive queen herself. By now the sun is high in the heavens and it is relentlessly, blisteringly hot. I am glad we started as early as we did. Once inside the gallery, it is relatively cool, and I am absorbed in the remarkable collection of paintings and sculpture – although in some respects, it is really kind of a 'look-what-the-Raj-did-for-you' compendium of treasures of the glory days of Empire.

The cool confines of the Bengal Club beckon like an oasis in the desert. Vatsala joins us here, and after a gin and tonic, which is pure manna, we have a leisurely and enjoyable lunch. I am able to thank Vatsala personally for last night's hospitality, to which she modestly demurs. Actually we cannot thank them enough for giving us such an introduction to this amazing city. They take us back to the hotel, where we pick up our luggage and take a cab to the airport.

CHAPTER 41

Still Thursday, October 7 Maureen Brown, our lively companion from Nepal, had to leave for Delhi a couple of days after we arrived in Kathmandu, and we suggested that she might like to stay at our place. She would be company for Hilary, and it would be much nicer for her. We got word to Tony, and tonight when we get home around 9.00pm we find Maureen still in residence.

Hilary is in bed, but comes racing downstairs – there are a lot of hugs and presenting of presents before she is bundled back to bed. Maureen tells us "that is some kid you've got there." This remark is not totally without ambiguity, and I wait anxiously to hear what kind of 'some kid' she is.

Maureen recounts that, on arrival, she was welcomed by her young hostess, who directed Muni to take her luggage, then offered her a Bloody Mary before lunch. This was followed by an afternoon at the High Commission pool, and a general introduction to the Compound. They became quite matey over the next few days, with Maureen helping out with a school project, and being assured by Hilary that she did not "flunk out" when overseeing homework. There is a certain amount of bursting buttons when I hear this positive account of my youngest's hospitality, and thank Maureen warmly for being such good company.

Friday, October 8 Back in Delhi, and back on the cocktail circuit. An American couple has invited us (and Ruth) to an elegant soirée this evening. It is all of that. He is, I believe, a business tycoon, seconded to some executive post in Delhi. They have a very grand house with a beautiful garden. Small tables are set up on a vast terrace, and everything is graciously done. Ruth is delighted to find herself at a table with a German couple, the von Sydows, and I gather the conversation flowed like the Rhine in spate.

Maybe it is the plethora of servants, maybe it is the times, or maybe it is the Raj legacy of dressing for dinner in the

This is ... something straight out of "King of the Khyber Pass"

jungle, but Delhi parties are quite formal, and Ruth once again congratulates herself on packing a couple of evening dresses after all, although she was convinced she would never wear them.

Saturday, October 9 Doug goes off to play golf, Hilary is in the American School swim meet, and I work on the next issue of *The Scoop*. When Doug returns we go to pick up Hilary for the Horse Show at the Polo Grounds – a big event.

At the American pool we find Hilary triumphant and festooned with ribbons, having acquitted herself well in the swim meet. A quick change into her riding clothes, and we arrive at the Polo Grounds in time for the opening ceremony.

It is spectacular. This is no tame dressage or fence jumping, but something straight out of *King of the Khyber Pass*. I believe at some stage or other, the Brits decided that pig-sticking was not quite the thing and that riders must content themselves with tent-pegging. It is all spine-tingling stuff to watch. A cavalry troop of superb-looking Sikhs go thundering across the field, spearing tent pegs at a gallop, and raising their swords with triumphant battle cries.

Major Singh's little group doesn't quite rise to the same level of excitement, but we cheer Hilary on in the Musical Chair Ride. The day concludes with a party at the American Commissary for the swim meet team.

Sunday, October 10 Doug has invited Paul Dingledine, head of the Activities Committee, for dinner tonight, and I rather enjoy the novelty of cooking in my own kitchen, with some idea of how things will turn out. I work on *The Scoop* in the morning, then Doug takes Ruth and Hilary into Old Delhi, while I prepare the dinner menu. After dinner, we have a pleasant evening of bridge. Ruth insists on doing the cleaning up, to which offer I make only a minimal protest.

Monday, October 11 Today is the day of my much dreaded speech to the French Group of the International Women's Club. It has been refined by my French mentor at the High Commission for grammatical faults, but I am still woefully nervous. However, *Les Deux Solitudes* goes quite well, and I even field a few post-speech questions. The Canadian film I finally came up with turned out to be really quite good, and certainly helped pad out the allotted time.

Tuesday, October 12 Realize Ruth has yet to see my favourite Delhi sight, the Qutb Minar, so we drive out there, and as usual I find something else I missed the last time. Ruth shows guarded interest, so we don't dally, but lunch in style at the Qutb Hotel.

Thursday, October 14 *"Free at last, free at last! Thank God Almighty!!"* It may seem a little pretentious for me to borrow Martin Luther King's shout of exultation over such trivial matters as having my French speech behind me, *The Scoop* distributed and the fair goodies priced. But it is lovely to have everything tidied up in my mind, and to know I can enjoy a morning at the Museum for my Arts of Asia course, an afternoon of swimming and tonight a wonderful roof party under the stars at the home of a particularly delightful Political Officer.

Saturday, October 16 A day of showing Ruth some hitherto unseen sights, and picking up things that have been ordered and promised and re-ordered and re-promised, but finally we get Ruth's new suit, her emerald ring and a pair of custom-made shoes.

Sunday, October 17 One of the guards, who has a French (Canadian) flair for cuisine has organized a 'Coq au Vin' night at the cabana. We happily sign up, and it is marvellous. We are still licking our fingers when it is time to leave for the Sound and Light Show at the Red Fort. It is, as always, a winner, and I feel my reputation as a hostess is rising to unwarranted heights.

Monday, October 18 Waken at 4.00am as today is the day scheduled for Kilmeny's arrival at the usual ghastly hour. Hilary, who has been badly missing her siblings, is already up. I rouse Doug and we are off. We gather up our eldest child with all the joy of doting parents, and return home. Instead of going to bed we all stay up talking and carry on with the day. As evening approaches and Tony does likewise with the pre-dinner drinks, Kilmeny can barely get past the olive, and goes to bed, followed shortly, I may add, by her mother.

Tuesday, October 19   There is a dinner at the Grenes, and Kilmeny is invited. She wears the new blue dress we gave her for her birthday. I find myself looking at her, perhaps for the first time, not as my daughter, but as an individual, stand-on-her-own person. It is a strange feeling, but accompanied by a certain glow of pride.

Wednesday, October 20   The demands of the up-coming fair takes me off to a meeting of the Committee at the Y, and I am so happy Kilmeny is on hand to take Ruth on her last minute rounds. I have to get going on the International Women's newsletter, pick up Hilary from school and take her to riding, and wonder what I would ever do if I also had to clean the house and make the meals. Yet, I did, 'in real life', did I not? Maybe I did, but did I do it all that well, I ask myself, as I recall the laundry basket of mounting ironing and hastily-made beds.

The day ends with a special farewell dinner for Ruth, and Tony does us proud. It has been a really great visit, and she has had a wonderful time, full of trips, exotic outings and elegant parties. We are all on the verge of tears. Ruth does not stop at the verge.

Thursday, October 21   Up at 3.00am to take Ruth to the airport. No point in rousing the household as goodbyes were said last night. On the way home, I am thinking along the lines of one door closing... In this case, if one Ruth goes, is another far behind? Ruth Baldwin is expected in another couple of days. She is a very close friend, and has been for a long time. A true 'friend of the bosom' as we used to say in my childhood. What worries me is whether I am going to be able to give her the same splendid time Ruth Number 1 had? Our planned trip to the Khyber Pass is now a bit iffy, and I am going to be up to my ears with the International Chrysanthemum Fair.

At home, I join the others for breakfast, then dash off to pick up Elizabeth Grene for the Museum Course. I love this exploration into India's past. We are studying the Indus Valley civilization at the moment, and I am bursting to talk about it, but where? It is not exactly cocktail party conversation. I can just see people stifling yawns, and looking desperately over my shoulder.

Afternoon bridge, and then the big news in the evening. We have been assigned a five-bedroom house near the Rhine in Bad Godesberg. I am, of course, delighted, but at the moment too tired to show it.

Friday, October 22 Diwali, and I give the servants a day off and enjoy the bliss of doing my own thing. This involves wandering around the house in a cool muslin nightie and drinking my tea in the living room. Doug is off to play golf with the 'Generals' at the Army Golf Club. In the evening we have supper on the upper terrace under the stars and watch the fireworks. It is lovely. Retire early and set the alarm for 3.00am for tomorrow's early arrival.

Saturday, October 23 These early morning comings are one of Delhi's crosses to be borne; we reluctantly pull ourselves out of bed. We arrive on time, only to find the plane has been delayed and will not be in for another couple of hours. Although it scarcely seems worthwhile, we go home and crawl back into bed. What seems seconds later, the alarm goes off again and we, bleary-eyed, drive out once more to Palam. Several flights have de-planed and people are milling around. No one looks like Ruth among the hikers and hippies and confused-looking 'group' tourists. Cancelled flights and delayed planes have added to the usual bedlam of Delhi airport – birds fly madly about and the swaddled, sleeping bodies on the floor are stumbled over, accompanied by the curses of the camel and the jackal. We check the arrival board, which is seldom, if ever, accurate and find that Ruth's plane is due in 15 minutes.

Doug spots her coming down the ramp, festooned with bags and looking anxious, as well she might. She is swallowed up in the crowd, and we wait, and wait, and wait. Doug decides to go all 'Pukkha Sahib', and seeks out someone in authority. It seems her luggage has been lost, and she cannot be admitted onto the sacred soil of India (ie beyond Palam airport) until it is found and checked through customs. I catch a glimpse of her looking hot and beginning to steam. Several centuries pass, while forms are filled out, and then, at last, she emerges, *with* her bag and an airport flunky who has found her luggage. He hovers all too noticeably, but Ruth is in no state to acknowledge him, and I dig around in my purse for a few rupees, which he snatches up and is gone. Welcome to India!

We take her home to the sanctuary of Vasant Vihar and give her a restorative cup of tea. As nobody is up, we drive her to the Golf Club and back along Shanti Path, impressive in the early morning light. Tony has breakfast waiting for us on our return, and then we tuck Ruth into her room, draw the curtains and leave her to recover.

She is up by the time we come back from golf, and Doug and the girls take her to Connaught Circus, while I work on *The Scoop*. Still suffering from jet lag and a bad tension headache, she retires early.

Sunday, October 24 It is fortunate that it is Sunday, as nobody has to get up until they feel like it. I discovered early on in my life as a 'Mem' that servants are a two-edged sword. You cannot keep them hanging about waiting for meals to be consumed – breakfast is at 8.00am, period and amen. I have already eaten when Ruth appears. I make her some tea and toast, give her a couple of aspirin and set her out on the shaded patio with a copy of the *The Times of India*. She perks up as her headache disappears, and we have a lovely long chat and peruse some maps for her planned jaunts.

I know her so well that I feel, quite correctly, that she is not ready to be rushed into too much activity. So after the *de rigueur* Sabbath Bloody Marys and cheese soufflé, we have a leisurely tour. Down the Rajpath, past the President's Palace, and on to see the always endearing 'Dancing Policeman'. He is such a feature of Delhi life, and I never grow tired of watching him twirl and bend, smiling the whitest of smiles in his beautiful brown face, as he directs traffic from his podium.

Thursday, October 28 My conscience is doing more than prick me. Ever since Ruth arrived, I have been dumping her on Kilmeny, who faithfully takes her to the pool, buys her lunch at the cabana or at the Ashoka, and waits for her wandering mother to return.

My days are filled with meetings at the IWC, ditto of the national conveners for the Fair, or it's my turn for bridge, and today there is a final pricing session for the Canadian booth. Ruth joins in on this latter event, which is good, as she meets a lot of women from the High Commission, and I send up a silent prayer that someone will invite her out. Everything worked so well for Ruth Number 1, and everything seems against Ruth Number 2. Ah me!

Friday, October 29 Take Ruth up to Cook's Travel to organize a number of outings – Kajaraho, Agra, etc. Would love to arrange for her to go to the Pushkar Camel Fair, but there again, the fates are against us, as there is a conflict of interest with other trips. After a long wait for Mr Vargas at Cook's, he finally appears, only to tell us we should have seen Mr Ambrose, the ticket man. Can we come back at 4.00pm?

We are jinxed, but I console Ruth by taking her to Old Delhi to see the Red Fort. We go for lunch at the Maiden's Hotel, which she loves, and then I return her to the Imperial and Cook's to await the elusive Mr Ambrose, while I hasten off to attend the IWC event at the Iranian Embassy. I would have skipped this, but have been told quite firmly that the Executive *must* attend.

We see a film on the Coronation of the Shah in 1967. Talk about realms of gold! It is a magnificent spectacle, but why did they wait so long, I ask in vain? He has been Shah since some time in the 1940s, but the question is unanswerable, and who knows, perhaps even a state secret. I could not help comparing this opulent film, with its images of solid gold canopies and jewel-encrusted robes with the one I showed on Canada. Leaping salmon and ice sculptures just don't measure up. It is dark by the time I leave; as I am on unfamiliar territory, I get hopelessly lost. More through luck than anything else, I somehow make my way back to the High Commission to gather up Doug from the TGIF festivities and home. Ruth packs, and we set the alarm for 4.15am to get her to the airport for the first of her Indian adventures.

Thursday, November 4 A visiting Canadian doctor and his wife have been assigned to our care. They are a pleasant couple about our age. Doug takes Dr H to the office, and Mrs H and I have a round of shopping, which is tops on her wish list. I detect that she is 'into' clothes, and we go to Raj Creations, Sumitra's and the Irwin Road shops. Lunch at the Imperial, and then a tour of the Janpath and the Cottage Industries. I ask her rather wistfully if she would be interested in going to the Qutb Minar, but she is enthralled with what she is doing, and ruins are just not her thing. I am happy she is happy. I leave her surrounded by silk kaftans and go to pick up the girls from riding. I hasten back, but when I arrive I find to my horror that she has disappeared.

Visions of Mrs H, her Hush Puppies dragging in the dust, being abducted into some distant seraglio, pass before my eyes. Unlikely and all as this scenario seems, where is she?

"The last time I saw your wife, doctor, she was looking at a kaftan – quite pretty really – sort of a pinky-mauve..." I am beginning to foment into a real panic as I search frantically among the stalls, and barely restrain myself from looking under them. It is then that I see her. She is emerging from a doorway, clutching numberless packages and wreathed in smiles. She has never had such fun, and shopping at Eaton's was never like this, and does she really have to go home? Yes, yes and yes, and under lock and key, too.

Ruth is due back tonight, and I leave word with Tony to be on tap. I have warned her that we are going to a dinner party, so she may have to take a cab. On our return, there is no sign of Ruth. I wait up for an hour or so, then finally go to bed.

Friday, November 5 I get up at 6.00am and, like an anxious mother, peek into Ruth's room in case she has returned, unheard and unseen. The light is on, and the bed turned down, but nobody is there. I feel a flutter of fear, and that awful sinking feeling mystery authors are always writing about. What to do? Doug sensibly suggests that we wait 24 hours, and see if there is any message.

Just as we sit down to breakfast, there is a rap at the door. It is Ruth in a state of outrage. That old familiar Indian Airlines trap has been sprung again. She had bought their $200-takes-precedent-over-kings-and-ambassadors ticket, not only to find herself bumped, but on deeper scrutiny to discover that they had made a complete dog's breakfast of her itinerary. The only decent thing they did apparently was to put her up in a hotel in Calcutta.

She is somewhat soothed by Tony making her a splendid breakfast, and by Doug phoning Cook's to tell them to get their act together. I drop her off at the travel agency, and come back to collect her in another hour. She has been placated with promises of red carpets all the way, and a guaranteed plane leaving at 5.45pm. What would be her pleasure for the rest of the afternoon, I ask, only to find when we get home that there is a message for me to pick up some jumble sale stuff the Brits have for me. Once again, Ruth and her desires are temporarily placed on the back burner. She is happy to accompany me for the ride, and we end up with tea on our patio, and a nice long companionable chat until we leave for the airport.

Hilary has been on a school trip to Nanital, and returns, having had a wonderful, if exhausting, time. She falls into bed, and is seen no more that evening.

Sunday, November 7 Doug requested that we remain in India until after Christmas, so that Hilary can finish her school term. The logic of this is unassailable, and the request is granted.

Today Doug's replacement is due in, a Dr Peter Webster. He is a bachelor, and has been assigned a spot in the Compound. There has been a bit of a flutter among the secretaries and single female officers, as unattached males are at a premium. Doug goes out to pick up Dr W at the usual witching hour but, predictably enough, he does not return with his charge until 7.30am. I make everybody breakfast, and give the newcomer a subtle once-over. He is a very nice, very personable young man, and I am sure a good doctor. I invite him over for dinner tonight, and find he is also very bright, and we have a really pleasant evening, although he drifts off mid-conversation toward the shank of the evening.

Monday, November 8 Ruth is due back today, but the time (being Indian Airlines time) is uncertain; she will phone or take a taxi. I go to French, play bridge with the Brits, work at the library, swim and take the girls riding. Home for dinner, but there's no sign of Ruth. We are just having our coffee, when Ruth bursts in – hot, frustrated and fuming yet again. She has been bumped twice (despite all the promised red carpets); they lost her bags (again) and language falters when it comes to describing her views on India's transport facilities. We bring her in, feed her drinks and dinner, and make much of her. She hated Benares, but was awed and overwhelmed by the Taj, and we exchange stories until she feels that perhaps her trip wasn't all that bad, when you come right down to it.

Tuesday, November 9 I feel a bit like the ferry man of legend, doomed to travel back and forth for all eternity, as I rise to take Ruth once more to the airport. It seems advisable, as despite her ranking in the 'kings-ambassadors' category, she is now fourth on the stand-by list, and there is no guarantee she will get on.

When we arrive, Ruth spots two American ladies who have been bumped along with her in the endless shuffle of Indian Airlines' cards. They are numbers two and three, and have high hopes. We fall into conversation and, rather dejectedly, they tell how they have been planning this trip for more than two years. Both are from Kansas; one is an architect, the other a teacher. They have never strayed far from their native cornfield, and this Asian experience was to have been the journey of a lifetime. So far, all they have seen of India have been queues and crowded airports.

I suggest we check with the desk about boarding priorities, and it turns out they will not get on this flight. This seems incredible when they are second and third on standby, but I know from past experience that there is no point in expostulating indignantly, or even asking "How come?" The response will just be another infuriating waggle of a dark head, and nothing will happen. I strongly suspect that palms have been crossed, but this is idle speculation and of no help to anyone. I prepare to take Ruth home with me, when I look over at the two forlorn figures, and the better me surfaces. I ask if they would like to come home with us for breakfast. The effect is electrifying. Their bags are gathered, and we are out at the car before I can say "You're welcome."

356

Doug is a little startled to find two complete strangers at our breakfast table, but he rallies like a gentleman, and Tony emerges with plates of bacon and eggs and cups of hot coffee. The ladies are overwhelmed and cannot thank us enough. The prospect of a day or more spent within the smelly precincts of the Delhi airport was almost more than they could face, and now, here they are being served a Yankee breakfast in a cool, clean and airy house. Words to this effect are reiterated between bites, and their gratitude is obviously boundless.

I leave Ruth entertaining them on the patio, while I dash off to the first engagement of the day. They are still here when I return, and we have a round of sherry, then lunch. We telephone the airport only to find they will not be able to leave until tomorrow, but they can charge a hotel. I drop them off at the Ashoka, and only narrowly escape further effusions of gratitude.

Thursday, November 11 Having got Ruth off (yes, really) yesterday morning, I launch into another round of pricing; lap up a session of the Museum course, and then attend a farewell bridge lunch for Enid Walker. Our usual foursome, including the delightful Amrijit Singh, is present, as well as another three tables of an international mix.

Friday, November 12 Monica and Hamish have returned from England, with Hamish's back operation safely behind him. She telephones to say she is going out today to collect the china we had both ordered and would I like to come.

Kilmeny joins me, and we drive out to the Bank House. I don't think Monica is looking all that sprightly, for the holiday has been fraught and she is suffering from jet lag. We collect our china, which I love. It is a complete tea set for eight, in white, with a pattern of small and discreet blue flowers. The fact that half the British contingent seems to have ordered the same pattern isn't going to matter a toss when we are all in different corners of the world. We take a tonga back to the Bank House, much to Kilmeny's delight. The horse is ancient and tired, and stumbles along over the rough road. The driver gets out his whip, but reckons without Monica. She berates him in smatterings of Hindi, and predicts an incarnation as an

357

Ruth ... bearing an elephant prodder like an avenging sword

abused beast of burden for the wretched man. I am only relieved that she does not snatch his whip and turn it on him. Kilmeny would have liked to linger in the Bank House's cool and scented garden, but we have to hurry back to pick up Ruth once more.

We arrive at the airport, and find (surprise, surprise) that the plane has not arrived. We are informed that, "It is delayed, oh my yes, and we do not know when it will come." We tool around to the Compound, and pick up Peter Webster to bring him home for dinner. I send a few prayers heavenwards that Ruth will show up.

The moon has risen above my poetic Kashmiri tree, and the drinks and toasted cashews are being passed, when there is a pounding at the door. I get up from the patio as Tony goes to open the door.

Ruth, hair a-tousle, swathed in a long Indian skirt and bearing an elephant prodder like an avenging sword, stands in the doorway.

"Jesus H Christ," she announces to no one in particular, "they've done it again."

There follows a tale of delayed take-offs, questionable tickets and a succession of sickening green sandwiches. She presents the elephant prodder as a gift, with a few suggestions as to where she would like to have put it. Once more, we figuratively clasp her to our consoling bosoms, and spirits are both served and soothed.

Saturday, November 13   It doesn't matter what needs to be done, I am determined to spend the day with Ruth who, after all, is one of my oldest and dearest friends. We go to all the most interesting shopping areas. Ruth buys a beautiful Kashmiri shawl, and a kind of Mogul fur hat for her son John. Then the entire household goes off to Old Delhi, for a more thorough tour, including the Jama Masjid and Chandni Chowk. Hilary keeps a weather eye on Ruth, lest she pale before the horrors that await her. Ruth, to her credit, does not turn a hair.

The Browns are having a dinner party tonight, and Ruth has been invited. I am so glad that she will have at least one Delhi party, but even here we are tripped up. Sheila has fallen prey to some awful bug, and can barely make it through dinner, retiring shortly thereafter. Doug Brown tries to carry on, but the spirit has gone out of the evening, and we soon all silently steal away.

Sunday, November 14 We try to cram in a few things like the Lodi Gardens and Humayun's tomb for Ruth, but I am feeling distinctly unwell (Sheila B's bug, perhaps). I even decline Ruth's invitation to take us all out for dinner. The rest go and have a good time, returning to tell me, in detail, everything they had to eat, which is definitely not a stomach settler.

Monday, November 15 Up at 4.00am to take Ruth to the airport for the last time. She assures me she had a marvellous time and it was all a great experience. She probably means it, but I feel regret over the cancelled trip to Afghanistan, and the comedy of errors that was the essence of her '$200-see-India-like-a-Rajah' tour.

Return home in time to get organized for my turn as the hostess of the French group. The directions were very sketchy (and said very quickly) but as far as I could gather the morning was to involve "game". I should have asked, but I thought it might have to do with a lecture by someone on subcontinental fauna. It doesn't. When they all stream in, it becomes obvious that the morning is not to be about game, big or otherwise, but about *games.*

We hastily get out card tables, dig out cards, resurrect a Scrabble set, a Monopoly board, and ditto for chess. It is all a little 'oops' in atmosphere, but dear Kilmeny leaps in, and in flawless French explains that her *mère* has just returned from the airport where she had to see someone off who was "very dear to her." It all sounds slightly like the end of a love affair, and there is a general sympathetic chorus of "ahs". I am out of my depth, and merely beam nervously on them all, and suggest we start to *jouer* like mad. Despite this confused and hectic beginning, the morning goes really well. My attempt at French-style 'yums' is a great success, as is the *café filtre.*

Wednesday, November 17 Kilmeny has been dying to spread her wings and see more of India. Since that first summer when

360

she fled from some of its more overt horrors, she has become inured, and anxious to make the most of this fleeting opportunity. Heather Gorman (Grindley's Bank) has a delightful niece, Grania Langdon-Down, who is the same age as Kilmeny and equally anxious for exploration. I arrange to pick her up and take both girls to the pool for a swim and lunch at the Cabana. They hit it off immediately, and Heather and I feel all the pride of a successful dating bureau. They come back to the house, get out maps, and plot an itinerary beginning with Lucknow.

Raj, of course, alerts her mother, who, with her usual efficiency, arranges to have relatives posted as a welcoming committee at the railway station. I am not sure this is exactly what the young travellers have in mind, but this morning we see Kilmeny off to meet Grania at the station for the 8.00 train. It does not have quite the ring of the 'No 5 Punjab Down', but then train schedules are not titled to suit romantics.

This afternoon there is a reception for a visiting dignitary from France, a Madame De something or other. The International Women's Club is out in full force. I am fearful of being caught up in one of those stilted and uneasy conversations, but Madame is such a charmer, that if she notices any gaucheries of syntax, she ignores them. I soon find that I am chatting away, with what might just pass as ease.

Friday, November 19 To date, the head of the Activities Committee has not been able to find anyone to take over *The Scoop*. Today he telephones to let me know that the new head of Immigration has agreed to do it, and I heave a sigh of relief, as I hope this means that I can turn the editorship over forthwith.

Saturday, November 20 Whenever we are having a party, I cannot help but wallow in the difference between Then and Now. Gone is the frantic atmosphere on the day of a major party at home – the long hours of food preparation, cleaning the loos, ironing linens and kicking things into the nearest closet before rushing up to get dressed.

None of that in this privileged life. I pick up a few last-minute things at the Commissary, and when I return the shamiana is up, and things are moving smoothly. I check on the kitchen, and Tony has just carved one of his spectacular table centres from a long squash.

As the day wanes, I go upstairs for a rest, have a leisurely, scented bath, get dressed, then give a last-minute check. The tables are set, candles are lit, and everything looks the way it ought. The first guests begin to arrive, and pretty soon the party is underway. It is very, very successful, and the evening has the right mood. I enjoy it as much as anyone. When the guests have taken their leave, Doug and I sit out under the stars, with a nightcap, and some left-over nibblies, while hands other than mine return the house to normalcy.

Tuesday, November 23 My fond hope that the new editor of *The Scoop* would somehow gather the whole thing under his wing proves to be ill-founded. Anne Morrissey has offered to help and comes over this afternoon to see how things are done. It sounds simple, but as I do 90 per cent of the writing, I cannot really explain how my mind works. (Come to think of it I never have been able to explain how my mind works.) I had thought I could press her into typing, but it turns out she can't type, so I am not sure the initiation has been all that fruitful.

Monica is having a party for Hamish's birthday, and we are invited. I love the Chartered Bank House – it is such an echo of past privileges somehow. It is really a great evening, with an excellent dinner and Hamish is no longer suffering so much distress since his back operation.

Wednesday, November 24 On the other side of the world, Peter is having his birthday. I wonder what he is doing, and would I approve? Of course I wouldn't approve, and would it be any different if I were there, making him an angel food birthday cake and blowing out candles? It is one of those days when I feel a terrible sense of distance – not just in miles, but a sort of spiritual disconnection.

As I am up at 4.00am, to see Doug off to Rajasthan, it evolves into a dawn-to-dusk day. I work away at *The Scoop* but, with one thing and another, I don't really get going until the afternoon. This time both the new editor and his assistant come to watch, and that is all they do – watch. I show them

362

what I can, but emphasize to Mr B that he will put his own stamp on the publication, and must not feel bound by any particular format. It goes without saying that I don't really get on with it until after they leave. Have dinner, and finally put it, and myself, to bed at 1.00am.

CHAPTER 42

Sunday, November 28 It seems strange, but Hilary and I are alone. We start some Christmas baking, then write a few of the rather offbeat Christmas cards we bought yesterday, after which Hilary helps me make up signs for our White Elephant Stall. Dinner at the ACSA Lounge and a movie.

Monday, November 29 A fascinating day. One of the guests at Hamish's birthday dinner was an elderly general, whose grandfather or great-uncle or whatever had been involved in the Siege of Delhi, and had left the general a map of the gun emplacements surrounding The Ridge. I have become really wrapped up in the Mutiny, and have read everything I can find.

He, the general, is interested in my interest, and promises he will get the map to Monica, so that we can tour and check out these historic sites.

Today is the day, and I go out to the Bank House in the afternoon, and Bolar Singh is ready at the wheel. Monica shows him the map, but although he looks wise and knowing, he obviously does not have a clue as to what we are talking about.

He drives us out to a deserted cemetery in the depths of Old Delhi. It is a place of long-ago heartache, and a testament of youth in another type of war. The cemetery is full of the graves of young clerks in the East India Company, the majority of whom were in their late teens or early twenties. It seems there was a particularly virulent strain of cholera at the time that struck in the morning and killed by nightfall.

Doug experienced an incident a few months ago that set him thinking back to this swift and vicious killer. A young Canadian doctor, who had just graduated and just been married, brought his bride to India to celebrate both events. He had always been fascinated by the subcontinent and had been boning up on Hindu philosophy and 'Holy Mother Ganga' and the purification of her waters for the believers. Heaven knows what possessed him, but he decided he would follow the faithful into the Ganges at dawn, and was dead by 5.00pm that afternoon.

Doug was notified, and began to wonder if the cause of death could have been a return of this virulent type of cholera that had killed so many newly arrived young men in the 19th century. He requested an autopsy report, which was promised but did not appear. Further inquiries brought more promises, but nothing else. Finally, when he demanded the report, and demanded it *now*, he encountered the proverbial stone wall. What autopsy? What report?

We conclude our tour of the cemetery, and are taken into some as yet unknown parts of Old Delhi. A careful scrutiny of the map reveals where the gun emplacements had to be. We locate an overgrown field, with some decaying buildings on the periphery. I am thrilled to see ancient chunks out of one of the buildings, from which has sprung abundant vegetation, and even the beginning of a tree. The line of trajectory would have followed exactly from the position of one of the besieging guns. We climb down into the field, and check our positions on the map.

First thing we know we are surrounded by a fascinated circle, all inquiring "What is it the Memsahibs wish to find?" and scratching vigorously at their dhotis. Monica says something about gun emplacements, which muddies the water no end.

"Oh no, no, no, there are no guns here – you are agents of the police perhaps?"

I cannot help but wonder how wide the recruitment of police agents must be. We deny any such involvement, and realizing that any further explanations would be useless, we thank them, just as if they had been of the greatest assistance, pass a few rupees around, and return to the car. As far as an exploration into military history, the afternoon has not been a total success, but as an echo of another time and an offbeat tour of Old Delhi, it has been marvellous.

Wednesday, December 1 Yesterday was the last meeting for our White Elephant booth, and today Hilary and I work on signs, gather bags and sort out things for the '5 paisa' table. Only another three days.

Friday, December 3 My faithful committee meets me at the YWCA, and we work like Trojans, setting up tables, putting up Canadian flags and posters, and generally getting organized for the morrow. I have pressed some of my British friends into service, and dear Eileen stays to help me lock up. Returning home, I find to my delight that Kilmeny has returned. She and Grania had *"the* most fantastic time", and are keen to set out again. I am so happy to see her and with practically no subtlety, direct her into immediate action for the cause. She helps me with last-minute items, before she begs off to go to bed.

Saturday, December 4 'F' day! Kilmeny, Hilary and I are down at the YWCA at 8.00am, and start setting things up. The rest of the Committee filter in as the morning progresses. A messenger comes from the Fair Chairman to say that there has been a change of plans. Mrs Gandhi will arrive at 11.00am for the official opening, and we can start selling at 11.30am. As we are all set up, a lot of the volunteers go out for coffee, and are just trickling back in when Mrs Gandhi arrives. She makes a tour of all the 'national' tables and is introduced to each convener. She pauses long enough at the Canadian booth to shake hands. Unbeknownst to me, a press photographer is nearby and snaps a picture. I glance over at Hilary. She is quite literally goggle-eyed, and gasps out that I have just had my picture taken shaking hands with Mrs Gandhi. I make an attempt to appear blasé, but actually feel somewhat exalted by this encounter with a head of state.

The sale goes really well, although without the anticipated crowds. The estimate is one-quarter to one-third fewer visitors than last year, attributable in part to the fact that we are vying with the Davis Cup, opening today in Delhi. Our booth realizes 7,743 rupees, which is fantastic and higher than last year, despite the lower attendance. We did not quite reach our goal of 10,000 rupees, but it will still go a long way. I am very pleased, feel I learned a lot and that it was a worthwhile effort. Absolutely wiped out by the time I gather up the girls and go home at 8.00pm.

Sunday, December 5 Pure undiluted heaven, with no

pressures. I wash all the sheets from the sale, and sort out the leftovers from our booth. Take the girls out for dinner as a thank-you for all their help.

Wednesday, December 8 It is Canada Day for the International Women's Club, and the Residence is decked out for the occasion. We have been practicing the Huron Carol, which is lovely, but is also difficult to make sound impressive with so slender a choir of uncertain sopranos. I can only describe it as 'thin', and the film we elect to show does not, perhaps, get across the essence of a Canadian Christmas. It is a black-and-white picture set in Montreal, and a bit short on Yuletide jollity, what with a driving wind blowing snow across something that closely resembles the Russian Steppes, and cars jammed up on St Catherine's Street, surrounded by an nimbus of exhaust.

Still, we ply the international community with Nanaimo bars and butter tarts, shortbread in the shape of maple leaves, and anything else we can think of that is even remotely ethnic. Mrs HE seems quite pleased, and it has been a solid effort, which, I guess, is what really counts.

Thursday, December 9 Not one of my better days. Doug is due to return home, and does not appear, nor does he send word. It is my turn for the British bridge, and only one table shows up, then half of the other, so it is a hit-and-miss-lend-a-dummy sort of affair. Then, too, Tony's refreshments lack style, to put it mildly. Come dinner, he passes off yesterday's soup and the remains of the bridge sandwiches – something he would never get away with if the Sahib were here.

Sunday, December 12 Word has come that Doug will be back tonight, so I spend the day writing Christmas letters like mad, and wrapping up presents already purchased. Ram Singh arrives to take us to the airport to meet Doug. The Sahib arrives laden with goodies – lengths of Thai silk, a gorgeous Indonesian cheese board, a beautifully carved 'Thinking Buddha' and a Santa-sack of odds and ends for Hilary's collection.

Wednesday, December 15 I am off to the wind-up meeting of the International Chrysanthemum Fair committee, being hosted by Mrs Mears (the over-all convener and the wife of the Dutch Ambassador) at the Netherlands Residence. The summation is that it was a huge success. I think again that despite the poverty of the market, despite the Davis Cup, despite the rock-bottom prices, the money raised will comfort, solace, feed, educate and succour countless numbers of Delhi's citizens, and a few surrounding villages. I think we all feel this, not, I hope, in a smug self-satisfied way, but as having climbed a few painful inches up India's mountain of social ills.

Thursday, December 16 The High Commissioner is hosting a farewell dinner for us at the Residence tonight, and we have been asked to pick out the guest list. They are mostly doctors, our British, American and Australian counterparts, of whom we are so fond; the Khoslas, the Nehrus, the incoming Dr Webster, our particular friends, the Barkers and the Parkers, and Kilmeny is also included. We are both terribly proud of her. I am not sure that it had all that much to do with us, but she is so bright and so attractive, and we can pretend that it did. It is an elegant and lovely evening, and very thoughtful of His Excellency.

Friday, December 17 One of life's dark days. It begins with visions of sugar plums – the twins are due to arrive, and Kunti Verman is hosting a farewell coffee party for me this morning. I love Kunti, who has been a marvellous president of the IWC, and one of the nicest people ever. As a matter of fact, I realize how much I cherish the women of this group – charming, elegant and highly intelligent. Any barriers of differing cultures have long since been swept away by the strength of genuine friendship. As the party is being given for me, no way can I miss it. All should be fine because the twins' plane is expected at 4.00am, and I am up betimes.

From past experience, I know to phone the airport rather than dash off, and sure enough, the flight has been delayed until 7.00am. Still lots of time. Kilmeny and I go, only to find that it is now scheduled for 10.00am. Maternal feelings conflict with social responsibilities, and Kilmeny tells me not to be silly.

She will drive me to the coffee party, and pick up the twins. I am in the process of getting dressed when the phone rings. Kilmeny answers it and I hear her say:

"But what about my brother and sister?"

I take it in, but I don't. It is a fear so awful that I don't want to move, in case any motion will bring on a catastrophe. Something else is said, but I don't hear it, and I don't want to hear it. Kilmeny is coming up the stairs and I brace myself. My insides disintegrate with relief as I hear my eldest release her frustrations.

"Mum, you'll never believe what that dumb airline has done! All that fussing about delay, and now they have flown the plane right over Delhi and on to Bangkok."

If they had flown the plane back to England, I would still have got down and kissed the ground. They had not crashed. My beautiful twins had not become tragic statistics. It is all I care about, and I only half hear Kilmeny's untangling of the facts of the incident.

It all involves lost time and air regulations about crew fatigue. As things turn out our two, and four other school children from England, were the only passengers for Delhi. A stop here would have messed up the airline schedule, and over-extended crew time. As a consequence, the six school children will now be put on another KLM flight in Bangkok, and will arrive around dinnertime. I cannot stop shaking for at least a half hour, but pull myself together and go off to the coffee morning. Mrs Mears has already heard the news, and apologizes to me personally for the iniquities of their national airline.

When we finally gather up our exhausted children (Martin, arriving from Winnipeg, has been up almost 72 hours), all they want to do is collapse into their respective beds.

Wednesday, December 22 Things are reaching a high point in preparations, still a little short of fever pitch, but busy enough. The girls go off for last minute shopping. Then Kilmeny, who finds herself in charge of this year's Christmas play at the High Commission, darts off to see about costumes, etc. Hilary accompanies Ann Morrissey to go to look for a Christmas tree.

369

"It is your Christmas, so I will give you a bargain ..."

I get a report from Ann on her tree-hunting jaunt with Hilary. Ann has a small son, aged three or four, for whom a Christmas tree is still one of life's magic moments, and it is absolutely essential that they have one. It is now only three days before Christmas, and the Delhi tree markets, sparse to begin with, are now almost depleted. The three of them approach, and Ann picks out one forlorn-looking specimen from an equally forlorn-looking batch.

"How much?"

"Very cheap, Memsahib, only 25 rupees." Ann makes a move toward her purse, but Hilary puts out her hand.

"25 rupees? 25 rupees? We will give you 10."

"Oh, Miss Sahib, there is no profit. This is a very fine tree, and worth twice what I am asking, but," and he shrugs resignedly, it is your Christmas, so I will give you a bargain at 20 rupees."

Hilary, with hands spread out in a gesture of incredulity, shakes her head. There are some urgent whispers from Ann that she must have a tree, and she will pay. "Just let's get a tree."

"Trust me, Mrs Morrissey," says my little street Arab, and turning to the vendor:

"12 rupees."

"Oh, I cannot let this fine tree go for such a price. 18 rupees, and it is sold."

"It is not worth it," Hilary retorts, "but we will make it 15 rupees, and that is the last word." By now Ann is in despair that her child will never have this scrawny shrub for his Christmas.

Hilary takes Ann by the hand and starts to walk away, as the vendor, who has enjoyed the game as much as Hilary, acknowledges a true trader and bows to the inevitable. 15 rupees exchange hands, and the tree is sold.

Around noon, I pick up Kilmeny again and we change for lunch. It is Doug's party for his staff, and we all gather at Claridge's. We have also invited the Grenes, the Kapurs, the Khoslas and the Tiernans. It goes very well, although there is an unspoken sense of sadness. We know we are all together for the last time, and wonder when, if ever, shall we meet again.

Kilmeny has been working on the annual play, and tonight

it is to be presented at the High Commission. Every child has a part; every parent is in attendance. Apart from some minor glitches, the children love being in it, the parents are entranced, and any flaws are happily forgotten. The evening concludes with carol singing around a real Canadian Christmas tree, and a gorging on mince tarts and eggnogs.

Friday, December 24 It is Christmas Eve in this strange desert land, so much more like the original than our own frozen north. Our last family member, Peter, arrives predictably late at 6.00am, and it is almost another two hours before he is released into the larger world of Palam Road, and we are on our way home. The poor boy barely has time to clear his head and get the sand out of his eyes before his father whips him out to the shops. The day is spent in a flurry of wrapping and whispering and hiding parcels until all is finally deposited where it ought to be under what passes for our Christmas tree. Hilary negotiated the purchase of this one, too, and all things considered did quite well. The tree is only mildly lopsided.

The whole family has been invited over to the home of the new Political Officer for a late afternoon grog party. There is a lovely atmosphere to the party, due to a charming house and delightful hosts. As there is plenty of what we always call 'V&V' (*viandes* and VO) only a light supper is needed when we return home. This is fortunate, as that is all we get. I cannot really blame Tony. He is, I think, in a bit of panic over this feast in which the Sahibs indulge once a year.

Saturday, December 25 Rumpled and sleepy-eyed people emerge one by one, and fuse into a family circle in the living room. A cup of eggnog works wonders, and we gather around the tree to open our presents. I am blessed with some exceptional gifts – a wide-angle lens for my camera, a beautiful brass-inlaid box, Kashmiri papier mâché, batik cushion covers, and the room is filled with "oohs and ahs". We are festooned with the traditional marigold wreathes by the staff, and they are presented with their bonus envelopes. There follows breakfast, the entertainment wallahs, and then we are off to the Parkers for a Christmas morning noggin.

Now an experienced Memsahib, I return and check on the kitchen. Tony hates it, but with all these alien dishes, it is the only way. A little more broth in the glutinous soup, increased basting for the turkey, and I skip out before the lowering brow of our cook.

The Barker family arrive, and it is a wonderfully happy Christmas night. They make a great hit with the young, and why not, accompanied as they are by two handsome young men. They enter into the family charades with maximum enthusiasm, if minimum talent, and it is well past midnight before Bolar Singh is summoned for the return to Old Delhi.

Sunday, December 26 Boxing Day this year is literally that. I spend it filling boxes with our household goods, our Indian treasures and things that we think are our Indian treasures. I work better on my own, and Doug retreats to the office, the children to the pool and the tennis courts, and I find myself dallying over special letters, a history of the Taj Mahal and generally deferring the finality of closing the lid on two years of our life. Rod Haney cycles over for his usual Sunday tea. He has been such a good companion and neighbour, and I shall miss our weekly wide-ranging discussions over our cha.

Monday, December 27 At my now daily task of packing, except for Monica coming to take me to Mr Butt's. Mr Butt is close to being a legend in his own time. He is a Kashmiri magnate and purveyor of rugs, crewelwork and all things bright and beautiful. I buy two crewelwork bedspreads and take a rug on approval.

Over lunch, Monica tells me a marvellous story about Mr Butt, which is faintly reminiscent of that old Charles Laughton film, *The Beachcomber*.

It seems that in days gone by, Mr Butt was not only an unsuccessful salesman, but a gambler, a lush and a con artist of surpassing skill. He also "out-paramoured the Turk", as Shakespeare put it, when it came to women. One day, into this disreputable life, there came a lady missionary from Concord, New Hampshire, bent on saving any soul that came within her orbit. Meeting a prime sinner like Mr Butt was the supreme challenge. Exactly how the resulting miracle came about is a

373

bit hazy, but the end of the tale is that they were married, after The Pledge had been duly sworn by the repentant Mr Butt. Now a pillar of the community, Mr Butt passes the collection plate in the American Methodist Church of a Sunday.

Back at my task, and then we all go off to Kim Chi's engagement party at the Veitches. She is Djung Veitch's beautiful daughter, and is an absolute lotus flower of a girl. She is engaged to a handsome young Canadian, and we all sincerely wish her well. After the party, we bring the Barkers and Peter Webster home with us for a nightcap. It is after midnight by the time they leave, and we are due up at 5.00am for tomorrow's morning departures.

Tuesday, December 28   The family separation begins. Kilmeny must return to a waiting job as a ski instructor on Seymour Mountain. Martin, too, has to leave for the annual dog-sled challenge and snowshoe race at St John's School. I have always hated change, and for the umpteenth time in my life, wish things could stay the same.

When I return from the airport, I can barely keep my eyes open, but I am saved from falling into the temptation of another hour's sleep by the arrival of the packers. What a mess! However, thanks to Peter and Barbara who pitch in, we somehow manage to get every inlaid plate, every carved chess piece tucked away, and the packers leave just before dinner, promising to return in the morning.

Wednesday, December 29   "The days dwindle down to a precious few..." I feel sadder and sadder as the hour approaches. So much has this strange, wonderful, maddening country become part of my life.

Monica pops in, and we sort out the godown to see if there is anything she would like. Last call of the day is to visit the Administrator's wife, who has become a particular friend. She is in bed with painful phlebitis. We are both in tears when I leave – me from sentiment, she probably from her terribly sore leg. In the evening, my Sunday visitor, Rod Haney, has asked us all over for dinner, and we say goodbye to a really good friend.

Thursday, December 30 Our last farewell 'do' has been arranged by our Dr M of the Punjab for 6.00pm this evening at the Ashoka Hotel. We are by now only too well aware that 6.00pm does not *really* mean 6.00pm, and so we fall in with Dermott Grene's suggestion that we all meet at their place for a little refresher before we join the party.

'We' includes the Tiernans and Peter Webster, and it is a well-fortified group that reaches the Ashoka some time after 7.00pm. The host's family is out in full force. Most of them we met on our trip through the Punjab. There is the Doctor and his wife, her sister and brother-in-law, a couple of related Brigadiers and a Lieutenant-General, as well as a couple of Indian doctors. No expense has been spared, and we no sooner arrive than drinks are passed around. Dr M beams and introduces everybody to everybody else, and then that is it.

I go through the usual monosyllabic conversations with the ladies. Inquiries after their families inform me, "They are well thank-you"; inquiries after their own health produce the same response.

I can see Barbara Tiernan tangling with a silent sister-in-law. She told me later that she learned everything about the lady's favourite curry "down to the last pea."

I abandon the distaff side to place myself beside the Brigadier. I fare no better here, and finally hit the nadir of all social conversation when I actually ask him: "How is the Indian army?"

The music plays but nobody dances. The drinks are passed, but none of the locals drink. Time goes by, conversation lags, but there is no suggestion of dinner. Dermott hisses in my ear that he has an ulcer that should be kept fed, and when did I think we were going to eat? Peter Webster entices me out on the dance floor for the purpose of asking me the same question. We had both detected the spoor of a waiter some time ago, which gave a flicker of hope, but nothing came of it.

It is reaching the point where the western personnel of the party are either going to get absolutely loaded or are going to faint dead away. Finally, around 11.00pm, Doug suggests to Dr M that perhaps we should have dinner, as he thinks some of the others may have to leave. Instantly waiters are summoned, places are assigned, and there is an unseemly rush to the table. I am sitting dead centre with Peter Webster. We look on covetously as waiters place bread rolls at either end of the table, but nothing in front of us. When eventually a basket of hot and fragrant buns are put at my right hand, I pick it up, feeling truly noble, and offer it to Peter, saying, "thy necessity is greater than mine."

He looks at me with what might pass for reverence.

"If I live to be a thousand, I shall never forget this gesture," as he falls upon the staff of life.

Friday, December 31 A strange sort of New Year's Eve. The house no longer looks like ours. The survival kit from the High Commission imparts a feeling of permanent impermanence. I go up to the Commission to make the obligatory round of farewells. This is almost as bad as leaving home two years ago.

The family has been invited for a Hogmanay bash at the Barkers, but somehow none of us has the heart for it. Monica suggests we come over this morning instead, which Peter, Barbara and I do. In true Delhi fashion, Bloody Marys are served, then we go to Maiden's for lunch. The Barkers have been wonderful friends, and we feel a genuine attachment that I somehow know will span time and distance.

We join Doug at home, and take everyone over to the ACSA Lounge. There is a party in progress, but the friends with whom Hilary has spent the day suggest we join them at the snack bar.

The end is the end, and we return home for the last time. We retire with our own thoughts to our own rooms. I cannot sleep, and hear the sounds of the chowkidar tapping the fence railing; his sign that the sahibs, the memsahibs, and all who lie within the high walls and behind the iron gates may rest well. He is on duty – oh my, yes.

CHAPTER 43

Saturday, January 1, 1977 New Year's Day, and we leave for the airport at 5.00am. Tony is on hand, and I give him his chit, payments for the staff until January 7, and a month's salary each for Muni and him. We thank him and say goodbye, but the constraint that has always been there remains. I feel sorry about this, but remind myself that I am the only wife to date at the High Commission who has not fired a servant. To be truthful, I am in two minds as to whether this is a virtue or pure spinelessness. In any event, I have couched Tony's reference in careful terms, and recommend him particularly to bachelors. Interfering wives are an anathema.

There are some things I will not miss about India, and the nauseating chartreuse luncheons of Indian Airlines are among them.

Once aboard, they are presented with the predestined inevitability of a Greek tragedy. The flight is mercifully short, and we arrive for our last two days on the subcontinent in Aurangabad, the City of Aurangzeb, last of the Mogul emperors.

Two days are not nearly enough time, with all the fascinating things that await us in this remarkable city: the Panchakki Water Mill and Gardens, the mausoleum Aurangzeb built for his wife and the mystical Hill of the Gods. The caves of Ellora and Ajanta, however, are our prime targets and we want to give them the full measure they deserve.

We book into the Ram International, and after lunch set out on our tour of discovery. There is a lot of financial palaver about getting a cab, but we settle on 85 rupees and start off. After a stop at Daulatabad, a rather interesting hill fort, we carry on to Ellora. The day is hot, and the dust billows up from the road. It is difficult to imagine that anything of interest lies ahead, but we suddenly turn a corner, and there, in a shimmering haze, is a bank of dry, sun-baked hills, wherein lie the fabled underground miracle of the caves of Ellora.

It is staggering, this poem of living stone, carved from the

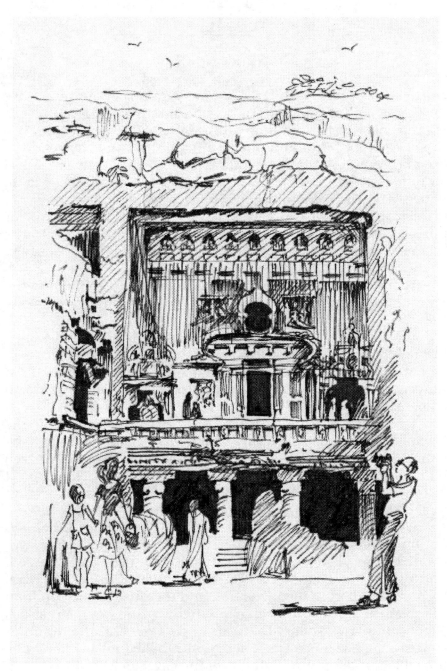

It is staggering, this poem of living stone

heart of the mountain. I have my guidebook at the ready, full of informative notes. I read out the text covering the ecumenical nature of the caves, Buddhist, Hindu and Jain; the Herculean labour required in the shifting of 200,000 tons of stone; the antiquity, the wonder. Fascinating and all as the statistics are, the atmosphere is that of the rising of a curtain for a first-rate play. I am transported from this burning Indian scene back to a Saturday afternoon matinee. I can almost smell the popcorn. Stewart Granger and Deborah Kerr (or someone of that ilk) have just found the lost city they have been seeking, and they gasp in awe at a Hollywood version of the same. Nothing, but nothing, in imagination could match what we now see.

Going through the main entrance into the Hindu temple of Kailasa, the late afternoon sun is slanting across an incredible rock face of primeval carvings – huge colonnades and phantom galleries, whose delicate traceries seem almost impossible given the thickness of the stone; an imposing statue of Lakshmi and carved icons of other gods from the Hindu pantheon. Towering stone elephants guard the cave entrances, and even after 13 centuries, the ceiling paintings are discernible.

Chronologically, the 12 Buddhist caves to the south are the oldest, dating back to the 7th century. The 17 central Hindu ones were built next, followed by the five post-Gupta Jain caves in the northern section. We have entered by the Hindu group, but as we feel nothing in the other Hindu caves could match Kailasa, we move on to investigate the Buddhist ones.

The Buddhist caves are comparatively spare when you consider them against the ornateness of the Hindu group. As with other Hindu art, the carvings are tightly concentrated and intricate, celebrations in stone of war and peace, battling deities, lush flora and romping fauna. There are more than a few rather explicit depictions of embracing couples, engaging in what Dr Kinsey described as man's favourite sport.

We explore several of the Buddhist caves, and even find one with a statue of the Hindu goddess of learning, surrounded by a number of worshipful Buddhist figures. This emphasizes once more the historic intertwining of the Asian faiths. In Cave Number 10, we find this meeting of the two religions again. We come upon a chaitya, the only Buddhist chapel in Ellora. There is an enormous image of Buddha, surrounded by pillars, whose engraved friezes show more Buddhist figures, but the cave itself is dedicated to an unofficial patron saint of Indian craftsmen, Viswakarma, the 'architect of the gods'.

Ellora is truly one of the most extraordinary experiences of our entire time in India, but enthralling as it is, we are beginning to flag in the breathless heat. A last determined sortie into the Jain caves, which give the impression of greater delicacy in both theme and execution, and we emerge once more into the contemporary world.

It is New Year's Day, and the Ram International is in party mood. There are balloons and streamers, and an orchestra plays *As Time Goes By*. Doug and I dance, and then he sweeps his middle daughter onto the floor. It is the beginning of a new year, and the end of an old one I shall not forget.

Sunday, January 2, 1977 After a lot of on-again, off-again business, we finally get a place on the bus going to Ajanta. We drive through the sun-bleached landscape, and when we are about halfway there, we stop at a village. Just when I am feeling I cannot bear to leave India, I get a therapeutic shot of reality. The village is the bottom of the Indian pits – filthy and fly-infested, with all the usual hacking and spitting and finger-nose blowing from the populace, plus all the clutching, begging and jumping in front of the cameras. I am beginning to see, as a distant oasis, the scrubbed streets of a small town in Germany.

We drive on, and stop at a lookout point to get our first glimpse of the Ajanta caves. They lie, embedded in a rock, that forms a giant horseshoe, and I can easily see how they could have been hidden all these centuries. Two thousand years of art and architecture lay buried in this wooded glade until a group of British officers on patrol came across the treasure trove in 1819.

We reach the caves around noon. It is in a spectacular setting, with the towering cliff, a thickly wooded gorge, and the cascading Waghora waterfall. The Ajanta restaurant, waiting for its victims, is beside the steps, and we are turfed into a grubby café, a-buzz with flies and the odours of past meals. We have been given an hour for lunch, but pick at some dubious curry and wander out among the beggars and eager salesmen, the latter hoping for a brisk trade in crystal and amethyst.

Ajanta, like Ellora, is a miracle of construction, but it is most noteworthy for its art, considered one of the world's most glorious collections of cave paintings. Somewhere in the second century AD, Buddhist monks found the cliff, and carved it to their purpose, in a less frenzied and intricate manner than those of the Hindu caves at Ellora. Some of the murals are a little disappointing as time has muted the once-vibrant glory of the paintings, but it is still awesome, and we wander around open-mouthed. Ajanta has a total of 29 caves, five fewer than Ellora, and they are also on a smaller scale, working as the carvers did on a much more restricted site. We see what we can in the time allowed, before we are escorted back to the bus. We drive to Aurangabad and into the rays of the setting sun. The fading light is almost symbolic of our almost last day in India.

Monday, January 3 I wake with some reluctance, knowing that it cannot be put off. Today we are really leaving India, this land that I have loved and hated, these people who have infuriated and enchanted me; this experience that has widened my horizons, changed my perceptions and taught me more of the story of man than I could ever have imagined.

But one more of what my friend Sheila always called JIS (Jolly Indian Surprises) lies ahead of us. We reach the airport to find our confirmed seats on the flight to Bombay have been cancelled. This announcement, made over Doug's protestations of "Confirmed, do you hear me, confirmed", is accompanied by some mutterings from officialdom that "Others had appeared, you see, and now we are helpless." Our connecting flight from Bombay to Karachi is due to leave at 8.00pm, and how, Doug, demands does Indian Airlines propose to deal with that? The answer is an unceremonious "take the bus."

Despite hot words (spoken and unspoken) what else can we do?

We will take the bus. Or so we think. It turns out that after we have loaded our mass of luggage onto the Indian Airlines bus, the driver refuses to take us, as we are "not enough",

381

there being just a handful of passengers. He would have to add to the cost per passenger, and the other passengers refuse to pay.

A heated discussion ensues about airlines and their responsibility for over-booking, for giving away confirmed seats, for every sin in the Christian, Hindu, Buddhist and Jain calendars. It is all to no avail – there is just a shaking of the head. Finally, I blow my stack and join in.

Every frustration, every evasion, every irritation I have ever felt in India comes together in a mighty outburst of indignation. Much moved by all this emotion, I am urged "not to be outraged." "Outraged does not begin to describe what I am feeling," I retort.

There is a change of tactics as I become icily calm, and bring out a notebook from my purse. I ask for names; I record things in my little black book. I tell them that a letter will be going to the Department of Tourism and Transport, where, I imply, we are not without influence. Copies of this letter will also go to the President and Director of Indian Airlines. I do everything but pull out my picture of Mrs Gandhi and me, hovering over white elephants at the International Fair. The words 'an international incident' are not actually spoken, but they hang like an unsheathed sword over their now shaking heads.

"Oh Memsahib what can we do? You have taken my unhappy name? Yes? Please to let me see what can be done."

What he saw, and what he did was to unearth a Government of India car (no doubt thinking of my close chums in Transport and Tourism). He is practically on his knees when he tells us it will cost 1080 rupees, but he has no doubt we will be repaid. Still muttering imprecations and empty threats, we load the car and are off in the heat and dust of a Maharashtra morning.

By noon, we reach Poona, and enjoy an air-conditioned lunch. This is followed by several vicissitudes, including an hour's hold-up due to road repairs, but miracle of miracles, we reach Bombay and its airport at 7.00pm.

Just as well as the hassle of leaving India is second only to the hassle of arriving in it. By the time we reach Karachi where we must de-plane, I am so sleepy, I keep nodding off in the departure lounge, and once on the faultlessly reliable JAL and heading for Cairo, I close my eyes and know no more.

The End

EPILOGUE

There are still times when, waking or sleeping, I dream I am back in India and wonder again at the persistence of its spell.

I left Canada with some reluctance and no little apprehension, and for a while suffered what I suppose one could only call a desert of the soul. Alien, not only to my surroundings, but to myself – a person without a purpose, a mother without her children, living in a home whose kitchen I feared to enter, in a country whose heart I had yet to know.

There were so many things I hated, but more that I loved. I hated a society that flaunted its whining beggars and clutching lepers; I detested the wheedling salesmen who dodged in front and followed behind, clinging like leeches until the last hope of a sale had died. Yet there was a kind of joyousness in the people and a beguiling charm that I found irresistible. I hated the betel-juice spittle that stained the streets and so many of the unattractive social habits of the general populace. But what was this, compared to a civilization that had seen the birth of two of the world's great religions, and to a people who have clung to their gods; honoured their traditions and lived, without complaint, the lives their karma dictated.

While I may carry with me images of the tragedy of India's social ills, I also see, in memory's eye, the Taj Mahal by moonlight, a sea of almond blossoms in a Kashmiri spring and the lights coming out across the Hoogley. They were all the things that became part of me; for slowly, slowly, I came to belong. I found my place in India – in the exploration of the land, in the study of its history, the magnificence of its architecture and the friendship of its people. And when I left it was with a broadened mind, a vastly enriched spirit and with my sandals dragging reluctantly in the Indian dust.

ACKNOWLEDGEMENTS

Special thanks are due to all those who laboured with me in the production of this memoir. To Carolyn Nicholson, whose inspired pen and sharp wit created the illustrations; to my daughter Kilmeny for her generous help in preparing the text for publication; to my son Peter, who rescued me from the toils of technology; to Adrienne Nicholson Chow for her invaluable help in the creation of the cover design; to Sally Jordan for her encouraging critiques in the early stages of writing; and, last of all, to my husband Douglas, whose endless patience saved the author from self-destruction.

ISBN 1-41204025-6

9 781412 040259